Ancient African Religions

Ancient African Religions

A History

ROBERT M. BAUM

OXFORD
UNIVERSITY PRESS

Oxford University Press is a department of the University of Oxford.
It furthers the University's objective of excellence in research, scholarship,
and education by publishing worldwide. Oxford is a registered trade mark of
Oxford University Press in the UK and in certain other countries.

Published in the United States of America by Oxford University Press
198 Madison Avenue, New York, NY 10016, United States of America.

© Oxford University Press 2024

All rights reserved. No part of this publication may be reproduced, stored in a retrieval system,
or transmitted, in any form or by any means, without the prior permission in writing of Oxford
University Press, or as expressly permitted by law, by license or under terms agreed with the
appropriate reprographics rights organization. Inquiries concerning reproduction outside the scope
of the above should be sent to the Rights Department, Oxford University Press, at the address above.

You must not circulate this work in any other form
and you must impose this same condition on any acquirer

Library of Congress Cataloging-in-Publication Data
Names: Baum, Robert M., author.
Title: Ancient African religions : a history / Robert M. Baum.
Description: New York : Oxford University Press, 2024. |
Includes bibliographical references and index.
Identifiers: LCCN 2024004613 (print) | LCCN 2024004614 (ebook) |
ISBN 9780197747063 (paperback) | ISBN 9780197747070 (hardback) |
ISBN 9780197747094 (epub)
Subjects: LCSH: Indigenous peoples—Religion. | Africa—Religion.
Classification: LCC BL2400 .B295 2024 (print) | LCC BL2400 (ebook) |
DDC 200.96—dc23/eng/20240129
LC record available at https://lccn.loc.gov/2024004613
LC ebook record available at https://lccn.loc.gov/2024004614

DOI: 10.1093/9780197747100.001.0001

Contents

List of Maps vii
List of Figures ix
Preface xi
Acknowledgments xiii

1. Introduction 1

2. Before Adam and Eve: African Religions from the Dawn of Humanity to the Neolithic Revolution 37

3. A Religious History of Ancient Egypt: From Unification to the Reforms of Akhenaten 69

4. Not out of Egypt: Africa from 3200 to 1200 BCE 119

5. Egypt and the Nile Valley before the Roman Occupation 137

6. Beyond the Nile Basin: African Religious History from 1300 BCE to the Dawn of the Common Era 161

7. Egyptian Religious Traditions under Foreign Domination: From the Roman Conquest to the Arab Conquest 185

8. North and Northeast Africa in the Age of Roman and Byzantine Domination: From the First Century BCE to the Lesser Hijra 211

9. The Sahara and the South: African Religious History from the Beginnings of the Common Era to the First Hijra 239

10. Conclusion 253

Bibliography 267
Index 291

Maps

2.1. Africa before 3200 BCE.	36
3.1. Egypt to the New Kingdom.	68
4.1. Africa beyond the Nile to 1200 BCE.	118
5.1. Egypt and the Nile valley to the Roman Conquest.	136
6.1. Africa before the Common Era.	160
8.1. North and northeast Africa to the Hijra, 622 CE.	210
9.1. Africa before the Hijra.	238

Maps were provided by Jonathan Chipman, Department of Geography, Dartmouth College.

Figures

2.1.	The Tsodilo Hills, northwest Botswana (photo by Lawrence Robbins).	45
3.1.	The Nile River and the adjacent desert (photo by Robert M. Baum).	85
3.2.	The Pyramids at Giza, Egypt (photo by Robert M. Baum).	90
5.1.	Ramesses Temple, Abu Simbel, Egypt (photo by Robert M. Baum).	139
5.2.	Images of enslaved Nubians being taken north into Egypt, Abu Simbel (photo by Robert M. Baum).	140
7.1.	Falcon image associated with the god Horus, Edfu, Egypt (photo by Robert M. Baum).	188
7.2.	Monastery of St. Simeon, seventh century, west of Aswan, Egypt (photo by Robert M. Baum).	196
8.1.	Roman sacrificial altar by a Christian church, Volubilis, Morocco (photo by Robert M. Baum).	220
8.2.	Menorah oil lamp, Volubilis, Morocco (photo by Robert M. Baum).	221
8.3.	Stele, Axum, Ethiopia, with the Church of Mary Our Lady of Zion in the background (photo by Robert M. Baum).	230

Preface

When I began my dissertation research on the religious and social history of the Diola of southern Senegal, there were few monographs that examined the history of indigenous African religions. Most historical studies of African religions focused on the history of Christianity and Islam in Africa. The exception was the historical study of ancient Egypt and the often-intense debates about the influences that Egypt exerted within the rest of Africa and within the Mediterranean world. Frequently overlooked were the influences of the rest of Africa in the development of Egyptian culture. As field research became central to African anthropology, some studies included historical materials, including African religious history. Until the 1950s, however, historians focused more on the history of outsiders in Africa than on the history of Africans themselves. This movement toward an African history of African peoples tended to overlook forces of religious change, until the 1970s. Even then, it focused on Africa since the nineteenth century. This volume seeks to establish a continent-wide perspective on what we have learned about this history. It examines the history of ancient African religions, from the evidence of actions that can be associated with religious activity, which can be traced back over 200,000 years, to the lesser *hijra* when a portion of the Muslim community at Mecca sought protection with the Christian ruler of the kingdom of Axum early in the seventh century. Although African societies play important roles in the early history of Judaism and Christianity, the primary focus of this study will be on those religious traditions created by African peoples.

This is the first volume of a projected four-volume study of the history of African religions. The second volume will examine the period from the seventh century and Africa's first contacts with Islam (several years before the Hijra) to the European initiation of the Atlantic slave trade in the fifteenth century. It will include a history of African religions in the Eastern Diaspora—Iraq and India. The third volume will examine the variety of religious changes that occurred during the period of the Atlantic slave trade, which persisted into the waning years of the nineteenth century. It will

xii PREFACE

continue discussion of the south and southwest Asian African diasporas and the formation of a more recent American Diaspora. The fourth and final volume will examine African religious history from the partition of Africa in the late nineteenth century, through the colonial era, decolonization, and to the present day.

Acknowledgments

In a project that has engaged the central questions of my entire career, the historical dynamism of African traditional religions, there are many people to thank. First, I would like to thank Richard Elphick, an African historian, and James Helfer (Stone), a historian of religions, for introducing me as an undergraduate at Wesleyan University to the complexity and richness of the history of religions, both within Africa and beyond. I would like to thank my thesis advisor, David Robinson, whose patient, enthusiastic, and sage advice improved my work and grew into a lifelong friendship. In my early career, two mentors stood out. Both passed on way too young. Alan Segal and Marilyn Waldman inspired me to take my research wherever it led and to address the issues it raised rigorously and creatively.

It is now fifty years since I first arrived in Senegal, beginning a lifelong engagement with the Casamance township of Kadjinol. To my adoptive brothers, Dionsal and Diongany Diedhiou, and my sister-in-law, Elizabeth Sambou, who welcomed me into their home and hearts, I feel a debt of gratitude that I can never return. To the priest-kings (Coeyi) of Kadjinol and Mlomp—Sikakucele Diatta, Siliungimagne Diatta, and Sebikuan Sambou—whose friendship and guidance will not be forgotten. In Egypt, I would like to thank Professor Hassan Hanafi of the University of Cairo for his introduction to Egypt and his introductions to people in Egypt. In Eswatini, I would like to thank the Sihlonganyane family for their friendship and their assistance in my research.

I am also grateful to the many universities and foundations that provided direct funding for this research, including the University of Missouri, Dartmouth College, and the Woodrow Wilson International Center for Scholars in Washington, DC. This book was written during the COVID-19 pandemic. I am grateful to my wife, Peggy, for sharing our isolation with my book manuscript and providing both moral support and editorial assistance during the long process.

I would like to thank Cynthia Read of Oxford University Press for first suggesting this project, Theo Calderara for directing the process of approving the manuscript, and Brent Matheny for guiding the manuscript into the production process. I would like to thank Ganga Balaji for her patience in the editorial process and to Leslie Anglin for copy-editing the manuscript. Thanks to Lawrence Robbins of Michigan State University for sharing his photographs of the Tsodilo Hills. I would like to thank Roger Arnold of African and African American Studies for his help with the technical aspects of assembling photographs. Thanks to Travis Ables for preparing the index. Finally, I would like to thank Jonathan Chipman of Dartmouth College's Geography Department for preparing the maps.

1
Introduction

In my work on the history of African religions, I have long been troubled (and sometimes amused) by the persistent claims of more traditional historians that one cannot succeed in such endeavors. Some have contended that African religions do not have a history unto themselves, apart from their interaction with the newer religious traditions of Islam and Christianity. They see African religions as rigid in their traditionalism, as contrasted with the change-oriented cultures of the West. Others concede that such a history exists, but the source materials, envisioned primarily as written documents, are insufficient to reconstruct such a history. This book speaks directly to these critics. By relying on the existing corpus of written texts, oral traditions, linguistic analyses, descriptions based on participant observation, and various types of archaeology, I demonstrate that African religious history is nearly as old as humanity itself. The history of African religions becomes in many ways like a pentathlon, expecting the scholar who conducts such research to work with written texts, to learn African languages, to live within a community where these religious traditions are practiced, to study material culture, both sacred and mundane, and a variety of archaeological sources from tree rings to stone circles and gravesites. Using all these materials scholars can provide the evidentiary basis for a rich history of African religions that addresses the complexity of these traditions and their abilities to be transformed over time. The idea of a fundamental difference between indigenous religions, including African religions, seen as outside of history, and world religions, seen as profoundly historical, cannot be sustained.

I have spent my entire academic career focused on the historical study of African religious traditions, not only their interactions with Christianity and Islam, but their history as far back as accessible sources will permit. In addition to teaching about African religions for over forty years, I have conducted archival and field research in Senegal for a total of five years, periodically, since 1973. This has resulted in the publication of two monographs focused on the history of Diola religion. The first of these, *Shrines of the Slave Trade: Diola Religion and Society in Precolonial Senegambia*, relies primarily on oral traditions and written texts to examine the religious and social history of a small community in southwestern Senegal. It looks at the ways in which a Diola religious tradition was created by drawing on older traditions of prior inhabitants as well as the ideas and practices of newcomer communities as they entered the region by the seventeenth century. It focuses on a single Diola subgroup, the Esulalu, who used their religious tradition to interpret and shape their participation in and provide protection from the Atlantic slave trade. This religious tradition also provided means of understanding and controlling the challenges of frequent warfare and raiding, ecological shifts such as droughts, and the outbreaks of epidemics affecting people and livestock.

My second book, *West Africa's Women of God: Alinesitoué and the Diola Prophetic Tradition*, examines a Diola tradition of direct revelation from the supreme being, Emitai ("Of the Sky"), who commanded prophets to teach. This challenges the nontheistic stereotypes of African religions, by focusing on a powerful supreme being who communicates directly to more than sixty individuals. I collected oral traditions concerning fifteen individuals, all of them men, from the precolonial era. However, since the colonial conquest, in the latter half of the nineteenth century, two-thirds of the forty-five prophets were women. Thus, we are looking at both the intensification and the transformation of a prophetic tradition in which a supreme being turned to women leaders to introduce innovations into a Diola religious system. This included important teachings reaffirming religious communities challenged by conversion to Christianity or Islam, frequent drought, and colonial powers' attempts to impose an agricultural system that would have locked Diola farmers into bonds of economic dependency.[1]

These books demonstrate the importance of historical reflection within African religious systems and the profound changes that are remembered in oral traditions. Together with my comparative work on African and other indigenous religious traditions, these historical works became the foundation of what will become a general history of African religions. I have also conducted research in other African countries, including Egypt, Morocco, Gambia, Liberia, Ghana, Ethiopia, Uganda, Tanzania, South Africa, Zimbabwe, Eswatini, Namibia, and Botswana.[2] This book will not be the

---

[1] Robert M. Baum, *Shrines of the Slave Trade: Diola Religion and Society in Precolonial Senegambia* (New York: Oxford University Press, 1999). Robert M. Baum, *West African Women of God: Alinesitoué and the Diola Prophetic Tradition* (Bloomington: Indiana University Press, 2016).

[2] This research was conducted with the aid of foundations and universities, including the Thomas J. Watson Foundation, the Social Science Research Council, the Fulbright-Hays Foundation,

first broad history of religion in Africa. There are many histories of African Islam and Christianity. I will draw on these works as well as historical and ethnographic monographs in these fields. However, the primary focus of this work will be on the history of indigenous African religions, at times in sustained interaction with the new Abrahamic religions. In contrast to Islam, Christianity, and Judaism, these religions were created in Africa, by African communities, and they have played a central role in sustaining the cultural identity of particular peoples. This does not mean that they did not influence or were not influenced by other indigenous religions, only that Africans perceived of them as received or created by their own ancestors, primarily for their own communities.[3] This book will serve as the first continent-wide history of African religions with a primary focus on the history of traditional or indigenous religions.

However, there are many scholars who are skeptical about the feasibility of such a history, particularly among European and American commentators. In his important book, *The Invention of Africa*, Valentin Mudimbe traced the history of Western representations of Africa from the ancient Greeks to contemporary academics.[4] Fundamental to these images are two assumptions: that Africa is a place without history and a place without religion. People without history or religion met the characteristics of what Aristotle labeled as brutish peoples, people who had incomplete souls, who were "natural slaves."[5] These representations reflect the nature of contact between the West and Africa, especially the Atlantic slave trade and the colonial conquest, which were legitimated by denying the rich vitality of

---

National Endowment for the Humanities, The Ohio State University, the American Philosophical Society, the American Council of Learned Societies, Iowa State University, University of Missouri, the Woodrow Wilson International Center for Scholars, and Dartmouth College.

[3] The term "indigenous" has generated its own controversies. How old must a religion be before it is considered "indigenous"? A category that includes religions created by Africans, Native Americans, and Australasians who had little contact with one another may share most fundamentally an experience of conquest and disdain that accompanied imperial domination since 1500. For some of the academic debates about the term, see Robert M. Baum, "Indigenous Religions," in *A Concise Introduction to World Religions*, ed. Willard Oxtoby and Alan F. Segal, 2nd ed. (Toronto: Oxford University Press, 2007), pp. 10–50. Robert M. Baum, "The Forgotten South: African Religions in World Religions Textbooks," *Religious Studies Review* 21 (January 6, 2006), pp. 27–30. James Cox, *From Primitive to Indigenous: The Academic Study of Indigenous Religions* (Aldershot, UK: Ashgate, 2007).
For a list of some of the major historical studies of Christianity or Islam in Africa, see footnote 19 later in this chapter.

[4] Valentin Mudimbe, *The Invention of Africa: Gnosis, Philosophy, and the Order of Knowledge* (Bloomington: Indiana University Press, 1988), pp. 69–77.

[5] Aristotle, *Politics*, ed. Louise Ropes Loomis (Roslyn, NY: Walter Black, 1942), pp. 251–258.

4 ANCIENT AFRICAN RELIGIONS

African cultures.[6] These images persist in the continuing denial of African contributions to the world's religious landscape and have been used to provide an intellectual underpinning to assertions of white supremacy and Western hegemony. Georg Friedrich Hegel provides an influential example of this type of representation in his *The Philosophy of History*, where he describes an Africa he never visited:

> Africa proper ... the land of childhood, which lying beyond the day of self-conscious history is enveloped in the dark mantle of night....
> But even Herodotus called the Negroes sorcerers, now in sorcery we have not the idea of a God, of a moral faith ...
> At this point we leave Africa ... For it is no historical part of the world, it has no movement or development to exhibit ... What we properly understand by Africa is the unhistorical, undeveloped spirit, still involved in the conditions of mere nature and which had to be presented here only as on the threshold of the World's History.[7]

As recently as 2007, a president of France, Nicolas Sarkozy, referred to Hegel's passage in a speech he made on an official visit to Dakar, Senegal. He said: "The tragedy of Africa is that the Africans have not fully entered into history."[8] The historian Bethwell Ogot claims that the presentation of ahistorical African traditional religions is part of "'the old excuse employed for a long time by western scholars to deny the existence of African history.'"[9] As anthropologist Randy Matory has noted, enslaved Africans were portrayed as the "opposite of the normal historical agent."[10] The denial of African religious systems and the denial of African history are closely related. To Westerners operating within an intellectual tradition that marginalized

---

[6] Philip Curtin, *The Image of Africa* (Madison: University of Wisconsin Press, 1964). William D. Cohen, *The French Encounter with Africans* (Bloomington: Indiana University Press, 1980). Okot P'Bitek, *African Religions and Western Scholarship* (Kampala: East African Literature Bureau, 1970). Chinweizu, *The West and the Rest of Us: White Predators, Black Slavers and the African Elite* (New York: Vantage Books, 1975). Mudimbe, *Invention*, p. 69.

[7] Georg F. Hegel, *The Philosophy of History* (New York: Dover, 1956), pp. 91, 93, 99.

[8] "Discours du Président de la République Française, Université de Dakar—Sénégal," July 26, 2007. Thanks to Laura Grillo for bringing this to my attention. "Africans Still Seething over Sarkozy Speech," *Reuters*, September 6, 2007.

[9] Bethwell Ogot cited in Terence Ranger and I. A. Kimambo, "Introduction," in *The Historical Study of African Religions*, ed. Terence Ranger and I. A. Kimambo (Berkeley: University of California Press, 1978), p. 3.

[10] J. Lorand Matory, *The Fetish Revisited: Marx, Freud, and the Gods Black People Made* (Durham, NC: Duke University Press, 2017), p. 42.

African history and religions, an African religious history seemed beyond the realm of possibility.

By the late nineteenth century, the growing quantity of descriptions of African religions gathered by ethnographers, missionaries, administrators, and travelers in Africa undermined the credibility of representations of Africa as a place without religion. As David Chidester has pointed out, Europe's "discovery" of African religions had an enormous impact on the growth of the new academic discipline of comparative religion, becoming the source of much of the raw material upon which foundational theories were based.[11] During this period, theorists like Charles de Brosses saw African cultures' primary importance as living museums where Western scholars could observe what their ancestors were like by what they saw as African cultures frozen in time. For example, the prominent anthropologist E. B. Tylor claimed that "The history of civilization teaches, that up to a certain point, savages or barbarians are like what our ancestors were and our peasants still are, but from this common level the supreme intellect of the progressive races has raised their nations to heights of culture."[12] Thus, African religions became a window into the nature of religious life before the birth of world religions. A century later, the well-known European historian Hugh Trevor-Roper attacked the growing field of African history in Tylorean terms:

> Undergraduates, seduced as always by the changing breath of journalistic fashion, demand that they should be taught the history of black Africa. Perhaps in the future, there will be some African history to teach. But at the present there is not, or very little, there is only the history of Europeans in Africa. The rest is largely darkness, like the history of pre-European, pre-Columbian America. And darkness is not a subject for history.... Tribes whose chief function in history, in my opinion, is to show the present an image of the past from which, by history, it has escaped.[13]

---

[11] David Chidester, *Savage Systems: Colonialism and Comparative Religion in Southern Africa* (Charlottesville: University Press of Virginia, 1996), pp. 3–29.

[12] E. B. Tylor, cited in Leroy Vail and Landeg White, *Power and the Praise Poem: Southern African Voices in History* (Charlottesville: University Press of Virginia, 1991), pp. 5–6.

[13] Hugh Trevor-Roper, *The Rise of Christian Europe* (New York: Harcourt, Brace, and World, 1965), p. 7. This attitude persists in more recent scholarship, which uses twentieth-century ethnographies of African societies to illustrate the impact of the Neolithic Age in Africa. Elise Boulding, *The Underside of History: A View of Women Through the Ages*, Vol. I (London: Sage, 1992), pp. 122–125.

As a result, most scholars who engaged in the study of African religions limited their historical work to the study of Islam and Christianity in Africa or the impact of colonial rule.

Some argued against the historical study of African religions because they saw them as part of "traditional societies," highly resistant to change and reliant on existing methods and practices to address new challenges rather than question fundamental paradigms. This would include functionalist anthropologists who emphasized synchronic approaches and systems that adjusted to disruptions by seeking to return to a social equilibrium. As Yves Person noted in his 1973 essay calling for more historical study of African religions:

> As to functionalism which triumphed between the two world wars in the Anglo-Saxon world, it is the clearest example of the refusal of history. It imposed the concept of "traditional society," as a machine made of well aligned pieces, which excluded all development, all movements over time. Traditional society had an unchanging character, the masters of functionalism, like Radcliffe-Brown and Malinowski, had formally prohibited anthropologists from wasting their time in doing "pseudo-history" or "speculative history."[14]

In response to severe challenges, however, like the colonial conquest, they might be unable to return to equilibrium. Instead, they were seen as brittle and breakable in the face of the challenges of the colonial era.[15] This would allow for a religious history that begins with the arrival of external catalysts for change, such as colonization, Christianity, or Islam, but not one that reflected internally generated or local forces.

With a very different emphasis, many structuralists argued that underlying apparent change were deep structures of thought that remained constant. In a now classic essay, De Craemer, Vansina, and Fox have illustrated this perspective: "The culture common to Central Africa that existed in precolonial times can be called 'classical'. Its core elements have remained remarkably intact in the face of enormous changes ... The common religion has been

---

[14] Yves Person, "Pour une histoire des religions africaines," in *L'Invention religieuse en Afrique: Histoire et religion en Afrique Noire*, ed. Jean-Pierre Chrétien (Paris: Karthala, 1993), p. 14. Translations of foreign titled texts are made by the author.

[15] On static models in the development of functionalist anthropology, see Brian Morris, *Anthropological Studies of Religion: An Introductory Text* (Cambridge: Cambridge University Press, [1987] 1998), pp. 123–131.

remarkably stable, perhaps for millennia." Change came at the level of new techniques of utilizing existing resources, but without changes at this deeper level of understanding."[16] For a religious history of the precolonial era, these images of equilibrium, continuity, and/or stasis are particularly strong. They reinforce the sense that there are inadequate sources for such a history, as well as the absence of what many in the West regard as a dominant force in world history, the West itself.[17]

This ahistorical view of African religions has been embraced by many scholars in religious studies as well. For example, in the most widely read textbook on African religions, the late John Mbiti wrote that African religious history begins with the penetration of Islam and Christianity and that there was little history before that time. "In the traditional set-up where the African concept of time is mainly two-dimensional, human life is relatively stable and almost static. A rhythm of life is the norm, and any radical change is either unknown, resented or so slow that it is hardly noticed." This was a view of "traditional" societies that dominated much of the social science literature until recently. Mbiti went on to discuss how change begins to become more rapid in the late nineteenth century and gains momentum "toward the middle of the twentieth."[18] Studies of African religions' interaction with Christianity or Islam continue to be the most common form of African religious history.[19] For example, Elizabeth Isichei wrote a book which presented itself as a history of African religions, which included detailed discussions of the history of Christianity and Islam in Africa, but only a brief, predominantly ahistorical presentation of African religious traditions in a final section of her work.

---

[16] W. J. Craemer, Jan Vansina, and R. Fox, "Religious Movements in Central Africa," in *Comparative Studies in Society and History* 18 (1976), p. 465. James Fernandez, *Bwiti: An Ethnography of the Religious Imagination in Africa* (Princeton, NJ: Princeton University Press, 1982), p. 9. Claude Levi-Strauss, *The Savage Mind* (Chicago: University of Chicago Press, 1965), p. 21.

[17] Eric Wolf, *Europe and the People without History* (Berkeley: University of California Press, 1982).

[18] John Mbiti, *African Religions and Philosophy*, 2nd ed. (Oxford: Heinemann, 1990), p. 211. For a critique of Mbiti's views on the history of African religions, see Ranger and Kimambo, "Introduction," p. 2.

[19] There are many histories of Islam in Africa, in West Africa, or in other areas. Nehemia Levtzion and Randall Pouwels, eds., *History of Islam in Africa* (Athens: Ohio University Press, 2000); J. Spencer Trimingham, *History of Islam in West Africa* (Oxford: Oxford University Press, 1969). Mervyn Hiskett, *The Development of Islam in West Africa* (London: Longman, 1984). Peter B. Clarke, *West African Islam* (London: Arnold, 1982). David Robinson, *Muslim Societies in African History* (Cambridge: Cambridge University Press, 2004). Vincent Monteil, *L'Islam Noir* (Paris: Editions de Seuil, 1971). Similarly, there are many histories of Christianity in Africa or in regional histories. C. P. Grove, *The Planting of Christianity in Africa* (4 vols.) (London: Lutterworth Press, [1946] 1964), Bengt Sundkler, *A History of the Church in Africa* (Cambridge: Cambridge University Press, 2000). Elizabeth Isichei, *A History of the Church in Africa: From Antiquity to the Present* (Grand Rapids, MI: Eerdmans, 1995).

She also claimed that African religious traditions are losing their place as distinct religious traditions, insisting that: "These religions still survive, though only a small and aging group in any African population would identify themselves first and foremost as traditionalist. Traditional religions survive, above all, in the hearts of Christians and Muslims, the *zar* spirit cult of Somalia and the Republic of Sudan is an example of the latter and the persistence of witchcraft among African Christians of the former."[20] Religious self-identification varies both within different contexts and with different interlocutors. This includes differences between urban and rural locations of interviews and the ethnic and religious identify of the surveyor. Traditional religions, albeit in decline, retain their viability in many parts of Africa.

World religions are seen as situated within history, but indigenous religions, including African religions, are seen as outside of the flow of history. For Mircea Eliade, one of the most prominent historians of religion in the twentieth century, indigenous religions are of interest in terms of patterns of symbolism, but world religions have an exclusive claim on religious history.[21] This is reflected in world religions textbooks which, if they include African religions at all, see them as a prologue to the study of more historical religions, placed in early chapters with ancient, prehistoric religions, or with other indigenous religions.[22]

Finally, there is a group of scholars who accept the idea of profound religious change but argue that the limited nature of the sources available before European written records would make it impossible to reconstruct. This would include religious studies scholars like Geoffrey Parrinder and anthropologists like Jack Goody. There is an implicit assumption behind many religious histories that they should start with an ethnographic baseline just before the European conquest and focus their histories on interaction with Islam, Christianity, and/or colonialism.[23] Before colonial rule, written documentation would only describe those events accessible to literate

---

[20] Elizabeth Isichei, *The Religious Traditions of Africa: A History* (Westport, CT: Greenwood, 2004), p. 4.

[21] We see this in the prominent role of African and other indigenous religions in Mircea Eliade's *Patterns of Religion*, 3 vols. (New York: New American Library, [1958] 1974); but their virtual absence from his multivolume *A History of Religions* (Chicago: University of Chicago Press, 1978). For a brief discussion of the world religions concept within the comparative study of religion, see Tomoko Masuzawa, "World Religions," in *The Encyclopedia of Religion*, ed. Lindsay Jones (Detroit, MI: Thomson/Gale, 2005), Vol. 14, pp. 9800–9804.

[22] Baum, "The Forgotten South."

[23] Geoffrey Parrinder, *West African Religion* (New York: Barnes and Noble, [1949] 1970). Jack Goody, *The Logic of Writing and the Organization of Society* (Cambridge: Cambridge University Press, 1986), pp. 7–8.

observers, foreigners to most African societies. It is within the colonial era, primarily a late nineteenth- and early twentieth-century phenomenon, that one finds considerable written documentation, traditionally the raw material for both the disciplines of history and of religious studies. Not surprisingly, it is where one finds the overwhelming majority of religious histories. Until recently, however, written sources were too limited in number and came from too narrow a group of authors to provide sufficient material for a history of religions, even for the relatively recent past.

Beginning in the 1950s, the late Jan Vansina, an anthropologist as well as a historian, provided an eloquent justification for and concrete evidence of the value of oral traditions as historical sources. This enabled the academic study of events that were beyond the view of literate observers for the first time.[24] As African historians adopted the techniques of gathering and interpreting oral traditions, in the 1960s, however, they shied away from applying such techniques to topics of religious change. Some historians who used oral traditions in other areas of historical inquiry seemed oddly reluctant to apply oral traditions to the history of religions. They suggested that oral traditions reflect present-day concerns of a society to such an extent that they eliminate most memories of significant religious change that challenge ideologies of continuity with the time of the "first ancestors." The fact that more "traditional" historians deemed oral sources unreliable may have encouraged oral historians to focus on larger states with more formalized traditions and less elusive topics like political and economic history in order to establish the legitimacy of the method on less empirically uncertain ground.[25]

This work is not the first to treat African religions historically. Several pioneers in African studies cleared the path for me and other members of a new generation of historians of African religions. Based on field research in the 1930s, E. E. Evans-Pritchard's anthropological studies of Nuer religion provided clear evidence of religious changes during the era of the Egyptian occupation of Nuer territory. In the nineteenth century, the Nuer witnessed a dramatic expansion of the category of spiritual powers he labeled as "spirits of the above"

---

[24] Vansina and his students' work in the study of oral traditions had an important impact in developing the field of African history beyond what Europeans saw of Africa, and it also influenced other fields of history to move beyond written documentation as their primary sources. It helped open fields of history whose primary actors had less access to written ways of documenting their activities and thoughts. Jan Vansina, *Oral Traditions: A Study in Historical Methodology* (Harmondsworth, UK: Penguin, [1971] 1973). Jan Vansina, *Oral Tradition as History* (Madison: University of Wisconsin Press, 1985).

[25] Person, "Pour une histoire des religions africaines," p. 17.

and of prophetic leaders who provided leadership for their communities in the name of these spiritual beings.[26] Evans-Pritchard concluded that:

> Nuer religion, like any other, has, of course, a history, but we can only trace it as far as it survives in the memories of the Nuer themselves, for reports by travelers ... are on this matter, slight and unreliable.... However, Nuer statements, supported by ethnological evidence, enable us to say with a fair degree of probability what have been the main lines of development during the last hundred years.[27]

In the early 1970s, works by Terence Ranger, I. Kimambo, and Robin Horton explored African religious history before colonization, addressing such issues as the history of particular spirit cults, changing concepts of the supreme being, and interaction with expansionary religions like Christianity and Islam within an Africa-centered context. Adding to the evidence of oral traditions, historians began to look at archaeological and linguistic evidence, art history, and ritual studies, and to read ethnographic data in new ways in order to reconstruct the early history of African religions, sometimes within a particular community. At other times it was on a more regional basis. This work has been strongly influenced by their pioneering efforts.[28]

Examining the Sources

There are many scholars who remain skeptical about the possibility of studying precolonial African religious history. They focus on the inadequacy of written sources and the unreliability of oral traditions before the nineteenth century. The earliest written sources were initially written in Egyptian hieroglyphics and were rich sources on ancient Egypt, with some value for neighboring communities, but offered little evidence concerning more distant places. Written sources on ancient Africa in European languages,

---

[26] E. E. Evans-Pritchard, *Nuer Religion* (Oxford: Oxford University Press, [1956] 1974), pp. 28–62 and 287–310.
[27] Evans-Pritchard, *Nuer Religion*, p. 311.
[28] Terence Ranger and I. Kimambo, eds., *The Historical Study of African Religions* (Berkeley: University of California Press, 1972). Robin Horton, "A Hundred Years of Change in Kalabari Religion," in *Black Africa: Their Peoples and Their Cultures Today*, ed. John Middleton (New York: Macmillan, 1970). Christopher Ehret, *History and the Testimony of Language* (Berkeley: University of California Press, 2011).

primarily Greek and Latin, focused on the North African coast and were limited to what was witnessed or heard about by the European authors. In such works as Herodotus's *The Histories*, there was a tendency to incorporate hearsay evidence into written texts about parts of Africa that they had never visited, regardless of how exotic the descriptions might sound.[29] There are a few texts and inscriptions in the southwest Arabian language of Sabean. Northeastern African writings, primarily in Ge'ez and Meroitic, provide description of the region, but only for the last two thousand years. Meroitic script has only been partially deciphered, reflecting the difficulties of using a language that is no longer spoken and which has no known relatives. Arabic sources were also quite limited and focused on North Africa, the Sahara, the Sahel, Ethiopia, and the Swahili coast of East Africa and primarily since the growth of Islam in the seventh century. Written sources in West African languages, in Ajami script, concentrated on the region since the ninth century. Although sources in Egyptian, Ge'ez, and Meroitic have substantial information related to the history of African religions, the authors of the few early narratives in European or Semitic languages rarely focused on religious issues, spoke other African languages, or stayed long enough to understand the cultures they described.

The lack of written sources makes the utility of oral traditions central to the historical study of African religions. Many historians and religionists question the depth or accuracy of oral traditions, especially in relation to religious change. Ultimately, this debate centers on the contrast between literate and oral, "traditional" and "modern," and change-oriented and resistant-to-change cultures. Some scholars assume that traditional societies and their oral traditions are unreflective. This image is reinforced by the methods of teaching adherents about African religions. One must be initiated in order to learn esoteric knowledge concerning specific religious cults as well as the reflective aspects of underlying concepts and theories. Beyond the education that is provided to groups of younger people in various stages of initiation, religious instruction is a highly personal process. This reflects a theory of knowledge in which esoteric knowledge is seen as a form of power. A seeker of this knowledge must demonstrate that he or she is able to handle power responsibly at both a personal level and on behalf of the community.[30] Situating

---

[29] Herodotus, *The Histories* (London: Penguin, 1972).
[30] Michael D. McNally describes a similar insistence among the North American Ojibway that only people who demonstrate the responsibility to use the power being offered them through religious

specific cults or ideas historically is among the more closely guarded areas of knowledge, particularly when one is initially told that these things have existed relatively unchanged since the time of the first ancestors. One must be sure that the hearer of such information can handle the resultant power. Among the Diola of Senegambia, to impart such knowledge to people without the right to know it or the responsibility to use it for the good of the community is referred to as "poisoning the ears" of the listener.[31] Many fledgling anthropologists, historians, and historians of religion, funded for a year's field research and with little more than a rudimentary knowledge of the language, gained access only to those materials that the elders deemed were appropriate to their neophyte status. Too often, the researchers concluded that they had received a full account and that the oral testimony itself was neither terribly detailed nor indicative of much secondary reflection, rather than admit the limitations of their field research.[32]

In many ways, the work of Jack Goody illustrates this ambivalence about the feasibility of conducting historical work on African religions the most clearly. On the one hand, Goody firmly believes that African religious traditions have been profoundly influenced by new religious cults which bring in "new ideas, new prohibitions, new taboos, and were never simply 'more of the same' . . . they often modified in significant ways the classificatory systems of the community into which they penetrated by introducing new moral and cosmological order."[33] In other contexts, however, he contends that oral traditions are not adequate for critical reflection on the significance of these events.[34] He argues that presentist perspectives so dominate oral history that they become an integral part of what he labels "cultural homeostasis: those innumerable

---

instruction in ways that strengthen the community will receive such education. Michael D. McNally, "Native American Site Visits in the Context of Service Learning," *Spotlight on Teaching*, American Academy of Religion, October 2004, p. vii.

[31] Baum, *Shrines*, pp. 15–23.
[32] Many researchers have stressed the importance of repeated visits over long periods of time as essential for overcoming the tendency to limit researchers' access to the more superficial accounts. For an example of this emphasis on repeated field research, see Andrew Apter, *Black Critics and Kings: The Hermeneutics of Power in Yoruba Society* (Chicago: University of Chicago Press, 1992), p. xiii. On my own field research methods, see Baum, *Shrines*, pp. 19–23. Robert M. Baum, "From a Boy Not Seeking a Wife to a Man Discussing Prophetic Women: A Male Fieldworker among Diola Women in Senegal, 1974–2005," *Men and Masculinities* 11 (2008), pp. 154–163. Robert M. Baum, "Setting Out on the Awasena Path: Conducting Field Research in Diola Communities in Senegal," *Mande Studies* 20 (2018), pp. 61–70.
[33] Goody, *Logic of Writing and the Organization of Society*, pp. 7–8.
[34] Jack Goody, *The Domestication of the Savage Mind* (Cambridge: Cambridge University Press, [1977] 1986), p. 27.

mutations of culture that emerge in the ordinary course of transmission from one generation to the next."[35] The late Jan Vansina criticized Goody's social functionalism and his idea of homeostasis: "At any given time traditions are perfectly congruent with the society. Any alteration in social organization or practice is immediately accompanied by a corresponding alteration in traditions.... For Goody the difference between the oral and the literate society is this homeostasis plus the claim that culture is totally homogeneous in oral society and heterogeneous in literate society."[36] Still Vansina expressed a similar skepticism about the study of religious history:

> Religious practice was so tied up with other institutions that it lacked sufficient autonomy and visibility to develop systematic traditions of its own. It is diffused throughout society. Furthermore, change in the representation and in the practice of ritual was so slow as often to be unconscious and hence could not be remembered. Where change was done slow ... the need to adhere to the new consensus effectively prevented development of traditions that would indicate what previous representations of ultimate reality might have been. Oral traditions are therefore sources that are not promising for intellectual history in general and religious history in particular except when they touch on the ideology of kingship.[37]

However, Vansina allowed for the possibility that acephalous societies, which carefully limit any concentrations of political power, might have richer oral traditions about religious history.[38] In such cases, royal reigns do not become the primary chronological signposts for major events. Rather, adoption of new shrines and changes in initiation rites are often perceived to be focal points for the cultural continuity of their societies. As Yves Person noted: "For stateless societies, where oral sources are often mediocre and the political tradition is inconsistent, it is often the study of religious phenomena of the microcosm, confronted early or late by the macrocosm, that instructs us the most clearly about the past."[39]

---

[35] Goody, *Domestication of the Savage Mind*, p. 14.
[36] Vansina, *Oral Tradition as History*, p. 120.
[37] Jan Vansina, *The Children of Woot: A History of the Kuba Peoples* (Madison: University of Wisconsin Press, 1978), p. 187. Jan Vansina, "History of God among the Kuba," *Africa* 28 (1983), p. 17.
[38] Jan Vansina, "Oral Tradition and Its Methodology," in *UNESCO General History of Africa, Vol. 1, Methodology and Prehistory*, ed. J. K-Zerbo (Berkeley: University of California Press, 1981), pp. 152–153.
[39] Person, "Pour une histoire des religions africaines," p. 24.

In many societies, each spirit cult has its own history, a founder, and a historical context in which it was created, as well as a changing role within the community. Contrary to Goody's claims, these are remembered, debated, and contested. Such things are often not disclosed to outsiders equipped with tape recorders, interpreters, and a limited schedule for field research. As I noted in reference to the Diola of Senegambia: "history provides a way to trace the origins of power back to the time of the first ancestors. Their relationships to a Diola past shape the relative importance of various cults, rituals, lineages, and property rights. Diola visions of that history become powerful forces in their understanding and ordering of their world."[40] Evidence of religious innovation challenges a fundamental image of African religions as consistent with the authority of the first ancestors who are seen as creating these traditions. It demonstrates that some practices, institutions, and ideas were created in more recent times, times that can be determined through the relationships to major natural events, studies of lineages, initiation rituals, and/or king-lists. To gain access to these types of oral testimony, individuals must demonstrate their ability to use this powerful knowledge responsibly, in ways that serve the community and its traditions.

Opponents of the use of oral traditions in African religious history emphasize what they see as the static nature of nonliterate cultures. This is part of an overstated contrast between tradition and modernity, between what Levi-Strauss calls the "hot" or the "cold" or the "raw and the cooked." The West is portrayed as embracing change and willing to challenge accepted theories and beliefs. They contrast their own societies with the "raw" indigenous societies' resistance to change, their quest for a return to social equilibrium and a reluctance to critically examine existing theories and beliefs.[41] In a path-breaking work, historian of science Thomas Kuhn questioned the dichotomy, demonstrating convincingly that the "hottest" in the West, scientists, are reluctant to challenge existing paradigms and often squeeze new evidence into preexisting theories. He cites the famous German scientist Max Planck, who wrote in his autobiography: "'a new scientific truth does not triumph by convincing its opponents and making them see the light, but rather because its opponents eventually die, and a new generation grows up that is familiar with it.'" Kuhn likens paradigm shifts to religious

---

[40] Baum, *Shrines*, p. 11.
[41] Levi-Strauss, *Savage Mind*, pp. 233–234. Claude Levi-Strauss, *The Raw and the Cooked* (New York: Octagon Books, 1969).

conversions.[42] The German Egyptologist Jan Assmann recommends an alternative that does away with the dichotomy, that we "regard cultures not as homogeneous wholes, but as both 'hot' and 'cold' and marked by both linear and cyclical time forms."[43] I would add that discourses of continuity or fidelity to older traditions remain central to many religions, not just within Africa. This entire work demonstrates the innovative aspects of African religions.

Three assumptions govern the resistance to the use of African oral traditions: their mythic qualities, the tendency to eliminate discordant events or ideas from oral narratives, and the lack of reflection about the significance of the changes that they describe. The mythic opposition includes anthropologist T. O. Beidelman, who argues that oral traditions primarily "reveal certain social or cultural 'truths' quite outside the sphere of the historical."[44] More recently he wrote about the "unchanging cosmological verities that provide coherence to how Kaguru analyze their society. These do not alter and are structurally the same in nearly all clan legends, even though particular details may vary."[45] Concerned that historians may be dismissive of mythic elements in oral traditions, Beidelman overlooks evidence of historical testimony concerning the development of Kaguru identity, migrations, and settlement patterns. Operating within a structuralist approach, he minimizes the importance of the contexts in which oral traditions develop or the ways in which they reflect critical issues in the evolution of a community's identity.

Other critics of oral traditions have emphasized the streamlining of traditions in which most of what is remembered from the past retains an importance to the narrator's society at the time of the narration. Things that seem

---

[42] Max Planck, cited in Thomas Kuhn, *The Structure of Scientific Revolutions*, 2nd ed. (Chicago: University of Chicago Press, 1970), p. 151. John Skorupski also questions this dichotomy which has profoundly influenced studies of indigenous religions. John Skorupski, *Symbol and Theory: A Philosophical Study of Religion in Social Anthropology* (Cambridge: Cambridge University Press, 1976), pp. 1–5, 194. In a more African-focused discussion, see Dan F. Bauer and John Hinnant. They suggest that many theorists underestimate both the openness of traditional societies and the closed tendencies of scientific communities. "Normal and Revolutionary Divination: A Kuhnian Approach to African Traditional Thought," in Ivan Karp and Charles Bird, eds., *Explorations in African Systems of Thought* (Washington, DC: Smithsonian, 1980), p. 233.

[43] Jan Assmann, *The Mind of Egypt: History and Meanings in the time of the Pharaohs* (New York: Holt, 1996), p. 15.

[44] T. O. Beidelman, "Myth, Legend, and Oral History: A Kaguru Traditional Text," *Anthropos* 65 (1970), p. 95. See also Luc de Heusch, *Le Roi Ivre ou l'origine de l'Etat* (Paris: Gallimard, 1972), pp. 363–364.

[45] T. O. Beidelman, *Moral Imagination in Kaguru Modes of Thought* (Bloomington: Indiana University Press, 1986), pp. 72, 82.

unimportant or contradict contemporary needs get forgotten or consciously weeded out of the narratives. This assumption rests on a notion of traditional societies as relatively homogeneous and faction-free, with little room for individual initiative. They tend to assume that contemporary needs can be boiled down to a few different groups and that individual perspectives would not produce distinctive narrative emphases. People have varied interests and different groups retain different aspects of the tradition and then introduce these elements back into other groups' narrative performances as the need or the desire arises. Peter Schmidt underscores this diversity of perspectives in reference to Buhaya oral traditions in Tanzania: "in the Buhaya religious system content and structure of oral traditions such as didactic myth, political history, and tales about the functions of shrines as mnenome differ considerably from the oral traditions of praise song singers who formerly related political history for the king. Recognition of different historiographic subsystems according to context helps to explain the development of different historical perspectives on Buhaya."[46] Furthermore, many students of oral traditions cite numerous examples of people recounting oral traditions that do not serve their individual or collective interests. Jan Vansina suggests that these elements, which seem to oppose the needs of the community, are particularly compelling as historical evidence. "When, however, traits or anecdotes run counter to fashion, they should be seen as reliable. These data resisted the trend to idealization."[47]

The remaining questions focus on a set of assumptions about the nature of oral cultures in contrast to literate cultures, especially their capacity for critical reflection. Both Walter Ong and Jack Goody have explored this dichotomy and have reached what I would regard as disturbing conclusions. Goody suggests that literate communities sustain a greater awareness of the contrast between the past and present. He contrasts that with people in oral cultures who cannot compare texts from different periods and therefore tend to think "mythically" about their past, whereas a "true" historical consciousness develops only with the existence of written texts.[48] He attributes this difference to the absence of the technology of writing; he does not believe that people in oral and literate cultures differ in any innate mental abilities. Goody and his colleague, Ian Watt, argue that:

[46] Peter R. Schmidt, *Historical Archaeologies: A Structural Approach in an African Culture* (Westport, CT: Greenwood, 1978), p. 7.
[47] Vansina, *Oral Tradition as History*, p. 29.
[48] Goody, *Domestication of the Savage Mind*, pp. 14–15.

But all their conceptualizations of the past cannot help being governed by the concerns of the present, merely because there is no body of chronologically ordered statements to which reference can be made. Myth and history merge into one. The elements in the cultural heritage which cease to have a contemporary relevance tend to be soon forgotten or transformed, and as the individuals of each generation acquire their own vocabulary, their genealogies, and their myths, they are unaware that various words, proper names and stories have dropped out, or that others have changed their meanings or been replaced.[49]

Goody and Watt draw on Maurice Halbwachs, whose work focuses on the shaping of memory by contemporary needs, though he only worked in literate cultures.[50] All three, however, seriously underestimate the diversity of historical needs and of individual historians in many cultures, as well as the considerable quantity of data retained in oral traditions that cannot be readily assigned to a contemporary function. The different emphases in oral histories may represent different "schools" of history. The assumption that history in oral cultures is only a mirror of present-day societal needs not only ignores similar influences on literate history but also confines oral historical knowledge far too narrowly within functionalist walls.[51]

Goody's writings on literacy influenced a student of rhetoric, Walter Ong, whose writings have influenced a scholarly generation's attitudes toward the "oral cultures" of the world. Lacking the fieldwork experience that informs Goody's work, however, Ong drew a less nuanced contrast between the oral and literate. For Ong, "oral" people live in an oral culture where "to think through something in non-formulaic, non-patterned, non-mnemonic terms, even if it were possible, would be a waste of time, for such thought, once worked through, could never be recovered with any effectiveness, as it could be with the aid of writing. It would not be abiding knowledge but

---

[49] Jack Goody and Ian Watt, "The Consequences of Literacy," in *Literacy in Traditional Societies*, ed. Jack Goody (Cambridge: Cambridge University Press, 1975), p. 34. This has been reaffirmed in Goody's *The Interface between the Written and the Oral* (Cambridge: Cambridge University Press, 1987), p. 220. Cults which bring in "new ideas, new prohibitions, new taboos, and were never simply 'more of the same.'"

[50] Maurice Halbwachs, *The Collective Memory* (New York: Harper, 1980). See also Paul Connerton, *How Societies Remember* (Cambridge: Cambridge University Press, 1989), pp. 2–6.

[51] For a critique of Halbwachs and Connerton, see Robert M. Baum, "Secrecy, Shrines, and Memory: Diola Oral Traditions and the Slave Trade in Senegal," in *Activating the Past: History and Memory in the Black Atlantic World*, ed. Andrew Apter and Robin Derby (New Castle upon Tyne, UK: Cambridge Scholars Press, 2010), pp. 139–156.

simply a passing thought, however complex."[52] He insists that education in oral cultures is quite different than in literate ones: "They learn by apprenticeship—hunting with experienced hunters for example—by discipleship, which is a kind of apprenticeship, by listening, by repeating what they hear, by mastering proverbs and ways of combining and recombining them, by assimilating other formulary materials by participation in a kind of corporate retrospective, not by study in the strict sense."[53] To Ong, oral cultures resist innovation and self-criticism, follow familiar paths, and hand down traditions from generation to generation. He describes oral people as living "very much in a present which keeps itself in equilibrium or homeostasis by sloughing off memories which no longer have present relevance."[54] Ong's work has shaped the image of "oral man" and oral cultures in many disciplines and applied to the study of many societies.[55]

Mircea Eliade rejects these claims of equilibrium or homeostasis in the history of religions. In *The Quest*, Eliade asserts that every culture "is constituted by a series of interpretations and revalorizations of its 'myths' or its specific ideologies."[56] Central to knowing these reevaluations is a knowledge of the languages within which these processes are expressed. African studies researchers who have worked in African languages and who have done extended research on multiple occasions have consistently found that local intellectuals analyze and debate issues raised by the oral knowledge that they transmit. Oral historians' ability to reflect on the significance of changes in ideas and practices demonstrates a far more highly developed capacity for memory than the writing-dependent theorists in literate cultures would allow.[57] For example, among the Diola of southern Senegal, elders work within a cyclical theory of history. The world has been created and destroyed many times. In each case, life returns with a single couple who remain in close contact with the supreme being, Emitai. As humans develop social institutions, they neglect the supreme being, become diverted by quests for wealth and power, and resort to witchcraft and other antisocial activities.

---

[52] Walter J. Ong, *Orality and Literacy: The Technologizing of the Word* (London: Methuen, 1982), pp. 35–36.
[53] Ong, *Orality and Literacy*, p. 9. He also equates oral cultures and traditional ones. See "World as View and World as Event," *American Anthropologist* 73 (1969), pp. 636–641.
[54] Ong, *Orality and Literacy*, p. 46. Goody, *Domestication of the Savage Mind*, p. 41.
[55] Vail and White, *Power and the Praise Poem*, p. xii.
[56] Mircea Eliade, *The Quest: History and Meaning in Religion* (Chicago: University of Chicago Press, [1969] 1984), p. 61.
[57] For a more detailed discussion of the use of oral tradition in my own work, see Baum, *Shrines*, pp. 8–12.

Eventually the world becomes so corrupted that Emitai decides to destroy it in an apocalypse called *Adonai*. Within this historical model, both the Atlantic slave trade and European colonization are seen as part of the downward pull toward destruction.

One finds other models for understanding such events within BaKongo thought, relating the arrival of Europeans to their vision of the world as two mountains, separated by the ocean.[58] The analysis of oral traditions provides a means of accessing a wider range of African perspectives on the history of religions than written sources alone. This will become evident in the course of this work. As Wim van Binsbergen suggests, the analysis of oral traditions, combined with a careful assessment of the symbolic context of these recitations, may provide a means of creating a new form of the "histories of ideas" that is quite different from those that have dominated Western academic practice."[59]

Archaeology also provides an important source for African religious history. Analyses of tree rings provide clues to cycles of drought and plentiful rainfall which have implications for religious history. Campsites offer clues to the types of foods consumed and hence the types of agricultural, fishing, or hunting cults that were present. Similarly, graves may provide clues about attitudes about death and the afterlife, which are central to most religious systems. Christopher Hawkes claims a certain utility to focusing on funerary practices. He notes that "Grave goods indicate a belief that the dead need material or equipment, as though they were still alive. But how much further can we go than that?"[60] Deliberate placing of bodies facing toward the rising or setting sun, burial in home sites or remote locations, and purposeful design of graves or tombs may offer clues about religious views of death. However, as Mark Smith insists, this must be done with caution.

> Although it is sometimes assumed that the practice of burial itself constitutes evidence of a belief in an afterlife, we should be cautious about linking the two without more proof of a connection between them. Some

---

[58] Baum, *Shrines*, pp. 58–59. Wyatt MacGaffey, *Religion and Society in Central Africa: The BaKongo of Lower Zaire* (Chicago: University of Chicago Press, 1986), pp. 42–61. "African History, Anthropology, and the Rationality of Natives," *History in Africa* V (1978), pp. 105–126.

[59] Wim van Binsbergen, "Lykota, Liya, Bankoya: Memory, Myth, and History," *Cahiers des Etudes Africaines* XXVII (1987), pp. 387–388.

[60] Christopher Hawkes (1954) cited in Lars Fogelin, "Delegitimating Religion: The Archaeology of Religion as Archaeology," in *Belief in the Past: Theoretical Approaches to the Archaeology of Religion*, ed. D. S. Whitley and K. Hays-Gilpin (Walnut Creek, CA: Left Coast Press, 2017), p. 131.

societies bury their dead but have no conception of posthumous existence. Conversely, others believe in an afterlife, but do not bury their dead. Internment of a corpse can be no more than a quick and simple way to dispose of it. Nor is the difference between burial and disposal always apparent, even to specialists. What to identify as graves, others think are simply rubbish pits, into which bodies have been thrown for the sake of conveniences.[61]

Ritual sites can be analyzed both in terms of the types of plants and animals offered at these locations and the types of materials left behind by ritual participants. Sites of rituals become important sources for religious history. As Joyce Marcus noted:

Since ritual must be performed over and over in prescribed ways to be effective, these repetitive performances can bring about patterning in the archaeological record. Archaeologists therefore need to locate the places where rituals were performed, draw inferences about why these places were considered appropriate for ritual, determine which non-perishable artifacts should be discarded there and consider which perishable artifacts might have been used, even when their recovery is unlikely.[62]

Curtis Maren and Zelalen Assefa argue that archaeological evidence can provide important insights into a variety of symbolic behaviors having religious significance: "burial of the dead, preparation of a human skeleton after death, or shaping functional objects with symbolic (communicative) goals in mind." They caution against overly confident interpretations, suggesting that although burial can have symbolic meanings, it can also have been done "simply to dispose of a rotting corpse."[63]

Changes in ritual locations, in ritual structures, and the paraphernalia left at such sites provide important information about religious history.

---

[61] Mark Smith, *Following Osiris: Perspectives on the Osirian Afterlife, from Four Millennia* (Oxford: Oxford University Press, 2017), p. 9.
[62] Joyce Marcus, "Rethinking Ritual," in *The Archaeology of Ritual*, ed. Evangelos Kyrickidis (Berkeley: University of California Press, 2007), p. 46.
[63] Curtis Maren and Zelalen Assefa, "The Middle and Upper Pleistocene African Record for the Biological and Behavioral Origins of Modern Humans," in *African Archaeology: A Critical Introduction*, ed. Ann Brower Stahl (Malden, MA: Blackwell, 2012), p. 116.

Unfortunately, remains are not evenly distributed. Objects from drier regions and rock objects are more likely to be preserved than objects from moister areas or from organic materials. In general, there is a serious lack of archaeological sites for West Africa and the Zaire basin before the second millennium BCE.[64] Western fascination with the wonder that was Egypt has led to more funding for archaeological work there than in other regions of Africa. Questions of political stability have also affected the ability of archaeologists to conduct research in many African nations.

Over the last half century, ethnoarchaeological approaches have become increasingly common. Examining material objects and ritual sites through an emphasis on the cultural meaning allows researchers to carefully interpret objects and places through cultural analysis. As Peter Schmidt noted in reference to his work in Tanzania: "One of the advantages of ethnoarchaeology is that it richly informs an otherwise inanimate material culture with cultural significance."[65]

Once written or oral interpretations are available to explicate archaeological evidence, then the investigations become much more nuanced. Until that time, assigning meanings to exclusively material evidence can be quite difficult. In the absence of local interpretations, material evidence can be suggestive, even strongly suggestive, but not conclusive. The scholar relying on material evidence often has trouble resisting the temptation of projecting from what he or she knows of more recent human activity back to ancient materials. Although some such interpretation is inevitable, it must be done rarely and as openly as possible.

Similarly, linguistic shifts can provide important clues concerning migrations of population groups, introductions of new technologies, and ideas concerning deities, spirits, and rituals. Shared words often suggest shared ideas among groups. Newer words, derived from older roots, provide evidence of new needs for verbal expression. Borrowed words may indicate religious or cultural influences that would be of value to the historian of African religions. Rates of linguistic change, what is known as

---

[64] Alisa Brady and Peter Robertshaw, "The Glacial Maximum in Tropical Africa 22,000–12,000 BP," in *The World at 18,000 BP, Volume One, Low Latitudes*, ed. Clive Gamble and Olga Soffer (London: Unwin Hyman, 1990), 121.
[65] Peter Schmidt, *Iron Technology in East Africa: Symbolism, Science, and Archaeology* (Bloomington: Indiana University Press, 1997), p. 164.

glottochronology, can help establish dates for such shifts. As linguistic historian Christopher Ehret suggests:

> The writing of history from language evidence begins with a fact, simple in statement but complex in its implications: every language is an archive. Its documents are the thousands of words that make up its lexicon. Each development of a new word, each shift in meaning or change in usage of an existing word, takes place for a human historical reason. Sometimes the reason may have been an ephemeral factor of taste or fashion, no longer recoverable.
>
> But more often than not, word histories have practical and discernable causes. New words come into use, and old words change meaning or add new meanings, because change takes place in the particular elements of human knowledge, belief, custom, or livelihood to which they refer.[66]

In a recent monograph, Rhonda Gonzalez provides a detailed analysis of the use of glottochronology in the study of early African history and the use of what she identifies as "median dating estimates."[67]

Jan Vansina urged caution about relying too heavily on glottochronology. He agreed that it provides evidence of important changes in terminology but rejected the idea that such changes could be dated with certainty. Vansina insisted that scholars cannot assume that languages change at a constant rate. Derek Nurse agreed: "linguistic change can be quite uneven, proceeding in fits and starts, and is directly affected by external circumstances."[68] Vansina preferred something he called "words and things," which is less chronologically precise but may be more accurate. He also rejected imagery in some historical works that suggest that languages split from one another. He saw them as beginning to diverge in a more gradual process. Finally, Vansina urged historians of ancient Africa to carefully cross-check linguistic, archaeological, oral, and written evidence.[69]

---

[66] Ehret, *History and the Testimony of Language*, p. 3, 52.

[67] Rhonda Gonzalez, *Societies, Religion, and History: Central East Tanzanians and the World They Created, c. 200 BCE to 1800 CE* (New York: Columbia University Press, 2009), pp. 22–27. She and other colleagues working on the early history of Bantu-speaking histories rely heavily on lexicostatistics and the work of Morris Swadesh. Catherine Symone Fourshey, Rhonda M. Gonzalez, and Christine Saidi, *Bantu Africa: 3500 BCE to Present* (New York: Oxford University Press, 2017), pp. 26–93.

[68] Derek Nurse, "The Contributions of Linguistics to the Study of History in Africa," *The Journal of African History* 38 (1997), p. 366.

[69] Jan Vansina, *Paths into the Rainforest: Toward a History of Political Tradition in Equatorial Africa* (Madison: University of Wisconsin Press, 1990), p. 16. Jan Vansina, *How Societies Are Born: Governance in West Central Africa Before, 1600* (Charlottesville: University of Virginia Press, 2004), pp. 7–11.

Still, language plays an important role in shaping human ways of classifying phenomena, and its influence can be quite long-lasting. As Emile Durkheim noted:

> Thus, the language of a people always has an influence upon the manner in which new things, recently learned are classified in the mind and are subsequently thought of; these new things are thus forced to adapt themselves to pre-existing forms. For this reason, the language which men spoke when they undertook to construct an elaborated representation of the universe marked the system of ideas which was then born with an indelible trace.[70]

Language shapes the ways that people construct their worlds and decide what is significant. With the search for proto languages, however, there are also problems of context. Although we can learn the root words that are shared between languages from word lists, it is difficult to establish the deeper meaning of terms, particularly when they have religious significance. Durkheim ascribed an importance to language that transcends word lists: "Language is not merely the external covering of a thought; it is also its internal framework."[71] Word lists by themselves, however, cannot reveal this internal structure and can lead to overly confident assertions of common ideas.

Africa in the Study of Religions

Having discussed the challenges and strengths of sources for the historical study of African religions, I turn to the question of whether Africans had "religion." From the beginning this question became entangled in debates about the origins of religion in general. This issue needs to be addressed at empirical, comparative, and theoretical levels. European visitors to Africa, beginning with the Portuguese, in the fifteenth century, provided limited commentaries on African religions. By and large, they came for other reasons—seeking sea routes to the East Indies on behalf of their Portuguese sponsors; engaging in trade in beeswax, gum Arabic, ivory, gold, and enslaved persons; or to

---

[70] Emile Durkheim, *The Elementary Forms of Religious Life* (New York: The Free Press, [1915] 1965), p. 94.
[71] Durkheim, *Elementary*, p. 94.

establish permanent trading stations on readily defensible ground on coastal islands or mainland promontories. In a few areas, most notably the Kingdom of Kongo, missionaries played a vital role, providing detailed descriptions of African rituals, with occasional glimpses into the central concepts that underlay their religious systems. Most travelers' accounts provided fragmentary evidence, taken out of its social or cultural context. Still, these travel memoirs and diaries, ships' logs, and missionary accounts became the raw material for the representation of African religions in Western imaginaries. They fueled the early modern speculation about the origins of religion in general and the nature of religious systems. These reports were collected into anthologies or thematic compendiums by such men as Charles de Brosses in France and Sir James Frazer in England.[72]

Despite the growing number of descriptions of African religious practices, some explorers, travelers, and administrators persisted in the idea that Africans had no religions at all. Sir Samuel Baker, who explored the Upper Nile in the 1860s, wrote with confidence about the Shilluk, Nuer, and Dinka people he encountered: "Without any exception, they are without a belief in a Supreme Being, neither have they any form of worship or idolatry; nor is the darkness of their minds enlightened by even a ray of superstition. The mind is as stagnant as the morass which forms its puny world."[73] One has to wonder how he was able to draw such conclusions without speaking the languages or staying in any one location for any sustained period. Baker looked for houses of worship and written texts, what he considered to be essential components of religious life. He found none.

As reports of African religious practices slowly reached interested readers of ethnographic and travel accounts in Europe and the Americas, theorists began to try to make sense of these descriptions. Influenced by the tendency since the late eighteenth century to develop a corpus of laws of society that paralleled the proliferation of natural laws about the universe, a group of armchair anthropologists took these reports and proposed laws

---

[72] Charles de Brosses, *On the Worship of Fetish Gods: Or, Parallel of the Ancient Religions of Egypt with the Present Religions of Nigritia* (1760), in *The Returns of Fetishism: Charles de Brosses and the Afterlife of an Idea*, ed. Rosalind C. Morris and David H. Leonard (Chicago: University of Chicago Press, 2017). Sir James Frazer, *The Golden Bough* (New York: Macmillan, 1935).

[73] Baker attributed this lack of religion to peoples whose religious systems have been studied in now classical anthropological and historical works by Evans-Pritchard, *Nuer Religion*. Godfrey Lienhardt, *Divinity and Experience: The Religion of the Dinka* (Oxford: Oxford University Press, 1961). Douglas Johnson, *Nuer Prophets: A History of Prophecy from the Upper Nile in the Nineteenth and Twentieth Centuries* (Oxford: Clarendon Press, 1994). Sir Samuel Baker, cited in E. E. Evans-Pritchard, *Theories of Primitive Religion* (London: Oxford University Press, [1965] 1984), pp. 6–7.

about the development of religion, usually seeing European practices at the apex of humanity's religious evolution. Africa was relegated toward the bottom, portrayed almost as a living laboratory where social scientists could see how early humanity sought to understand the spiritual forces that circulated in the world, though most of them never encountered the peoples they theorized about.[74] The earliest of these theorists was Charles de Brosses, who claimed that the origins of humanity's religious expressions came from "power objects" that were sometimes traded with the Portuguese along the West African coast. Religious practitioners consecrated these objects and thought that they contained spiritual powers that could effect change in the world. The Portuguese called them *feitiços*, which de Brosses translated as "fetish," from which the theory of the fetishist origins of religion was born. The term initially referred to popular forms of magic in the Middle Ages and was used to describe highly valued material items in West African trade and West African religious practice.

> These divine Fetishes are nothing other than the first material object that each nation or individual have seen fit to have ceremonially consecrated by Its priests: a tree, a mountain, the sea, a piece of wood, a lion's tail, a stone, a shell, salt, a fish, a plant, a flower, an animal of a certain species, such as a cow, goat, elephant, or sheep, in short, anything of this sort that one could possibly imagine. They are so many Gods, sacred objects, and also talismans for the Negroes, who also worship them . . . in an exact and respectful manner, address their wishes to them, offer them sacrifices, carry them in procession, if it is possible, or wear them on their persons with great marks of veneration and consult them on any significant occasion.
>
> They *regard* them as titularies of men and as powerful safeguards against all sorts of accidents. They swear on them, and this is the only vow that these perfidious peoples dare not violate.[75]

Regardless of their material content, de Brosses claimed that fetishes were seen as valuable, powerful, and sacred. Although Africans certainly saw

---

[74] On armchair anthropologists, see E. E. Evans-Pritchard, *Theories of Primitive Religion* (Oxford: Clarendon Press, 1965), p. 6. The idea that prehistoric religions can be understood by *looking* at present-day indigenous religions persists, particularly in reference to hunting and gathering groups like the San. For a recent example, see Denise Carmody and John Carmody, *Original Visions: The Religions of Oral Practices* (New York: Macmillan, 1993), pp. 3–5. For a discussion of nineteenth-century German evolutionary social theory, see Matory, *Fetish Revisited* p. 42.

[75] Brosses, *On the Worship of Fetish Gods*, p. 48.

the possibility of concentrating spiritual power in certain objects, they did not conceive of such power actually being contained by an object. Similar beliefs were found in Abrahamic traditions, from the veneration of Christian or Muslim relics, to the Jewish practices of placing Holy Scripture above each entryway into one's home. De Brosses, however, saw African fetishism as a lower spiritual state than the monotheism of Western religions.[76] Later theorists introduced other stages. Auguste Comte added an intermediary stage of polytheism and Sir Edward Burnett Tylor added a preliminary stage of animism, both of which they would have thought had African examples.[77] Andrew Lang believed that ancestor worship was the primal religion. Both the concerns with the origins of religions and the idea of the evolution of religion in discrete stages reflected the influence of Charles Darwin's theories of evolution and a desire to justify European imperial expansion in Africa, the Americas, and Asia.[78]

There is a second type of question about the existence of something called "religion" in Africa. This issue can be broken down into two areas. First, there is the question of whether scholars can assume the existence of something called "religion" cross-culturally, given the term's close association with Christianity and the Roman world. Second, there is the question of the relevance of this category for the study of African cultures. In a now classic essay, the late historian of religion Jonathan Z. Smith challenged scholars engaged in comparative research, to question their assumption of a category of religion in all societies:

> While there is a staggering amount of data, of phenomena, of human experiences and expressions that might be characterized in one culture or another, by one criterion or another, as religious—there is no data for religion. Religion is solely the creation of the scholar's study. It is created for the scholar's analytic purposes by his imaginative acts of comparison

---

[76] William Pietz, "The Problem of the Fetish, I," *RES: Anthropology and Aesthetics* 9 (1985), pp. 4–17. Rosalind C. Morris and David H. Leonard, *The Returns of Fetishism: Charles de Brosses and the Afterlives of an Idea* (Chicago: University of Chicago Press, 2017).

[77] Graham Harvey has recently tried to redeem the term "animism," as a focus on relations among persons, a view of all beings and aspects of the environment, such as rocks or mountains, as subjects, but I think his definition is so far from Tylor's as to demand a new term. See Graham Harvey, *Animism: Respecting the Living World* (London: Hurst and Company, 2017), pp. xvii–xxiv, 3–30. For a thoughtful critique of the new animism, see Daryl Wilkerson, "Is There Such a Thing as Animism?" *Journal of the American Academy of Religion* 87, no. 2 (June 2017), pp. 289–311.

[78] Benjamin Ray, *African Religions: Symbol, Ritual, and Community* (Englewood Cliffs, NJ: Prentice Hall, 1976), pp. 5–6. Evans-Pritchard, *Theories*, pp. 6–28.

and generalization. Religion has no independent existence apart from the academy.

He then challenges comparativists to stipulate exactly what they mean when they use the English term "religion" or its cognates in related languages.[79] Talal Asad raises a similar challenge to anthropologists: "The anthropological student of *particular* religions should therefore begin from this point in a sense unpacking the concept which he or she translates as 'religion' into heterogeneous elements according to its historical character."[80]

These are very different questions than the one posed by Hegel or Baker. They are raised in a specifically African context by the historian Louis Brenner. He points out that "most African languages did not include a word which could be convincingly and unequivocally translated as 'religion'" until contact with Christians and Muslims, who already had such a concept. "Nonetheless, most studies of African societies treat 'religion' as an institutionally and conceptually distinct category of analysis as if the author knew precisely what it was, not only for himself, but for the members of the societies under study as well."[81] Although Brenner is correct that many African religions do not have a single term that corresponds to what Westerners refer to as "religion," there is clear evidence for ideas and practices and their places within African cultural systems that would significantly overlap with what Westerners mean by "religion." The Egyptologist Jan Assmann agrees about the term: "The ancient Egyptian language has no word for 'religion', but the many treatments of Egyptian have encountered no difficulties in determining their subject, the relevant phenomena are clearly distinct within what remains to us of Egyptian culture."[82]

Following Smith's and Asad's challenges, in the Diola language, the only African language that I speak fluently enough to address this question, there are four terms that I associate with the English term "religion": *makanaye* (customs), *boutine* (path), *kainoe* (thought), and *awasena* (one who performs

---

[79] J. Z. Smith, *Imagining Religion: From Babylon to Jonestown* (Chicago: University of Chicago Press, 1982), p. xi.
[80] Talal Asad, *Genealogies of Religion: Discipline and Reasons of Power in Christianity and Islam* (Baltimore: Johns Hopkins University, 1993), p. 54.
[81] Louis Brenner, "Religious Discourses in and About Africa," in *Discourse and Its Disguises*, ed. Karin Barber and de Moraes Fabias (Birmingham: Centre for West African Studies, University of Birmingham, 1989), p. 87.
[82] Jan Assmann, *The Search for God in Ancient Egypt* (Ithaca, NY: Cornell University Press, 2001), p. 7.

rituals).[83] The association of these terms with what I mean by religion closely resembles the late Ninian Smart's idea of a catchment of seven characteristics that define what he means by religion in his comparative studies.[84]

It should be pointed out that what religion means is quite different within a single culture depending on whether one is engaged in scholarly study, what kind of scholarly study, and whether one is an adherent and, if so, what type of adherent. To many scholars, religion is a bounded phenomenon, focused on the sacred and not the profane, whereas to a significant number of adherents, there is nothing that is truly profane. Religion may be less a distinct entity than a perspective on the entirety of life.[85] It is the assumption of this work that all cultures have something that corresponds to what Westerners refer to as "religion," not as something distinct and separate from other forms of human experience, but as a distinct aspect of systems of thought, fundamentally charged with the interpretation and bestowing of meaning on the experiences of life. As the historian Suzanne Langer noted, human beings cannot sustain themselves without the ability to explain their world. This is a central task of African religious systems, just as it is in other cultures.[86] Even when people consider themselves to have rejected "religion" in the form of its most salient beliefs, that is, a belief in a particular deity, they remain profoundly influenced by core ideas and issues, modes of perception, and ways of posing questions.

Over the past two centuries of scholarly study of African religions, there have been periodic attempts to establish a basic description of African "religion" as if the well over a thousand different religious systems could be boiled down into one template. Neither de Brosses nor Tylor had sufficient data to distinguish among different African religions. De Brosses considered them fetishist; Tylor placed them in the animist category. As people became aware that there were spiritual entities, a new debate emerged, a debate concerning the importance of a supreme being and its relationship to other

---

[83] For a more detailed discussion of these Diola terms, see Baum, *Shrines*, pp. 36–37.

[84] Ninian Smart, *Worldviews: Cross-Cultural Explorations of Human Beliefs*, 3rd ed. (Upper Saddle River, NJ: Prentice Hall, 2000), pp. 8–10. Stephan Quirke deals with the problem in a different way for his study of ancient Egyptian religion, emphasizing their sense of place, their relationships with other people and other peoples, and to the forces that influence our lives, as the key aspect of what he means by "religion." Stephen Quirke, *Exploring Religion in Ancient Egypt* (Chichester, UK: Wiley, Blackwell, 2015), p. 1.

[85] Baum, *Shrines*, p. 35.

[86] Suzanne Langer, cited in Clifford Geertz, "Religion as a Cultural System," in Clifford Geertz, *The Interpretation of Cultures* (New York: Basic Books, 1973), p. 89. Robin Horton, "African Traditional Thought and Western Science," in *Patterns of Thought in Africa and the West*, ed. Robin Horton (Cambridge: Cambridge University Press).

types of spiritual beings. Missionaries had found that wherever they worked, when they asked people about their name for the supreme being, they always had an answer. As missionary reports became increasingly numerous, it became clear that most African religions had a sense of a single deity who began the process of creating the universe. However, these supreme beings were, in many cases, assisted by lesser spirits or divinities. Based on the observed reality that these lesser divinities, spirits, and ancestors received more ritual attention than did the supreme being, outside observers concluded that African supreme beings were inactive and were overshadowed by the various types of lesser spirits. They referred to African supreme beings as *deus otiotus* or as remote deities. The existence of lesser spirits led some to conclude that African religions were polytheistic, a step below the Abrahamic monotheistic religions, as described by Auguste Comte and later evolutionary theorists.[87]

African Christian theologians were deeply troubled by this condescension toward African religions. In response, E. Bolaji Idowu developed the idea of "diffuse monotheism," suggesting that many lesser divinities of Yoruba religion, the 401 orisha, were manifestations of the one deity, Olorun or Oludumare.[88] John Mbiti, J. F. Danquah, and other African Christian commentators sought to demonstrate that African religions were monotheistic as well.[89] The Ugandan poet and philosopher Okot P'Bitek criticized the entire debate about African monotheism and polytheism as having more to do with Christian scholars' preoccupation with the idea that Christians are monotheists in the face of Greek, Jewish, and Muslim critiques than it does with ordinary practitioners of African religions.[90] Since the time of ancient Greek philosophers, intellectuals have valued monotheism over polytheism and African intellectuals sought to associate their religious heritage with the more prestigious terminology. One could argue that monotheism is an ideal type; even the most adamantly monotheist traditions, Judaism and Islam, have beliefs in other *theos*, be they angels for both Jews and Muslims, Satan (Iblis) for some Jews and most Muslims, and *djinn* (spirits) for many Muslims.

---

[87] On the idea of a remote supreme being, see Diedrich Westermann, quoted in Rosalind Shaw, "The Invention of African Traditional Religion," *Religion* 20 (1990), p. 344. Shaw, "Invention," pp. 330–353. Ray, *African Religions*, pp. 5–7, 50–52.

[88] E. Bolaji Idowu, *Olodumare: God in Yoruba Religion* (New York: Wazobia, [1962] 1994), pp. 102, 204. E. Bolaji Idowu, *African Traditional Religion* (London: SCM Press, 1973), p. 135.

[89] John Mbiti, *Concepts of God in Africa* (New York: Praeger, 1976). J. B. Danquah, *The Akan Doctrine of God: A Fragment of Gold Coast Ethics and Religion* (London: Cass, 1965).

[90] Okot P'Bitek, *African Traditional Religions and Western Scholarship* (Kampala: East African Literature Bureau, 1970), p. 88. Ray, *African Religions*, pp. 14–16.

In the 1940s, a Belgian Catholic missionary, Father Placide Tempels, sought to shift the focus, arguing that African religions concentrated on a disembodied power, *la force vital* (life force or vital force). His work was criticized for suggesting that underlying African religious practice was a philosophical set of concepts, focusing on both the augmentation and diminution of life force and the importance of the extended family and community in African religious life.[91]

In the 1970s, the sociologist Robin Horton set out what he called his "basic African cosmology," as a prelude to his theory explaining religious conversion that dominated African religious history in the late twentieth century. He began with what he called a two-tiered cosmology.

> In the first tier we find the lesser spirits, which are in the main concerned with the affairs of the local community and its environment—i.e., with the microcosm. In the second tier we find a supreme being concerned with the world as a whole—i.e., with the macrocosm. Just as the microcosm is part of the macrocosm, so the supreme being is defined as the ultimate controller and existential ground of the lesser spirits.[92]

Horton saw a close connection between African supreme beings and macrocosmic experience, lesser spirits with microcosmic experience. He incorporated a historical dimension, allowing for a greater or lesser emphasis on a supreme being depending on the nature of economic activity and social relations. Trade, pastoralism, or other activities relying on extensive travel or interaction with outsiders Horton saw as encouraging a monolatric emphasis. Similarly, subsistence farming with its local orientation supported a focus on lesser spirits. Horton assumed that, since most Africans live in rural areas and concentrate on agriculture, the microcosm and lesser spirits tended to dominate African religious life. He saw supreme beings as usually remote from the daily concerns of most African religionists and morality as the responsibility of the lesser spirits of the second tier. Horton claimed:

> The essence of the pre-Modern situation is that most events affecting the life of the individual occur within the microcosm of the local community, and that this microcosm is to a considerable extent insulated from the

---

[91] Placide Tempels, *Bantu Philosophy* (Paris: Presence Africaine, 1946).
[92] Robin Horton, "African Conversion," *Africa* 41 (1971), p. 101.

macrocosm of the wider world. Since most significant interaction occurs within the local community, moral rules tend to apply within the community rather than universally—i.e., within the microcosm rather than within the macrocosm. Given the association of lesser spirits with microcosm and supreme being with macrocosm, it follows from these facts that the former will be credited with direct responsibility for most events of human concern, will be the primary guardians of morality, and will be credited with direct responsibility for relatively few events of human concern, will have no direct association with morality and will seldom be approached by human beings.[93]

There are a number of problems associated with this theory. First, Horton assumes that the supreme being and the lesser spirits are in opposition; an increase in one leads to a decrease in the other, a kind of zero-sum game of religious activity. Local and regional crises may lead to an intensification of religious activity at all levels. Furthermore, he exaggerates the localism of precolonial Africa. Many African states and cities were multiethnic, had thriving cults of local deities, and engaged in significant amounts of long-distance trade. To provide one example, that of San groups of the Tsodilo Hills of Botswana's Kalahari: "The families here not only grew their own subsistence food; they also may have traded surplus cattle and specularite for smelted copper and iron, for seashells from the Atlantic and Indian Oceans, and for glass beads from the Middle East ... clearly reveals that the inhabitants were anything but isolated. Indeed, Tsodilo is being gradually elevated into its proper place as a pivotal center for first millennium trade, despite its location in the middle of the dry Kalahari Desert."[94] Even the most isolated areas of the Kalahari were involved in long-distance trade that ultimately linked African societies with trading partners beyond the continent.

Some of the most important shrines of the supreme being were in relatively remote areas that could easily be associated with Horton's microcosms. He also seems unaware of the crucial role that supreme beings play in judging people after death, something described as common within Atlantic coastal communities from Senegal to Congo. It is the supreme

---

[93] I will discuss Horton's theory of conversion later in this work. Horton, "African Conversion," p. 101. Robin Horton, "On the Rationality of Conversion," *Africa* 45 (1975), p. 219.

[94] Alec Campbell, Larry Robbins, and Michael Taylor, eds., *Tsodilo Hills: Copper Bracelet of the Kalahari* (East Lansing: Michigan State University Press, 2010), p. 7. The South African film *The Gods Must Be Crazy* suggested a similar isolation for their late twentieth-century descendants.

being, Emitai, who decides in a Diola cosmos, who becomes an ancestor, and who is banished as a phantom. Among the Yoruba, it is Olorun or Oludumare who determines one's fate in the afterlife, whether one will be reborn and what kind of life one can look forward to after being reborn.[95] This suggests that in many African religions the supreme being plays a critical role in the ultimate issue of morality: judgment after death. Furthermore, in many West African religions, the supreme being is associated with rain. Adequate rainfall is a source of major religious concerns in much of the Sahel and Sudanic regions and is central to the survival of both herding and farming communities.

Similarly, Horton assumes a greater homogeneity of his second tier than actually exists. Rather than two tiers, I would argue, there is a continuum from the supreme being to the most immediate ancestors. Lesser spirits or deities range from powerful gods associated with the heavens or earth, thunder clouds and blacksmiths, to more local deities associated with particular places, local warriors, and local boys' and girls' rites of passage. Ancestors provide the most intimate connection with the spiritual world, providing life to their descendants before they died and ongoing counsel and assistance for their descendants once they have crossed over to the realm of the dead. Different African religious systems emphasize different aspects of this continuum, but there is no direct correspondence between the degree of localism and the focus of religious veneration.

Horton seems unaware that the supreme being is quite capable of entering the microcosm of local affairs. Diola elders describe the intervention of Emitai in a war between two quarters of the same township, a war in which Divinity favored the side that had been morally wronged. Here again is a concrete example of a supreme being intervening on moral issues, even though they are of strictly local importance.[96] Similarly, Diola elders describe soldiers going off to fight in the First World War, carrying consecrated soil from local spirit shrines to protect them on European battlefields. Traditional priests developed new rituals to protect their youth from harm on the battlefields of Western Europe. More dramatically, the ability of Yoruba deities, the orisha, to cross the Atlantic Ocean despite the horrors of the Middle Passage, suggests that African spirits were not confined to any microcosm, but reemerged in cults of Shango, Oshun, Ogun, Yemaya, and Eshu

---

[95] Baum, *Shrines*, p. 39. Simon Bockie, *Death and the Invisible World: In Kongo Belief* (Berkeley: University of California Press, 1993).
[96] Baum, *Shrines*, pp. 95–98. Baum, *West African*, pp. 52–53.

from the Caribbean to Brazil, becoming important religious influences in Santeria, Vaudou, Candomble, and Macumba. Finally, he ignores the ability of lesser spirits to thrive in such macrocosmic environments as the Greek and Roman empires.

This work focuses on the historical study of African religious traditions. I define African religious traditions as religions created in Africa, by African people, and closely associated with ideas of cultural identity. I will not try to develop a basic African cosmology but recognize that there are some regional similarities in African religious traditions. For example, religious traditions of the Upper Guinea Coast have similarities, particularly in contrast to traditions of Lower Guinea or the Sudanic region. Still, even among groups that outsiders consider to be one ethnic group—that is, the Yoruba, Shona, or Diola—there are considerable variations among subgroups affecting not only religious practices but the underlying concepts that are associated with them.

Throughout this study, I will examine African traditions' sustained interaction with religions that originated outside of Africa. In the case of Judaism, there is a debate about whether its origins can be traced back to Moses's Egypt or Abraham's Sumer, but there has been a close connection between African communities and Jewish communities according to both Hebrew and other sources. Christianity traces its presence in Africa back to the narratives concerning the flight of Jesus, Joseph, and Mary to Egypt. The Islamic connection to Ethiopia precedes the Hijra by several years. Of the major traditions originating outside of Africa, only Hinduism is a recent presence, primarily affecting African religious history since the mid-nineteenth century. However, religious traditions that African communities created remain the central focus of this work.

Finally, I should point out some terms that have different implications in different disciplines, with negative connotations to people outside the comparative and historical study of religions. For example, the term "myth" often implies an untrue or fabulous story and the label of "mythomaniac" could be applied to some politicians, but within the academic study of religion it refers to a sacred narrative, a tradition handed down within a religious community that is widely seen as having an authoritative and, often, extra-human source. This term facilitates comparative work by suggesting that such sacred narratives as Yoruba creation myths are comparable with Genesis and with the Rig Veda. What it does not do is suggest anything about the truth claims of a particular myth, only that it occupies a similar position as sacred traditions in other religions.[97] The same is true of the term "cult," which has acquired a negative meaning of a small, authoritarian movement, frequently led by a charismatic leader. Historians of religions use the term in its older meaning of a particular set of rituals and a community of shared religious focus that is directed to a particular deity, spirit, or power as an important part of a religious tradition. So using a term such as "blacksmith cults" does not suggest anything negative about a community which invokes the powers of fire and the artisanal skills of masters of iron.

Structure of the Work

This study is organized chronologically, beginning with what we can know about the religious practices of the earliest human beings, who originated in Africa. This chapter continues through the Neolithic Revolution and the rise of sedentary villages and towns. The source material for this chapter is primarily archaeological. In Chapter 3, I move on to a discussion of ancient Egyptian religious history, from the unification of Egypt to the religious reforms of Akhenaten. Source material includes archaeological evidence and both written texts and written versions of oral traditions. Chapter 4 analyzes the history of ancient African communities outside of the Nile valley, from the end of the fourth millennium until the latter part of the second millennium BCE. This section relies on archaeology, linguistic analysis, and a few written texts.

In Chapter 5, I return to the Nile valley of ancient Egypt and Nubia, from the suppression of Akhenaton's reforms until the Roman conquest of Egypt and Lower Nubia. Chapter 6 examines the history of African religions beyond the Nile valley, through the Hellenistic era. Chapter 7 examines the sustained interaction among Egyptian religious traditions, Judaism, and Christianity under various forms of Roman rule, before the spread of Islam into the region. Chapter 8 focuses on the history of North and northeast Africa until the arrival of Muslim asylum-seekers at the Ethiopian court in Axum, in the early seventh century. Chapter 9 traces the religious history of West, East, Equatorial, and southern Africa until the early seventh century. Finally, Chapter 10 reflects on the broader significance of these changes in religious thought and practice, from the origins of humanity to the end of the pre-Islamic era.

---

[97] Eliade, *Quest*, pp. 72–73. Smith, *Imagining Religion*, p. 66. Kenelm Burridge, *New Heaven, New Earth: A Study of Millenarian Activities* (Oxford: Basil Blackwell, 1969), pp. 62–69.

A continent-wide history of African religions cannot hope to be comprehensive. I will focus my analysis on those areas illuminated by the richest sources, be they archaeological, written, or oral in nature. Thus, my efforts to analyze African religious history are limited to where the most extensive and best work has been done. Political instability, physical remoteness, and inequities in the way research monies are allocated all affect my ability to see in those areas where I have not worked directly. My late friend and colleague Marilyn Waldman was fond of telling anecdotes about the legendary Persian religious teacher Mulla Nasrudin, who often used humor to shed light on complex problems of human existence. She began her last book with the following anecdote: "A neighbor found Mulla Nasrudin crawling around under a streetlamp. Asked why, the Mulla replied, 'Because I lost my ring across the street.' 'Then why are you looking under the lamp?' 'Because the light is better here.'"[98] I hope that my looking where "the light is better" will prove more successful than Nasrudin, but there are limits to the available sources and their accessibility and, as a result, to what historians can see. Much work needs to be done, and it will never be complete. This book represents a first effort toward a continent-wide history of African religions, focused primarily on the indigenous religions of Africa.

---

[98] Idries Shah, *The Exploits of the Incomparable Mulla Nasrudin*, quoted in Marilyn R. Waldman, *Prophecy and Power: Muhammad and the Qur'an in the Light of Comparison* (Sheffield, UK: Equinox, 2012), p. 1.

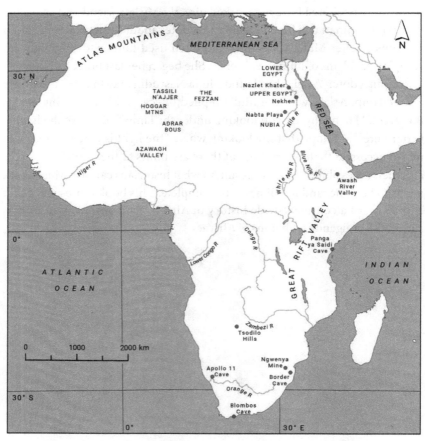

Map 2.1. Africa before 3200 BCE (courtesy of Jonathan Chipman).

2
Before Adam and Eve

African Religions from the Dawn of Humanity to the Neolithic Revolution

We begin where humans began: on the African continent. This chapter examines the earliest evidence suggesting human practices that could be considered as having a religious dimension. It is difficult to establish human motivations from the silent material remains examined by archaeologists. However, the study of early burial locations provides tangible evidence of human concerns about their fates after death. These are central to most religious systems. The prominence of such materials for the earliest phases of human religious history does not eliminate the possibility of other religious thought; rather, it highlights the difficulty of accessing it from archaeological evidence. Even before the emergence of *Homo sapiens*, some of our hominin ancestors carefully laid their deceased relatives to rest, suggesting that specific practices were needed to ensure a safe transition to whatever form of afterlife was envisioned. This discussion remains limited to the examination of durable remains: graves, stone objects, bones, and so on. It begins a complex process of analysis of material goods and places of archaeological importance, inferring the earliest human rituals and providing glimpses into the religious concepts that informed them. Examinations of ancient ritual sites also provide evidence of early religious activity. Finally, linguistic analysis offers insights into religious concepts and practices, particularly in the Equatorial region, where extensive comparative and historical research has been conducted.

This chapter is not, however, focused on the theoretical debates about the origins of religions; whether religions originated in dreams, visions, the veneration of unusual places or objects, or whether we have long been genetically programmed for "religion." Although such issues have attracted scholarly debate for over two centuries, answers to these questions remain a matter of speculation. The available archaeological and linguistic evidence cannot resolve them. Instead, I concentrate on the earliest indications of religious activity without assuming that thought about what one might consider religion began at the same time as the material evidence associated with graves. As the archaeological record became increasingly complex, so did the evidence suggestive of religious practices. For this very early history, I utilize a minimalist definition of religion, borrowed from the classic work by André Leroi-Gourhan: "it is simply based on manifestations of concerns appearing to surpass the material order." He provides the specific example of the use of ocher to adorn bodies and objects, though it did not serve a mundane, practical purpose.[1] This chapter examines the limited archaeological traces concerning hunters and gatherers; the impact of the Neolithic Revolution; the beginnings of animal husbandry and farming as human occupations; and the religious consequences of these transformative changes. The chapter ends before the discovery of the oldest written records and the establishment of the First Dynasty of a unified Egypt. Within the chapter, I examine African religious history in what has often been labeled as prehistory. However, there has never been a period before history, when humans did not shape their world, only a lack of evidence of the changes they engendered.

As paleoanthropologists found fossil remains and early stone items made by our hominin ancestors, they determined that humanity began on the African continent, most likely close to the Great Rift Valley of eastern Africa. It was in this area of wooded grasslands that *Australopithecus* separated from ape-like predecessors (*Ardipithecus*) about five million years ago. Evolutionary geneticists also confirm that *Homo sapiens sapiens* emerged on the African continent.[2] If our ancestors, from Lucy (*Australopithecus afarensis*) to the first *Homo sapiens*, lived in Africa, then it stands to reason that the first human activity that could be labeled as "religious" also began on the continent. As J. David Lewis-Williams and T. A. Dowson have suggested: "If the 'Out of Africa' hypothesis is correct ... it is in Africa that we shall find clues that point to the earliest manifestations of 'spirituality' ... if only we can spot them. The problem is that we do know what they may look like."[3] As René Descartes's famous proof for human existence ("I think therefore I am") defines humans, above all, as thinkers, and the anthropologist Clifford Geertz has emphasized the human quest for meaning, then it follows that the first human thought from religious perspectives also came from Africa.[4] Paleoanthropologists'

---

[1] André Leroi-Gourhan, *Les religions de la préhistoire* (Paris: Presses Universitaires de France, [1964] 1990), p. 5. Translation by Robert M. Baum.
[2] Lawrence M. Robbins, personal communication, November 2021.
[3] J. D. Lewis-Williams and T. A. Dawson, *San Spirituality: Roots, Expressions and Social Consequences* (Cape Town: Double Story, 2003), p. 5.
[4] Clifford Geertz, "Religion as a Cultural System," in Geertz, *The Interpretation of Culture* (New York: Basic Books, 1972). See also Leroi-Gourhan, *Les religions de la préhistoire*, p. 6.

cognitive studies challenge the antiquity of this claim, however, by suggesting that only *Homo sapiens* evolved sufficiently to be capable of the abstract thinking or the ability to link multiple cognitive domains associated with religious ideas. Steven Mithen asserts that the creation of art, science, and religion all required a high level of cognitive integration and critical reflection.[5] Some scholars insist that this only occurred in the last 60,000 years. Moving away from strictly cognitive approaches, archaeologists Christopher Henshilwood and Francesco d'Errico propose an "adaptive" hypothesis in which they argue that symbolic behavior arose as a result of "a fundamental change in human behavior . . . when symbolism became inherent in material culture. This innovation which demonstrates the ability for sharing, storing, and transmitting coded information within and across groups, has played a crucial role in creating, maintaining and transmitting the social conventions, beliefs, and identities that characterizes all known human societies."[6]

The idea of early humans thinking about religious issues, however, is difficult to prove. We only have the testimony of religious sites, artifacts, preparations of the dead and their graves, and the remains of what could be ritual offerings. We have no direct testimony of individuals before the invention of writing. Still, we can cautiously infer from what we know of later humanity that people think about what they do, that they seek to develop systematic ways of knowing their world, that they use ritual activity to enhance the predictability and controllability of that world, and that they think about ways to legitimate such activity.

Due to the absence of written sources, the limited quantity of material remains, and the difficulties in attributing thought and motivation to such materials, there is very little evidence concerning religious activity before the Neolithic Revolution.[7] At the present stage of research, there is no extant material supporting the idea that the Australopithecus practiced anything that could be readily associated with religious activity. The earliest evidence focuses on members of the genus *Homo*, which emerged around two and a

---

[5] Ilkka Pyysiäinen, *How Religion Works: Toward a New Cognitive Science of Religion* (Leiden: Brill, 2003), pp. 196–236. Steve Mithen, *The Prehistory of the Mind: The Cognitive Origins of Art, Religion, and Science* (London: Thames and Hudson, 1998), pp. 11, 209, 210, 215.

[6] Francesco d'Errico and Christopher S. Henshilwood, "The Origin of Symbolically Mediated Behavior: From Antagonistic Scenarios to a Unified Research Strategy," in *Homo Symbolicus: The Dawn of Languages, Imagination, and Spirituality*, ed. Henshilwood and d'Errico (Philadelphia: John Benjamin, 2011), p. 49.

[7] On the difficulties of interpreting religious motivations from material remains and archaeology's cautious approach to such matters, see Pierre de Maret, "Archaeological and Other Prehistoric Evidence of Traditional African Religious Expression," in *Religion in Africa*, ed. Thomas D. Blakely, Walter E. A. van Beek, and Dennis L. Thomson (London: James Currey, 1994), pp. 183–185.

half million years ago. Some paleontologists argue that *Homo erectus*'s skills at creating Acheulian stone tools suggest that these hominins were capable of symbolic thought and speech. Others question this theory, claiming the connection between technical skills and capabilities of symbolic thought and/or language have not been established.[8] This is supported by the fact that neither *Homo habilis* nor *Homo erectus* have left any known traces of religious activity.

Paleolithic Religions

Still, before the emergence of *Homo sapiens sapiens*, our hominin ancestors made special preparations—that is, ritual preparation of the dead. The recently discovered human ancestor, *Homo naledi*, lived well before the emergence of *Homo sapiens*, beginning around two million years ago. Recent discoveries at the Rising Star Cave, near Johannesburg, South Africa, indicate that these hominins (between 236,000 and 335,000 BP) took great pains to dispose of the dead in inaccessible places, protecting them from anyone who would disturb their remains or use them nefariously against the group or the individual.[9] Fifteen different individuals were left in the cave, at various times over a considerable period of time. What this says about attitudes toward death or an afterlife is difficult to ascertain. Still, we can determine that the preservation of such remains—their treatment as something other than food or unpleasant items that must be discretely disposed of—suggests some thought about what events come to pass with the ending of a life.[10] James Shreve reports from his discussions with the archaeological team that discovered *Homo naledi*: "Having excluded all other explanations, Berger and his team were struck by the improbable conclusion that bodies of *Homo naledi* were deliberately put there by other *Homo naledi*. Until recently, only *Homo sapiens* and possibly some archaic humans such as the Neanderthals are known to have buried their dead in such a ritualized manner." There were no signs of human habitation in this area of the caves, no bones of other animals, nor any sign that they had been washed into

---

[8] "Homo Habilis," in *Encyclopedia Britannica*, 2018, https://www.britannica.com/topic/Homo-habilis. Kevin Shillington, *History of Africa*, rev. ed. (New York: St. Martin's Press, 1995), p. 8.

[9] James Shreve, "Mystery Man," *National Geographic* 228 (October 2015), pp. 53, 34–35. John Noble Wilford, "New Species in Human Lineage Is Found in a South African Cave," *New York Times*, August 10, 2015. E-mail communication from Professor Jeremy de Silva, Dartmouth College, Hanover, New Hampshire, 2017.

[10] Leroi-Gourhan, *Les religions de la préhistoire*, p. 54.

the area.[11] Lee Berger and his archaeological team assessed the importance of this deliberate catchment of the dead by *Homo naledi*:

> We propose that funerary caching by H. naledi is a reasonable explanation for the presence of remains in the Dinaledi and Lesedi Chambers. Mortuary behaviours, while culturally diverse, are universal among modern human cultural groups.... We have no information about whether H. naledi was a symbolic species, although with the possibility that it manufactured Middle Stone Age tool kits, we do not rule out such abilities. But symbolic cognition is not likely to have been necessary to have sustained a repeated cultural practice in response to the physical and social effects of the death of group members.[12]

Although the absence of such practices does not preclude the existence of religious thought about death and the afterlife, the existence of such practices is highly suggestive. Other evidence of early religious activity has been found in graves that can be dated back 500,000 years, although their meaning cannot be determined with certainty.[13]

With the emergence of *Homo sapiens*, between 350,000 and 100,000 years ago, comes evidence of a ritual preparation of the body, daubing it with red ocher, placing the bones in a special way, and pointing the head either toward the east or west, toward the rising or setting sun.[14] These actions suggest that, even by the Middle Paleolithic Era (250,000–70,000 BP), rituals expressed a concern with the transition from life to death and that they linked this to the cycles of sunrise and sunset. Recent excavations at Panga ya Saidi Cave (see map 2.1), along the coast of Kenya, revealed the grave of a two- or three-year-old child that has been dated to approximately 78,000 BP. This is the

---

[11] Shreve, "Mystery Man," p. 53. Amy Ellis Nutt, "Scholars Identify New Human Ancestor," *Washington Post*, September 11, 2015. Museum text from Maropeng Cradle of Man Museum, Sterkfontein, South Africa, visited by the author in January 2018. Paul H. G. M. Dirks et al., "Geological and Taphonomic Context for the New Hominin Species Homo Naledi from the Dinaledi Chamber, South Africa," *eLife*, September 10, 2015,

[12] Lee R. Berger, John Hawks, Paul H. G. M. Dirks, Marine Eliot, and Eric Roberts, "Homo Naledi and Pleistocene Human Evolution in Subequatorial Africa," *eLife*, May 9, 2017.

[13] Ocher is a soft mineral containing a considerable amount of iron oxide. Ian Watts, "Ochre in the Middle Stone Age: Ritualised Display or Hide Preservatives," *South African Archaeological Bulletin* 57 (2002), p. 1. Jacquetta Hawkes, *Prehistory, Volume I, Part One, History of Mankind: Culture and Development* (New York: New American Library, 1963), p. 192. Mircea Eliade, *A History of Religious Ideas, Volume 1, From the Stone Age to the Eleusinian Mysteries* (Chicago: University of Chicago Press, 1978), p. 9.

[14] Gregory J. Wightman, *The Origins of Religion in the Paleolithic* (Lanham, MD: Rowman and Littlefield, 2015), p. 217.

oldest known deliberate burial in an "excavated grave" that has been found in Africa. Furthermore, a covering was placed tightly around the child's body. Traces of ocher were found on the child's bones. The grave was initially excavated and then filled in with a different type of soil.[15] At the Border Cave in South Africa's KwaZulu-Natal Province, excavations reveal the existence of shallow graves, deliberately set apart from people's living spaces, dating back 70,000 years. A reddish-brown stain *on the* bones indicates that the bodies were adorned with ocher before burial. "A perforated Conus shell" was also found by the grave, providing at least some indication of the preservation of human adornments in the burial process.[16]

Excavations at the Blombos Cave in South Africa revealed ocher pieces etched with X marks in patterns, between lines, which are estimated to be 70,000 years old. David Lewis-Williams suggested that this could be the world's oldest example of art or of a symbolic object.[17] This challenged Steven Mithen's claim that the mental capacity to work symbolically, to create art or, for that matter, to create religion, did not emerge until approximately 60,000 years ago.[18] Painted rocks, shell beads, and other ornaments were also found in the cave, suggesting that the people who left artifacts there had a capacity for artistic and symbolic thought. In northwestern Eswatini (Swaziland), archaeologists discovered Middle Stone Age tools deep inside an ancient mine, as well as near the surface. Archaeological investigations of the Old Ngwenya Mine found that early inhabitants of the region were mining hematite, from which ocher was extracted 41,000 to 43,000 years ago. A site in the Matobo Hills of present-day Zimbabwe yielded a stone palette and paints dating back 40,000 years which might have had a ritual use.[19] These minerals could have been used to adorn bodies in burial sites, to add to snake venom to coat arrowheads, and to provide paints for southern African

---

[15] Maria Martinon-Torres, Michael Francesco d'Errico, and D. Petraglia, "Earliest Known Human Burial in Africa," *Nature* 593 (May 5, 2021), pp. 95–100.

[16] Paul Pettitt, *The Paleolithic Origins of Human Burial* (New York: Routledge, 2011), p. 73. Peter Mitchell, *The Archaeology of Southern Africa* (Cambridge: Cambridge University Press, 2002), p. 99.

[17] J. David Lewis-Williams, *San Rock Art* (Athens: Ohio University Press, 2013), p. 25. Christopher Stuart Henshilwood, *Holocene Prehistory of the Southern Cape, South Africa: Excavations at Blombos Cave and the Blombos Pontein Nature Reserve* (Cambridge: Cambridge Monographs in African Archaeology, #75, 2008), p. 25. Curtis Maren and Zelalen Assefa, "The Middle and Upper Pleistocene African Record for the Biological and Behavioral Origins of Modern Humans," in *African Archaeology: A Critical Introduction*, ed. Ann B. Stahl (Oxford: Blackwell, 2012), p. 116.

[18] The ability to think symbolically and to create art is often associated with the Upper Paleolithic Age, beginning around 50,000 BP, rather than the Middle Paleolithic, which is suggested by some of the evidence cited here. Pyysiäinen claims that such capacities only emerged 40,000 years ago. Mithen, *The Prehistory of the Mind*, p. 11. Pyysiäinen, *How Religion Works*, p. 217.

[19] David Coulson, "Trust for African Rock Art," www.Africanrockart.org.

rock art.[20] As the use of red colors in rituals became increasingly common, ocher may have been associated with power, life, blood, spirit, and flesh.[21]

Archaic *Homo sapiens* may have been involved in the defleshing of corpses. Excavations of human remains from the Awash River valley in Ethiopia (close to where Lucy was found) have found corpses with gouge marks made from a stone tool in the frontal portions of the cranium, dating back 600,000 years. This could be indicative of ritual cannibalism, the consumption of portions of human bodies to acquire their powers or to honor their memories. It could also have the more mundane function of removing flesh from the corpse for food or to avoid unsanitary decomposition prior to reburial. It is also possible that the flesh removals could have been linked to a cult of ancestors.[22]

Archaeological discoveries made over the last twenty-five years strongly suggest that the oldest known ritual site in the world may have been discovered in northwestern Botswana. This area, the Tsodilo Hills, consists of five massive hills that rise out of a flat and arid plain, northwest of the Okavango Delta. These include a Male Hill, which is the steepest, and a Female Hill, which is the largest. Archaeologists suggest that this area has been inhabited by "anatomically modern humans" for over 100,000 years.[23] Large numbers of stone tools have been recovered in the area, indicating that people used the area as a base for hunting expeditions as early as the Middle Stone Age. Many of the stones used to make these tools originated a significant distance from Tsodilo, indicating that long-distance trade networks already existed in the region.[24] Lawrence Robbins claimed that the early inhabitants of the Tsodilo Hills already dipped their arrows in poison that they prepared themselves

---

[20] I visited the site of the mine and its museum in January 2018. Bill Baird, "Strange Earths: Ancient Mining in Swaziland," *The Edinburgh Geologist* 42. George J. Coakley, "The Mining Industry of Swaziland," *United States Geological Survey* 27, no. 1 (2000). Mithen, *The Prehistory of the Mind*, p. 182.

[21] Wightman, *The Origins of Religion in the Paleolithic*, pp. 4, 182.

[22] W. Arens has suggested that the idea of cannibalism, in both ritual and nonritual situations, is grossly overstated and may reflect Western preoccupations with the subject more than activity of various human groups to whom it has been attributed. *The Man-Eating Myth: Anthropology and Anthropophagy* (New York: Oxford University Press, 1979). Paul Pettitt, *The Paleolithic Origins of Human Burial* (New York: Routledge, 2011), p. 49.

[23] Larry Robbins, Mike Murphy, and Alec Campbell, "Windows into the Past: Excavating Stone Age Shelters," in Campbell et al., *Tsodilo Hills: Copper Bracelet of the Kalahari*, ed. Alec Campbell, Larry Robbins, and Michael Taylor (East Lansing: Michigan State University Press, 2010), p. 63. Lawrence H. Robbins, "Sebilo: 19th Century Hairdos and Ancient Specularite Mining in Southern Africa," *International Journal of African Historical Studies* 49, no. 1 (2016), p. 105.

[24] D. J. Nash, Sheila Coulson, J. S. Ullyott, M. Babutsi, L. Hopkinson, and M. P. Smith, "Provenancing of Silcrete Raw Materials Indicates Long-distance Transport to Tsodilo Hills, Botswana during the Middle Stone Age," *Journal of Human Evolution* 63 (2013), pp. 286–287.

for use in hunting.[25] The hills are covered with rock paintings of geometric designs, wild animals, human beings, and more recent ones of domestic animals, approximately 4,500, in total, some of which are thousands of years old.[26] When Laurens van der Post visited the Tsodilo Hills, he described them as the Louvre of the Kalahari. He also noted that all his equipment jammed whenever he tried to film there, something he associated with the mystical quality of the place. More recently, James Suzman described them as "small mountains that rise as a vast rocky cathedral complex out of the otherwise unremitting flatness of the Northern Kalahari."[27] The hills remain sacred to local Khoisan-speaking peoples and to some Bantu language speakers. San oral traditions trace the creation of humans to the Tsodilo Hills in general and animals to the Female Hill.[28] Both the Ju/'hoansi (Khoi san) and the Hambukushu (Bantu speakers) associate Tsodilo with spiritual forces linked to rain.[29] Toward the end of the Middle Stone Age, specularite was being mined for ocher in the Tsodilo Hills, and it may well have been used in burial rituals, though no Middle Stone Age burial sites have yet to be found in this area (see Figure 2.1).

The Female Hill also houses a cave, known as the Rhino Cave, because of a painting of a rhinoceros near the cave's entrance. It is quite small, eleven meters long and no more than five meters wide. It could hold fifteen people within its shelter. The north wall is covered with rock paintings.[30] According to archaeologists Nick Walker and Sheila Coulson, the south wall of the cave is dominated by the carved image of a tortoise head or a

---

[25] Lawrence H. Robbins, Alec C. Campbell, George A. Brook, Michael L. Murphy, and Robert K. Hitchcock, "The Antiquity of the Bow and Arrow in the Kalahari Desert: Bone Points from White Paintings Rock Shelter, Botswana," *Journal of African Archaeology* 10, no. 1 (2012), pp. 7–20.

[26] Sheila Coulson, Sigrid Staurset, and Nick Walker, "Ritualized Behaviour in the Middle Stone Age: Evidence from the Rhino Cave, Tsodilo Hills, Botswana," *Paleoanthropology* (2011), p. 19. Robbins et al., "The Antiquity of the Bow and Arrow"; interview with Lawrence Robbins, Okemos, Michigan, August 2021.

[27] Laurens van der Post, *The Lost World of the Kalahari* (New York: Pyramid Books, [1958] 1968), pp. 185–212. James Suzman, *Affluence without Abundance: The Disappearing World of the Bushmen* (New York: Bloomsbury, 2017), p. 21.

[28] Alec Campbell, "Visiting Tsodilo: Preparing the Imagination," in *Tsodilo Hills: Copper Bracelet of the Kalahari*, ed. Alec Campbell, Larry Robbins, and Michael Taylor (East Lansing: Michigan State University Press, 2010), p. 21. Michael Taylor and Alec Campbell, "The Source of Life," in Campbell et al., *Tsodilo Hills*, p. 29.

[29] Alec Campbell, "The Hills and Rain Making," in Campbell et al., *Tsodilo Hills*, p. 27. It is also a Christian pilgrimage site, where people seek the healing waters of local springs. Sheila Coulson, Philip Segadika, and Nick Walker, "Ritual in the Hunter-Gatherer/Early Pastoralist Period: Evidence from Tsodilo Hills, Botswana," *African Archaeological Review* 33, no. 2 (June 2016). Larry Robbins, Alec Campbell, George Brook, and Michael Murphy, "World's Oldest Ritual Site? The 'Python Cave' at Tsodilo Hills World Heritage Site, Botswana," *Nyame Akuma* 67 (2007), pp. 2–6.

[30] Lawrence H. Robbins, Michael L. Murphy, Alec Campbell, and George A. Brook, "Excavations at the Tsodilo Hills Rhino Cave," *Botswana Notes and Records* 28 (1996), pp. 23–45. Coulson et al., "Ritualized Behavior in the Middle Stone Age," 2011, pp. 23, 46–49.

Figure 2.1. The Tsodilo Hills, northwest Botswana (photo by Lawrence Robbins).

snake. This was later identified as a python because of its prominence in San creation myths in southern Africa. This image is a large rock with over three hundred cupules and grooves ground into it, giving the appearance of scales on a cylindrical body, a pointed head, an eye, and a cleft suggesting a mouth.[31] At various times of day, during the winter months, sunlight shines through an opening in the cave onto the image, sometimes creating patterns of light resembling the head and horns of an animal. Highlighting its presence, in the glow of an evening campfire, the snake appears to move in an undulating manner.[32]

According to Coulson, rituals could have taken place in this small, enclosed area. Ocher powder, which was often used in rituals, has been found in cave debris. Behind the image of the python emerging from the rock wall of the cave is a small chamber where ritual leaders could have hidden. From

---

[31] Some of the cupules and grooves are extremely old, while others are more recent. Sheila Coulson, "The Secret of Rhino Cave," in *Dangerous and the Divine: The Secret of the Serpent*, ed. Wouter Welling (Amsterdam: KIT, Afrika Museum, 2012), pp. 121–125. For a variety of photographs of the snake, do an Internet search for "Python Cave, Tsodilo Hills, Photos."

[32] George A. Brook, L. Bruce Railsback, Alec C. Campbell, Lawrence H. Robbins, Michael L. Murphy, Greg Hodgins, and Joseph McHugh, "Radiocarbon Ages for Coatings on Cupules Ground in Quartzite Bedrock at Rhino Cave in the Kalahari Desert of Botswana, and Their Paleoclimatic Significance," in *Geoarchaeology: An International Journal* 26, no. 1 (2011), pp. 61–82. Interview with Lawrence Robbins, August 4, 2021.

there, they could have made sound effects for a ritual, or they could have made a dramatic entrance into the cave at a particular moment in the ritual drama.[33] Coulson openly acknowledges the difficulties of dating objects and sites in the Middle Stone Age, but he suggests that the snake image could date to as early as 70,000 years ago, which would make it the oldest known religious sanctuary in the world and the location of its oldest known rituals. This, too, challenges some evolutionary scientists who argue that humans did not evolve sufficient brain capacity to create religious practices and articulate religious ideas until about 60,000 years ago.[34]

Some archaeologists question whether this image is actually a snake and whether the rock carving dates back 70,000 years. Lawrence Robbins and his team of archaeologists, who were the first to conduct excavations there, believe that the cupule-covered image remains "enigmatic in relative age and function." A similar stone form was covered with cupules/depressions at the nearby Depression Cave, but it contained no animal images. Furthermore, they maintain that there is insufficient evidence for a claim that this is the world's oldest ritual center.[35] However, Gregory Wightman points out that snakes play a prominent role in local San sacred traditions. According to Mathias Guenther, Khoi-San associated snakes with the trickster deity, Haiseb, who created them from his severed penis.[36] Furthermore, shamans can assume the shape of snakes during what has been called the

---

[33] Coulson et al., "Ritual," p. 49. Coulson et al., "Ritualized Behavior in the Middle Stone Age," pp. 20, 37. Wightman, *The Origins of Religion in the Paleolithic*, pp. 202–208. John Kinahan described a similar ritual in the Namib Desert during the first millennium of the Common Era. John Kinahan, *Namib: Archaeology of an African Desert* (Woodbridge, Suffolk, UK: James Currey, 2022), p. 205.

[34] The Research Council of Norway, "World's Oldest Ritual Discovered—Worshipped the Python 70,000 Years Ago," *Science Daily*, November 30, 2006. Brian Handwerk, "'Python Cave Reveals Oldest Human Ritual, Scientists Suggest," *National Geographic News*, December 22, 2006. Maren and Assefa, "The Middle and Upper Pleistocene African Record," p. 116. Pyysiäinen, *How Religion Works*, p. 215.

[35] Wightman, *The Origins of Religion in the Paleolithic*, p. 202. Robbins does not dispute the idea that people lived in and around the Tsodilo Hills for 100,000 years but rejects the idea that it is a carved image of a snake. Furthermore, he dates the oldest rock art to within the last 10,000 years. Lawrence H. Robbins, Michael L. Murphy, George A. Brook, and Alec C. Campbell, "Archaeology, Paleoenvironment and Chronology in the Tsodilo Hills White Painted Rock Shelter, Northwest Kalahari, Botswana," *Journal of Archaeological Science* 27, (2006), p. 30. . Robbins et al., "Windows into the Past," p. 60. Larry Robbins, Alec Campbell, George Brook, and Michael Murphy, "World's Oldest Ritual Site? The 'Python Cave' at Tsodilo Hills World Heritage Site, Botswana," *Nyame Akuma* 67 (2007), pp. 2–6. On the difficulty of dating rock carvings, see David Coulson and Alec Campbell, *African Rock Art: Paintings and Engravings on Stone* (New York: Harry Abrams, 2000), pp. 74–77. Brook et al., "Radiocarbon Ages"; Robbins, personal communication, August 4, 2021.

[36] Mathias Guenther, *Tricksters and Trancers: Bushman Religion and Society* (Bloomington: Indiana University Press, 1999), pp. 103, 187. Wightman, *The Origins of Religion in the Paleolithic*, p. 202. Kinahan, *Namib*, p. 7. David Lewis-Williams and Thomas Dowson, *Images of Power: Understanding Bushman Rock Art* (Johannesburg: Southern Book Publishers, 1989), pp. 130–131. Renaud Ego, *San: Art rupestre de; Afrique australe* (Paris: Société Nouvelle Azim Biro, 2006), p. 206.

trance dance.[37] Wightman also accepts the idea that the rock carving is approximately 70,000 years old, making the Python Cave roughly contemporaneous with the engraved pieces of ocher found at South Africa's Blombos Cave and newer than the intentional burial at a cave in coastal Kenya. These ocher slabs had often been cited as an early example of artistic and symbolic production. A sculpted image of a python could be seen as performing a similar role.[38]

In the Middle Paleolithic Era, excavations in the Nile Valley of Upper Egypt, dating back from around 55,000 BP, include the grave of a six-year-old child, buried in a sitting position in a shallow grave, and looking in an easterly direction. Although based on only one grave, it appears that the body was placed there deliberately, suggesting ideas about an afterlife and its relationship to the movement of the sun.[39] A more recent burial at Nazlet Khater was dated to between 34,400 and 31,500 years ago. The grave pit was covered with boulders and the body was buried facing west, the direction that later Egyptians associated with the land of the dead. This site also includes a two-faced ax adjacent to the body, the earliest known burial of grave goods which could be useful in a life after death. David Phillipson has noted similar evidence of what he calls the "ritualized disposal of the dead" in northeastern Ethiopia.[40] However, archaeologist Mark Smith cautions scholars not to assume that burial indicates a belief in an afterlife. Conversely, the absence of deliberate burials does not exclude such beliefs.[41] Although burial itself does not assure religious speculation about death or the afterlife, the deliberate placing of the dead in distinct postures and positioning the face either toward the rising or setting sun are strongly suggestive of such concerns.

In the Maghreb of northwestern Africa, burial sites associated with the Iberomaurusian Era (18,000–5500 BCE) included stone cairns, burial pits, and stone-lined depressions. The bodies appeared to have been deliberately

---

[37] Robbins et al., "Windows into the Past."

[38] Paul S. C. Tacon, "Identifying Ancient Religious Thought and Iconography: Problems of Definition, Preservation, and Interpretation," in *Becoming Human: Innovations in Prehistorical Material and Spiritual Cultures*, ed. Colin Renfrew and Iain Horley (Cambridge: Cambridge University Press, 2009), p. 63.

[39] Pierre M. Vermeersch, "Middle and Upper Paleolithic in the Egyptian Nile Valley," in *Southeastern Mediterranean Peoples between 150,000 and 10,000 Years Ago*, ed. Elena A. A. Gareen (Oxford: Oxbow Books, 2010), p. 74.

[40] David W. Phillipson, *Ancient Ethiopia, Aksum: Its Antecedents and Successors* (London: British Museum Press, 1998), p. 34. Mark Smith, *Following Osiris: Perspectives on the Osirian Afterlife from Four Millennia* (Oxford: Oxford University Press, 2017), p. 10.

[41] Mark Smith, *Following Osiris: Perspectives on the Osirian Afterlife from Four Millennia* (Oxford: Oxford University Press, 2017), pp. 9–10.

placed in a flexed or extended position and were often covered with ocher. Both the sites and the attention to the bodies indicate a concern with deceased persons after their deaths.[42]

During this period, rainfall increased in the desert areas west of the Nile, allowing people to return to this region for hunting and gathering. In an area of intermittent desert ponds, known as Nabta Playa, archaeologists discovered a small complex of standing stones, ten in number, each between two and three meters high, and a small circle of stone slabs and "two slab-covered tumuli, one of which had circles, have been found nearby. Some of these circles may have been used to chart the movement of the sun, hence the seasons and the timing of summer rains."[43] The stone circles and the slab-covered tumuli containing a bull may well indicate a ritual site, though a more precise meaning remains elusive. Still, the presence of seven of these sites, one containing the remains of an entire young cow, strongly suggests a religious purpose. By 6000 BCE, people had made the transition to agricultural production, growing barley, which allowed both larger and more stable settlements while highlighting the need for predictable rainfall.[44]

Historical linguistic analysis provides strong evidence that Niger Congo, the largest family of languages in Africa, originated in the wooded savannah of the Niger and Benue River valleys, between 10,000 and 20,000 years ago. By 10,000 BP, the Bantu branch of Niger-Congo had formed a distinct cluster in the Benue and Cross river valleys. Supporting this is the claim that Bantu languages' closest cousins are found in eastern and east/central Nigeria. The Nilo-Saharan language family appears to have originated around Lake Chad around 15,000 BCE. By 8000 BCE, the Afro-Asiatic language family had probably developed in northeast Africa. Only the Semitic branch of its six major language clusters developed outside of Africa, in the southwest Asian areas immediately across the Red Sea. Khoisan languages appear to have

---

[42] David Litell, "Late Pleistocene/Early Holocene Maghreb," in *The Encyclopedia of Prehistory, Volume I, Africa*, ed. Peter N. Peregrine and Melvin Ember (New York: Kluwer Academic, 2001), p. 132. Courtlandt Canby with Arcadia Kocybala, *A Guide to the Archaeological Sites of Israel, Egypt, and North Africa* (New York: Facts on File, 1990), pp. 181, 241.

[43] Stan Hendricks and Pierre Vermeersch, "Prehistory: From the Paleolithic to the Badarian Culture [c. 7,000,000–40,000 BCE]," in Ian Shaw, *The Oxford History of Ancient Egypt* (Oxford: Oxford University Press, 2000), p. 34. Vivian Davies and Renée Friedman, *Egypt Uncovered* (New York: Stewart, Tabori, and Chang, 1998), p. 20.

[44] Brian M. Fagan, *People of the Earth: An Introduction to World Prehistory* (New York: Harper/Collins, 1995), p. 284. Fred Wendorf and Romuald Schild, "Nabta Playa and Its Role in Northeastern African Archaeology," *Journal of Anthropological Archaeology* 17 (1998), p. 108.

developed in the northern Namibia/ northern Botswana region, around 10,000 BCE.[45]

Rock art provides another perspective on Paleolithic religion, especially in the Saharan and southern African regions. Rock art has been dated back as far as 28,000 BCE, well before the domestication of livestock and the cultivation of crops but continued to be produced well into the nineteenth century. Important sites have been found in North and Northeast Africa, the mountainous regions of the Sahara Desert, East, and Southern Africa, most of which predates the Common Era. At the Apollo 11 Cave, in southern Namibia, rock paintings, possibly 30,000 years old, depict images of various animals, including a cat-like creature with human legs. Such art suggests an ability to think symbolically about the images being portrayed, which is an important aspect of religious conceptualization. The abundance of such paintings led John Masson to claim that this cave was a ritual site of considerable significance to the Middle Stone Age artists who created them.[46]

Unfortunately, much of the discussion of rock art has been done with little attention to dating the engravings or paintings. This reflects the difficulty of establishing dates for the creation of these types of art.[47] However, a tendency to utilize ethnographic descriptions since the nineteenth century to interpret early rock art has added to the difficulty of using it historically. For example, some scholars have interpreted lines painted in such a way that they appear to emanate from a person's head, as examples of shamanic power or what the !Kung call *n/um*.[48] Similarly, paintings of human figures with animal heads have been interpreted as representing shamanic experience or the manifestation of zoomorphic deities.[49] These interpretations grow out of much more recent observations projected back

---

[45] Derek Nurse, "Contributions," pp. 373-374, 389.

[46] Apollo 11 Cave received its name when an archaeologist found it during the Apollo 11 moon landing in August 1969. John Masson, "Apollo 11 Cave in Southwest Namibia: Some Observations on the Site and its Rock Art," *The South African Archaeological Bulletin*, Vol. 61, # 183, June 2006, pp. 76-89. Brian M. Fagan, *People of the Earth: An Introduction to World Prehistory*, New York: Harper Collins, 1995, p. 208. Lewis-Williams, *San Rock Art*, p.27. David Coulson, Trust for African Rock Art.

[47] David Coulson and Alec Campbell, *African Rock Art: Paintings and Engravings on Stone*, New York: Henry N. Abrams Inc., 2000, pp. 74-76. David Lewis-Williams and Sam Challis, *Deciphering Ancient Minds: The Mystery of San Bushman Rock Art*, London: Thames and Hudson, 2011, p. 42. Maret, "Archaeological," p. 186. Masson, "Apollo," p. 84

[48] J. David Lewis-Williams, *The Rock Art of Southern Africa*, Cambridge: Cambridge University Press, 1983, pp. 21, 23. I saw rock paintings depicting humans with lines coming out of their heads at Ngamikurira in Zimbabwe, in September 1992. Sharon Steadman, *The Archaeology of Religious Cultures and Their Beliefs in Worldwide Context*, Walnut Creek, CA: Left Coast Press, 2009, p. 86, Marion Wallace with John Kinahan, *A History of Namibia*, London: Hurst, 1998, p. 27.

[49] Coulson and Campbell, p. 117. Steadman, p. 86.

to a distant past. As Peter Lane suggested, this is highly problematic: "the form of analogical modeling is rooted in the deep-seated western belief that hunter-gatherers like the San represent the timeless and essential qualities of humans as <u>biological beings</u>. As such they are thought to live lives closely resembling those of ancient hunters."[50] Peter Garlake also criticizes the weaknesses of this approach: "San art, like San beliefs and practices, was almost certainly more diverse and changeable in its significance than Lewis-Williams allows. His insistence on a uniformity of belief, practices, and modes of representation is inherently improbable."[51]

Nevertheless, some of the rock art, of uncertain dates, depict dances by men and women in southern Africa, including some people with liquid (possibly blood) coming out of their noses and some people who apparently fell to the ground in a trance state. Similarly, explicit paintings of a woman with her legs spread apart may indicate some kind of fertility ritual.[52] Maret cites David Lewis-Williams analysis of southern African rock art: "'The trance dance itself, the capture of the rain animal and the experiences, symbols and metaphors of trance were prominent among the artists' subject matter. I believe further that the trancers and the artists were, for the most part, one and the same.'"[53] As early as 1873, a San elder described to J. M. Orpen a link between trance dance, death, and the acquisition of spiritual powers and that these powers were associated with particular animals represented in rock art.[54] Though difficult to date accurately, it appears that these rock paintings illustrate connections between dance and trance and concerns with women's fertility in the early periods of rock artists among hunters and gatherers in southern Africa.

The extensive rock art in the central Saharan mountains near Tassili, dating as far back as 10,000 years, provides examples of hunting peoples and wildlife usually associated with West Africa, south of the desert. Some drawings, often done in ocher or white pigment, depict domesticated animals including cattle, sheep, and goats. Others include men and women dancing in what appears to be ritual performances, and a man slitting the throat of a cow in what could be a ritual sacrifice. Some of the dancers appear

---

[50] Peter Lane, "Barbarian Tribes and Unrevealing Gyrations: The Changing Role of Ethnographic Imagination in African Archaeology," in Ann Stahl, ed. *African Archaeology*, Malden MA: Blackwell, 2015, p. 25.
[51] Peter Garlake, *Early Art and Architecture of Africa*, Oxford: Oxford University Press, 2002, p. 42.
[52] Coulson and Campbell, *African*, pp. 86, 117. Lewis-Williams and Dowson, p. 68,
[53] David Lewis-Williams, cited in Maret, "Archaeological," p. 187.
[54] J. M. Orpen cited in Lewis-Williams and Dowson, p. 69.

to have been wearing masks. The frequent paintings of men with large phalluses having coitus with women or receiving fellatio from animals suggest a focus on powers associated with male fertility.[55] David Coulson suggests that the depiction of "round headed persons" that "appear to float through space" could indicate a familiarity with shamanic experience. Steven Mithen claims these same people are shown as worshipping at sun rise. [56] People were buried in rock-lined tumuli, which have been found in many places throughout the region.

Similar rock engravings have been found in the Eritrean and Tigrayan highlands of Northeast Africa. Men with elaborate headdresses, often with erect penises, dance in close proximity to a number of wild animals. This suggests a ritual link between hunting and male fertility. [57]

Paleolithic evidence of religious activity is limited to graves, cemeteries, ritual sites, as well as various types of rock art. These sites are more common in North, East, and Southern Africa; they are quite sparse in Equatorial and West Africa, where acidic soils dissolved burial remains. Although there are dangers in the over-interpretation of such sources, these locations provide evidence of increasingly elaborate preparations of both bodies and tombs. As Gordon Childe has noted: "The arbitrary peculiarities of implements, weapons, ornaments, houses, burial rites, and ritual objects are assumed to be the concrete expression of common social traditions that bind the people together."[58] With *Homo naledi* one finds the deliberate removal of the dead from the places where people lived and their internment in places that were difficult to access. With *Homo sapiens sapiens,* one finds the persistent use of ocher to adorn the bodies of the dead, suggesting that its bright red color carried meanings beyond simple adornment. One also finds that early humans decorated these ocher bars, as early as 70,000 years ago, suggesting some kind of special meaning. Archaeologists also provide evidence of early ritual sites, most notably the Rhino Cave, which suggests the

---

[55] Jeremy Swift, *The Sahara,* Netherlands: Time-Life International, 1979, pp. 52-61. Jean-Loïc Le Quellec, *Rock Art in Africa: Myth and Legend,* Paris: Flammarion, 2004, pp. 13-58. Arthur P. Bourgeois, "Masking in Sub-Saharan Africa," in Theodore Celenko, ed. *Egypt in Africa,* Indianapolis: Indianapolis Museum of Art, 1996, p. 69.

[56] David Coulson, Trust for African Rock Art. Steven Mithen, *After the Ice: A Global Human History, 20,00-5,000 BC,* London: Weidenfeld and Nicholson, 2003, p. 493.

[57] Zelalem Teka, "Distribution and Significance of Animal Rock Art in Eritrea," in Peter R. Schmidt, Matthew C. Cantor, and Zelalem Teka, eds. *The Archaeology of Ancient Eritrea,* Trenton: The Red Sea Press, Trenton, 2008, p. 66.

[58] Gordon Childe cited in K. R. Dark, *Theoretical Archaeology*, Ithaca: Cornell University Press, 1995, p. 89.

ritual supplication of spiritual beings associated with serpents, in a sanctuary where the movement of the sun illuminated the serpent sculpture in different ways at different time of the year. Rock paintings suggest the use of dance and carved masks, as well as the experience of trance and spirit possession in the Sahara and in southern Africa. These disparate, but widely distributed materials provide the earliest evidence of what we could consider to be religious activities on the African continent.

Neolithic Religions

Although hunting and gathering were the primary occupations of our ancestors until the relatively recent past, animal husbandry and the cultivation of crops began approximately 12,000 years ago. They had a profound effect on virtually all aspects of human societies and cultures. The domestication of cattle, goats, sheep, and poultry allowed for more regular access to a food supply than hunting and gathering alone could provide. The domestication of food animals also led to limitations on population mobility, making it more difficult to follow game animals in company of their animal herds. It also tended to encourage regular transhumant patterns, alternations between wet season and dry season pastures rather than the following of game animals. For the first time, accumulation of property beyond people's immediate needs became an important objective of work. The planting of crops demanded that people settle in fixed communities long enough to gather in the harvest. This more sedentary existence, however, generated a need for more cooperative tasks such as barriers to livestock entering fields and irrigation and drainage systems to ensure proper amounts of moisture. This required greater security against raids from non-sedentary communities. It also generated surpluses of food which not only encouraged the expansion of artisanal industries, but also supported the creation of specialized offices for political and religious leaders and functionaries. Collectively these changes are known as the Neolithic Revolution, which began in some areas in the twelfth millennium BCE.[59] However, hunting and gathering remained important sources of food and other material goods. This section focuses on the history of

---

[59] Jacques Vandier, Christiane Northcart and Jean-Louis de Cenid, *L'Egypte avant les Pyramides: 4è millenaire*. Paris: Editions des Musées Nationales, p. 14.

African religions, since the beginnings of African agriculture, but prior to the invention of writing. In some areas, however, agriculture never became important sources of economic activity.

Capsian culture in a moister Sahara provides the earliest evidence of cattle and sheep herding, as early as 7000 BCE. Planting of various forms of millet and fonio seem to have spread out from the Sahara to the North African littoral and toward the Nile Valley. In Capsian sites (6000-3500 BCE), there is some evidence of secondary burials in which partially decomposed bodies and bones were gathered up and reburied in a different place. This suggests an on-going concern with the fate of the dead.[60] In the Atlas Mountains of Morocco, rock paintings focused on rams, which could refer to their use as sacrificial animals or as symbolizing a deity represented by the image of a ram. Such ram deities were quite common in North Africa, the Sahara, and the Nile Valley. In the Hoggar, a mountainous area of the central Sahara, images of rams and of owl's heads have been found in burial tumuli. At Abelessa, archaeologists have found figurines of women with large breasts and large hips, drawing attention to their fertility and life-giving powers. Similar female statuettes have been found in other parts of the Atlas Mountains.[61] Later images in the Atlas Mountains, around 4000 BCE, rock engravings of goats with orbs between their horns resembled later images of the Egyptian supreme deity, Amun.[62]

Studies of the Nile Valley during this period of early agricultural settlements, have focused on graves and cemeteries as the best-preserved archaeological evidence of concepts of death and the afterlife. As Mark Smith has noted:

> In the absence of written documents, scholars have turned to other types of evidence in seeking to elucidate the first Egyptians' conceptions of the afterlife: the size, form, and location of cemeteries, tombs, and graves, the position in which a dead person was buried, the orientation of the body

---

[60] Lutell, "Late Pleistocene," p. 132. Phillip C. Naylor, *A History of North Africa: From Antiquity to the Present*, Austin: University of Texas Press, 2009, p. 5.

[61] Muzzolini, p. 167. Henri Lhote, *Les Touargegs du Hoggar (Ahoggar)*, Paris: Payot, 1955, pp. 78-79. Bernard Rosenberger, in Jean Brignon, et. al. *Histoire de Maroc*, Casablanca: Librairie Nationale, 1967, p. 14.

[62] Alfred Muzzolini, *L'Art rupestre préhistorique des massifs centraux Saharan*, Oxford: Cambridge Manuscripts in African Archaeological Research, 1986, pp. 94-99.

and the monument enclosing it, the treatment of the corpse, the objects deposited in the tomb alongside the dead, representations on tomb walls, possible traces of ritual activity, including the presence of human or animal sacrifices, as well as differences between the burials of individuals of varying social status. Additionally, evidence from non-funerary contexts has been utilized, e.g. rock art from the desert regions to the east and west of the Nile Valley.[63]

Archaeologists have noted strong similarities in burial practices between the areas of Lower and Upper Egypt (south of the Delta) and the Nubian region of northern Sudan and southern Egypt. Maria Gatto has noted similarities in the deposit of grave goods between the Western Desert and the Nile Valley. She attributes that to a circular movement of peoples from the desert areas to the Nile Valley during drier periods, and migration from the Nile Valley to Western areas during wetter periods of the Holocene Era. Ana Navajas Jiménez suggests that the Holocene Era, Sixth Millennium, cultures of the Western Desert and the Middle Nile represented the northern limits of Nubian culture.[64] There is insufficient evidence, however, to determine whether the shared burial practices were a result of Egyptian influences moving south or early Nubian influences affecting the northern reaches of the Nile Valley. The dry climate of the Nile Valley provided evidence of another ritual practice, male circumcision. Preserved remains of foreskins, dated back to the early Sixth Millennium provide evidence for the longevity of this rite of male initiation.[65]

The first Egyptian agricultural settlements have been identified with the Badarian culture of Middle Egypt, from as early as 4800 BCE and as recently as 4000 BCE. Badarian people lived in small villages along the Nile and practiced a mixed economy, including a heavy reliance on fishing and farming of emmer wheat; a lesser role for herding cattle, sheep, and goats; and for hunting. Excavations of Badarian cemeteries, usually situated at some distance from the inhabited villages, reveal graves in which bodies were placed

---

[63] Mark Smith, pp. 8 = 9.

[64] Maria Carmela Gatto, "The Nubian Pastoral Culture as Link between Egypt and Africa: A view from the Archaeological Record," in Karen Exell, ed. *Egypt in its African Context: Proceedings of the Conference held at the Manchester Museum, University of Manchester, 2-4 October 2009*, Oxford: Archaeopress, 2011, pp. 21-22. Ana I. Navajas Jiménez, "The predynastic Bas primigeniusas as a Royal Image of Territory, Boundaries, and Power in an African Context," in Exell, ed. op. cit. p. 31

[65] Susan, Bailey, "Circumcision and Male Initiation in Africa," in Theodore Celenko, ed. *Egypt in Africa*, Indianapolis: Indianapolis Museum of Art, 1991, p. 88.

on mats and covered with brush, baskets, skins or, even, linen.[66] As Patricia Spencer noted concerning the Badarian burials:

> The dead had been placed in graves covered over originally by brushwood and low mounds of earth that had collapsed onto the burials, many of which had been robbed in antiquity. Most of the bodies were in fetal positions – unlike the extended burials of the dynastic period – but with their faces to the west, indicating that they shared the Egyptian theory of "the west" being the abode of the dead. They had grave goods which consisted of tools, slate palettes, cosmetic items, clay and ivory figurines, stone vessels, and an abundance of pottery of distinctive types . . . . . Petrie recognized straight-away that they were excavating an unusual cemetery that did not conform to regular Dynastic customs – there were no hieroglyphics (or any other kind of) inscriptions, and no grave goods that were recognizably "Egyptian."[67]

Although the bodies were placed on a simple mat, pottery was placed alongside the body, in the grave. This is one of the earliest examples of grave offerings, probably placed there to accompany the deceased into the afterlife.[68] Barbara Watterson noted: "Bodies were buried with hands, containing a few grains of cereal, cupped in front of mouths in preparation for their first meal in the afterlife."[69] Domestic animals, (dogs, oxen, sheep, and goats) and gazelles, all apparently sacrificed, were placed in separate graves around some of the human tombs. Offerings of bread have also been located. Mourners placed leather bags of emmer wheat and barley at the feet of the deceased. As John Taylor has noted these ritual offerings provide "clear signs of a belief in the survival" after death.[70] In some cemeteries, it appears that men

---

[66] A. Jeffery Spencer, *Early Egypt: The Rise of Civilisation in the Nile Valley*, Norman: University of Oklahoma Press, 1995, p. 25. Michael Rice, *Egypt's Making: The Origins of Ancient Egypt, 5000-2000 BC*, London: Routledge, 1991, pp. 27-28.

[67] Patricia Spencer, "Petrie and the Discovery of Early Egypt," in Emily Teeter, ed. *Before the Pyramids: The Origins of Egyptian Civilization*, Chicago: Oriental Institute of the University of Chicago, 2011, p. 18. See also: David Wengrow, *The Archaeology of Early Egypt: Social Transformations in North Africa, 10,000 to 2650 BC*, Cambridge: Cambridge University Press, 2006, p. 27. B. G. Trigger, "The Rise of Egyptian Civilization," in B. G. Trigger, B. J. Kemp, D. O'Connor, and A. B. Lloyd, *Ancient Egypt: A Social History*, Cambridge: Cambridge University Press, 1983, p. 27.

[68] Hendrickx and Vermeersch, "Prehistory," p. 40. F. DeBono, "Prehistory in the Nile Valley," in J. Ki-Zerbo, ed. *Methodology and African Prehistory, Volume I UNESCO General History of Africa*, London: Heinemann, 1982, p. 645. Fagan, *People*, p. 285.

[69] Barbara Watterson, *The Egyptians*, Oxford: Blackwell, 1997, p. 32.

[70] John H. Taylor, *Death and the Afterlife in Ancient Egypt*, Chicago: University of Chicago Press, 2001, p. 13.

and women were buried separately. Wealthier individuals were buried in a special section of the cemetery and the grave goods were more elaborate.[71] Their mourners often placed ivory or clay figurines of women, emphasizing their breasts and pubic areas, which suggest a link to the mysteries of motherhood and fertility, which would be important in a life to come.[72]

Similar burials were reported for Middle Egypt, including the Fayyun, west of the Nile Valley, where the dead were buried on mats, within the village settlements.[73] Beginning around 4000 BCE, the Amratian culture (also referred to as Naqada I) immediately following the Badarian, included bodies wrapped in animal hides or linen.[74] These graves also yielded figurines, including representations of women with prominent breasts and hips, which emphasized women's reproductive powers. Some of these female figures had cow's horns which suggested links to Hathor, the goddess of female sexuality and fertility. Ithyphallic figures embodied male fertility. Figurines with wooly dreadlocks have also been found in the Amratian graves, suggesting sustained contact with or the physical presence of people more commonly associated with sub-Saharan Africa.[75] Large clay palettes with decorations in the forms of animals may have had some religious significance.[76] Sacrifices of domestic animals were limited to men's graves, but sacrifices of gazelles were found in both men and women's tomb areas.[77] Amulets in the shape of hippopotami have also been found, possibly indicating a protective role of a deified form of this source of ivory from the Nile.[78]

---

[71] Hendrickx and Vermeersch, "Prehistory," p. 40.
[72] Douglas J. Brewer, *Ancient Egypt: Foundations of a Civilization*, Harlow, UK: Pearson, Longman: 2005, p. 80. Beatrix Midant-Reynes, *The Prehistory of Egypt: From the First Egyptians to the First Pharoahs*, Oxford: Blackwell, 2000, p. 156. Mark Smith, p. 17. Trigger, "Rise," p. 27. Michael Rice, *Egypt's*, p. 28. A. J. Spencer, *Early*, p. 23. Simon Najovits, *Egypt, The Trunk of the Tree, Vol. I: The Contexts*, New York: Algora Publishing, 2003, p. 12.
[73] John Philipson, *African Archaeology*, Cambridge: Cambridge University Press, 2008, Third Edition, p. 197. A. J. Arkell, *The Prehistory of the Nile Valley*, Leiden: Brill, 1975, p. 32. Wilson Wetterstrom, "Foraging and Farming in Egypt: The Transition from Hunting and Gathering to Horticulture in the Nile Valley," in Thurston Shaw et al., eds., *The Archaeology of Africa: Foods, Metals, and Towns* (London: Routledge, 1993), pp. 216–217. Lars Fogelin, "Delegitimizing Religion: The Archaeology of Religion as Archaeology," in David S. Whitley and Helly Hays-Gilpin, eds. *Belief in the Past: Theoretical Approaches to the Archaeology of Religion*, Walnut Creek, CA: Left Coast press, 2008, p. 131.
[74] Taylor, *Death*, pp. 47, 79.
[75] Arkell, *Prehistory*, pp. 36–37. Stan Hendricks and Pierre Vermeersch, "Prehistory: From the Paleolithic to the Badarian Culture [c. 7,000,000–40,000 BCE]," in Ian Shaw, *The Oxford History of Ancient Egypt* (Oxford: Oxford University Press, 2000), p. 17. Najovits, *Egypt, The Trunk of the Tree*, p. 12.
[76] Some have suggested that the jackal amulets may indicate the worship of Anubis, but that cannot be confirmed. Mark Smith, p. 68. Jeffery Spencer, *Early Egypt*, p. 31.
[77] Wetterstrom, p. 219. Rosalie David, *Religion and Magic in Ancient Egypt*, London: Penguin, 2002, p. 52.
[78] Watterson, p. 36.

The Nile Delta region excavations at Merimda revealed clay figurines from about 4100 BCE, including the oldest representation of a human being found in Egypt. This was an image of a human head, with holes cut into it to place bird feathers representing beard hair and hair on the male figure's head. The specific religious significance of this image, if any, cannot be ascertained.[79] Other burial goods, including tools, suggest a sense that people would need these items in the afterlife. Families of the deceased often buried the dead under their houses.[80] Just south of the Delta, and slightly more recent, El Omari grave sites, dating back to about 3200 BCE, reveal distinctions between the graves of the rich and the poor. The bodies of poor people were wrapped in rough fabric. Wealthier individuals had stone mounds erected over their graves. In both cases the dead were placed on their left side and faced west, toward the setting sun. By this time, settlements like El Omari had become dependent on the cultivation of wheat and other grains as their primary sources of food.[81] In contrast to Middle and Upper Egypt, fewer material objects were found in the graves. El Omari grave sites, however, often included a small clay pot placed near the face, arms, or legs. One grave contained a skeleton still holding a staff that resembled scepters used by the rulers of the early Egyptian dynasties. Some scholars have suggested that this was the grave of a village headman. Graves of men tended to be placed on the west side of the graveyard; women and children on the east.[82] At nearby Maadi, cemeteries included separate burials of dogs and gazelles, similar to Badarian practice. This site also contained the earliest copper tools and weapons found in northern Egypt.[83]

During the Second Naqada period, beginning in 3600 BCE, the Nile Valley experienced growing urban populations, centered in large towns like Nekhen (Hierakonpolis) and Naqada. Grave sites reveal increased use of copper, gold, and silver, as well as growing distinctions between rich and poor within the cemeteries. The wealthy frequently were interred in tombs made of brick, while the poor continued to be buried in older types of graves.[84] Shards of jars from Palestine, once filled with olive oil or wine,

---

[79] Barbara Watterson, *The Egyptians*, Oxford: Blackwell, 1997, p. 30. Hendrickx and Vermeersch, p. 39.
[80] Canby with Kocybala, p. 157.
[81] Fagan, *People*, pp. 383-384.
[82] Midant-Reynes, pp. 119-121. B. G. Trigger, "The Rise of Egyptian Civilization," in B. G. Trigger, B. J. Kemp, D. O'Connor, and A. B. Lloyd, *Ancient Egypt: A Social History*, Cambridge: Cambridge University Press, 1983, p. 24-25. Michael Rice, *Egypt's*, p.29.
[83] Trigger, "Rise," pp. 25-26.
[84] Rosalie David, *Religion and Magic in Ancient Egypt*, London: Penguin, 2002, pp. 43, 61. Canby with Kocybala, p. 113. Marc Van De Mieroop, *A History of Ancient Egypt*, Malden, MA: Wiley-Blackwell, 2011, p. 37.

found in the greaves of wealthier individuals, indicate the importance of long-distance trade in these luxury goods, as early as the Fourth Millennium. Some graves of wealthier people included ceramic funerary masks. Animal graves surrounded these graves. They could include elephants, wild bulls, domestic cattle, hippopotami, hartebeests, or baboons. Their symbolic meaning remains elusive.[85]

Michael Rice has suggested that concepts of gods, initially as abstract forces represented by staffs covered in cloth, developed during this period.[86] For example, the city of Nekhen, focused on a sanctuary for the worship of an early form of the falcon god, Horus.[87] According to Barbara Watterson, the existence of Horus cults in both Upper and Lower Egypt was one of the reasons it became closely associated with royalty in a united Egypt.[88] Given the extensive use of writing once Egypt was united, around 3200 BCE, archaeologists have suggested that writing developed during the Naqada II and Naqada III period, just prior to the unification of Egypt.[89] Christiane Zivi-Coche claims that early written texts, including the Pyramid Texts (c. 2600 BCE), indicate that there were well established cults of some of the earliest Egyptian deities in the Pre-Dynastic Era. These may have included Ptah, Atum, Neith, Hathor, Isis, Osiris and Seth. Small sanctuaries for these deities and perhaps others for whom we have no record were made of relatively non-durable materials such as wood, reeds, mats, bricks, or adobe.[90] Fekri Hassan claims that female deities were particularly prominent throughout the Fourth Millennium.[91]

In the Nile Delta region, Buto, the capital of Lower Egypt, was a major ritual center protected by a cobra goddess, Wadjyt. Slightly further south was the ritual center of Sais, associated with the goddess Neith. The vulture goddess, Nekhbet, was associated with a town of the same name in Upper

---

[85] Renée Friedman, « Herakonpolis » in Emily Teeter, ed. *Before the Pyramids: The Origins of Egyptian Civilization*, Chicago: Oriental Institute of the University of Chicago, 2011, p. 39. Van De Mieroop, pp. 31, 33.
[86] Michael Rice, *Egypt's*, p. 49. Jeffery Spencer, *Early Egypt: The Rise of Civilization in the Nile Valley*, Norman: University of Oklahoma Press, 1948, 48.
[87] Brian Fagan, *Egypt of the Pharaohs*, Washington: National Geographic, 2002, p. 44. Friedman, "Herakonpolis," p. 42.
[88] Barbara Watterson, *The Gods of Ancient Egypt*, New York: Facts on File, 1986, pp. 99-100, 136.
[89] Jeffery Spencer, *Early Egypt*, pp. 39-62.
[90] Christiane Zivie-Coche, *Book I Pharaonic Egypt* in Françoise Dunand and Christiane Zivie-Coche, *Gods and Men in Egypt, 3000 BCE to 395 CE* (Ithaca, NY: Cornell University Press, 2004), pp. 72-73. This is supported by Jacques Vandier, *La Religion Egyptienne* (Paris: Presse Universitaires de France, 1949), p. 33. David, *Religion*, pp. 54-58.
[91] Fekri A. Hassan, "Primeval," pp. 307-310. Elise Boulding, *The Underside of History: A View of Women Through Time*, Vol. I (London: Sage, 1990), p. 158.

Egypt.[92] Barbara Lasko suggests that in the Pre-Dynastic Era, Nekhbet "could well have been regarded as a creator or a supreme mother goddess, in the entire southern half of Upper Egypt, at least."[93] Henri Frankfort has argued that each community had a "rainmaker," a ritual specialist who could control the Nile flood. Given the paucity of rainfall in Lower Egypt and the independent causes of the Nile floods, I suspect that this religious leader was less a rain priest and more connected to the river's waters and its ability to inundate the valley with fertile soils.[94] By the end of the Naqada II period, during the reign of a king called Scorpion, in Upper Egypt, just before Narmer united the two kingdoms, one finds the earliest evidence of irrigation systems, an engraving of the king operating an irrigation device.[95] The growth of irrigation systems may have placed greater demands on governmental services and increasing pressure for the unification of the two Egyptian kingdoms.

Further south, in Nubia, excavations reveal the existence of elaborate cemeteries by 10,000 BCE. In addition to tools and beads, these graves often contained carved figurines, which could indicate the idea of servants accompanying the dead into the next world or the representation of deities that they might encounter.[96] At one such cemetery, at Jebel Sahada, the bodies of fifty-eight individuals were buried in shallow pits covered with slabs of sandstone. The bodies were consistently buried in a "flexed positioning of the bodies toward the rising sun [which] is seen as having a religious significance."[97] Nearly half of those buried showed cut marks on bones and, in some cases, chert points were still embedded in the bones, suggesting violent deaths.[98] By 4000 BCE, evidence of cattle sacrifices, associated with cemeteries of what archaeologists call the A Group Complex of Lower Nubia, indicate both the domestication of cattle and more elaborate ritual activities,

---

[92] Barbara Mertz, *Red Land Black Land: Daily Life in Ancient Egypt* (New York: Dodd, Mead, and Company, 1978), p. 22. Gay Robins, *Women in Ancient Egypt* (Cambridge, MA: Harvard University Press, 1993), p. 23. Fekri Hassan, "Primeval," p. 312.

[93] Barbara S. Lesko, *The Great Goddesses of Egypt* (Norman: University of Oklahoma Press, 1999), p. 60.

[94] Trigger, "Rise," p. 48. H. Frankfort, 1948.

[95] Rosalie David, *Religion and Magic in Ancient Egypt*, London: Penguin, 2002, p. 11.

[96] A. Muzzolini, "La 'Neolithisation' du nord de l'Afrique," in Olivier Aurenche and Jacques Cauvin, eds. *Neolithisations: Proche et Moyen Orient, Méditerranée orientale, nord de l'Afrique, Europe méridionnale, Chine, Amérique du Sud*, Lyon: CNRS, 1989, p. 167.

[97] Lawrence H. Robbins, "Eastern African Advanced Foragers," in Joseph O. Vogel, ed., *Encyclopedia of Precolonial Africa: Archaeology, History, Linguistics, Cultures, and Environment*, Walnut Creek, CA: Altamira, 1997, p. 340.

[98] Stan Hendrickx and Pierre Vermeersch, "Prehistory: From the Paleolithic to the Badarian Culture (c. 70,000–4000 BC)," in Ian Shaw, ed., *The Oxford History of Ancient Egypt* (Oxford: Oxford University Press, 2000), pp. 29–30.

including more lavish grave goods for wealthier individuals. In the Dongola Reach area of central Nubia, bodies were placed on beds of red and yellow ocher in the graves. In many instances, mourners placed sacrificed lambs alongside the body of the deceased.[99] Places for ritual offerings were often placed on the west or south side of the tombs.[100]

Based on his excavations of a Nubian cemetery at Questal (circa 3300 BCE), Frank Yurco has concluded that Lower Nubia had royal mortuary cults that may have influenced the development of the pharaonic cults in Egypt. An incense burner found by a grave was decorated with an image of a king wearing the white crown of Upper Egypt, protected by a falcon god that may have been a precursor of Horus.[101] These grave goods were associated with the A-Group Nubian kingdom called Taseti, the Land of the Bow. This suggests considerable cultural exchanges between Upper Egypt and Nubia before the unification of Egypt and the possibility of Nubian influence in the development of a ruler protected by a falcon god. [102] By 3000 BCE, graves in this area included stone vessels, copper axes, and other tools. They also found jewelry and amulets worn around the necks of the dead and small figurines of fired mud. Some of these figures featured images of women with exaggerated buttocks and hips, with little attention to facial features, hair, or breasts. This may reflect an emphasis on women's power to give birth. These figurines were especially found in graves of women and children.[103]

At Kadera, a Neolithic site north of present-day Khartoum, a cemetery was found containing 200 graves, which showed clear economic variation. Graves of wealthier people contained elaborate grave goods, including carved hippopotamus ivory, carnelian bead necklaces, and stone palettes. Poor people had no grave goods.[104] At Kadruka, wealthier graves included elaborate offerings of human figurines and hippopotamus ivory. Some graves included stelae on top of the graves. Some of the graves at Kadruka and Kadera, may have been accompanied by human sacrifices as a part of the

---

[99] Sandro Salvatori and Donatella Usai, eds. *A Neolithic Cemetery in the Northern Dongola Reach: Excavations at Site R12*, Oxford: Archaeopress, 2008, pp. 58. 74.

[100] Bruce Williams, "A Perspective for Exploring the Historical Essence of Ancient Nubia," in W. V. Davies, ed. *Egypt and Africa: Nubia from Prehistory to Islam*, London: British Museum Press, 1989, p. 75.

[101] Frank Yurco, «Egypt and Nubia: Old, Middle, and New Kingdom Eras, » in Edwin Yamauchi, ed. *Africa and Africans in Antiquity*, East Lansing: Michigan State University Press, 2001, pp. 30-32.

[102] Frank J. Yurco, "Egypt and Nubia: Old, Middle, and New Kingdom Eras," in Edwin Yamauchi, ed. *Africa and Africans in Antiquity*, East Lansing: Michigan State University Press, 2001, pp. 31-33.

[103] Marjorie M. Fisher, et al. *Ancient Nubia: African Kingdoms of the Nile*, Cairo: American University in Cairo, 2012, p. 13. *Midant-Reynes, pp. 222-223*.

[104] Fisher, p. 14.

burial ritual. The existence of multiple bodies in a single grave, with no signs of re-opening the grave; the emphasis on a single centrally-located body adjacent to another body interred next to the grave goods, which presumably belonged to the central figure, are cited as evidence of this practice. Hearths, suggesting communal cooking, were also found in these cemeteries which could have been used for funerary feasts. Dogs were buried at the four corners of the rectangular cemetery.[105] These grave goods indicate a growing emphasis on material possessions necessary for the afterlife and a growing emphasis on ritual sacrifice to assist them in their journeys.

In the fourth millennium BCE, farming and herding were important economic activities in many parts of a much moister Saharan region. Black African farmers dominated many of the small settlements, and with growing aridity of the Sahara, these communities concentrated around oases, still populated by their descendants, the Haratin. Distinctly African varieties of domesticated cattle appear in the mountainous regions of northern Niger, just south of the Algerian border, as early as 3500 BCE. Evidence includes a skeleton of an African cow at Adrar Bous and rock art from the Hoggar, the Fezzan and Tassili.[106] Andrew Smith claims this provides evidence of a cattle cult in the Sahara during the Neolithic Period. The presence of short horn cattle by the Fifth Millennium refutes the theory that the Nile Valley was the source of Saharan cattle. Rather, Saharan people domesticated them during a period of sufficient rainfall, that the region could support animal grazing. Excavations at the Saharan site of Tushka, in southwestern Libya, yielded the burial of several wild cattle skulls, suggesting that wild cattle had some kind of ritual significance. Burial sites in the Atlas Mountains contain evidence of defleshing practice similar to those of the Awash River Valley.[107] There is some evidence of sorghum cultivation in the Hoggar and Fezzan, as well. Mourners wrapped the bodies of the dead in animal hides before burial. Graves were covered by stone cairns during this period.[108] This suggests the importance of the living returning to the graves of their deceased relatives.

---

[105] Steffen Wenning, *Africa in Antiquity: The Art of Ancient Nubia and the Sudan, Volume II, The Catalogue*, Brooklyn: Brooklyn Museum of Art, 1978, pp. 23-24. Midant-Reynes, pp. 225-230.

[106] J. Desmond Clark, Patrick Carter, Dianne Gifford-Gonzalez, Andrew Smith, "The Adrar Bous Cow and African Cattle," in J. Desmond Clark, et. al. editors, *Adrar Bous: Archaeology of a Central Saharan Granite Ring Complex in Niger*, Tervuren: Royal Museum for Central Africa, 2008, pp, 355-368.

[107] Bernard Rosenberger "Des Origines aux Almoravides," in Jean Brignon, et al. *Histoire du Maroc*, Casablanca: Librairie Nationale, 1967, p. 15.

[108] B. Wai Andah, "West Africa Before the Seventh Century," in G. Mokhtar, ed. *Ancient History of Africa, Volume II, UNESCO General History of Africa*, Paris: UNESCO, 1981, pp. 598-599. Andrew B. Smith, *African Herders: Emergence of Pastoral Traditions*, pp. 100, 108. David J. Mattingly, "The

In the Eastern Sahel and Central Sudanic zones of West Africa, there is linguistic evidence of a shared culture by 6000 BCE. Christopher Ehret claims that in this "Sudanic religion there is but a single level of the preternatural, a single spiritual force or Presence associated symbolically and perhaps literally also with the sky and the rain."[109] This linkage of a supreme being with the sky and rain remains common throughout the Sudanic region where droughts are a common occurrence.

Other sources on the Central Sudan focus on burial practices and agriculture. As in the case of the Badarians, northern Nigerian mourners placed their dead facing west. Desmond Clark excavated a grave in which a head rested on a giraffe vertebra and a necklace of ostrich shell beads adorned the neck of the deceased.[110] Further to the south, in the Azawagh valley, large settlements of people herded cattle, goat, and sheep, supplementing these activities with hunting, fishing, and probably millet cultivation. During the Fourth Millennium, burial preparations included placing the bodies of the dead in graves with their knees flexed. A few pots and ivory beads were found in the graves. Extensive buried remains of cattle, sheep, and goats that had been sacrificed suggest a religious significance to these domestic animals.[111] By 3200 BCE, however, the Azawagh River had dried up and the settlements abandoned. Excavations in northern Ghana reveal the farming of cowpeas/black-eyed peas and the gathering of palm kernels in what is known as the Kintampo culture by 3100 BCE. Other than the use of ocher on bodies of the dead as early as 10000 BCE, however, little has been found that could indicate any kind of religious practice.[112]

In eastern and southern Africa, items buried in people's graves provided the earliest clues to Neolithic religious life. By 6000 BP, southern African

---

African Way of Death: Burial Rituals Beyond the Roman Empire," in David L. Stone and Lea M. Stirling, eds., *Mortuary Landscapes of North Africa*, Toronto: University of Toronto Press, 2007, p. 140. Fiona Marshall and Elizabeth Hildebrand, "Cattle Before Crops: The Beginning of Food Production in Africa," in *Journal of World Prehistory*, Vol 16, #2, 2002, p. 107.

[109] Christopher Ehret, *An African Classical Age: Eastern and Southern Africa in World History, 1,000 BC to AD 400*, Charlottesville: University Press of Virginia, 1998, p. 145.

[110] Andrew Smith, Andrew Agrilla, Allison Galloway, "Burials and Human Skeletal Materials from Adrar Bous," in Clark, et. al. pp. 369-387.

[111] Susan Keech McIntosh, "The Holocene Prehistory of West Africa," in Emmanuel K. Akyeampong, ed. *Themes in West African History*, Oxford: James Currey, 2006, p. 22.

[112] Museum of Archaeology, University of Ghana, Legon, visited by the author in February 2018. Derek J. Watson, "Bosumppa Revisited: 12,500 Years of the Kwabu Plateau, Ghana, as Viewed 'from on the top of the hill,'" p. 461.

grave goods included tools, jewelry, and painted stones. John Phillipson suggests that these grave goods are evidence of a belief in an afterlife, at least "a belief that the dead would have some use for such objects."[113] By 5000 BP, East African burial sites included ceramic representations of cattle, leopards, and hippopotami, all suggesting an economic and/or religious significance that would lead them to be included in grave goods.[114] At Gogoshiis Qabe in southwestern Somalia, S. A. Brandt excavated a grave of at least one person buried with thirteen pairs of Kudu horns from the Early Holocene Era (c. 8000 BCE). Brandt argues that the uniqueness of this find suggests that the deceased was either a hunter or a leader of unusual prominence within his community. Brandt also found evidence of secondary burials in which "the individual most likely died at some other locations, and the remains of the person were subsequently reburied at the rock shelter."[115] This idea of a reburial also is suggestive of elaborate concepts of an afterlife.

Since the Fifteenth Century of the Common Era, Equatorial Africa's vast rainforest and wooded savannahs have reinforced European images of it as the "ahistorical region of Black Africa," *par excellence*. Despite this image of a window into the lives of prehistoric peoples, both archaeological and linguistic evidence provide important indicators for the early history of religions in the region.[116] In Equatorial Africa, the limited archaeological excavations have yielded a possible ritual site in the Lower Congo region and a burial site in Cameroun. In Lower Congo, a Neolithic site yielded very large containers capable of providing food and possibly fermented drink for a large group of people. Hans-Peter Wotzka offers the hypothesis that large crowds gathered for "initiation rituals, perhaps in connection with chthonic cults, [which] took place there."[117] In Cameroun, burial sites reveal intentional burials in rock shelters and internment pits. In one grave a child was found lying on his left side "in a contracted position with the head resting on a pillow in the form of a large stone slab." Other sites reveal two women who were buried back-to-back and numerous examples of ocher being used on

---

[113] John Phillipson, *African Archaeology*, Cambridge: Cambridge University Press, 2005, Third Edition, p. 108.
[114] Stanley Ambrose, "East African Neolithic," in Peter N. Peregrine and Melvin Ember, eds. *Encyclopedia of Prehistory, Volume I, Africa*, New York, Kluwer, 2001, p. 100.
[115] Robbins, "Eastern African," p. 339.
[116] Robert Cornevin and Henry Stanley cited in Jan Vansina, *Paths in the Rainforest: Toward a History of Political Tradition in Equatorial Africa*, Madison: University of Wisconsin Press, 1996, p. 3.
[117] Hans-Peter Wotzka, "Central Africa Neolithic," in Peter N. Peregrine and Melvin Ember, eds. *Encyclopedia of Prehistory, Volume I, Africa*, New York: Kluwer Academic, 2001, p. 50.

the corpses of the deceased.[118] All of this evidence suggests intentional burial and concern for the protection of the bodies of the dead.

In Equatorial Africa for this period, however, the most well-known evidence comes from historical linguistic analysis, associated with the expansion of Bantu language speakers, their migration from the area between the Benue and Cross rivers of southeastern Nigeria, east and south into Cameroun and neighboring countries. Their migrations may have resulted from demographic pressure from Nilo-Saharan groups that moved into the Sahel and Sudanic regions of West Africa as the Sahara became more arid.[119] At the end of this period, more than five thousand years ago, Bantu speakers split into Eastern and Western linguistic groups. At that time farming was primarily limited to the savannah areas and population density remained quite low. In the heart of the Equatorial Forest, hunting and gathering activities prevailed throughout this period prior to the third millennium BCE.[120] All dates, however, must be seen as tentative because one cannot assume a constant rate of linguistic changes.

Relying on linguistic analysis, Catherine Fourshey, Rhonda Gonzales, and Christine Saidi claim that a Proto-Bantu language had developed from the Eastern Benue cluster of languages by 3500 BCE. They suggest that Bantu-speaking peoples already made distinctions between ancestral spirits and territorial spirits, the former retained in the memories of their living descendants and the latter associated with particular geographical areas.[121] They identified a common root word associated with spirits, though they may be reading more recent ethnographic or travelers' descriptions into their interpretation of their evidence for the sake of providing a narrative of what these ancient traditions looked like. Thus, they talk about the ways in which ancestors must be venerated, their ability to bless and to punish, and their relationship to fertility, all of which may be extrapolations from more recent evidence. Their linguistic analysis suggests that there was a

---

[118] Hans-Peter Wotzka, "Central Africa Neolithic," p. 50.

[119] Jan Vansina, "Inner Africa (circa A.D. 500-1800)," in Alvin Josephy, ed. *The Horizon History of Africa*, New York: McGraw Hill, 1971, V. 2, p. 272.

[120] Jan Vansina, *Paths in the Rainforests: Toward a History of Political Tradition in Equatorial Africa*, Madison: University of Wisconsin Press, 1990, p.49. _____, *How Societies are Born: Governance in West Central Africa Before 1600*, Charlottesville: Press of the University of Virginia, 2004, p. 23. Kairn Klieman. *"The Pygmies were our Compass:" Bantu and Batwa in the History of West Central Africa, Early Times to c. 1900*, Portsmouth, NH: Heinemann, 2003, p. 43.

[121] Catherine C. Fourshey, Rhonda M. Gonzales, and Christine Saidi, *Bantu Africa: 3500 BCE to Present*, New York: Oxford University Press, 2018, pp. 5, 46-47. Rhonda M. Gonzales, *Societies, Religion, and History: Central-East Tanzanians and the World They Created, c. 200 BCE to 1800 CE*, New York: Columbia University Press, 2009, p. 94.

proto-Bantu word for supreme being, *Nyambe,* which was in use by 3500 BCE. It was derived from an older Niger-Congo verb, "to begin," which they claim was in use 1500 years earlier.[122] Maret reports that there are also words for lesser spirits and for something that is forbidden or taboo in proto-Bantu languages. Fourshey, Gonzales and Saidi also claim that there was a term for lineage and, more specifically, for matrilineage in Proto-Bantu by 3500 BCE. This would suggest that Bantu-speaking peoples were organized around extended kinship groups, traced initially through the maternal line. A shared term for patrilineage appears to be 500 years newer than the term for matrilineage.[123] Their analysis also yields evidence suggesting that male circumcision was practiced by Proto-Bantu speakers by the mid-fourth millennium BCE and that there was a shared term for age cohort that suggests the existence of age grades of circumcised males. This is supported by archaeological evidence cited by Wotzka for Lower Kongo.[124]

It should be pointed out, however, that what we have are terms for spirits, a supreme being, lineages (both matrilineal and patrilineal), male circumcision, and age sets. These terms, by themselves, cannot yield a sense of the role of ancestors or the supreme being, their relationship to one another, or living people, or the structure of initiation rituals. Linguistic evidence demonstrates the longevity of these ideas or practices, but not what they meant to the people involved. Still, the analysis of long-standing vocabulary at the root of many Bantu languages provides exceptional paths into understanding the earliest of African religious practices.[125]

Conclusion

Mortuary remains provide the clearest evidence of ancient African religious history. As Huntington and Metcalf explain: "The diversity of cultural reaction is a measure of the universal impact of death. But it is not a random reaction; always it is meaningful and expressive."[126] Archaeological evidence from the first millennia of the Neolithic Revolution, reveal a growing

---

[122] Fourshey, et. al., pp. 54-55. Maret, "Archaeological," pp. 192-195. Gonzales, p. 91.
[123] Fourshey, Gonzales, and Saidi. pp. 57-58.
[124] Ibid. p. 82. Wotzka, "Central Africa," p. 50.
[125] For a discussion of the strengths and weaknesses of linguistic approaches to African history, see Derek Nurse, "The Contributions of Linguistics to the Study of History in Africa," *Journal of African History,* Vol. 38, 1997, pp. 359-391.
[126] Huntington and Metcalf cited in Paul Pettitt, *Paleolithic,* p. 2.

emphasis on personal property being placed in graves alongside the deceased. In many cases bodies were deliberately placed on a north south axis, with their faces looking toward the rising or setting sun. This suggests a linkage between the movements of the sun and the transitions of human existence. This expressive intentionality provides significant evidence of beliefs in the importance of respecting the dead and preparing them for a life after death. As Leonard Lesko noted in regard to pre-dynastic Egypt, "Already in pre-historic times, burial customs indicated a belief in life after death which would have required that the body be preserved along with some household furnishings and food offerings. The expectation of hope was for a life after death that was not unlike human existence in this world. The location of tombs and position of the bodies in their graves became traditional, and the traditions may have been more or less religious."[127] This is echoed by archaeologist, John Taylor:

> During the Badarian and Naqada I-II cultures (c. 4400-3200 BC), the corpse was usually laid in an individual pit-grave....Gifts for the dead were placed with the body... The essentially practical character of most of the objects provided – ceramic and stone jars of food and drink, maceheads, flint knives and other tools and weapons, cosmetic palettes and personal jewelry – indicate that at this stage the afterlife was regarded as an extension of earthly existence, a state in which the deceased would experience the same needs and require the same comforts as those in life.[128]

Some of the figurines found in graves represented concerns about female fertility. These images empathized large breasts, hips, and buttocks, and a carefully demarcated genital area. Similarly, Saharan rock paintings of men with large phalluses engaging in coitus with women or receiving fellatio from animals draws attention to the power of male fertility.

Other sources also shed light on religious practices in these early stages of African history. Archaeological sites in the Tsodilo Hills and the Nile Valley strongly suggest the existence of religious sanctuaries, from a period as early as 70,000 years ago. Caves with carved images and places where people tracked the movements of the sun offer clear possibilities of ancient ritual practice. The frequency of rock art paintings of eland in southern Africa,

---

[127] Leonard Lesko, "Egyptian Religion: An Overview," in Lindsay Jones, ed. *Encyclopedia of Religion*, Volume 4, Detroit: Thomson Gage, 2005, p. 2703.
[128] Taylor, *Death*, p. 13.

hippopotami and wild cattle in the Nile Valley, indicate the importance of hunting and possibly the veneration of zoomorphic deities. The abundance of rock art illustrating humans dancing, some with rays emanating from their heads and others with blood coming out of their noses, may be signs of altered states of consciousness. Deliberate marking of ocher piecess, as found at South Africa's Blombos Cave, reinforces this idea of early *Homo sapiens'* use of symbolic decoration. Francisco d'Errico and Christopher Henshilwood noted the importance of the emergence of symbolic action.

A fundamental change in human behavior occurred when symbolism became inherent in material culture. This innovation, which demonstrates the ability for sharing, storing, and transmitting coded information within and across groups, has played a crucial role in creating, maintaining, and transmitting the social conventions, beliefs, and identities that characterize all known human societies.[129] Small kingdoms emerged in the Nile Valley by the fifth millennium BCE, but we know little about the religious role of the monarch or his advisors.

Linguistic analysis of the Bantu language family, closely associated with population movements beginning nearly six thousand years ago, provide a different perspective, on the longevity of terminology related to the supreme being, lesser spirits, ancestors, and certain forms of social organization and male initiation. Word lists and linguistic analysis can suggest the diffusion of concepts which are defined in terms of parallels with terms from living languages. Although we are still a long way away from local interpretations of what these terms meant in the lives of the people who used them, they point the way towards a history of African religions even before the establishment of centralized kingdoms or written languages.

In the next chapter we turn to religious practices in ancient Egypt. Guided by written texts, the historian of religion can, for the first time utilize contemporary explanations of their ritual activity, of ritual sites, and their concepts of spiritual forces and spiritual beings that shape their world.

---

[129] Francisco d'Errico and Christopher Henshilwood, "The Origin of Symbolically Mediated Behavior: From Antagonistic Scenarios to a United Research Strategy," in Christopher Henshilwood and Francisco d'Errico, eds., *Homo Symbolicus: The Dawn of Language, Imagination, and Spirituality*, Philadelphis: The John Benjamin Co, 2011, p. 49.

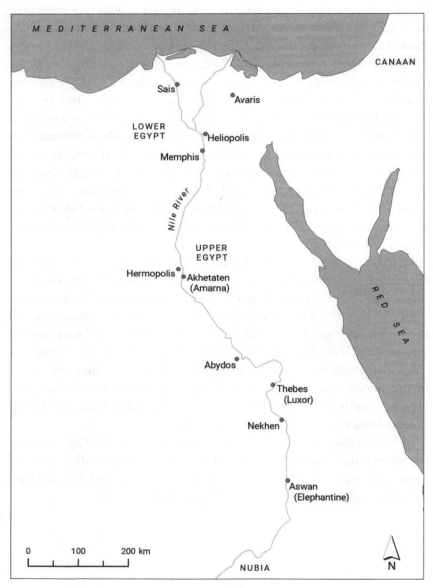

Map 3.1. Egypt to the New Kingdom (courtesy of Jonathan Chipman).

3
A Religious History of Ancient Egypt

From Unification to the Reforms of Akhenaten

Egyptian civilizations occupy a central place in the history of ancient Africa, casting a long shadow over more contemporary debates about the nature of African and Western civilizations (see Map 3.1).[1] Over five thousand years after the unification of Egypt, scholars argue about the racial composition of Egyptian society, its influence in the development of Western civilization, and its relationship to the rest of Africa. Modern commentators often project the racial concerns of their era back into debates about whether Egyptians were "black" or "white," whether there was a multiracial society, and whether social and political stratification corresponded to what twentieth- and twenty-first-century people imagine when they talk about race. There are similar debates about the influence of ancient Egypt on Greek and other Mediterranean cultures and religions. Some commentators on world history have insisted on a steady westward trajectory from Mesopotamia to Israel, Greece, and Rome, stubbornly overlooking the openly acknowledged influence of Egypt on ancient Greek sciences, philosophy, and the arts.[2]

---

[1] I would like to thank the students in my "Introduction to African Religions Course," for reading this chapter and providing feedback. Comments by Camryn Foltz and Sam Lefkowitz were particularly valuable.

[2] Martin Bernal has argued for an important Egyptian influence in the development of both Minoan and Classical Greek civilizations. Martin Bernal, *Black Athena: The Afroasiatic Roots of Western Civilization* (New Brunswick, NJ: Rutgers University Press, 1987). James S. Putnam, *Egyptology: An Introduction to the History, Culture, and Art of Ancient Egypt* (New York: Quintet Publishing, 1990), pp. 98–100. Théophile Obenga, *Ancient Egypt & Black Africa: A Student's Handbook for the Study of Ancient Egypt in Philosophy, Linguistics, & Gender Relations* (London: Karnak House, 1992), pp. 61–63. Cheikh Anta Diop, *Egypte Ancienne et Afrique Noir* (Dakar: IFAN, 1989), p. 474. Cheikh Anta Diop, "Histoire primitive d'humanité: Evolution du monde noir," *Bulletin de l'IFAN*, Tome XXIV, ser B, no. 3 and 4 (1962), pp. 524–529. E. A. Wallis Budge in many ways provides the context in which Bernal and Diop developed their critiques. Budge argues against the possibility of North African races in particular or African languages in general of developing the capacity of metaphysical thought that he associates with such Greek philosophers as Aristotle. E. A. Wallis Budge, *The Gods of Ancient Egypt*, Vol. I (New York: Dover Books, [1904] 1969), p. 143. Georg Friedrich Hegel is closely associated with the idea of world civilizations moving steadily westward. See G. F. Hegel, *The Philosophy of History* (New York: Dover Books, 1956). Miriam Lefkowitz is Bernal's best-known critic, though she does not use Budge's racial arguments. Miriam Lefkowitz, *Not out of Africa: How Afro-Centrism Became an Excuse to Teach Myth as History* (New York: New Republic and Basic Books, 1997).

Other commentators have suggested that it was the pharaoh, Akhenaten, rather than the Hebrew patriarch, Abraham, who developed the first monotheistic religious tradition, one that went on to inspire what became Judaism, Christianity, Islam, and Bahaism. Sigmund Freud's controversial book, *Moses and Monotheism*, was an early and influential argument for the idea that Moses's teachings derived primarily from the continued influence of Akhenaten. Yosef ben Johannan has also claimed an Egyptian origin of Mosaic teachings and therefore an African origin to what has been inaccurately described as the Abrahamic tradition.[3] Self-described Atenists also traced the origin of monotheism to Akhenaten and the worship of the solar disk, Aten, not to Abraham or Moses.[4] Ahmed Osman takes a different tack, suggesting that Moses was Akhenaten, and that he was deposed and sought refuge in Sinai, as Moses, before returning and leading the Exodus of his followers. He suggests that Akhenaten was the child of Amenhotep III with a Hebrew maid.[5] It is important to point out, however, that there is no evidence that either Egyptians or Hebrews came up with the oldest form of monotheism, since we know far too little about the early history of religious thought in the rest of the world.

In contrast to Akhenaten, there is no undisputed evidence that either Abraham or Moses was a historical figure. Only scriptures claim to be firsthand sources of their existence. As Jan Assmann has noted, "We cannot be sure that Moses ever lived because there are no traces of his earthly existence outside the tradition..." Akhenaten's..." religion, however, spawned no tradition but was forgotten immediately after his death. Moses is a figure of memory but not of history, while Akhenaten was a figure of history, but not of memory."[6] The teachings of Akhenaten have variously been described as a monotheistic reform of Egyptian religion or as an ancient heresy, but his teachings were vigorously suppressed by the pharaohs who succeeded him.[7] This may have reflected the importance of temple patronage and food distribution to local communities through festivals rather than concerns about

---

[3] Sigmund Freud, *Moses and Monotheism* (New York: Vantage, 1959). Yosef ben-Jochannan, *African Origins of the Major Western Religions* (Baltimore: Black Classics Press, [1970] 1991). Yosef ben-Jochannan, *African Mother of Western Civilization* (Baltimore: Black Classic Press, 1988), p. 354.

[4] Anonymous letter addressed to Robert Baum et al., McConaugh, Georgia, December 2018.

[5] Ahmed Osman, *Moses: Pharaoh of Egypt: The Mysteries of Akhenaten Revealed* (London: Grafton Books, 1996).

[6] Jan Assmann, *Moses the Egyptian: The Memory of Egypt in Western Monotheism* (Cambridge, MA: Harvard University Press, 1997), p. 2.

[7] David P. Silverman, ed., *Ancient Egypt* (New York: Oxford University Press, 1997), pp. 128–129.

heresy. How accessible these teachings would have been to someone like Moses, nearly a century after Akhenaten, remains difficult to establish.

Furthermore, the argument that Akhenaten was the source of Western monotheism has been vigorously rejected by adherents of the Abrahamic religions, by many historians of religions, and by scholars of the ancient Near East.[8] The continued association of Aten with the sun's rays is just one example of the differences with ancient Hebrew views of the supreme being, which had few associations with natural forces working in the universe. Still, it is possible that the monotheistic currents surrounding Akhenaten's reform could have influenced or reinforced monotheistic tendencies in the Hebrew tradition. The Egyptian origin of Moses's name and the book of Exodus's description of his knowledge of Egyptian traditions and his influential role at the Egyptian court all suggest that Moses was at least exposed to Egyptian religious thought. As Chancellor Williams reminds us, Abraham, Joseph, and Moses all spent considerable time in Egypt.[9] And when the ancient Hebrews despaired that Moses had abandoned them at the foot of Mount Sinai, they created a golden calf that may have had ties to the Egyptian Apis bull, the creator god Ptah, and the fertility goddess Hathor.[10] More difficult to determine is Moses's own ethnicity. The biblical book of Numbers describes Moses as marrying an unnamed Ethiopian woman, which his siblings, Aaron and Miriam, strongly opposed. According to this narrative, God punished Miriam by turning her leprously white, forcing Aaron to pray for their forgiveness for condemning Moses's marriage. This tradition suggests a sense of color consciousness among the ancient Hebrews and a divine mandate to reject such racial distinctions. It also suggests, however, an absence of perceived ethnic difference between Moses and other Hebrews.[11]

There is more agreement about the role of Egypt in Africa, with longstanding theories that much of African civilization grew out of Egyptian influences. Here again the harshest debate is about whether those great shapers of African civilizations, who came from Egypt, were white or

---

[8] Donald B. Redford, *Egypt, Canaan and Israel in Ancient Times* (Princeton, NJ: Princeton University Press, 1992).

[9] Exodus 2:10–11. Chancellor Williams, *The Destruction of Black Civilization, Great Issues of a Race from 4500 B.C. to 2000 A.D.* (Chicago: Third World Press, 1987), p. 35. The Ben Ezra Synagogue, in Coptic Cairo, built in the ninth century CE, is reported to have been built on the site where the pharaoh's daughter found the infant Moses floating down the Nile in a reed basket. I visited the synagogue in May 2000.

[10] Assmann, *Moses the Egyptian*, p. 72.

[11] Numbers 12.

black, both anachronistic projections, but with much at stake for the past two centuries of debates about race and history.[12] Advocates of white influence south of the Sahara often embraced the Hamitic Hypothesis, a theory popularized in the late nineteenth century that claimed that small groups of Hamites left Egypt, intermarried with African elites, and introduced everything that represents civilization into these societies. As Bruce Trigger noted: "The rulers of Kush generally were portrayed as 'Caucasoid' (Hamitic) when Kush was being described as a source of civilizing influence for the rest of sub-Saharan Africa, but these same rulers were characterized as Blacks when the region's achievements were considered in relation to those of ancient Egypt."[13] For example, C. G. Seligman claimed that the Shilluk he encountered in the Anglo-Egyptian Sudan derived an idea of sacred kingship from similar ideas of the ancient Egyptians. He went on to claim that "the civilizations of Africa are the civilizations of the Hamites." Seligman claimed that Hamites were white, "pastoral Europeans," and they could conquer Africa because they were "quicker witted."[14] Similarly, the Jungian anthropologist Eva Meyerowitz claimed that Akan religion and culture of Lower Guinea were of "non-Negro African origin." For Meyerowitz, Akan civilization came from Egypt.[15] Such theories were used to legitimate the colonization of the African continent during the late nineteenth and twentieth centuries.

Proponents of the Hamitic Hypothesis went as far as to try to demonstrate that African ruling elites were lighter in skin color and had more facial features in common with Caucasians than Africans of more humble circumstances. Such projections had tragic consequences in the countries of

[12] Robin Derricourt, *Inventing Africa: History, Archaeology, and Ideas* (London: Pluto Press, 2011), pp. 103–129.
[13] Bruce G. Trigger, "Nubian, Negro, Black, Nilotic?" in *Africa in Antiquity: The Arts of Ancient Nubia and the Suda: Volume I, The Essays*, ed. Sylvia Hirchfield and Elizabeth Riefenstahl (Brooklyn, NY: The Brooklyn Museum, 1978), p. 28.
[14] Bruce G. Trigger, "The Rise of Ancient Egypt," in *Ancient Egypt: A Social History*, ed. B. G. Trigger et al. (Cambridge: Cambridge University Press, 1992, p. 48. Robin Law, "The 'Hamitic Hypothesis' in Indigenous West African Thought," *History in Africa: A Journal of Method* 36 (2009), p. 94. C. G. Seligman, *The Races of Africa* (London: [1930] 1960), pp. 61–100. Andrew Reid, "Ancient Egypt and the Sources of the Nile," in *Ancient Egypt in Africa*, ed. David O'Connor and Andrew Reid (London: UCL Press, 2002), pp. 66–70. Christopher Wrigley, "Speculation on the Economic Prehistory of Africa," *Journal of African History* I, no. 2 (1960), p. 189.
[15] Eva Meyerowitz (1960, p. 235), cited in Caleb A. Folorunsa, "Views of Ancient Egypt from a West African Perspective," in *Ancient Egypt in Africa*, ed. David O'Connor and Andrew Reid (London: UCL Press, 2003), p. 88. Sir Harry Johnston, *The Divine Kingship in Ghana and Ancient Egypt*, 1902, p. 487. D. Olderogge, "Migrations and Ethnic and Linguistic Differentiation," in *UNESCO General History of Africa, Volume 1, Methodology and African Pre-history*, ed. J. Ki-Zerbo (London: Heinemann, 1981), p. 273.

Rwanda and Burundi, where German and Belgian administrators applied such distinctions to the tense relationship between Tutsi and Hutu social classes in these colonial societies.[16] John Roscoe described a similar distinction between "Negro-Hamitic" pastoralists and what he considered "Negro" agriculturalists in the Bunyoro kingdom in Uganda.[17] In some variations of the Hamitic Hypothesis, it was Semites—Hebrew, Phoenician, or Arab— who migrated south. Scholars have cited the practice of infant male circumcision as evidence of Hebrew influence on Yoruba culture, for example. Arab origins have been included in genealogies of many predominantly Muslim groups and even some non-Islamic communities.[18]

Some Afrocentric scholars also claimed that Egypt was the most important source of African civilizations, though they insisted on describing this Egypt as "black." Molefi Kete Asante, one of the most influential Afrocentric scholars, asserts that Egypt was a black African culture and that "The foundation of all African speculation in religion, art, ethics, moral questions and aesthetics, are derived from systems of knowledge found in ancient Egypt. To some extent it is this foundation, rather than the Greeks, that has made a lasting impact on the western world."[19] Asante draws heavily on the work of the Senegalese linguist and archaeologist Cheikh Anta Diop. However, Diop compared the similarities of other African and Egyptian cultures without suggesting in which direction the cultural influences flowed.[20]

Both proponents of the Hamitic Hypothesis and certain Afrocentric theorists attributed everything that represents civilization, in societies south of the Sahara, to Egyptian initiatives. These theorists deprived the peoples of

---

[16] Timothy Longman, *Christianity and Genocide in Rwanda* (Cambridge: Cambridge University Press, 2010), pp. 60–66.

[17] John Roscoe, *The Bakitra of Banyoro* (Cambridge: Cambridge University Press, 1923), pp. 6, 7, 13. For a critique of the Hamitic Hypothesis, see Felix A. Chami, "Diffusion in the Studies of the African Past: Reflections from New Archaeological Findings," *African Archaeological Review* 24 (2007), pp. 2–3.

[18] Reverend Samuel Johnson, *History of the Yoruba: From Earliest Times to the Beginning of the British Protectorate* (Lagos: CMS Bookstore, 1921), pp. 3–5. Olumode Lucas, *The Religion of the Yoruba*, cited in Chief (Dr.) M. A. Fabunmi, *An Anthology of Historical Notes on Ife City* (Lagos: John West Publishing, 1985), p. 11. Nehemia Levtzion, *Ancient Ghana and Mali* (London: Methuen, 1973). D. T. Niane, *Soundiata: An Epic of Old Mali* (London: Longman, 2006). Roscoe, *Bunyoro*, cited in *Ancient Egypt in Africa*, ed. David O'Connor and Andrew Reid (London: UCL Press, 2003), p. 67. Joseph J. Williams, *Hebraisms of West Africa: From Nile to Niger with the Jews* (New York: The Dial Press, 1930), 44, 50, 245.

[19] Molefi Kete Asante, *Kemet, Afrocentricity, and Knowledge* (Trenton, NJ: Africa World Press, 1990), pp. 47, 14.

[20] Cheikh Anta Diop, "The Origins of Ancient Egyptians," in *Ancient Civilizations of Africa, Volume II, UNESCO General History of Africa*, ed. G. Mokhtar (London: Heinemann, 1981), pp. 26–57. Diop, *Egypte Ancienne et Afrique Noir*, pp. 474, 491. Diop, "Histoire primitive d'humanité."

most of Africa of significant agency in the creation of their own civilizations. David O'Connor and Andrew Reid have noted the positive aspects of linking African civilizations to the civilization of ancient Egypt, but they expressed this concern: "it still seems to argue that, subsequent to the influx of Egyptian-derived innovation, Sub-Saharan Africa has been without history, unable to change and indeed culturally stagnating."[21] Chancellor Williams has gone as far as to assert that the weaknesses of African societies at the time of the Atlantic slave trade and European colonization were a direct result of the conquest and isolation of an ancient Ethiopia that was the source of ancient Egyptian civilization, first by the Greeks and Romans, and then by Arab empires which isolated the rest of Africa from these ancient centers of civilization.[22] Whether it was white people or black people who traveled south, it is Egypt rather than the rest of Africa that is held up as the source of civilization.

I contend that it is just as likely that black African societies from a less arid Sahara or from the Upper Nile had a profound influence in the development of Egyptian civilization. As Saharan peoples migrated into the Nile valley, they carried with them their religious cults and their skills in animal husbandry. Zoomorphic gods are found in rock art of the Sahara and eastern Africa, as well as in ancient Egypt. For example, images of rams have been found in the southern Maghreb and the central Sahara, dating back to 6000 BCE. These images suggest a precursor to Egyptian ram deities, even Khnum, who was said to be the deity entrusted with the creation of humans.[23] Izak Cornelius suggests that Bes, the chubby dwarf deity who protects pregnant women, may have come from Punt in the Horn of Africa.[24] Elaborate ways of burying the dead have also been found in these areas. Donald Redford has noted the influences of sub-Saharan African technologies, such as ivory carving, as well as archaeological evidence of population movements from

---

[21] David O'Connor and Andrew Reid, "Introduction: Locating Ancient Egypt in Africa: Modern Theories, Past Realities," in *Ancient Egypt in Africa*, ed. David O'Connor and Andrew Reid (London: UCL Press, 2003), p. 8.

[22] Williams, *Destruction of Black Civilizations*, pp. 55, 297.

[23] Ram deities are also common in West Africa, though of uncertain vintage. Philip E. L. Smith, "The Late Paleolithic and Epi-Paleolithic of Northern Africa," in *Cambridge History of Africa, Volume I, From the Earliest Times to c. 500 BCE*, ed. J. Desmond Clark (Cambridge: Cambridge University Press, 1982), p. 398. A. H. Zayed with J. Devisse, "Egypt's Relations with the Rest of Africa," in *Ancient Civilizations of Africa, Volume I UNESCO General History of Africa*, ed. G Mokhtar (Paris: UNESCO, 1981), p. 151.

[24] Izak Cornelius, "From Bes to Baal: Religious Interaction between Egypt and the East," in *Pharaoh's Land and Beyond: Ancient Egypt and Its Neighbors*, ed. Pearce P. Creasman and Richard H. Williams (New York: Oxford University Press, 2017), p. 212.

south to north and from the western deserts of Libya and the Sahara into the Nile valley. E. Wallis Budge claims that there is a black African base to Egyptian religion, suggesting that basic concepts and ritual practices originated in black communities of the Upper Nile valley and the Saharan regions. Nicolas Grimal gets more specific by arguing that Egyptian religion was based on a totemic system associated with towns and provinces of Pre-Dynastic Egypt, a practice that has been described in similar ways in many areas of Africa. Brian Fagan suggests that a collection of cattle cults, including the fertility goddess Hathor, had their origins in Saharan communities who moved to the Nile valley, along with their cattle, as the Sahara became more arid.[25] Chief (Dr.) M. A. Fabunmi reverses the claims of Egyptian origins, insisting that the Yoruba city of Ile-Ife was the ultimate home of civilization: "The British received their civilization from Rome, Rome from Greece, Greece from Persia, Persia from Chaldea, Chaldea from Babylon, the Babylonians and the Hebrews from Egypt, the Egyptians and the Tyrrheneans from Ile-Ife in Yorubaland."[26]

What is lacking and contributes to this focus on the "wonder that was Egypt" is the abundance of written documents and archaeological sites that allow us to understand far more about ancient Egypt than about the rest of the continent in antiquity. Kathryn Howley added: "A distinct lack of archaeological evidence for native Nubian religious practices . . . exacerbates the impression of Nubia as a passive recipient of Egyptian ideas." There can be little doubt that influences flowed in both directions.[27] As Peter Shinnie contended: "It must be made clear, though, that in many cases there is no certainty that in these common elements we may not be seeing Africa's legacy to Egypt as Egypt's legacy to Africa. The resemblances which can be found in cultural, social, and religious spheres between Egypt and other parts of Africa cannot of themselves tell us which way these influences may have travelled."[28]

---

[25] Redford, *Egypt, Canaan*, p. 7. Reid, "Ancient Egypt and the Sources of the Nile," p. 70. Nicolas Grimal, *A History of Ancient Egypt* (Malden, MA: Blackwell, [1992] 2008), p. 40. Brian Fagan, *Egypt of the Pharaohs* (Washington, DC: National Geographic, 2001), p. 38.

[26] Fabunmi, *Anthology*, p. 159,

[27] Kathryn Howley, "Egypt and Nubia," in *Pharaoh's Land and Beyond: Ancient Egypt and Its Neighbors*, ed. Pearce P. Creasman and Richard H. Wilkinson (New York: Oxford University Press, 2017), p. 220. A. Hamir Zayed, "Egypt's Relations with the Rest of Africa," in *Ancient Civilizations of Africa*, Vol. II, *UNESCO General History of Africa*, ed. G. Mokhtar (London: Heinemann, 1981), pp. 148–152. Elizabeth Isichei, *The Religious Traditions of Africa: A History* (Westport, CT: Praeger, 2004), p. 12. Ana I Navajas Jiménez, "The Predynastic Bas primogenius as a Royal Image of Territory, Boundaries, and Power in an African Context," in *Egypt in Its African Context*, ed. Karyn Exell (Oxford: Archaeopress, 2011), pp. 32–33.

[28] P. L. Shinnie, "Meroe: The African Heir of Ancient Egypt," in *Ancient Egyptian Civilization*, ed. Brenda Stalcup (San Diego: Greenhaven Press, 2000), p. 189.

As archaeological evidence of the early history of the Sahara and the upper Nile regions increases, this can be argued with greater specificity.

Historical linguistic analysis does not shed much light on the question of the direction of cultural influences. According to the most influential classifier of African languages, Joseph Greenberg, ancient Egyptian was probably one of the early languages of the Afro-Asiatic family, which included Semitic, Cushitic, Berber, and Chadic languages stretching from northern Nigeria to the Fertile Crescent. Their shared origins made theories about Egyptian borrowings from Semitic languages difficult to establish. Similarly, ancient Egyptian influences in Chadic or Berber languages become difficult to extract from their shared history. What it does suggest, however, is that for millennia this area has constituted a single linguistic zone, dominated by languages which share common origins.[29]

Although Herodotus called Egypt "the gift of the Nile," it was also endowed with the gift of location, a crossroads between Africa and the Mediterranean world, between Africa and the Middle East. It was protected by increasingly arid deserts to its east and west, but it enjoyed relatively easy access to the upper Nile valley, to trans-Saharan trade routes, and to the Red Sea.[30] It was the crossroads of the ancient world, subject to influences from and able to exert influence upon all of the cultural zones that were adjacent to it.[31] Judging from the paintings on papyrus scrolls, on coffins, and in various types of burial structures, Egypt was a multiracial society, with portrayals of black, reddish-brown, and white people and divinities.[32] It was not consistently racially stratified along the lines of European-dominated societies since the fifteenth century. Racial hierarchies appear quite fluid, and different ethnic groups with varying complexions controlled royal governments in different dynasties. Intermarriage between Nubians and Egyptians appears

---

[29] Trigger, "Rise of Ancient Egypt," p. 11. Joseph Greenberg, *The Languages of Africa* (Bloomington: Indiana University, 1966), pp. 43–61.

[30] For a discussion of Egypt's location as a crossroads of the ancient world, see Barry J. Kemp, "Old Kingdom, Middle Kingdom, and Second Intermediate Period, c. 2686–1552 BC," in *Ancient Egypt: A Social History*, ed. B. G. Trigger et al. (Cambridge: Cambridge University Press, 1992), pp. 125–149.

[31] Redford argues for both sub-Saharan and Palestinian influences on early Egyptian culture. Redford, *Egypt, Canaan*, p. 7.

[32] This is confirmed by Cheikh Anta Diop. He describes a population divided among three racial groups: Negroid at 36 percent, Mediterranean at 33 percent, and Cro-Magnon at 11 percent. The remaining 20 percent are racially mixed or undetermined. Diop, "Histoire primitive d'humanité," p. 484. See also Aidan Dodson, *Monarchs of the Nile* (Cairo: American University in Cairo Press, 2000), p. 4. Frank J. Yurco, "Egypt and Nubia: Old, Middle and New Kingdom Eras," in *Africa and Africans in Antiquity*, ed. Edwin M. Yamauchi (East Lansing: Michigan State University Press, 2001), p. 48. G. Mokhtar, "Introduction," in *Ancient Civilizations of Africa*, ed. G. Mokhtar (London: Heinemann, 1981), p. 14.

to have been fairly common and to have attracted little controversy. As Michael Rice has noted, a number of the early rulers, including Khufu and Djoser, appeared to have more African racial features. Other rulers had more Mediterranean features.[33] Resentments of some dynastic shifts may have focused more on a perception of new dynasties being foreign rather than of different skin color.[34]

Agricultural societies developed in the Nile valley and the Fayyun by the fifth millennium BCE, gradually using the surpluses of their rich farmland to support larger state structures and a high degree of economic specialization. By the beginning of the fourth millennium, clusters of villages had bonded together to form small states. By the end of the fourth millennium, these states became united, initially as kingdoms of Lower Egypt (the delta) and Upper Egypt (the valley, north of Nubia). Their control focused on the black lands, fertile and well-watered areas enriched by the Nile's annual floods. State control of irrigation and flood control systems contributed to the bolstering of political authority. These public works required strong administrative structures capable of organizing the necessary labor power and of providing military protection. Both to the west and the east of the Nile valley lay the red lands, rich in minerals, including gold, but dry and sparsely populated, with only an occasional oasis where agricultural production could take place. These deserts provided a modicum of defense to the agricultural communities of the valley, preventing the movement of large armies into the region.

Ancient Egyptian history was marked by a series of dynasties, about forty in all, grouped together in the Archaic Period, the Old Kingdom, Middle Kingdom, and New Kingdom, each of which was separated from the others by an intermediate period characterized by political instability and the breakdown of centralized authority. Throughout the ancient period, however, Egypt remained a hierarchical society, divided between nobility, scribes, and priests; and artisans, peasants, and slaves.[35] Priests served as administrators; the temples they controlled became administrative centers. Given the close association of political authority and the royal cults, each shift of kingdom had important religious consequences. In theory, at least,

---

[33] Michael Rice, *Egypt's Making: The Origin of Ancient Egypt* (London: Routledge, 1990), pp. 201, 221.
[34] Donald B. Redford, *From Slave to Pharaoh: The Black Experience of Ancient Egypt* (Baltimore: Johns Hopkins University Press, 2002), p. 6.
[35] H. W. E. Saggs, *Civilization before Greece and Rome* (New Haven, CT: Yale University Press, 1987), p. 27.

it was the pharaoh who appointed the priests of all the major temples within his domains. In practice, however, he only appointed the primary priests and left appointments of their subordinates to his clerical appointees.[36] The continual, though variable, relationship of the pharaohs to divinity—in the form of Horus, Re, Re-Atum, or Aten—and their role as high priest of the kingdom underscored the theocratic nature of the Egyptian state. As Herodotus noted: "'They [the Egyptians] are religious to excess, beyond any nation in the world.'"[37]

The available source materials reinforce the tendency to focus on the various kingdoms, their courts, and local elites. They left the most elaborate burial monuments, the most extensive grave goods, and hieroglyphic texts, which reflected the concerns and ideas prevalent among the upper classes and the priesthoods. Scholars know far less about the religious concerns or daily lives of the vast majority of commoners who derived their living from farming, trade, or artisanal occupations. They knew even less about the daily life of enslaved groups in Egyptian society. Sources on women's lives are also scarce, though there are some materials on women rulers and priestly attendants. Engraved or painted artwork, on the walls of tombs, portrays scenes from daily lives of all these groups, however idealized. Adding to the difficulties in tracing a broad religious history is the problem that many of the available texts, often engraved in pyramids, other burial sites, or monuments, provide dates for the particular texts, but not whether they represent the first iteration of these materials. This is particularly challenging in analyzing the conflicting cosmologies associated with early Egyptian religious centers. Leonard Lesko noted: "Because it is impossible to know when each of the cosmogonic myths and cosmological concepts originated and how long each of them was present, there is a tendency to ignore the problem."[38]

This chapter is an exercise in reading against the grain, of developing a history of Egyptian religions from sources that stress the importance of continuity and stasis. Throughout the two millennia discussed here, different cosmologies and deities competed for dominance but continued to serve as a potential resource when the ideas and practices associated with

---

[36] Byron R. Shafer, "Temples, Priests, and Rituals: An Overview," in *Temples of Ancient Egypt*, ed. Bryan R. Shafer (Ithaca, NY: Cornell University Press, 1997), p. 9. Elise Boulding, *The Underside of History: A View of Women Through Time* (London: Sage, 1987), p. 158.

[37] Emily Teeter, *Religion and Ritual in Ancient Egypt* (Cambridge: Cambridge University Press, 2012), pp. 3–4.

[38] Leonard Lesko, "Ancient Egyptian Cosmogonies and Cosmologies," in *Religion in Ancient Egypt: Gods, Myths, and Ancient Practice*, ed. Byron E. Shafer (Ithaca, NY: Cornell University Press, 1991), p. 122.

them were needed by Egyptian people. In some cases, attempted religious changes imposed by royalty were unsuccessful and older traditions returned to prominence. In many instances, new deities, new cosmologies, and new concepts of the good life drew on older concepts, while presenting new ways of thinking about matters of ultimate concern. Underlying ancient Egyptian religion, however, were persistent fears of disorder and chaos. Most ancient Egyptians saw Ma'at, the goddess of order and justice, as a bulwark against disorder associated with the god Seth, other trickster deities, and the desert wilderness that dwarfed the slender, fertile, and vulnerable Nile valley. Egypt's kings also served as an opponent of the forces of disruption.

This chapter focuses on the Old and Middle Kingdoms, prior to 1300 BCE, but it continues through the religious reforms introduced by Akhenaten during the New Kingdom. It examines religious changes that can be documented in the written and material culture of ancient Egypt, as Egyptian visions of the origins of the universe, of gods and goddesses, burial and the afterlife, the roles of priests and laity and men and women changed along with changes in political, economic, and social life. These changes can be documented in the shifting centers of royal religious patronage and changes in cosmogonic myths that emphasized different deities. Written sources, however, tend to stress the stability of Egyptian beliefs and practices while minimizing disruptions.[39] Additional perspectives come from archaeological evidence involving homes, family altars, and the more modest tombs of ordinary Egyptians.

The earliest written documents, dating from the Old Kingdom, provide some evidence about religious life prior to the unification of Egypt, in what is often referred to as the Pre-Dynastic Era, corresponding roughly to the fourth millennium. These writings, collectively known as the Pyramid Texts, were carved on the walls of the Saqqara pyramids and date primarily to the Fifth Dynasty.[40] Some of the deities described in Old Kingdom texts appear to have been worshipped prior to the unification of Lower and Upper Egypt and the emergence of the First Dynasty. The royal Sed festivals also had their roots in the Pre-Dynastic Era. Some of these deities served as patron deities of specific towns or villages and were associated with particular animals, assuring the prosperity and fertility of the community.[41]

---

[39] David O'Connor, "New Kingdom and Third Intermediate Period, 1552–664 BC," in *Ancient Egypt: A Social History*, ed. B. G. Trigger et al. (Cambridge: Cambridge University Press, 1992), p. 186.

[40] Marc Van De Mieroop, *A History of Ancient Egypt* (Malden, MA: Wiley-Blackwell, 2011), p. 86.

[41] Redford, *Egypt, Canann*, p. 9. Alejandro Jiménez Serrano, "Royal Festivals in the Late Predynastic Period and the First Dynasty," BAR International Archaeological Services 1076

A falcon deity, possibly a precursor of Horus, was associated with Nubian Group A monuments at Questal.[42] One must keep in mind, however, that most of the written documents were produced by small groups of scribes, priests, and the nobility. Few writers describe ordinary people, and very few documents survive that were written by members of the lower classes. Our views of gender are also skewed by a preponderance of what we think are male authors. Because so many documents come from tombs, such as the Pyramid Texts and the *Egyptian Book of the Dead*, scholars tend to focus on elaborate Egyptian views of death, the afterlife, and the ritual preparations for both.[43] How accurately that reflects the central concerns of Egyptian religion remains uncertain. Stephen Quirke claims that the enduring focus of Egyptian religion was ensuring ma'at (justice), working for what is right, and ensuring offerings to the gods and the ancestors.[44]

Archaic (3100–2686 BCE)

Toward the end of the fourth millennium BCE, King Narmer (identified as Menes by the Greeks) united the kingdoms of Lower Egypt and Upper Egypt into a single polity. His successor, Aha, established the capital at Inb-Hd, better known by its Greek name, Memphis, located in the border area between Upper and Lower Egypt.[45] These early rulers of a united Egypt emphasized the importance of intermarriage between nobility of Upper and Lower Egypt.[46] For example, Aha married a woman named Neithotep (may the goddess "Neith be appeased") and established a shrine for Neith in the area of Seis in the Nile delta.[47] Even before the unification and during the First Dynasty, Egyptians revered Neith, who was seen as a creator god and a protector of kings.[48] Local deities who were

---

(Oxford: Archaeopress, 2002), pp. 4, 42. Rosalie David, *Religion and Magic in Ancient Egypt* (London: Penguin, 2012), p. 54.

[42] Yurco, "Egypt and Nubia," p. 31.
[43] Trigger, "Rise of Ancient Egypt," pp. 54–55.
[44] Stephen Quirke, *Exploring Religion in Ancient Egypt* (Chichester, UK: Wiley-Blackwell, 2015), p. 8.
[45] He is referred to as Menes in Herodotus's history. Ancient Egyptian was written without vowels. Silverman, *Ancient Egypt*, p. 22. Barbara Watterson, *The Egyptians* (Oxford: Blackwell, 1997), p. 42. Cyril Aldred, *The Egyptians*, 3rd ed. (London: Thames and Hudson, 1998), p. 81.
[46] Paul Johnson, *The Civilization of Ancient Egypt* (New York: Atheneum, 1978), p. 25.
[47] Grimal, *History of Ancient Egypt*, p. 50.
[48] Susan T. Hollis, "Neith," in *Encyclopedia of Women and World Religion*, Vol. 2, ed. Serinity Young (New York: Macmillan Reference, 1999), pp. 714–715.

worshipped in particular towns and districts (nomes) dominated local religious practice. Local priests performed daily rituals for the gods, who, in turn, protected their host communities. For example, Nit, a war goddess, was associated with the town of Sais. Osiris, initially a god associated with vegetation, received veneration at Busiris. His brother, Seth, was associated with the Upper Egyptian town of Ombos.[49]

From the time of the First Dynasty through much of the Old Kingdom, Memphis served as both an administrative center and as a site of royal temples. It lent its name to the earliest known cosmogony of a united Egypt. During this period, Ptah served as both the creator god and the principal deity of Memphis.[50] The Memphis Theology described him: "Thus Ptah was satisfied after he had made all things and all divine words. / He gave birth to the gods. / He made the towns. . . . / He established the nomes [provinces]. / He placed the gods in their shrine. / Thus were gathered to him all the gods and their kas, / Content, united with the Lord of the Two Lands."[51] The Memphis Theology emphasized the god's ability to imagine a world and then to create it through the force of his will and the power of his speech. All was unformed, without separation between the earthly and heavenly realm, a watery and chaotic universe. There were no gods, no humans, no life. Nun was seen as pure potentiality, the source of all matter, the "mother of mothers and the father of fathers."[52] As Ptah emerged from Nun, his first words began the process of creation.

> There took shape in the heart, there took shape in the tongue the form of Atum. For the very great one is Ptah, who gave [life] to all the gods and their *kas* (spirits) through this heart and through this tongue.[53]

---

[49] William C. Hayes, *The Scepter of Egypt: A Background for the Study of the Egyptian Antiquities in the Metropolitan Museum of Art, Part I, From the Earliest Times to the End of the Middle Kingdom* (New York: Harvey N. Abrams, 1953), pp. 75–76.

[50] Although the Memphite Theology is associated with the earliest dynasties of a united Egypt, the fullest text of it was found on an eighth-century BCE stone engraving. Lesko, "Ancient Egyptian Cosmologies and Cosmogonies," p. 90. Aldred, *Egyptians*, p. 82.

[51] Fagan, *Egypt*, p. 56.

[52] Françoise Dunand and Christiane Zivie-Coche, *Gods and Men in Egypt, 3000 BCE to 398 CE* (Ithaca, NY: Cornell University Press, 2002), pp. 44–48.

[53] This text was carved on a black granite stone called the Shabaka Stone (c. 700 BCE), but the older dialect of ancient Egyptian suggests that the original text was from the Old Kingdom, Shabaka Stone, British Museum #498, lines 53–54. Translated with M. Lichtheim, cited in David, *Religion and Magic in Ancient Egypt*, p. 87. Henri Frankfort, *Ancient Egyptian Gods* (New York: Harper and Row, [1948] 1961), p. 23. Jan Assmann, *The Mind of Egypt: History and Memory in the Time of the Pharaohs* (New York: Metropolitan Books, 1990), pp. 39–43.

As Mircea Eliade noted: "It is surprising that the earliest Egyptian cosmogony yet known is also the most philosophical. For Ptah creates by his mind ('his heart') and his word (his 'tongue')."[54]

The first major temple established at Memphis was Ptah's; the most powerful priests in the Archaic Period were his priests. Ptah was particularly associated with the growing importance of the artisan classes in the unified Egyptian kingdom.[55] Apis was a manifestation of the creator god Ptah, who appeared in the form of a bull, a symbol of strength and fertility, and was closely associated with the city of Memphis.[56] Ptah's high priest served as an important counsellor to the king and directed the various artisanal organizations, ranging from sculptors and potters to Jewelers and smiths.[57] Seshat was a goddess associated with learning, dating back to the First Dynasty and described on the Palermo Stone. She recorded the actions of human beings on leaves of a Tree of Life and played a role in measuring out the buildings of temple complexes.[58] By the Second Dynasty, the sun god, Re, whose cult was centered at Iwun (Heliopolis), became increasingly important, alongside Ptah.[59] During the first three dynasties of a united Egypt, royal burials were concentrated in Abydos, which later became a center of the Osiris cult. In traditions reported in the Middle Kingdom, Osiris was also seen as the first Egyptian king.[60]

Already in the Archaic Period, Egyptian concepts of life and death were quite complex. They understood human beings as having several noncorporeal components, in addition to the human body itself. These included the *akh*, "an aspect of the sun, a luminous element that permitted the dead to join the stars when they passed into the hereafter; it was the form in which the power—the spirit—of the gods or the dead manifested itself." This suggests a divine presence in all humans. The *ka* was the vital force, initially only of royalty, necessary to achieve eternal life. Different kinds of beings possessed different quantities of *ka*. The sun god, Re, was said to possess fourteen *ka*. At death, the *ka* was separated from the body. It was

---

[54] Mircea Eliade, *A History of Religious Ideas, Volume 1, From the Stone Age to the Eleusinian Mysteries* (Chicago: University of Chicago Press, 1978), p. 89.
[55] Rice, *Egypt's Making*, p. 190. Lesko, "Ancient Egyptian Cosmologies and Cosmogonies," p. 90.
[56] W. B. Emery, *Archaic Egypt* (Harmondsworth, UK: Penguin Books, 1961), pp. 124–126.
[57] Rice, *Egypt's Making*, p. 170.
[58] Emery, *Archaic Egypt*, p. 126. Joann Fletcher, *The Egyptian "Book of Living and Dying": The Illustrated Guide to Ancient Egyptian Wisdom* (London: Duncan Baird, 2002), p. 10.
[59] Rice, *Egypt's Making*, p. 197.
[60] David O'Connor, *Abydos: Egypt's First Pharaohs and the Cult of Osiris* (London: Thames & Hudson, 2012), p. 27.

seen as a force linked to both male and female powers of reproduction and to the ancestors.[61] The *ba*, often translated as "soul," was a kind of spiritual double, which left the body at death, but reunited with it after the completion of the mummification process. During the Archaic Period, it was mostly associated with royalty. A shadow was another kind of spiritual double with a separate existence from the body. Finally, there was the person's name itself, which represented the power of the spoken word, initially by the parents who provided the name and then reinforced each time the name was used by someone else.[62]

Beginning in the thirtieth year of his reign, the king's vital force was periodically reinvigorated through the performance of the Sed festival. Described as a royal jubilee celebration, this ritual of renewal reaffirmed the monarch's relationship to the god Sed, represented as a jackal. The ritual was said to have been performed at least since the reign of King Narmer, who united Upper and Lower Egypt. The Sed festival required elaborate preparations and was held as the annual flood began on the Nile.[63] Its timing reflected the desired connections between the resurgent river and a reinvigorated king. After the death of a king, royal funerary rituals focused on reuniting the *ka* with the pharaoh's body to ensure his immortality.[64] During the First and Second Dynasties, royal graves were surrounded by subsidiary graves of people who died at approximately the same time as the king. At the tomb of King Djer, six hundred subsidiary graves were found, the largest number at any of the Archaic royal burial sites. These included "subsidiary wives and servants with their equipment.... To accompany the king into the next world, and so achieve immortality by ministering to him in the hereafter." It remains unclear whether they were sacrificed to accompany the king into the afterlife or felt social pressure to end their lives and continue their roles as royal servants.[65] There are no signs of any violence or resistance in these subsidiary graves. The kings themselves were buried in more elaborate royal tombs known as *mastabas*. These tombs contained multiple chambers

---

[61] John H. Taylor, *Death and the Afterlife in Ancient Egypt* (Chicago: University of Chicago Press, 2001), p. 19.
[62] Grimal, *History of Ancient Egypt*, pp. 105–108. Taylor, *Death*, pp. 23–24.
[63] Alejandro Jiménez Serrano, "Royal Festivals in the Late Predynastic Period and the First Dynasty," British Archaeological Research, m. 1076 (Oxford: Archaeopress, 2002), p. 42.
[64] Fagan, *Egypt*, p. 89.
[65] Aldred, *Egyptians*, p. 85. Watterson, *Egyptians*, p. 48. Rice, *Egypt's Making*, p. 123. Johnson, *Civilization of Ancient Egypt*, p. 31.

and were first constructed during the Second Dynasty, in the reign of King Khaseckhemway around 2675 BCE.[66]

Artisans' graves were far more modest. They, too, however, included personal belongings such as the tools that they needed to ply their trades. Presumably, the deceased would use their tools in service for their patrons in the world to come.[67]

Old Kingdom (2695–2196 BCE)

The period known as the Old Kingdom was a time of growing economic prosperity, political centralization, and state control of Nubian areas of the Upper Nile and coastal areas of the Eastern Mediterranean.[68] The Nile itself played a central role. The year began with the onset of the annual floods, followed by the season of planting, and an arid season, until the end of the year. The annual flood was so important that a major god, Hapy, was associated with the floodwaters rather than the river itself. Hapy was portrayed as a heavy-set male with a pot belly and large breasts, somewhat androgynous, emphasizing his links to fertility and prosperity.[69] Reliance on the Nile flood also reinforced farmers' reliance on the Egyptian state for the maintenance of irrigation systems (see Figure 3.1).

During the Old Kingdom, two additional cosmologies emerged: one associated with Heliopolis (Iunu) and a second associated with Thebes. These cosmologies shared many assumptions about the nature of the universe and the gods and people who acted within each. Both cosmogonic traditions began with formless waters from which a creative force emerged. Each of them, however, stressed different deities, deities associated with particular towns and their temples, and different methods of creation.[70] Theologians at Heliopolis, near Memphis, developed a new vision of an Egyptian pantheon, identified with Horus, previously considered a sky god, who became closely associated with the kings of a unified Egypt. By the Fourth Dynasty,

---

[66] Silverman, *Ancient Egypt*, p. 168.
[67] Dominic Valtello, "Craftsmen," in *The Egyptians*, ed. Sergio Donadoni (Chicago: University of Chicago Press, 1997), p. 36.
[68] Jaromir Malek, "The Old Kingdom (c. 2686–2125 BC)," in *The Oxford History of Ancient Egypt*, ed. Ian Shaw (Oxford: Oxford University Press, 2000), p. 90.
[69] Dunand and Zivie-Coche, *Gods and Men in Egypt*, p. 345. David, *Religion and Magic in Ancient Egypt*, p. 9. Silverman, *Ancient Egypt*, p. 19.
[70] David, *Religion and Magic in Ancient Egypt*, pp. 61–62.

Figure 3.1. The Nile River and the adjacent desert, west of Aswan, Egypt (photo by Robert M. Baum).

pharaohs were seen both as the embodiment of Horus and the son of Re, the sun god.[71]

In traditions associated with Heliopolis, it was Atum who was created from the semen and the fingers of Nun-Ptah.[72] This Heliopolitan Cosmogony (c. 2800 BCE), found in the Pyramid Texts, focused on nine deities, known collectively as the Ennead. In this tradition, the sun god, initially identified as Atum Kheprer, emerged from the primal waters, onto a rock known as Benben. Models of this rock appeared in many temples of the Archaic Period and the Old Kingdom. Atum or Re began the process, creating other gods, through masturbation and ejaculating the male god, Shu, and the female god, Tefnut. In some accounts, he spits them out. In both cases, the lesser gods are created from the deity's fluids. After creating them, Atum wrapped his arms around each new deity in order to transmit his *ka* or life force. Tefnut and Shu, the first divine couple, created Geb, the earth god, and Nut, the goddess of the sky. This identification of the earth as a male deity and the sky as

---

[71] Silverman, *Ancient Egypt*, pp. 22, 24.
[72] David P. Silverman, "Divinity and Deities in Ancient Egypt," in *Religion in Ancient Egypt*, ed. Byron Shafer et al. (Ithaca, NY: Cornell University Press, 1991) p. 34. Lesko, "Ancient Egyptian Cosmologies and Cosmogonies," p. 96. Dunand and Zivie-Coche, *Gods and Men in Egypt*, pp. 14–15.

female is unusual in the comparative study of religions. Barbara Watterson claimed that Geb was androgynous. At his shrine in Heliopolis: "Geb was worshipped as a bisexual god and credited with having laid the Great Egg from which the sun emerged at the beginning of time in the form of the Benu bird.... One of Geb's epithets was the 'Great Cackler,' a reference to the cackle he gave as he produced this Egg!"

Geb and Nut created four deities, the male gods Osiris and Seth and their wives/sisters Isis and Nephthys.[73] Seth was associated with the red, desert lands and Osiris with the rich black soils of the Nile valley and delta. Re created human beings from his own tears, which some saw as something of an afterthought. This suggests that humans share in the divine creative fluids.[74] Distressed by the continued rebelliousness and treachery of humans, Re withdrew from the world, but he sent his daughter, the Eye of Re in the form of Sekhmet ("she who is powerful"), the lion goddess, to punish humans. Recoiling from the violence, Re relents to some extent and sends the inventor of writing and the patron god of scribes, Thoth, to help them.[75]

The cosmogony associated with Thebes and based on the Coffin Texts, dating from around 2000 BCE, shifts the emphasis from Ptah to Nun and introduces a less abstract method of beginning the process of creation. Nun was uncreated; it was the primal waters, but all the gods were created from it.[76] Nun began the process of creating divinities by masturbating. From this primordial act, Nun, the first to emerge from the waters, created a male deity, Shu, and a female deity, Tefnut. They were the first sexually differentiated deities. Shu was associated with air and dryness. Tefnut was associated with moisture. Shu and Tefnut became the parents of the earth god, Geb, and the sky goddess, Nut. In turn, they had four children, the gods Osiris and Seth, and the goddesses Isis and Nephthys. As this cosmology developed, the "divine hand" of Nun's fertile masturbation became associated with a goddess of that name, and eventually with Hathor, the goddess of female sexuality and, in the New Kingdom, with the God's wife of Amun. Thoth was an equally ancient god, associated with the moon and with the sciences and writing. The

---

[73] Barbara Watterson, *The Gods of Ancient Egypt* (New York: Facts on File, 1984), p. 55. Lesko, "Ancient Egyptian Cosmologies and Cosmogonies," pp. 91–92. Jacques Vandier, *La Religion Égyptienne* (Paris: Presses Universitaires de France, 1949), p. 33. Fletcher, *Egyptian "Book of Living and Dying,"* p. 11. David, *Religion and Magic in Ancient Egypt*, pp. 84–85.

[74] Fletcher, *Egyptian "Book of Living and Dying,"* p. 12.

[75] Fletcher, *Egyptian "Book of Living and Dying,"* pp. 12–13. Visit to the National Gallery of Art exhibit, "The Quest for Immortality: Treasures of Ancient Egypt," 2002.

[76] Obenga, *Ancient Egypt & Black Africa*, pp. 31, 37–38. Silverman, *Ancient Egypt*, pp. 120–121.

presence of both gods demonstrates that even in the Old Kingdom, science and the pursuit of knowledge were highly valued.[77]

In other myths, conflict emerges between the four sibling gods, particularly the brothers, Osiris and Seth. According to some traditions, Osiris had an affair with Nephthys, his sister and Seth's wife, and she gave birth to Anubis, the jackal god associated with the preparation of the dead and their final judgment.[78] Seth tricked Osiris, getting him to lie down in a coffin where Seth slew him, scattering his body parts all over Egypt. Given Egyptian concerns about the importance of preserving the physical bodies of the dead before they enter the land of the dead, Seth's deliberate dissection of Osiris's body was particularly heinous. Wherever parts of his body were found people created a ritual center, or they justified the existence of an older ritual center by linking it to the Osirian myth. With Osiris's demise, death entered the world. His wife and sister, Isis, went around collecting all his body parts and were able to revive him long enough for him to father Isis's son, Horus. Isis described her unusual role: "I have acted as a man; I was a woman. In order to make [Osiris] survive on earth, his name."[79] Through her selfless search for all of her husband's body parts and her determination to revive him long enough to bear his child, she embodied an Egyptian maternal ideal. With her taking control of the body of Osiris for purposes of procreation, however, she took on a role that most Egyptians associated with paternity. Unaware of her pregnancy, Seth tried to enslave Isis, but Thoth helped her escape. Isis hid her pregnancy from the other gods, remaining in seclusion in a remote, swampy area of the Nile delta. She raised her son to become a mighty warrior. Horus eventually defeated his uncle, became king, and was recognized as such by a council of the gods.[80] In these myths, gods betray their brothers and their spouses, seek to enslave one another, and exhibit all the treachery associated with the worst of humanity. However, Isis exemplifies the ideals of female power as manifested in marriage and motherhood.

---

[77] Gay Robins, *Women in Ancient Egypt* (Cambridge, MA: Harvard University Press, 1993), p. 17. Jennifer H. Wagner, "Shu," in *The Ancient Gods Speak: A Guide to Egyptian Religion*, ed. Donald B. Redford (Oxford: Oxford University Press, 2002), p. 335.

[78] Mark Smith, *Following Osiris: Perspectives on the Osirian Afterlife from Four Millennia* (Oxford: Oxford University Press, 2017), p. 6.

[79] Quoted in Susan Tovar Hollis, "Isis," in *Encyclopedia of Women and Religion*, Vol. I, ed. Serinity Young (New York: Macmillan, 1999), p. 488.

[80] This story of Osiris, Seth, and Horus is related in its most complete form during the Roman period early in the second century CE, by Plutarch. O'Connor, *Abydos*, pp. 35–36. Lesko, "Ancient Egyptian Cosmologies and Cosmogonies," pp. 92–93.

The cult of Osiris and the close association of Horus with the king of Egypt took on a new importance during the Fifth Dynasty. Devotees of Osiris claimed that the Egyptian king could become one with Osiris in the afterlife.[81] It drew on the older cult of the god Sokar and absorbed the deity Khentiamentiu, who had been closely associated with death and the afterlife.[82]

Egyptian kings were seen as intermediaries between humans and divinities, between the earthly and heavenly realms. They channeled the life-giving powers of gods to humans. In some traditions, Osiris was regarded as an actual human ruler, who introduced much of Egypt's cultural arts and established justice in his realm, before becoming a deity.[83] It is unclear to what extent other pharaohs were seen as "divine kings" or as sacred persons. Rosalie David rejects the idea of Egyptian divine kingship, suggesting instead that "the king did not actually become the god, but took on his attributes and enabled the god through him to become accessible to mankind."[84] This is supported by a text attributed to King Senruset I: "He [the god Hor-akhty] who created me as one who should do that which he had done, and to carry out that which he had commanded should be done. He appointed me herdsman for this land for he knew who would keep it in order for him."[85] The Pyramid Texts include many prayers asking Amun to strengthen the life force of the pharaohs so they could live a long life and sustain a strong kingdom.

Osiris's son Horus grew from a sky god to become closely identified with the kings and the royal families. Indeed, one of the king's names was called his Horus name. They performed the most important rituals designed to preserve the order of the universe and keep the world from descending into chaos.[86] Osiris became king of the underworld, a force for order, who supervised the process of judgment after death. On the other hand, Seth's love of chaos and rebellion, associated with the wilderness of the desert and

---

[81] R. T. Rundle Clark, *Myth and Symbol in Ancient Egypt* (London: Thames and Hudson, [1959] 1991), pp. 124, 196.
[82] Smith, *Following Osiris*, p. 544.
[83] Smith, *Following Osiris*, p. 103. O'Connor, "New Kingdom and Third Intermediate Period," p. 293.
[84] David, *Religion and Magic in Ancient Egypt*, p. 77. Lesko, "Ancient Egyptian Cosmologies and Cosmogonies," p. 92.
[85] Barry J. Kemp, "Old Kingdom, Middle Kingdom, and Second Intermediate Period in Egypt," in *Cambridge History of Africa*, Vol. I, ed. J. Desmond Clark (Cambridge: Cambridge University Press, 1982), p. 667.
[86] Robins, *Women in Ancient Egypt*, p. 21.

violent storms, embodied one of the earliest known examples of the trickster deity within the history of religions.[87]

Although tombs have provided many of our earliest insights into the concerns of Egyptian religious traditions, during the Old Kingdom, these tombs developed their most elaborate architectural manifestations, in the construction of the Pyramids. The oldest, the Step Pyramid of Saqqara, was the resting place of King Djoser, who came to power in 2667 BCE, at the beginning of the Third Dynasty. His body was placed in a subterranean chamber, beneath the massive structure of a multilevel pyramid.[88] According to many historians, Imhotep designed and supervised the construction of Djoser's pyramid, while serving as high priest to the sun god, Re, and chancellor to the king. As Dietrich Wildung suggests, Imhotep was "the first individual we know" in Egyptian history.[89] Imhotep was deified during the New Kingdom as the god associated with architecture, science, and medicine.[90] This suggests a fluidity to the boundary between humans and deities that is more typical of sub-Saharan African religious traditions. For example, oral traditions of the Yoruba suggest that most orisha, lesser deities, once lived on earth as human beings. Many Bantu-speaking communities have religious traditions that stress the importance of kings and cultural heroes who assumed significant spiritual roles after death.

An admonition attributed to Prince Hardjedef (approximately 2300 BCE) stressed the importance of one's final resting place: "'Make good your dwelling in the graveyard, make worthy your station in the West ... the house of death is for life.'"[91] The pyramids constituted the largest tombs in the ancient world and included elaborate chambers to house the tombs of pharaohs, food offerings, and models of servants who could help them in the afterlife (see Figure 3.2). These small images of servants, first noted around 2100 BCE, were made of painted limestone or ivory in the shape of a mummy and could be activated in the afterlife after invocations of special prayers.[92]

---

[87] O'Connor, "New Kingdom and Third Intermediate Period," p. 197.
[88] Malek, "The Old Kingdom," p. 91. Vandier, *La Religion Égyptienne*, p. 145.
[89] Dietrich Wildung, *Egyptian Saints: Deification in Pharaonic Egypt* (New York: New York University Press, 1977), p. 31.
[90] Dodson, *Monarchs of the Nile*, p. 24. A. Abu Bakar, "Pharaonic Egypt," in *Ancient Civilizations of Africa*, Vol. II of UNESCO *General History of Africa*, ed. G. Mokhtar (London: Heinemann, 1981), p. 91. John P. O'Neill, ed., *Egyptian Art in the Age of the Pyramids* (New York: Metropolitan Museum of Art, 1999), p. 13. Aldred, *Egyptians*, p. 98. Rice, *Egypt's Making*, p. 175. Toby Wilkenson, *Lives of the Ancient Egyptians* (London: Thames and Hudson, 2003), pp. 34–35.
[91] Taylor, *Death*, p. 136.
[92] Taylor, *Death*, pp. 112–135. Rice, *Egypt's Making*, p. 130.

90　ANCIENT AFRICAN RELIGIONS

Figure 3.2. The Pyramids at Giza, Egypt (photo by Robert M. Baum).

In many cases, amulets were placed inside the wrappings of the body or within the coffin, which could protect the deceased as he or she rested and along the journey to the afterlife.[93] The walls were engraved with ritual texts and expositions on Egyptian concepts of death. Grouped together, they became known as the Pyramid Texts.[94]

Each of the pyramids became a cult center where people sought to provide the king and his family with food and other needs in the afterlife through offerings in this world. The mummified body of the king, placed deep within the pyramid, would emerge each day to eat the offerings left near a niche carved to look like a false day.[95] In the Old Kingdom, only the kings could achieve eternal life.[96] Religious foundations, each with its own set of priests, ensured the proper conduct of rituals in honor of the deceased monarch. Daily offerings of meat, grain, and beer were provided for deceased kings.[97] Imhotep built cult chapels and a site for the Heb Sed ritual that reinvigorated

---

[93] Taylor, *Death*, p. 202.
[94] Vivian Davies and Renée Friedman, *Egypt Uncovered* (New York: Stewart, Tabori, and Chang, 1998), p. 92.
[95] Davies and Friedman, *Egypt Uncovered*, p. 80.
[96] David, *Religion and Magic in Ancient Egypt*, p. 77.
[97] Trigger, "Rise of Ancient Egypt," pp. 89–90.

the pharaohs, within the temple complex of Saqqara.[98] Within these temple complexes, artisans placed statues of the deceased monarchs where their *kas* could dwell after death.[99] In close proximity to the Pyramids were temples of Ma'at and Anubis. Ma'at was the goddess of order and justice, whose feather was placed on a scale opposite the heart of the deceased at their final judgment. The son of Osiris, Anubis, was the god who supervised the mummification practices, including the removal and preservation of internal organs in canopic jars, carefully kept near the body that was dried, wrapped in linen and medicines, and placed inside a coffin.[100] During this period, Abydos shifted from being a burial site for kings, to a ritual center focused on Khentamentiu, a local deity who had been worshipped there since the First Dynasty, and who eventually became associated with Osiris.[101]

During the Fourth Dynasty, Re, the sun god, became closely associated with royal authority. Under the direction of the pharaoh, temples dedicated to Re, marked by obelisks, became increasingly common.[102] From his main temple at Heliopolis, Re's priests exercised increased religious and political power and the sacred aspects of the king declined.[103] By the end of the Old Kingdom, Egyptians associated the creative power of the universe with Re. He was frequently referred to as Atum-Ra and was said to die each night and be reborn from his mother, Nut, each morning.[104] He was the presiding judge of the human soul at death. He was the deity who could expunge one's guilt for wrongdoing and, after weighing the soul on the scales of justice, allow the dead to enter the boat that would carry them west to the land of the dead.[105] Jan Assmann has argued that Re empowered pharaohs "on the earth of the living forever and eternity, to judge between people and to satisfy the gods, to create what is Right, to annihilate what is Evil."[106] Re was opposed by Apophis, an enormous water snake who could drink the celestial waters dry, thereby preventing the passage of the boat that carries the sun on its daily

---

[98] O'Neill, *Egyptian Art*, p. 15.
[99] O'Neill, *Egyptian Art*, p. 41.
[100] Taylor, *Death*, p. 65. Malek, "The Old Kingdom," p. 105.
[101] O'Connor, *Abydos*, p. 28.
[102] Malek, "The Old Kingdom," p. 109.
[103] Watterson, *Gods of Ancient Egypt*, p. 52.
[104] Vandier, *La Religion Égyptienne*, p. 33. In some older traditions, it is the goddess Neith who gives birth to the sun each morning. E. O. James, *The Ancient Gods: The History and Diffusion in the Ancient Near East and the Mediterranean* (New York: Capricorn Books, 1964), p. 84.
[105] Barbara Mertz, *Temples, Tombs, and Hieroglyphs: A Popular History of Ancient Egypt* (New York: HarperCollins, 2007), p. 99. Rice, *Egypt's Making*, p. 206.
[106] Jan Assmann, quoted in Quirke, *Exploring Religion in Ancient Egypt*, p. 8.

journey.[107] Several Fourth Dynasty rulers, including Menkaure and Khufu (Cheops), "share a nobility of African cast of features."[108]

Prophets became an increasingly important part of Egyptian religion during the Old Kingdom. These were individuals who claimed to speak for the gods as a result of privileged communication, often through dreams.[109] A man named Neferti claimed that a god had told him that the ruling dynasty would come to a disastrous end, but that Egypt would eventually be restored to glory. "'He who possessed no property is now a man of wealth. The poor man is full of joy. Every town says: let us suppress the powerful among us. He who had no yoke of oxen is now possessor of a herd. The possessors of robes are now in rags.'"[110] He also describes the land "destroyed without a remnant, not even the dirt under one's fingernails has remained of that which he has ordained."[111] The possibility exists that the king, Amenemhat I, who founded the Middle Kingdom's Twelfth Dynasty and was identified by name as the savior of Egypt, may have commissioned the text and tied it to a prominent personage associated with older dynasties to underscore his importance.[112] In the prophecy his mother was described as Nubian and he was born at Hierakonpolis.

Oracles that could predict the future or give advice about future plans were regularly consulted by Egyptian kings, as well as by the nobility, priests, and ordinary working people and farmers.[113] Some oracles derived their authority from privileged communications from various deities. They often responded to specific questions with yes or no answers. In some cases, responses were said to come directly from statues of the gods which emitted sounds that could be interpreted by a priest.[114] Kings and generals often consulted oracles before going to war. Soldiers performed acts of ritual protection, cast spells, and used amulets to protect themselves and defeat their enemies. Execratory texts have been found, directed against Nubian soldiers from Wawat and Yam.[115]

---

[107] Assmann, *Mind of Egypt*, p. 101.
[108] Rice, *Egypt's Making*, p. 207.
[109] Dunand and Zivie-Coche, *Gods and Men in Egypt*, pp. 27, 133.
[110] Cited in Sir Alan Gardiner, *Egypt of the Pharaohs* (London: Oxford University Press, 1961), p. 109.
[111] Cited in Assmann, *Mind of Egypt*, p. 108.
[112] John Baines, "Society, Morality, and Religious Practice," in *Religion in Ancient Egypt: Gods, Myths, and Personal Practice*, ed. Byron E. Shafer (Ithaca, NY: Cornell University Press, 1991), p. 170. Dodson, *Monarchs of the Nile*, p. 56.
[113] Baines, "Society, Morality, and Religious Practice," p. 170. Assmann, *Mind of Egypt*, p. 114.
[114] Teeter, *Religion and Ritual*, pp. 106–111.
[115] Yurco, "Egypt and Nubia," p. 45.

At the larger temples, priests were organized into specialized groups, each with different ritual responsibilities. The major priests controlled large tracts of land which provided a variety of agricultural products for offerings at their temples.[116] The king was considered the high priest of major temples and appointed the most important priests; others were recruited locally and were organized in a clear hierarchy. The *hem-ka*, servant of *ka*, were among the lower ranking priests who carried the offerings in funerals, supervised the endowment funds for tombs, and ensured that daily offerings were made there. Lector priests read "specialized religious texts in both temple and mortuary rituals." They had to be precise, both in the enunciation of these texts and the timing of the performance. They were initially drawn from the nobility, but these offices became increasingly open to other literate people during the Middle Kingdom. They participated in rituals that facilitated the journey of the dead to become transfigured spirits, or akhs. In major temples, the lectors were supported by God's Fathers, often as many as three such priests. Temple rituals emphasized priestly purity, which entailed abstinence from sexual relations and food avoidances specific to a particular deity.[117] Priests often played important roles in the administration of the kingdom and as teachers. For example, during the Sixth Dynasty, the scribe Pepy-nakht served as head of the priestly orders at several royal pyramids and as judge at Nekhen, before ending his career as overseer of foreigners at Elephantine (Aswan). Temples housed important libraries and served as centers for education and scholarly activities.[118] Scribes at temple-based workshops produced beautiful religious manuscripts often on papyrus.[119] The temples also housed the statues of their deities, who dwelled within their sacred precincts.

The first known women priests were members of the royal family and were described during the Fourth Dynasty, around 2650 BCE. Women served as priests (*hemet netjer*) both at major temples and in more local cults. Most of them served ritual roles in the worship of goddesses, including Neith and Hathor, where they filled a majority of the priestly offices.[120] Beginning around 2500 BCE, nonroyal women could also serve

---

[116] Ben Harig, "Administration: Temple Administration," in *The Oxford Encyclopedia of Ancient Egypt*, Vol. I, ed. Donald B. Redford (Oxford: Oxford University Press, 2001), pp. 21–22.

[117] Teeter, *Religion and Ritual*, pp. 21–23. Saggs, *Civilization*, p. 27. Sergio Pernigotti, "Priests," in *The Egyptians*, ed. Sergio Donadoni (Chicago: University of Chicago Press, 1997), p. 143.

[118] Shafer, "Temples, Priests, and Rituals," p. 9. Yurco, "Egypt and Nubia," p. 43.

[119] Alessandro Roccati, "Scribes," in *The Egyptians*, ed. Sergio Donadoni (Chicago: University of Chicago Press, 1997), p. 79.

[120] Robins, *Women in Ancient Egypt*, p. 142. David, *Religion and Magic in Ancient Egypt*, p. 306. Boulding, *Underside of History*, p. 159.

as priests, participating in the worship of Ptah and Thoth.[121] Women may have also played important roles in household rituals designed to enhance fertility and to ensure safe pregnancies and childbirths. Fertility figurines with prominent pubic areas and large hips and breasts were placed on altars to the goddess Hathor, as well.[122] Although there is no evidence of female genital cutting during the Old Kingdom, Egyptians did circumcise adolescent boys, as early as the Sixth Dynasty.[123] Priests performed circumcisions as part of male initiation rituals.

The Hermopolitan Cosmogony was first articulated by priests who worked in the Upper Egyptian ritual center of Hermopolis. Their teachings about the origins of the universe emphasized eight primary gods, the Ogdaad, who collectively created an egg, which they left on a mound in the primal waters of Nun. These eight gods were organized in four pairs with the male deity clearly dominant. Thus, one finds Nun, the god of primal waters, and his wife, Naunet; Huh (infinity) and Hauhet; Kuk, the god of darkness, and his wife, Kauket; Amun, the god of air/wind, and Amaunet. Unlike the males, the female deities were not associated with natural forces. The male deities were described as having frogs' heads, reflecting the marshy quality of the primal world. The female deities were associated with snakes' heads. Amun was known as "the Hidden One" or "the Secret One," whose original name remained unknown. Creation began at the site of the city of Hermopolis, where the primal hillock emerged from the waters. In some versions of this cosmogony, a lotus flower grew on the primal hillock. Re emerged from it as the sun god and organized the world as we know it. The nocturnal closing of the lotus blossom and its opening each morning recalled the movements of the sun and hence the movements of the sun god, Re. Thoth, the Ibis-headed god of writing and history, was closely associated with Hermopolis.[124]

---

[121] Barbara Lesko, "Ancient Egyptian Religion," in *Encyclopedia of Women and Religion*, Vol. 1, ed. Serinity Young (New York: Macmillan, 1999), p. 32. Barbara Lesko, *The Great Goddesses of Egypt* (Norman: University of Oklahoma Press, 1999), p. 240.

[122] Silverman, *Ancient Egypt*, p. 85.

[123] Susan Bailey, "Circumcision and Male Initiation in Africa," in *Egypt in Africa*, ed. Theodore Celenko (Indianapolis: Indianapolis Museum of Art, 1996), pp. 88–89. Joyce Tydesley, *Daughters of Isis: Women of Ancient Egypt* (London: Penguin, 1995), p. 156.

[124] Vandier, *La Religion Égyptienne*, pp. 34–35. Niels Nielsen et al., *Religions of the World*, 3rd ed. (New York: St. Martin's Press), p. 49. Dunand and Zivie-Coche, *Gods and Men in Egypt*, pp. 49–50. Vincent A. Tobin, "Amun and Amun-Re," in *The Ancient Gods Speak: A Guide to Egyptian Religion*, ed. Donald B. Redford (Oxford: Oxford University Press, 2002), p. 80. Courtlandt Canby with Arcadia Kocybala, *A Guide to the Archaeological Sites of Israel, Egypt, and North Africa* (New York: Facts on File, 1990), p. 147.

The Great Hymn to Khnum offers an alternative description of the creation of humans, from clay shaped on Khnum's potter's wheel.

> Forming all humans on his wheel,
> their speech differs in each country and in that of Egypt.
> For the Lord of the Wheel is their father, too ...
> and making all that is in their lands,
> as his mouth spat out, they were born
> as his wheel turns every day without pause.[125]

This cosmogony gradually developed a focus on Amun, who came to be seen as the embodiment of both male and female fertility.[126] Throughout the Old Kingdom, these sacred traditions coexisted, influencing one another and the temple rituals related to these myths. Ritual centers for the worship of Ptah at Memphis, Abydos for Osiris, and Re at Heliopolis competed for religious patronage and political influence.

First Intermediate Period (2181–2125 BCE)

Rivalries between Hierakonpolis and Thebes characterized much of this uncertain period. Prolonged drought may have contributed to growing political instability and social dissatisfaction in most areas of the Nile valley. Despite the breakdown of centralized authority and problems of political instability, the First Intermediate Period produced important religious texts that demonstrated considerable reflection about people's responsibilities to one another.[127] Toward the end of this period, in the Tenth Dynasty, a document attributed to King Akhtoy illustrates a growing consciousness of the complexities of ethical behavior and judgment after death. He wrote the "Instruction for Merikare," to his son, warning him not to commit acts of sacrilege in war and to always revere the sun god, Re. He then goes on to describe the importance of a proper place in the world to come and its dependence on his being a righteous ruler.

---

[125] *The Great Hymn to Khnum*, cited in Fletcher, *Egyptian "Book of Living and Dying,"* p. 211.
[126] Fletcher, *Egyptian "Book of Living and Dying,"* pp. 14–15. Dunand and Zivie-Coche, *Gods and Men in Egypt*, p. 51.
[127] Rundle Clark, *Myth and Symbol in Ancient Egypt*, p. 17.

The soul goes to the place it knows; it does not stray on its road of yesterday. Decorate your mansion of the West. Establish your place of the necropolis with straight-forwardness and just dealing, for it is on that that their hearts rely. More acceptable is the character of the straightforward one than the ox of the evildoer. Act for God, that he may do the like for you, with offerings for replenishing the altars and with caring. It is that which will show forth your name, and God is aware of the one who acts for him. Provide for people, the cattle of God, for he made heaven and earth for their liking. He repelled the greed of the waters; he made the winds in order that their nostrils might breathe; [for] they are likenesses of him that came forth from his flesh. He shines in the sky for their liking; he has made vegetation, small cattle, and fish for them to nourish them. He has killed his enemies and slain his own children, because they planned to make rebellion. He makes daylight for their liking, and he sails around in order to see them. He has raised up a shrine behind them, and when they weep, he hears. He has made them rulers even from the egg, a lifter to lift [the load] from the back of the weak man. He has made for them magic to be weapons to oppose what may happen.[128]

He instructs his son to rule by following these moral principles: "Do right as long as you are on earth, calm the afflicted, oppress no widow, expel no one from his earthly possessions. Do not kill, but punish with beatings or imprisonment. Then shall this land be well established. Leave vengeance to God. More acceptable to Him is the virtue of one who is upright of heart than the ox of the wrongdoer."[129] Ethical behavior by the ruler brings prosperity and tranquility to all his domains.

This emphasis on ethical behavior reinforced the idea that the possibility of eternal life extended beyond the nobility to most Egyptians. As John Taylor noted: "In the first Intermediate Period this path to new life became available to all Egyptians, each of whom could be individually identified with Osiris; from this time onwards the name of the dead were regularly preceded by that of Osiris."[130] The extension of the idea of eternal life to ordinary people provided a new emphasis on the importance of ethical behavior while providing new perspectives on the purpose of life. This broader access to an afterlife also led to increasing ritual attention on procuring the

---

[128] Instructions for Merikare, cited in Lesko, "Ancient Egyptian Religion," p. 103. Johnson, *Civilization of Ancient Egypt*, p. 136.
[129] Cited in Aldred, *Egyptians*, p. 126.
[130] Taylor, *Death*, p. 27.

assistance of ancestors to help their living descendants and protect them against their enemies.[131] Accompanying this extension of the possibility of an afterlife was a new emphasis on *ma'at* (just actions) and judgment after death. The turbulence of this period diminished the prestige of the rulers, opening ideas of afterlife to those previously excluded. Amun became an important deity, with its main ritual center at Thebes, whose influence dramatically increased during this period.

Middle Kingdom (2125–1650 BCE)

The Eleventh Dynasty, based at Thebes, blocked the Herakanpolitan effort to dominate Egypt and establish their own authority, ushering a long period of political and economic prosperity that became known as the Middle Kingdom. Their primary deity, Montu, was a local war god who remained unknown in other areas of Egypt. The new dynasty enjoyed the support of northern priests and scribes who assisted them in unifying the kingdom. Nubian culture was a strong influence among the rulers and the professional classes of the Eleventh Dynasty. Rulers of the Twelfth Dynasty, initially based in Thebes, also worshipped Montu. When they decided to move their capital further north, however, they allowed a new cult of the creator god, Amun, to incorporate many of the powers associated with Montu.[132] During the Middle Kingdom, Amun took on many of the attributes of more local gods, such as the fertility god Min, associated with the city of Coptos. Amun also became the national god associated most closely with the Old Kingdom and Re, the sun god of Hermopolis. Under the leadership of King Amenemhat, the founder of the Twelfth Dynasty, Amun became Amun-Re. He was linked along with the other gods of the Ogdaad, in the city of Thebes, the place of origin for many of the Middle Kingdom's rulers. Re worked through the king to ensure justice and to defeat chaos:

> Re has set up the king on the earth of the living forever and ever
> to speak justice to the people, to satisfy the gods,
> for the generation of ma'at, for the destruction of *isfet* [chaos].[133]

---

[131] Nicole Harrington, *Living with the Dead: Ancestors, Worship, and Mortuary Ritual in Ancient Egypt* (Oxford: Oxbow Books, 2010), pp. 34–35.

[132] Lesko, "Ancient Egyptian Religion," pp. 103–104. Aldred, *Egyptians*, p. 129. Tobin, "Amun," pp. 18–19.

[133] Assmann, *Mind of Egypt*, p. 187. Quirke, *Exploring Religion in Ancient Egypt*, p. 8.

Amun-Re was said to be capable of assuming any form and containing within himself all the other gods.[134] A hymn to Amun-Re describes him as a bull:

> The sweetness of thee is in the northern sky;
> The beauty of thee carries away hearts;
> The love of thee makes arms languid;
> The beautiful form relaxes the hands;
> And hearts are forgetful at the sight of thee;
> THOU ART the sole one WHO MAKES [all] that is;
> [The] solitary sole [one] who made what exists;
> From whose eyes mankind came forth;
> And upon whose mouth the gods came into being.
> He who made herbage [for] for cattle,
> And the fruit tree for mankind, . . .
> He who gives breath to that which is in the egg;
> Gives life to the son of a slug,
> And makes that on which gnats may live, . . .
> Who supplies the needs of the mice in their holes,
> HAIL TO THEE, WHO DID ALL IS,
> Solitary sole one with many hands.[135]

Cosmologies associated with the Middle Kingdom gave increasing importance to the god Osiris and extended the possibility of a blissful afterlife beyond royalty to include the nobility, priests, and professional classes of ancient Egyptian society. The *ba* became associated with each individual, not just the royal family. Although it lacked a physical form, it could travel and eat after death, but it had to return to the mummified body of the deceased.[136] Much of this material is found in what became known as the Coffin Texts, which describe the experience of the deceased: "Every god

---

[134] Lesko, "Ancient Egyptian Religion," p. 104. Donald Redford, *Akhenaten: The Heretic King* (Princeton, NJ: Princeton University Press, 1984), p. 162. Silverman, "Divinity and Deities," p. 39. David, *Religion and Magic in Ancient Egypt*, p. 155. James K. Hoffmeyer, *Akhenaten and the Origins of Monotheism* (Oxford: Oxford University Press, 2015), pp. 47–48. Watterson, *Gods of Ancient Egypt*, p. 139.

[135] "A Hymn to Amon-Re," in *The Ancient Near East*, ed. William H. McNeill and Jean W. Sedlar (New York: Oxford University Press, 1968), p. 210.

[136] Gae Callender, "The Middle Kingdom (c. 2055–1669 BC)," in *The Oxford History of Ancient Egypt*, ed. Ian Shaw (Oxford: Oxford University Press, 2000), pp. 179–182. Aldred, *Egyptians*, p. 129. Taylor, *Death*, p. 20.

you served on earth you will [now] see face-to-face."[137] A panel of gods judged the dead. Individuals judged as bad were eaten by ravenous gods, but those who were judged to have led good lives were allowed to enter the Field of Reeds.[138]

Abydos became a center of the Osiris cult, where an annual procession was held from what was said to be the tomb of Osiris. Rulers of the Twelfth Dynasty linked Osiris with Abydos's most important local deity, Khentamentiu, and merged their spiritual powers. Khenamentiu was often represented in human form, but with a jackal's head. King Senwosret I built a new temple for this composite deity. Wealthy people built mortuary monuments at Abydos, even when their graves were elsewhere, linking them to the cult of Osiris.[139] Ordinary people created "soul houses," small clay structures which were kept in people's homes to assist their dead relatives on their journeys to the land of the dead. Their families made offerings of meat, bread, animals, and libations to assist the dead.[140]

Popular views of the afterlife and its implications for ordinary people, unfortunately, remain undocumented. There was a growing emphasis on acts of personal piety, household shrines, and local worship, independently of priestly elites. Particularly prominent among the household cults were deities who protected the welfare of the home and had a special role in the protection of pregnant women. Often described as an ugly dwarf, the ithyphallic god Bes protected the home against malevolent spirits that could cause miscarriages. He could also bring joy to his devotees. Small figurines and murals portraying Bes have been found in the excavations of ancient houses. The hippopotamus god, Tawaret, and Hathor, the goddess of fertility, also protected women in the home.[141] Royal tombs included images of human servants, known as *shabtis*, which could be made out of wood, wax, faience, clay, or stone, that could be awakened through special prayers once their master had reached the land of the dead.[142]

During the Middle Kingdom, individuals could commission statuary or stelae associated with themselves and their families to establish an ongoing

---

[137] Assmann, *Mind of Egypt*, p. 170.
[138] David, *Religion and Magic in Ancient Egypt*, p. 160.
[139] O'Connor, *Abydos*, p. 7. Van de Mieroop, *History of Ancient Egypt*, p. 139.
[140] Exhibit on Egypt's Middle Kingdom, Boston Museum of Fine Arts, visited by the author, November 19, 2017. Van De Mieroop, *History of Ancient Egypt*, p. 120.
[141] O'Connor, *Abydos*, p. 181. Putnam, *Egyptology*, p. 52. Dunand and Zivie-Coche, *Gods and Men in Egypt*, p. 129. David Frankfurter, *Religion in Roman Egypt: Assimilation and Resistance* (Princeton, NJ: Princeton University Press, 1998), p. 124.
[142] O'Connor, *Abydos*, pp. 28, 182.

relationship with a particular deity's temple. Worshippers particularly patronized shrines of Amun established within their homes.[143] Some of these statues were associated with scribes, mayors, or civic leaders. Statues of distinguished leaders, not only kings, could receive offerings of food and beverages through rituals that were remarkably similar to those performed for the gods.[144] During this period, there is increasing evidence of the use of amulets designed to protect their users or beseech a god to do his or her bidding. "Magicians" carved into stone portions of the amulet, or wrote on papyrus paper placed within it, the purpose of the object and its relationship to deities or other forms of spiritual power.[145]

Women played less important roles in the priestly organizations of the Middle Kingdom. Women's most prominent ritual roles were as temple musicians and singers.[146] Generally, they could not lead temple rites for male deities, but often focused on their female consorts, Hathor, Isis, and Mut.[147] Even there, male priests became increasingly important. Despite the close association with fertility, sexuality, pregnancy, and childbirth, the cult of Hathor in the Middle Kingdom restricted its priesthood to men and to royal women.[148]

Prophecies continued to be important in Egyptian religious life. A Middle Kingdom text, "The Admonitions of an Egyptian Sage," attributed to a man named Ipuwer, describes a period of corruption and disasters culminating in an invasion by "Asians" (Hyksos). Ipuwer prophesized that a righteous king would ascend the throne and rid Egypt of invaders and corrupt practices, leading to a period of "happiness and prosperity."[149]

Second Intermediate Period (1750–1560 BCE)

This period witnessed the installation of a "foreign" dynasty, the Hyksos, often identified as "Asiatics" because they originated in Palestine or Syria.

---

[143] Johnson, *Civilization of Ancient Egypt*, p. 131.
[144] Dunand and Zivie-Coche, *Gods and Men in Egypt*, p. 77.
[145] E. A. Wallis Budge, *Egyptian Magic* (New York: Dover Books, [1901] 1971), p. 27.
[146] Robins, *Women in Ancient Egypt*, p. 145.
[147] Robins, *Women in Ancient Egypt*, pp. 177–178. Barry Kemp, *The City of Akhenaten and Nefertiti: Amarna and Its People* (London: Thames and Hudson, 2012), p. 25.
[148] Lesko, "Ancient Egyptian Religion," p. 32. Silverman, *Ancient Egypt*, p. 86. B. Lesko, *Great Goddesses of Egypt*, p. 241.
[149] Alan Gardiner, *The Admonitions of an Egyptian Sage: From a Hieratic Papyrus in Leiden* (Leipzig: T. C. Hinrichsasche, 1909), pp. 5–11.

They conquered large areas of Lower Egypt, early in the seventeenth century BCE, and controlled much of Egypt for about one hundred years. They introduced the chariot, which became a staple of the Egyptian military. In terms of religious practices, the Hyksos embraced much of the religious and cultural practices which had been prevalent in the Middle Kingdom, especially the worship of Amun. They also introduced some of the divinities they had known in Canaan, including Baal, Resheph, Anath, and Astarte, all of whom were welcomed in Egypt. Baal was often associated with the god Seth, who remained influential in Upper Egypt.[150] The Hyksos established a temple for Seth at their capital of Avaris. In turn, the Egyptians embraced the worship of the war goddesses Astarte and Anat as daughters of Re and wives of Seth.[151] The worship of these goddesses persisted long after the Hyksos departed. The Egyptian god Amun, however, became the deity most closely associated with resistance to Hyksos's foreign rule.[152]

New Kingdom (from 1560 BCE)

In 1560 BCE, Amosis ended the Second Interregnum by driving out the Hysksos and establishing the first of a series of dynasties that became known as the New Kingdom. His Eighteenth Dynasty was based at Thebes, the center of Egyptian resistance to Hyksos domination and the primary ritual center of the god Amun. A series of monarchs, including the most famous female ruler, Hatshepshut, consolidated authority over much of Egypt, Nubia, and parts of Palestine. Hatshepshut initially ruled as regent for a young Thutmoses II, who was fathered by her husband, but who had a far less influential mother. She also held the priestly office of God's Wife of Amun, one of the few powerful religious offices open to women in the New Kingdom.[153] After seven years as regent, Hatshepshut was able to consolidate both ritual and political authority in her own right, ruling a united Egypt and expanding the size and magnificence of the temple areas at Luxor and Karnak. Facilitating such construction projects were slaves captured in Egypt's new expansion into Palestine/Syria and Nubia.[154]

---

[150] David P. Silverman, "Divinity and Deities," p. 39.
[151] Cornelius, "From Bes to Baal," p. 215. Watterson, *Gods of Ancient Egypt*, pp. 115–116.
[152] Vincent A. Tobin, "Amun," in *The Ancient Guides Speak: A Guide to Egyptian Religion*, (Oxford: Oxford University Press, 2002), p. 19
[153] Silverman, *Ancient Egypt*, p. 87.
[154] Redford, *Akhenaten*, p. 9.

To bolster her claims to the throne, she said that it was the god Amun who was her actual father. He had disguised himself as Hatshepshut's royal father but revealed his true identity to her mother before having sexual relations with her. In addition to her devotion to Amun, Hatshepshut also patronized the cult of Hathor and her various manifestations. This included the temple she constructed, dedicated to Pakleh, a goddess portrayed with a lion's head and who was linked to desert areas near Thebes. The Ptolemies later linked her to Artemis, the Greek goddess of the hunt.[155] Amun inspired her to send an expedition to Punt, both to purchase incense and to acquire live trees that could be transplanted near the Egyptian capitol of Thebes. Sheldon Harvey describes the importance of incense in Egyptian religious practice:

> Just as burnt food offerings might nourish divine beings through their scent or essence, So too was the burning of aromatic resins thought to satisfy and bring pleasure to the gods. The mention of incense in Egyptian texts evokes two aspects of divinity: the vital pleasure that the gods take in smelling the scent of aromatic gums as well as the power of incense to transform human made places and things into ones worthy of divine inhabitation.

Egyptian priests and their associates used incense to purify the statues of the gods and the sacred spaces within the temples. Mourners used incense to purify the bodies of the dead.[156]

Amun commanded his "daughter" to create the Opet Festival, an elevenday celebration at the peak of the Nile flood. This involved a procession of statues of Amun and his wife, Mut, and their child, Khonsu, from Amum's temple at Karnak to Luxor. It also included a reenactment of the "divine impregnation of the king [Hatshepshut's] mother."[157] Amenhotep III claimed a similar divine origin. Amun-Re appeared to Mutemwia in the image of her husband, Thutmose IV: "he found her (Mutemwia) as she was resting in the beauty of her palace. She awoke on account of the aroma of the god.... He went to her straightaway ... and he caused her to see him in his form as a god ... she rejoiced at the sight of his beauty, and love of him coursed

---

[155] Joyce Tyldesley, *Hatchepshut: The Female Pharaoh* (London: Viking, 1996), pp. 155, 173.

[156] Stephen P. Harvey, "Interpreting Punt: Geographic, Cultural, and Artistic Landscapes," in *Mysterious Lands: Encountering Ancient Egypt*, ed. David O'Connor and Stephen Quirke (London: UCL Press, 2003), pp. 82–83.

[157] Nicholas Reeves, *Akhenaten: Egypt's False Prophet* (London: Thames and Hudson, 2001), pp. 33–38. Alan Gardiner, *Egypt of the Pharaohs,* (London: Oxford University Press, 1961), p. 186.

through her limbs. The palace was flooded with the god's aroma; all his fragrances were [of] Punt." Then Mutemwia spoke: "to this august god, Amun-Re, Lord of the thrones of the Two Lands. How great is your power...? Your dew permeates all my limbs. And then the majesty of this god did all that he desired with her. "Finally, he tells her: "Amenhotep, ruler of Thebes, is the name of this child I have placed in your body."[158]

Amun remained the central deity in the early part of the Eighteenth Dynasty. The great hymn of Amun, composed during the reign of Amenophis II, underscores the importance of this deity:

> (O Thou) who madest mankind and createst animals . . . creator of the tree of life and herbage which nourishes cattle . . . maker of what is above and what is beneath, he brightens the two lands, ferrying across heaven in peace . . . who made the whole earth, and distinguished natures for every god . . . Hail to thee, thou Re, lord of truth, whose shrine is hidden, lord of the gods, thou Khepry who resides in the authoritative fiat that creates the gods, thou Amun who makest mankind and distinguishes their forms, maker of life, separating one man's color from his fellow's, who hears the prayer of him who has been wronged, with gracious heart when called upon.[159]

Royally appointed first and second prophets supervised the rituals dedicated to Amun, but under the continuous scrutiny of the pharaohs.[160] The first pharaohs of the Eighteenth Dynasty expanded a temple complex at Karnak, at the northern edge of Thebes, dedicated to Amun, who was linked to the sun god, Re. For other major deities, the pharaohs of the Eighteenth Dynasty increasingly appointed members of the royal family as the primary temple priests.[161]

It was Thutmoses IV who increased the Egyptian ritual focus on new aspects of the divine powers of the sun. The sun god, Reharakhte, appeared to him in a dream. Thutmoses IV attributed his rise to power to the assistance of this deity. He also emphasized the divinity of Aten, the sun disk and

---

[158] Cited in Lawrence W. Berman, "Overview of Amenhotep III," in *Amenhotep III: Perspectives on His Reign*, ed. David O'Connor and Eric H. Cline (Ann Arbor: University of Michigan Press, 2001), p. 4.
[159] S. Hassan, *Hymnes religieux du moyen empire* (Cairo, 1928), cited in Redford, *Akhenaten*, p. 163.
[160] Redford, *Akhenaten*, p. 160. Dunand and Zivie-Coche, *Gods and Men in Egypt*, p. 103.
[161] Aidan Dodson, *Amarna Sunset: Nefertiti, Tutankamun, Ay, Horemheb, and the Egyptian Counter-Reformation* (Cairo: American University in Cairo Press, 2009), p. 6.

its rays.[162] Amenhotep III ruled over Egypt from about 1388 until 1348. He both expanded and secured the boundaries of his empire. He chose the customary five titles that reflected both his major accomplishments and the patronage of his primary divine supporters, invoking Horus, the Two Ladies who were divinities reflecting Upper and Lower Egypt, Golden Horus, king of Upper and Lower Egypt, and son of Re.[163] The titles invoked powerful forces associated with the pharaoh, which ensured the unity and prosperity of the kingdom. Amenhotep built new temples dedicated to Thoth, Ptah, Khnum, and Nekhbit.[164] During his reign, Egypt dominated Nubia and Palestine, as well as the Nile valley from Upper Egypt to the Mediterranean. His chief wife, Tiye, who was of Nubian ancestry, enjoyed particular importance during his reign, often depicted in equal size to her husband, Amenhotep III.[165]

In the early years of the New Kingdom, there was increasing speculation about the nature of the afterlife for ordinary people and the role of ancestors. In the homes of craftsmen of the village of Deir el-Madina, people erected altars to perform rituals requesting that their ancestors provide them with various types of assistance in meeting the challenges of their daily lives.[166] During this period, a collection of papyrus texts concerning the ritual preparations to ensure a good afterlife were gathered together. The earliest known text of the *Book of Living and Dying* dates from 1500 BCE, but it draws on a variety of sources, including the Pyramid Texts, which are a thousand years older. Better known as *The Egyptian Book of the Dead*, it was widely attributed to Thoth, who was the god associated with scribes and with writing.[167] It includes over two hundred illustrated texts describing prayers and rituals written on papyrus and placed by the body of the dead that could "help them pass through the dangers of the underworld and attain an afterlife of bliss in the Field of Reeds, the Egyptian heaven."[168] What R. Faulkner translates as "spells," but I would interpret as prayers, included lengthy, though formulaic defenses of the lives of the dead: "Behold,

---

[162] Redford, *Akhenaten*, pp. 20, 171. Dodson, *Amarna Sunset*, p. 2.
[163] Redford, *Akhenaten*, p. 35.
[164] Redfield, *Akhenaten*, p. 43.
[165] Van de Mieroop, *History of Ancient Egypt*, p. 194. Christiane Desroches-Noblecourt, *Life and Death of a Pharaoh: Tutankhamum* (London: George Rainfield, 1964), pp. 116–117.
[166] Davies and Friedman, *Egypt Uncovered*, p. 178.
[167] R. O. Faulkner, edited by Carol Andrews, *The Ancient Egyptian Book of the Dead* (Austin: University of Texas Press, 1995), p. 11. David, *Religion and Magic in Ancient Egypt*, p. 261. Johnson, *Civilization of Ancient Egypt*, p. 139.
[168] Faulkner, *Ancient Egyptian Book of the Dead*, p. 27.

I have come to you, I have brought you truth, I have repelled falsehood for you. . . . I have not done what the gods detest, I have not calumnied a servant to his master, I have not caused pain, I have not made hungry. . . . I have not killed, I have not commanded to kill, I have not made suffering for anyone, I have not lessened the food offerings in the temple." These food offerings were provided to nourish the *ka*, the vital force of each deceased person.[169]

It concludes with a detailed explanation of his respect for the ritual requirements of the gods and for the lands reserved for the gods.[170] This text provided vivid descriptions of the process of judgment after death, presided over by Osiris and assisted by Ma'at and her set of scales. She would weigh the heart of the deceased against the weight of a feather she placed on the scales. A heavy heart would tilt the scales away from a favorable judgment. The authors of these texts extended the possibility of eternal life to all Egyptians.[171] Apocalyptic thought is also found within the *Book of Living and Dying*. Spell 175 describes the creator, Amun, saying he will destroy the world after billions of years: "'I will destroy all that I have made: this world will return to Nu, to the limitless waters like its original state.'" Only the power of Atum and Osiris will remain, embodying the source of all things and the power of renewal. This suggests that even if Atum destroys the world, it can be restored by these two powerful gods.[172] It also provides the earliest known text mentioning pharaonic circumcision, an initiation ritual for girls that involved the most radical form of female genital cutting.

Another work, written by the scribe Kenherkhopshek at Deir el-Medina, focused on the oracular qualities of dreams. Gods and ancestors could communicate with people through dreams, providing them with insights about the success or future ventures or the origins of current problems. This work provided a guide to dream symbolism, the first of its kind in ancient Egypt. For example, he suggested that "'If a man see himself in a dream dea—God. It means a long life. . . . If a man sees himself in a dream drinking warm beer. . . . It means suffering.'"[173]

---

[169] Phillip C. Naylor, *A History of North Africa: From Antiquity to the Present* (Austin: University of Texas Press, 2009), p. 22.
[170] Spell 125, in Faulkner, *Ancient Egyptian Book of the Dead*, pp. 29–31.
[171] Silverman, "Divinity and Deities," pp. 48, 73.
[172] Silverman, *Ancient Egypt*, p. 131.
[173] Davies and Friedman, *Egypt Uncovered*, p. 184.

The Reforms of Akhenaten

In 1373 BCE, Amenhotep IV succeeded his father, who had ruled for thirty-nine years. Amenhotep found an empire that was secure and prosperous. He became pharaoh when he was still a young man, who had been educated primarily in the royal court. Though born by his father's chief wife, Tiye, he was something of a loner, deemed ugly by the reigning ideas of masculinity that held sway in the Eighteenth Dynasty. As a boy, he had received less attention from his parents than his older brother, the presumptive heir, who died prematurely. He shared some of the attributes of a *homo religiosus*, who was often identified as a liminal figure by virtue of his social isolation and unpopularity, which facilitated numinous experience.[174] He appointed his personal butler, Parennefer, as "overseer of the prophets of all the gods," but critics claimed that he chose him more for his personal loyalty than his religious acumen. Parennefer supervised the ritual offerings at all the major temples under royal supervision and diverted increasing amounts of offerings to the temples dedicated to Aten.[175] He was also concerned about the persistent influence of the priesthood of Atum as a challenge to royal authority.

Soon after ascending to the throne of a united Egypt, Amenhotep IV introduced a series of reforms that sought to revolutionize Egyptian religious life. He decided to invest the full authority of his rule as pharaoh to emphasize a deity associated with the physical aspect of the sun's rays, known as Aten. His predecessors, Tuthmosis IV and Amenhotep III, had devoted increasing attention to this solar deity.[176] Initially, Amenhotep wanted to make it the paramount deity in Egyptian religious life. He built a massive new temple dedicated to Aten, at Karnak, adjacent to the temple of Amon-Re, whom he planned to replace. Under the guidance of Amenhotep IV, Aten was no longer presented in human or animal form, but as the rays of the sun extending from the solar disk ending in an outstretched hand which would hold these powerful rays out to the pharaoh.[177] The Aten was described as eternal, the "Aten who begets itself. Yours is continuity, as it is for your son

---

[174] Redford, *Akhenaten*, p. 233. Reeves, *Akhenaten*, p, 8.
[175] Redford, *Akhenaten*, p. 60.
[176] William J. Murnane, ed., *Texts from the Amarna Period in Egypt* (Atlanta: Scholars Press, 1995), p. 20.
[177] Dodson, *Monarchs of the Nile*, pp. 96–98. Grimal, *History of Ancient Egypt*, p. 227. Reeves, *Akhenaten*, p. 106.

Wamre [Akhenaten]."[178] This suggests that it was the Aten that emerged by its own thought from the primal waters and began the process of creation. Amenhotep IV eschewed the traditional five-part title of the pharaoh and adopted the title '"he who rejoices in the horizon in his name 'Sunlight that is in the Disc.'" He built beautiful new temples to Aten, incorporating his symbol of rays of light emanating from the sun disk and ending in hands offering their power to the pharaoh. He also allowed an unusual influence to his primary wife, Nefertiti, whose name means "the beautiful one is come." She was a frequent subject of monumental art and was portrayed affectionately with Akhenaten and their children. She was shown making offerings alone to Aten and physically disciplining groups of female slaves.[179] Both actions were usually reserved for the king.

In the fifth year of his reign, he announced plans to establish a new capital at a previously uninhabited area along the Nile, at Amarna. He called the city Akhetaten, "the horizon of Aten." Some commentators claimed that this was part of an ambitious plan to create a sacred urban landscape based on Aten's revelation to his son, the pharaoh. Aten chose the site of Amarna, specifying the exact locations of his temples, the royal palaces, and the primary roads.[180] Akhenaten claimed that "it is the Aten, my Father, who advised me concerning the place of Akhetaten. No official ever advised me concerning it, nor have any people of the entire land advised me concerning it, to tell me a plan for making Akhetaten in this distant place." A wadi to the east of his new capital created a gap in the eastern escarpment from which one could have a perfect view of the first light of dawn and the "horizon of Aten" [Akhetaten].[181] As Jan Assmann points out—*akhet*—the term usually translated as "horizon" refers to a place of transition between realms, where the heavens and the earth meet and the sun emerges from the underworld.[182] It cannot be a coincidence that Amarna was close to the old ritual and political center of Hermopolis.

Other commentators claimed that part of his motivation was to diminish the entrenched power of the priesthood of Amun and other deities. Nicholas

---

[178] Tomb of Chamberlain Tutu, South Wall, in Murnane, *Texts*, p. 192.
[179] Redford, *Akhenaten*, p. 78. Wilkenson, *Lives*, pp. 196–199.
[180] Kemp, *City of Akhenaten and Nefertiti*, pp. 32, 34, 37. Boundary Stela, cited in Arthur Weigall, *The Life and Times of Akhnaton, Pharaoh of Egypt* (New York: Cooper Square Press, [1922] 2000), pp. 82–86.
[181] Akhenaten cited in David P. Silverman, Josef W. Wegner, and Jennifer H. Wegner, *Akhenaten and Tutankhamun: Revolution and Restoration* (Philadelphia: University of Pennsylvania Museum of Archaeology and Anthropology, 2005), pp. 44, 27.
[182] Assmann, *Mind of Egypt*, p. 58.

Reeves described the power of these priests at "Amun's temple, serviced by vast agricultural estates, administered by an immense bureaucracy and controlling numberless serfs and slaves, gradually growing in influence to take in shipping, manufacturing, mining, and other worldly concerns. The Egyptian king's constant battle was to hold the influence of Amun's troublesome priests—now controlling a state within a state—firmly in check."[183] During his visit he announced that he would establish a burial site for himself, his family, and court along with a collection of mortuary temples at Amarna. Akhenaten brought in 20,000 laborers to construct a new city, complete with temples, palaces, and residential neighborhoods for the workers themselves.[184]

Shortly after he began the project he changed his name from Amenhotep, "Amun is satisfied," to Akhenaten, "incarnation of Aten" or "useful to Aten."[185] In his ninth year as pharaoh, he adopted a title, "(Living) Re-Horakhty-who-rejoices-in-the-horizon-in-his-name-of-Shu-Re-who-is-in-the-Aten."[186] As they consolidated their reforms, Akhenaten and his supporters claimed that the Aten was the only god as noted in "The Great Hymn of the Aten":

> How manifold are your deeds!
> They are hidden from sight,
> O sole god, there is no other!
> You make the earth, as you desired, you alone.[187]

It could only be worshipped through rituals conducted under the auspices of pharaoh. These rituals, however, were much simpler, though food offerings remained an important part.[188] Like other deities, Aten received offerings of beef, bread, beer, wine, and edible plants. Furthermore, he claimed that he was the son of Aten and that Aten owned the office of pharaoh. Hymns to the

---

[183] Reeves attributes this influence to the priests' involvement with resistance to the Hyksos and their support of Hatshepshut's claim to be Amun's daughter and, therefore, a legitimate pharaoh. Reeves, *Akhenaten*, p. 45. Tyldesley, *Hatchepshut*, p. 32.
[184] Kemp, *City of Akhenaten and Nefertiti*, p. 17.
[185] Redford, *Akhenaten*, p. 62. Putnam, *Egyptology*, p. 35.
[186] Aidan Dodson, *Amarna Sunrise: Egypt from Golden Age to Age of Heresy* (Cairo: American University in Cairo Press, 2014), p. 52.
[187] Cited in David, *Religion and Magic in Ancient Egypt*, p. 225.
[188] Dodson, *Monarchs of the Nile*, pp. 96–99. Dodson, *Amarna Sunrise*, p. 9. Redford, *Akhenaten*, pp. 141, 179. Weigall, *Life*, p. 83.

Aten were inscribed on the walls of the great tombs of Amarna, celebrating the power of the one, universal god:

> You rise from the eastern horizon and have filled every land with your beauty.
> You are fair, great, dazzling, and high over every land.
> Your rays enclose the lands to the limit of all that you have made.
> You are Re, having reached to the limit of them and subdued them (for) your beloved son.
> Although you are far away, your rays are on earth and known.
> When you set in the western horizon,
> the land is in darkness in the manner of death . . .
> You bring into being fetuses in women,
> you make fluid in people.
> You give life to the son in the womb of his mother and calm him with that which stops his weeping, . . .
> You made an Inundation in the underworld,
> You bring it forth as you wish to cause the people to live,
> Since you made them for yourself,
> The Lord of all of them, wearying for them,
> The lord of every land, rising for them,
> The Aten of the day, great of majesty.[189]

Temples of Aten differed from older sanctuaries to the gods. They were open to the sky, allowing Aten's life-giving rays to fall directly on the participants. There were no anthropomorphic or zoomorphic images of the Aten during Akhenaten's reign.[190]

Akhenaten is often described as a heretical king, but it would be more accurate to see him as one of the leaders at the beginning of a worldwide period of religious reform that Karl Jaspers labelled as the Axial Age. This was a time when long-standing religious practices were criticized, reformed, or abandoned in favor of more universal and reasoned forms of religious thought. Jaspers, however, did not place ancient Egypt within his list of Axial Age civilizations. Despite this omission, however, Akhenaten's

---

[189] "Great Hymn to the Aten," cited in Dodson, *Amarna Sunrise*, pp. 122–126.
[190] Teeter, *Religion and Ritual*, p. 49. Reeves, *Akhenaten*, p. 91.

focus on the importance of proper conduct, critical reflection on older religious practices and a transcendent deity, which Benjamin Schwartz suggested were characteristic of the Axial Age, could place Akhenaten's teachings in a category of ultimately unsuccessful reform movements, types that would have been more successful later in the Axial Age more narrowly defined.[191] Akhenaten's teaching that the Aten created all life and that he was the god of all nations suggests that his work fit within the thrust of these movements. He sought to eliminate other forms of religious worship, even discouraging the worship of Osiris, but he supported the practice of placing *shabtis* in graves. They were images of wives and servants who could be brought to life in the world to come.[192] Few sources describe the nature of Akhenaten's communications with the deity, Aten, though Akhenaten does claim that it was Aten who showed him the location of his new capitol at Amarna.

He encouraged a more naturalistic form of art, including more personalized forms of his own image and that of his primary wife, Nefertiti, as well as displays of physical affection between the pharaoh and his wife and both of them with their children. After losing one of his daughters while she was quite young, Akhenaten allowed himself to be portrayed on the walls of his tomb, in a devastated state of mourning.[193] Akhenaten emphasized the importance of *ma'at*, truth and justice. He was described as the "prince of maat" and his city of Akhetaten as "the city of maat." A god's father (a high priest), Aye, claimed that Akhenaten "has placed Maat in my innermost being. My abomination is falsehood."[194] Finally, he emphasized the universality of Aten, a god of all peoples, as described in the "Great Hymn to the Aten. "'The countries of Syria, Nubia, the land of Egypt, you set every man in his plane, You supply their requirements, Each one has his food, and his time of life is reckoned. Their tongues, their natures as well; for their skins are distinct for you made the foreign people to be distinct, You made an

---

[191] S. N. Eisenstadt, "Introduction: The Axial Age Breakthroughs: Their Characteristics and Origins," in *The Origins and Diversity of Axial Age Civilizations*, ed. S. N. Eisenstadt (Albany: State University Press of New York, 1986), pp. 1–25. Benjamin I. Schwartz, "The Age of Transcendence," *Daedalus* 104, no. 2 (1975), pp. 2–3. Eric Weil, "What Is a Breakthrough in History," *Daedalus* 104, no. 2 (1975), pp. 24–25.
[192] Silverman et al., *Akhenaten and Tutankhamun*, p. 39.
[193] Putnam, *Egyptology*, pp. 35–38, 49. Barbara Mertz, *Red Land Black Land: Daily Life in Ancient Egypt* (New York: Dodd, Mead, and Company, 1978), p. 40.
[194] There is similar testimony about the importance of ethics and a commitment to justice by Akhenaten by his Chamberlain, Tutu. W. J. Murnane, ed., *Texts of the Amarna Period in Egypt* (Atlanta: Scholars Press, 1995), pp. 11–112, 192.

inundation in the underworld, You bring it forth, as you wish to cause the people to live.' "[195]

Redford questions whether Akhenaten's emphasis on reason and the sustaining of the universe were too cold and mechanical to gain widespread acceptance. He questions a presentation of Aten that lacked compassion for humanity.[196] Akhenaten's rejection of elaborate myths about the god Aten may have contributed to a sense of a stark and dour aspect of his religious reforms. Simultaneously, however, the lack of elaboration of a rich narrative emphasized the world-sustaining properties of the sun in a carefully reasoned way. Akhenaten's emphasis on a solitary and universal deity places him within the leaders of this reformist age, even though his teachings did not endure.

Although Akhenaten has been celebrated as an important leader of a monotheistic tendency within Egyptian religion, his teachings also established a degree of centralized control over Egyptian ritual life that was unprecedented in Egyptian history. Accompanying his reforms, Akhenaten ordered the confiscation of many temple-controlled lands and closed many of the temples dedicated to other deities. As Toby Wilkinson noted: "Temples were closed, priesthoods were disbanded, monuments to gods other than Aten were systematically defaced."[197] This was not the case of Osiris, however. His name was not removed from monuments, nor were his rites prohibited. Akhenaten did not support the Osiris cult, but he did not suppress it.[198] This concentration of religious authority, however, may have paved the way for massive resistance to Akhenaten's reforms and the thorough repudiation of his reforms within a few decades of his passing. Akhenaten also abolished the temple festivals for other deities, depriving most Egyptians of the opportunity to participate in major festivals or to enjoy the elaborate meals associated with temple rituals. These were important ways to involve ordinary people in temple worship. Under Thutmose III, Akhenaten's immediate predecessor, there were fifty-four festival days at Karnak alone.[199] Akhenaten and his supporters did little to develop myths or sacred traditions that would allow people to

---

[195] Dodson, *Amarna Sunrise*, p. 125.
[196] Redford, *Akhenaten*, p. 175.
[197] Toby Wilkinson, *Lives of the Ancient Egyptians* (London: Thames and Hudson, 2007), p. 189. David, *Religion and Magic in Ancient Egypt*, p. 218.
[198] Smith, *Following Osiris*, p. 278.
[199] Teeter, *Religion and Ritual*, p. 56.

readily identify with the reformist tradition. One must keep in mind that Akhenaten's reformist policies were most fully implemented in Amarna itself and were not as widely effective in outlying areas.[200]

Reversing Reforms

Although Akhenaten's successors did not immediately suppress the worship of Aten, they did allow the worship of other gods, especially Amun. Semenkhare, who succeeded Akhenaten and was his son-in-law, tried unsuccessfully to use the revival of Amun worship to strengthen the Egyptian state.[201] During his short reign of three years, pressure built to allow the return of the cult of Amun-Re. In the "Graffito for the Tomb of Pere," an artisan addressed pharaoh Semenkhare (Ankhkepure) and offered a prayer to Amun-Re:

> Come back to us, O Lord of Continuity. You were here before anything had come into being, and you will be here when they are gone. As you have caused me to see the darkness that is yours to give, make light for me so that I may see you. As your Ka endures and as your handsome beloved face endures, you shall come from afar and cause thy servant, the scribe Pawah, to see you. Grant him the condition of "Re awaits him," for indeed, the following of you is good.[202]

Semenkhare's successor, Tutankhaten, initially decided to follow the teachings of his father, Akhenaten. He was still a boy when he ascended the throne. Aten was worshipped, but as his reign endured, other deities were brought back into ritual attention. Marking this change, in the second year of his reign, Tutankhaten changed his name to Tutankhamun and moved his capital back to Thebes, following the advice of key advisors.[203] He issued an edict in which Tutankhamun attributed the political and economic troubles of his reign to the neglect of other deities. He was praised as the restorer of many temples who spent his reign making new images of the old gods. This

---

[200] Redford, *Akhenaten*, pp. 169, 180, 204. Grimal, *History of Ancient Egypt*, pp. 230–232. Wilkinson, *Lives*, p. 190.
[201] Kemp, *City of Akhenaten and Nefertiti*, p. 15.
[202] "Graffiti from the Tomb of Pere," cited in Murnane, *Texts*, p. 208.
[203] Redfod, *Akhenaten*, pp. 305–320. Wilkinson, *Lives*, p. 214.

suggests that many of the old images had been destroyed during the iconoclastic reforms of Akhenaten.[204] According to a stela describing the reign of Tutankhamun, many of the challenges of his reign were directly linked to the neglect of other gods:

> When his Person appeared as king, the temples and the cities of the gods and goddesses, staring from Elephantine [as far] as the Delta marshes ... were fallen into decay and their shrines were fallen into ruin, having become mere mounds overgrown with grass. Their sanctuaries were like something that had not come into being and their buildings were a footpath ... for the land was in rack and ruin. The gods were ignoring this land: if an army [was] sent to Djahy to broaden the boundaries of Egypt, no success of theirs came to pass; and if one prayed to a god to ask something from him, he did not come at all; and if one beseeched any goddess in the same way, she did not come at all. Their hearts were weak because of their bodies, and they destroyed what was made.

Tutankhamun restored the temples and statues and appointed new priests from leading families. He sent male and female slaves to work in the temples and female dancers and singers to perform in their celebrations.[205] Even though Tutankhamun supported the renewal of the older cults, some felt that his relative lack of success and even the premature deaths of members of the royal family reflected the neglect of most of the Egyptian gods and goddesses. Tutankhamun died suddenly, around the age of twenty, apparently of natural causes. He ruled about ten years.[206] Although he brought back other Egyptian deities, Aten remained. The back of his throne included an image of Tutankhamun and his wife basking in the lifegiving rays of Aten.[207]

Tutankhamun was succeeded by Aye, who may have been married to Nefertiti's sister. Under Tutankhamun, Aye had served as chief priest and royal chamberlain. He only ruled for three years but continued the revival of the older cults.[208] His successor, Horemheb, however, decided to close

---

[204] Redford, *Akhenaten*, pp. 208–209.
[205] Restoration inscription of Tutankhamun, cited in Murnane, *Texts*, p. 213.
[206] Wilkinson, *Lives*, p. 215.
[207] Anna Maria Donadoni Rivera, *Egypt: Classic Art Tours: The Valley of Kings* (London: Atlantis), pp. 32–33.
[208] Howard Carter, *The Tomb of Tutankhamun* (New York: E. P. Dutton, [1954] 1972), p. 10.

the temples of Aten. He leveled the temples and stelae, used the carved and engraved stone blocks (known as *talatat*), to fill in the ground for new temples dedicated to Amun and other deities, and sought to remove all evidence of Akhenaten's religious movement. He leveled the city of Amarna (Akhehaten) and removed Akhenaten's name from stelae, wall engravings, and kings' lists.[209] Horemheb's family origins remain obscure, but it appears that he served as a major general and then as regent for Tutankhamun before becoming pharaoh in his own right.[210] He chose to be coronated during the Opet festival, which was dedicated to Amun. Horemheb died without heirs, but he chose a military colleague as his successor, who began the Nineteenth Dynasty.

Horemheb and his successors effectively suppressed the religious reforms of Akhenaten. Egypt reaffirmed its commitment to a pantheon with Amun-Re as its most powerful deity. This revived Amun-Re, however, was perceived of as a god who reigned not only over Egypt, but the world beyond and his creative powers extended to the creation of all humanity.[211]

Despite the existence of an apocalyptic tradition, the restoration of an Amun-centered religion emphasized a regular cycle of death and rebirth. The sun-god, Amun-Re, embodied this process, being born with the sunrise and dying with the sunset.

> Every sunrise was a repetition of the "first occasion," the creation of the world in the beginning. Ra himself went through a daily cycle of death and rebirth, at sunset he entered the nether world, where he was regenerated and from which he was reborn in the morning as Ra-Harakhty. Light could not exist without darkness; without death there could be no regeneration and no life. To go with the sun-god the dead were also reborn; they joined Ra on this daily journey and went through the same cycle of death and rebirth.

The pharaoh conducted rituals that facilitated the journey of the sun. Osiris, as god of the underworld, became increasingly associated with Re as he underwent his journey of birth, death, and rebirth.[212]

---

[209] Redford, *Akhenaten*, pp. 67–69, 227. Reeves, *Akhenaten*, p. 93. Assmann, *Mind of Egypt*, p. 215.
[210] Dodson, *Amarna Sunset*, p. 109.
[211] Redford, *Akhenaten*, p. 163. Wilkinson, *Lives*, pp. 235–236.
[212] Jacobus van Dijk, "The Amarna Period and the Later New Kingdom (1352–1069 BC)," in *The Oxford History of Ancient Egypt*, ed. Ian Shaw (Oxford: Oxford University Press, 2000), p. 273.

Conclusion

This chapter analyzed the racialization of debates about the origins of ancient Egyptian civilization and its influence, both within Africa and in the Mediterranean and Near Eastern worlds. It suggests, as much as the existing evidence allows, that religious and cultural influences moved in both directions between Egypt and the rest of Africa. This breaks with much of the established literature by rejecting the assumption that all of these influences flowed out of a white or black Egypt, to become the source of all African civilizations. Zoomorphic deities, including a ram with a disk between its horns, may well indicate influences from the rest of Africa on the development of Egyptian religion. Specific influences from Saharan and upper Nilotic cattle cults are also probable. Evidence of population movements from Libya, the central Sahara, and the Upper Nile into Egypt provides additional support for this argument. Although the relationship of Egypt to the rest of Africa remains a controversial subject, the study of Egypt provides us with the longest and most detailed evidence for a history of religions in the ancient period.

Although many of the primary and secondary sources concerning the history of religions in ancient Egypt stress continuities of thought and practice, there is abundant evidence of major changes. Egyptian texts provide clear indications of the waxing and waning influences of various deities, their cults, and their priesthoods. Each of these deities was associated with different places and various forces of nature. Myths depicted gods and goddesses with distinct characters who engaged in struggles against other deities. Different cosmologies associated with priestly groups at the various capitals and ritual centers competed with one another for dominance but also influenced and were shaped by the others. They described different modes of creation, each with profound implications for the nature of the world and of people within it. The rise of the Osiris cult initially strengthened the sacred qualities of the Egyptian kings, but it gradually became a force for the extension of ideas of judgment and afterlife for an increasing number of Egyptians. By the New Kingdom the possibility of eternal life, once reserved to royalty, had been extended to most people in ancient Egypt. During the same period, however, priestly roles for women became more restricted. Women's rights to serve as priests were restricted to goddess worship, and then to the role of temple singers and musicians. This was true, despite the prominence of a number of women rulers, including Hatshepsut, who claimed to be the daughter of Amun and who ruled in her own right. By the New Kingdom, women were excluded from all major priestly offices, except the role as God's Wife of Amun. Especially during the Second Intermediate Period, Egypt accepted deities who had been worshipped by the Hyksos, most notably Baal and Astarte, who were incorporated within the Egyptian pantheon.

The most deliberate, though short-lived efforts to transform Egyptian religion were led by Akhenaten, who had begun life as Amenhotep IV. Sources are largely silent on the religious experiences that shaped Akhenaten's teaching, but he sought to impose the exclusive worship of the Sun Disk, the Aten. He saw the Aten in universal terms, the sole god, not only for Egyptians, but for Syrians and Nubians, for all the nations. He suppressed the worship of other deities and withheld support of their festivals, a major source of connection for ordinary people to Egyptian religious life. His emphasis on his role as the exclusive intermediary between people and the Aten, however, impeded the spread of the new teachings beyond Akhenaten's new capital at Amarna. His desire to retain control of this religious reform undermined its ability to develop a grassroots following and sustain a lasting transformation along the lines of an Axial Age breakthrough. It remains unclear how effective he was in displacing the worship of Amun and lesser deities, but their priests reasserted their authority as soon as Akhenaten died. Tutankhamun allowed the worship of other deities to resume and returned the capital to Amun's ritual center at Thebes. Horemheb went beyond that—seeking to destroy any record of Akhenaten's reign, his teachings, and the worship of the Aten. What remained, however, was Akhenaten's teaching that the supreme being of the Egyptians was universal, a divinity for all peoples. Although the movement did not succeed in implanting a reformed tradition in ancient Egypt, Akhenaten stands alone as one of the earliest religious reformers within any global history of religions.

Map 4.1. Africa beyond the Nile to 1200 BCE (courtesy of Jonathan Chipman).

4
Not out of Egypt

Africa from 3200 to 1200 BCE

This chapter examines the history of African religions during the second and third millennia BCE. It parallels the previous chapter on the history of ancient Egyptian religion, but the geographical focus shifts to the rest of Africa (see Map 4.1). Sources are far more limited, however. During this period there were written descriptions of Nubia, Punt, and Libya, primarily from Egyptian perspectives. Otherwise, researchers are limited to linguistic and archaeological evidence or written sources from more recent periods looking retrospectively at this period of African religious history. Furthermore, archaeological research has been less extensive outside of Egypt proper. Funding for such research beyond the Egyptian and Nubian Nile was spotty and focused on the Ethiopian highlands and East Africa's Great Rift valley. This reflects Western preoccupations with the origins of humanity and Ethiopia's long-standing role in the margins of the history of the oldest Abrahamic religions.

Since the Neolithic Revolution, permanent or semi-permanent settlements developed in most of Africa. These communities could sustain surplus quantities of food and support political and religious specialists. As pastoralism spread, this, too, allowed for limits on migration and greater occupational specialization. Accompanying this increasing diversity of economic activities, African communities created a growing range of religious institutions and ritual specialists to guide them. Spirits associated with success in fishing, herding, and farming developed to assist people in pursuing their livelihoods. New forms of healing cults were created to address the problems of diseases associated with greater population densities and a lag in the development of sanitary facilities. The close involvement of spirits and their cults in the healing and economic arts provided a clear basis for the growth of religious sanctions in the governance of local communities. Linguistic analysis reveals evidence of concepts of a supreme being, lesser spirits, and ancestors, as well as some clues about social organization and ritual activity, especially in Equatorial Africa.

Ancient African Religions. Robert M. Baum, Oxford University Press. © Oxford University Press 2024.
DOI: 10.1093/9780197747100.003.0004

Northeast Africa

Nubia and the Ethiopian highlands contain the richest ancient archaeological sites outside of Egypt. As in the Egyptian case, tombs provide the most detailed evidence regarding religious life for this period. This means, however, that most evidence concerns the wealthier classes. It also facilitates the creation of an image of these African religious traditions as focused on death, funerary rituals, and concepts of the afterlife. Nubia extended along the Nile valley, between the First Cataract at Aswan (Elephantine) and the Sixth Cataract, just north of present-day Khartoum. Located south of Upper Egypt, Nubia had extensive interactions with its northern neighbors, conducting trade and being subjected to frequent military incursions, slave-raiding, and even military occupation for long periods. Conversely, Nubians also conquered Egypt, contributing Nubian dynasties to Pharaonic Egypt, serving in the Egyptian army and administration, and intermarrying with Egyptian men and women. Egyptians introduced various deities and deified monarchs into Nubian religious life, and Nubians introduced some religious cults into Egypt. The attention of scholars, however, has tended to focus on Egyptian influences on Nubia—"the Egyptianization of Nubia." As Kathryn Howley has noted: "A distinct lack of archaeological evidence for native Nubian religious practices ... exacerbates the impression of Nubia as a passive recipient of Egyptian ideas."[1]

By 4000 BCE, agriculture had spread to the Nubian areas of the Nile, especially between the Third and Fourth Cataracts. Outside of the graves described in Chapter 2, little archaeological evidence can be associated with this period's religious practices. Janice Yellin characterized early Nubian worship "of their gods on hilltops and in caves."[2] As early as the First Dynasty, Egyptian armies raided the region, seizing captives, but not occupying territory. In the Middle Kingdom, Egyptians fortified key trade routes that led to the rich gold mines of the Nubian region.[3] By 3000 BCE, there was evidence that Nubians buried their dead, like their Egyptian counterparts,

---

[1] Kathryn Howley, "Egypt and Nubia," in *Pharaoh's Land and Beyond: Ancient Egypt and Its Neighbors*, ed. Pearce Paul Creasman and Richard H. Wilkinson (New York: Oxford University Press, 2017), p. 220.

[2] Janice W. Yellin, "Nubian Religion," in *Ancient Nubia: African Kingdom on the Nile*, ed. Marjorie Fisher (Cairo: American University in Cairo Press, 2017), p. 125.

[3] Brian M. Fagan, *People of the Earth: An Introduction to World Prehistory*, 8th ed. (New York: Harper/Collins, 1994), p. 395. E. A. Wallis Budge, *A History of Ethiopia, Nubia, and Abyssinia*, Vol. I (Oosterhout, The Netherlands: Anthropological Publications, [1928] 1970), pp. 11, 13–14. Cyril Aldred, *The Egyptians* (London: Thames and Hudson, 1998), p. 83. Yellin, "Nubian Religion," p. 126.

in graves that included items placed with the deceased for use in the life to come. Graves in this area included stone vessels, copper axes, and other tools. Archaeologists also found jewelry and amulets worn around the necks of the dead and small figurines of fired mud. Some of these figures featured images of women with exaggerated buttocks and hips, with little attention to facial features, hair, or breasts. This may reflect an emphasis on women's power to give birth. These figurines were especially found in graves of women and children.[4] Within Lower Nubia, at least, grave sites indicate relatively little economic differentiation during this period. There was greater economic variation within grave sites in Upper Nubia.[5] Near present-day Khartoum graves of wealthy people included carved ivory, jewelry made from precious stones, and other personal items. Remnants of sacrificed animals were also found near the graves of wealthy individuals, but not in more modest burials. Graves of the poor were not provided with valuable personal effects.[6]

By 2300 BCE, the kingdom of Kerma had gained control of the rich agricultural lands of the Dongola Reach and the gold mines in the nearby hills. Its ability to control long-distance trade generated considerable wealth for Kerma's dominant classes.[7] At times, Kerma was perceived of as a military threat to Egypt. Donald Redford describes Kerma as "a vibrant native culture, promoting its own forms with little essential influence from outside. Apart from pharaonic Egypt, Kerma represents the earliest autochthonous efflorescence of high culture on the African continent."[8] The people of Kerma were described as venerating mountains, caves, and large rock places that evoked a sense of the numinous within a mundane landscape. These were places where they could communicate with sacred powers. The city itself was dominated by an imposing mud brick temple known as a *deffufa*, where animal sacrifices were performed. Open air sacrifices addressed to the sun were performed on the rooftops of *deffufas*.[9] Images of rams on amulets and images found in graves suggest that these may have been associated with a

---

[4] Marjorie M. Fisher et al., *Ancient Nubia: African Kingdoms of the Nile* (Cairo: American University in Cairo, 2012), p. 13. Midant-Reynes, *Ancient Nubia*, pp. 222–223. Steffan Wenning, *Africa in Antiquity: The Arts of Ancient Nubia and the Sudan, Volume II, The Catalogue* (New York: Brooklyn Museum of Art, 1978), pp. 23–24.

[5] Michael A. Hoffman, *Egypt before the Pharaohs: The Prehistoric Foundations of Egyptian Civilization* (New York: Knopf, 1979), p. 260.

[6] Fisher, *Ancient Nubia*, p. 14.

[7] Fagan, *People of the Earth*, p. 395.

[8] Donald B. Redford, *From Slave to Pharaoh: The Black Experience in Ancient Egypt* (Baltimore: Johns Hopkins University Press, 2004), p. 33.

[9] Graham Connah, *African Civilizations: An Archaeological Perspective*, 2nd ed. (Cambridge: Cambridge University Press, 2001), p. 33. Howley, "Egypt and Nubia," p. 220. Vivian Davies and Renée Friedman, *Egypt Uncovered* (New York: Stewart, Tabori, and Yang, 1999), p. 126.

particular deity.[10] Nubian images of rams were eventually incorporated into the cult of Amun-Re within Nubia. Nubian royal women played important roles in the leadership of Kerma and Napata.[11]

Cemeteries associated with Kerma showed clear signs of economic differentiation. Historians suggest that Kerma's burial practices were primarily Nubian in origin, but they did show some degree of Egyptian influence, which increased over time.[12] Nubians built mud-brick chapels in the cemeteries, with walls decorated by images of wild animals, giraffes, elephants, and rhinoceros. Nubian corpses were placed on beds rather than in coffins. Some of the more elaborate beds had legs carved to resemble cows' legs.[13] Mourners placed personal property of the dead on or near the bed to accompany them into the afterlife.[14] They sacrificed sheep and goats on the floor at the foot of the bed.[15] Elaborate royal tombs covered with stones and grave goods have also been found. Royal tombs included as many as four hundred graves of servants and members of the court, both men and women, who seem to have been buried at the same time as the king. Some graves included remains of sacrificed rams and large numbers of cattle skulls adjacent to the human graves.[16] Redford described the royal graves: "The rulers were buried in . . . circular tumuli more than eighty-five meters in diameter and three to four meters in height. The corpse was laid upon a bed of costly material equipped with a headrest and sometimes covered with an ox hide. Silver crowns, weapons, sandals, fans, and edibles accompanied the deceased on his last journey, and hundreds of servants went to their deaths as human sacrifices to his future well-being."[17] Shrines in cemeteries of ordinary people suggest the existence of ancestor cults. Remains of animals killed in ways suggestive of ritual sacrifice reinforce this idea. Particular animals may have been

---

[10] Denise M. Doxey, Rita E. Freed, and Lawrence M. Berman, *MFA Highlights of Ancient Nubia* (Boston: Museum of Fine Arts Publications, 2018), pp. 25, 30–31. Alfred Muzzolini, *L'Art rupestre préhistorique des massifs centraux Saharien*, Cambridge Monographs in African Archaeology, BAR #378 (Oxford: Archaeopress, 1986), pp. 94–97, 102.

[11] Joyce Tyldesley, *Hatchepsut: The Female Pharaoh* (London: Viking, 1996), p. 48.

[12] Howley, "Egypt and Nubia," p. 220. Robert W. July, *A History of the African People*, 4th ed. (Prospect Heights, IL: Waveland Press, 1992), p. 26.

[13] I saw some Nubian grave beds at the Boston Museum of Fine Arts special exhibit on Nubia, November 2019. Howley, "Egypt and Nubia," pp. 220–221. Bruce Williams, "A Perspective for Exploring the Historical Essence of Ancient Nubia," in *Egypt and Africa: Nubia from Prehistory to Islam*, ed. W. V. Davies (London: British Museum Press, 1987), p. 75.

[14] Connah, *African Civilizations*, p. 31.

[15] William Y. Adams, *Nubian Corridors to Africa* (Princeton, NJ: Princeton University Press, 1979), p. 198.

[16] Wenning, *Africa in Antiquity*, pp. 25–28. Frank J. Yurco, "Egypt and Nubia: Old, Middle, and New Kingdoms Eras," in *Africa and Africans in Antiquity*, ed. Edwin M. Yamauchi (East Lansing: Michigan State University Press, 2001), p. 65. Connah, *African Civilizations*, p. 31.

[17] Redford, *From Slave*, p. 33. See also Howley, "Egypt and Nubia," p. 220.

associated with specific clans. The Kerman people placed bodies in graves with their arms and legs drawn up, so that knees and elbows almost touched one another. Pottery, jewelry, and beads were placed in the graves, reinforcing the idea that the deceased would need these objects in the afterlife.[18]

During the Kerma period, Nubian elites became increasingly familiar with Egyptian deities, especially Amun. However, they incorporated them within a Nubian religious system. Although Egyptians depicted Amun in human form, Nubians represented him as having a ram's head on a human body or just as a ram.[19] Nubian deities included Dedwen, a falcon god associated with the Egyptian Horus; Anukis; and Satis, all of whom were eventually incorporated into Egyptian theologies. Anukis and Satis were linked to the creator of human beings, Khnum, who was associated with the border city of Elephantine (Aswan). Satis was identified as Khnum's consort and Anukis as their daughter. All of them were associated with fertility and the annual flood of the Nile.[20] Sculptures of seated females, from the early second millennium, portray women with scars between their breasts and on their hips, suggesting the practice of ritual scarification as part of a rite of passage into adulthood.[21]

During the period of Hyksos domination, Kerma expanded its power within Nubia and cultivated a strong relationship with the "Asiatic" rulers of Egypt. With the reunification of Egypt in the New Kingdom, pharaohs turned their attention to the reoccupation of Nubia, seeking to control Nubia's resources, sparking resistance by Nubians, including revolts in the Lower Nubian areas where Egyptian administrations had been established.[22] In a letter from Amenophis II to his viceroy in Nubia, the pharaoh warned: "'Do not trust the Nubians, but beware of their people and of their witchcraft.'" Whether Nubians regarded themselves as practitioners of witchcraft or practitioners of ritualized forms of resistance remains unclear.[23] The tendency to describe such activities as witchcraft, itself, can be considered a form of repression by a powerful state. Shortly after 1500 BCE, the armies of King Thutomose I destroyed the Nubia capitol of Kerma.[24]

---

[18] David Edwards, "African Perspectives on Death, Burial, and Mortuary Archaeology," in *The Oxford Handbook of The Archaeology of Death and Burial*, ed. Sarah Tarlow and Liv Nilsson Slutz (Oxford: Oxford University Press, 2013), pp. 210–212. Yurco, "Egypt and Nubia," p. 65.
[19] Yellin, "Nubian Religion," p. 126. Jan Assmann, *The Mind of Egypt: History and Memory in the Time of the Pharaohs* (New York: Henry Holt, 1996), p. 318.
[20] Yurco, "Egypt and Nubia," p. 85. Alred, *Egyptians*, p. 30. Yellin, "Nubian Religion," p. 127.
[21] Werner Gillan, *A Short History of African Art* (New York: Facts on File Publishing, 1984), p. 59.
[22] Arielle P. Kozloff, *Amenhotep III: Egypt's Radiant Pharaoh* (Cambridge: Cambridge University Press, 2012), p. 70. Redford, *From Slave*, p. 38.
[23] Eddi Bresciani, "Foreigners," in *The Egyptians*, ed. Sergio Donandoni (Chicago: University of Chicago Press, 1997), pp. 225, 226.
[24] Marc van de Mieroop, *A History of Ancient Egypt* (Malden, MA: Wiley-Blackwell, 2011), p. 152.

Egyptians introduced the worship of the sun god, Amun-Ra, and cults focused on the divinity of the pharaohs. According to Howley, several pharaohs were deified in Nubia, but not in Egypt.[25] This was also true of Queen Tiye, mother of Akhenaten.[26] Amenhotep III had a temple built at Soleb, the "first Egyptian temple dedicated not to a long-standing venerable god, but to a specific king as deity." Amenhotep III was associated with the moon god, Khonsu.[27] The Egyptian hippopotamus goddess, Tawarut, who protected pregnant women, was introduced into Nubia, though in Nubia she was portrayed with wings.[28] Pharaoh Senwosret III became the patron god of Nubia. During this period, Egyptians established a major ritual and administrative center at Napata.[29] A rugged massif at Gebel Barakel became a ritual center and was claimed to be the primal mound of many Egyptian creation myths. Nubians claimed that one end of the mountain, a stone formation, took the form of a uraeus, described as a rearing cobra, a symbol of the Egyptian monarchy.[30] Egyptians called it "the pure mountain" and associated it with the supreme deity, Amun. Thutmoses III was credited with relatively benign rule over the region, including some degree of tolerance of Nubian religious practices, but that was not the case of his successors.

In contrast, Akhenaten violently suppressed a Nubian revolt while attempting to extend his religious reforms to Nubia. He ordered Amenhotep III's temple at Soleb defaced, removing all mention of Amun from the temple walls, although he retained statuary celebrating his father's reign. He also retained statuary of Queen Tiye, who was presented as a manifestation of the goddess Hathor.[31] He built a temple complex called Gem-aten, south of Kerma, where the solar deity, Aten, could receive worship.[32] Akhenaten's teaching as found in the "Hymn to Aten" stressed the equality of Egyptians, Nubians, and Syrians, something that would have found support in Kerma. Still the exclusive focus on Aten was not successful among Nubians. Reflecting the increasingly repressive rule of Egypt over Nubia, Rameses's massive temple at Abu Simbel included images of Nubian captives being carried north

---

[25] Yurco, "Egypt and Nubia," p. 85. Howley, "Egypt and Nubia," p. 222.
[26] Nicolas Grimal, *A History of Ancient Egypt* (Malden, MA: Blackwell, [1992] 2008), p. 222.
[27] Kazloff, *Amenhotep III*, p. 169.
[28] Howley, "Egypt and Nubia," p. 221. Redford, *From Slave*, p. 47.
[29] Timothy Kendall, "Sudan's Kingdom of Kush," *National Geographic* 178, no. 5, (1990), p. 103.
[30] Davies and Friedman, *Egypt Uncovered*, pp. 96–99.
[31] Kozloff, *Amenhotep III*, p. 172. W. Raymond Johnson, "Akhenaten in Nubia," in *Ancient Nubia: African Kingdoms on the Nile*, ed. Marjorie Fisher, Peter Lacovera, Sahiman Ikrem, and Sue d'Auna (Cairo: American University in Cairo Press, 2012), pp. 92–93.
[32] N. M. Sherif, "Nubia Before Napata (3100 to 750)," in *UNESCO General History of Africa, Volume II, Ancient Africa* ed. G. Mokhtar (London: Heinemann, 1981), p. 26. Johnson, "Akhenaten in Nubia," p. 92.

in chains, presided over by stern and powerful statues of the pharaoh.[33] As Arielle Kozloff noted: "These Nubian fortresses were venues for the display and ritual killing of war prisoners and criminals. . . . Likely the indigenous population [Nubian} were well aware of the temple's symbolism."[34]

Near the Red Sea coastal areas of present-day Eritrea or Djibouti was the kingdom of Punt. Its exact location remains unknown, but Egyptian chronicles describe it as a major trading nation which supplied Egypt with myrrh for temple offerings. Its smoke carried prayers up to the gods.[35] Presumably, commoners made similar use of myrrh for household rituals. Egyptians also purchased ivory, gold, and ebony from merchants who might have been reselling goods received from countries further south.[36] Men and women from Punt served as household servants in wealthy Egyptian homes. The Egyptian god Bes, who protected the harmony of the home and of women in childbirth, was said to have originated in Punt. On the other hand, Egyptians introduced the worship of Hathor into Punt.[37]

Recent archaeological discoveries, concerning a group known as Gash between 3000 and 1500 BCE, provided evidence of segmentary lineage-based societies in the Gash River delta near present-day Kassala in northeastern Sudan. They traded with Nubian and Upper Egyptian communities along the Nile and with the Ona of highland Eritrea.[38] At Mahal Teglinos, a major administrative and ritual center, members of dominant lineages among the Gash had stone stelae erected upon their graves, some of which were over a meter high. They were adorned with remains of animals that had been sacrificed in their honor. The Gash were involved in trade in frankincense, gold, and ivory along Red Sea trade routes and may have been associated with the Land of Punt.[39]

Ancient Ethiopian civilization centered on the highlands of present-day Ethiopia and Eritrea. This was an area of unusually temperate climate where

---

[33] Personal observation, Abu Simbel, June, 2000. Budge, *History of Ethiopia*, pp. 16, 19.
[34] Kozloff, *Amenhotop III*, p. 172.
[35] Aldred, *Egyptians*, p. 115. David W. Phillipson, *Ancient Ethiopia: Its Antecedents and Successors* (London: British Museum Press, 1998), p. 38.
[36] Tyldesley, *Hatchepsut*, pp. 144, 147.
[37] Bresciani, "Foreigners," p. 239.
[38] Jack Philips, "Punt and Aksum: Egypt and the Horn of Africa," *Journal of African History* 38 (1997), p. 439.
[39] Rodolfo Fattovich, "The Development of Ancient States in the Northern Horn of Africa, 3000 BC to 1000 AD," *Journal of World Prehistory* 23 (2010), p. 155. Rodolfo Fattovich, "At the Periphery of the Empire: The Gash Delta," in *Egypt and Africa: Nubia from Prehistory to Islam* ed. W. V. Davies (London: British Museum Press, 1987), p. 45. Kathryn A. Bord and Rodolfo Fattovich, "Processes of State Formation in Egypt and Ethiopia," in *Africa and Africans in Antiquity*, ed. Edwin M. Yamauchi (East Lansing: Michigan State University Press, 2001), p. 281. Rodolfo Fattovich, "Aksum and Habasha: State and Ethnicity in Ancient Northern Ethiopia and Eritrea," Boston University African Studies Center Working Papers, #228, 2000, p. 11.

important food crops, including teff, were first domesticated. Scholars frequently asserted that Ethiopian civilization was entirely derived from the peoples of southern Arabia and, less often, from Egypt. For example, E. Wallis Budge boldly declared that "The facts of history show that the Abyssinians borrowed everything of importance from the nations round about them. Their oldest civilization they owed to the Himyarites and Yamanites, and their language is closely allied to that of the peoples in the south of the Arabian Peninsula."[40] The earliest known Ethiopian dynasty was the Arwe Dynasty, which was seen as having a foreign origin. Its people revered snakes as a symbol of wisdom. A second dynasty was founded around 1370 BCE, by Za Besi Angabo, which dominated the Ethiopian highlands for approximately 350 years. This was the dynasty of Queen Makeda, which Ethiopian traditions associate with the Queen of Sheba.[41]

Northeastern Africa had developed its own religious traditions, but as early as five thousand years ago, these traditions were influenced by sustained contact with their neighbors in Egypt, the eastern Sudan, and South Arabia. Most of the sources, both textual and archaeological, already reflected these influences.

North Africa

The North African littoral included areas with a Mediterranean climate and sufficient rainfall to support a variety of agricultural activities. The interior of North Africa was not as arid in the third millennium BCE but faced increasing desertification throughout the second and first millennia. From the end of the fourth millennium until the beginnings of the first millennium, Berber peoples dominated North Africa west of the Nile valley and nearby oases. Their collective label came from the Greeks, who identified North African peoples as strange, as foreigners.[42] They identified themselves as Mazices or Imazighen, meaning "freeborn."[43] Throughout this period, however, people

---

[40] Budge, *History of Ethiopia*, p. xvi.

[41] William Hansberry, *Pillars in Ethiopian History: The William Leo Hansberry African History Notebook, Volume I*, ed. Joseph E. Harris (Washington, DC: Howard University Press), pp. 41–42.

[42] Reuben G. Bullard, "The Berbers of the Maghreb and Ancient Carthage," in *Africa and Africans in Antiquity*, ed. Edwin M. Yamauchi (East Lansing: Michigan State University Press, 2001), pp. 183–184.

[43] Gabriel Camps, *Les Berbères: Mémoire et identité* (Paris: Editions Errance, 1987), p. 15. Phillip C. Naylor, *A History of North Africa from Antiquity to the Present* (Austin: University of Texas Press, 2009), p. 4.

identified as black practiced agriculture in the mountainous regions of the Hoggar and Tassili of the central Sahara.[44]

Although sources are limited before the establishment of Carthage in the early first millennium BCE, it appears that the ancient peoples of the region venerated spirits associated with unusual rock formations and springs. They also used rituals to assist dead relatives in their journey to the life after death. Early Libyans buried their dead on their sides, covering the bodies with red ocher. They often placed food offerings in the graves. Mourners also placed amulets in the graves both to fend off malevolent forces and to assist the dead on their journeys to the afterlife.[45] Imazighen sacrificed animals to honor the dead and to seek their assistance. Some people would spend the night at a tomb, a rite known as incubation, in the hope of receiving a dream that would provide insight into or assistance with a particular problem.[46] Tassili rock art includes numerous portrayals of dancers, suggesting that the peoples of the ancient Sahara used dance in religious rituals. Similarly, paintings of people wearing animal masks may have had ritual significance.[47] Moroccan cemeteries, dating back to the third millennium, include large quantities of grave goods, especially tools and pottery that would be useful in the afterlife, and elephant ivory ornaments. Susan Searight argues that these graves show a Saharan influence. Near Tetouan, on Morocco's Mediterranean coast, standing stone circles surround large tumuli, measuring fifty-five meters across, that were later modified during the Punic Age.[48] These stone circles may have been used to chart the movement of the sun, suggesting a religious significance to solar activity.

Early North African sources reflect a prolonged interaction between peoples identified as Berber or Imazighen, who were engaged in animal husbandry, and black oasis communities of sedentary farmers, each with their own religious traditions. Their religious complementarity reflects the economic symbiosis of farmers and herder/traders in northern Africa.

---

[44] Alfred Muzzolini, *Les Images rupestres du Sahara* (Toulouse: By the author, 1994), pp. 2r, 78.
[45] J. des Songes, "The Proto-Berbers," in *UNESCO General History of Africa, Volume II, Ancient Africa*, ed. G. Mokhtar (London: Heinemann, 1981), pp. 435–438.
[46] Des Songes, "Proto-Berbers," p. 438.
[47] Muzzolini, *Les Images*, pp. 249, 256.
[48] Susan Searight, *The Prehistoric Rock Art of Morocco: A Study of Its Extension, Environment, and Meaning*, BAR International Series, 1310 (Oxford: Archaeopress, 2004), pp. 30, 34.

West Africa

Fishing and oyster-gathering communities existed along the coast of present-day Senegal as early as the fourth millennium.[49] Beyond coastal shell middens, archaeological sources for ancient West Africa are particularly sparse. Based on historical linguistic analysis, scholars believe that speakers of the earliest form of a Niger-Congo language were settled in the Niger River basin by 10,000 BCE.[50] By the end of the third millennium BCE, coastal languages in the Rio Nunez area in the Upper Guinea began to diverge from one another. By 3000 BCE, proto-Mel languages had split into proto-Bukigo and Highland languages.[51] Cultivation of sorghum, fonio, and other grains suitable to the savannah developed by 3500 BCE.[52] In the inland delta area of the Niger and along the Gambia and Casamance Rivers, West African peoples domesticated an African species of rice, known as *Oryza glaberimma*, by around 1500 BCE.[53] This began a process of producing religious traditions focused on the labor-intensive production of rice as a staple crop. These cults also concerned the fertility of the land, livestock, and, by extension the fertility of humans in the community.

By 1800 BCE, the southern Saharan community of Tichitt cultivated millet, herded cattle, and engaged in long-distance trade as a source of wealth and power. They continued to dominate the southwestern Sahara until the middle of the first millennium BCE.[54]

Some of the earliest archaeological evidence from West Africa came from Kintampo in a transitional area from forest to grasslands between 1500 BCE and 1100 BCE.[55] The twenty-eight Kintampo sites revealed farming areas in the wooded river valleys as far south as present-day Accra, on the Guinea Coast. The

---

[49] D. W. Phillipson, "Early Food Production in Sub-Saharan Africa," in *The Cambridge History of Africa, Volume I, From Earliest Times to c. 500 BC*, ed. J. Desmond Clark (London: Cambridge: Cambridge University Press, 1982), p. 776.

[50] Rhonda Gonzalez, *Societies, Religion, and History: Central East Tanzanians and the World They Created c. 200 BCE to 1800 CE* (New York: Columbia University Press, 2009), p. 32.

[51] Edda J. Fields, "Before 'Baga': Settlement Chronologies of the Coastal Rio Nunez Region, Earliest Times to 1000 C.E.," *International Journal of African Historical Studies* 37 (2004), p. 249.

[52] Fagan, *People of the Earth*, p. 289.

[53] B. Wai Andah, "West Africa before the Seventh Century," in *UNESCO General History of Africa, Volume II, Ancient Africa*, ed. G. Mokhtar (London: Heinemann, 1981), p. 606. A. Portères, "Berceaux agricoles sur le continent, Africain," *Journal of African History* 3 (1962), pp. 195–218.

[54] Kevin C. MacDonald, "A View from the South: Sub-Saharan Evidence for Contacts between North Africa, Mauritania, and the Niger, 1000 BC–A. D. 700," in *Money, Trade, and Trade Routes in Pre-Islamic North Africa*, ed. Amelia Dowler and Elizabeth Galvin (London: British Museum Press, 2011), pp. 72–73.

[55] Phillipson, "Early Food Production," pp. 781–782.

creators of this culture herded dwarf cattle and goats that could resist African sleeping sickness that was endemic in forested areas. They also exploited oil palms for a variety of uses and farmed cowpeas, yams, and cocoyams.[56]

As West Africans turned increasingly to farming and the herding of animals, ritual actions turned toward securing the fertility of the land, livestock, and people. Sacrifices of animals and offerings of libations of water, milk, palm wine, and millet beer became important to these ritual activities.

Equatorial Africa

Based on the analysis of linguistic similarities, historians have concluded that the proto-Bantu speakers originated in the Upper Benue River valley. The Bantu-speaking peoples of Equatorial Africa expanded into the borderlands between present-day Cameroun and Nigeria, approximately seven thousand years ago. Malcolm Guthrie's efforts to recreate the history of Bantu languages suggest that before Bantu speakers began to disperse they had developed the practice of animal husbandry, within a series of grassland settlements but had not yet learned how to work with iron.[57] Before they began their migrations, Bantu speakers shared concepts of lineage, ancestors, and witchcraft, given the common derivation of these terms throughout the Bantu language family. They shared terms for healer (*nganga*) and for a drum that became associated with the healing process (*ngoma*). Still we know little about what these terms actually meant within systems of thought prevalent in these societies.[58] By 3000 BCE, proto-Bantu speakers had separated into two groups, Eastern and Western Bantu in the area east of the Cross River.[59]

---

[56] B. Wei Andah, "West Africa before the Seventh Century," in *Ancient Civilizations of Africa, Volume II of UNESCO General History of Africa*, ed. G. Mokhtar (Paris: UNESCO, 1981), pp. 605–607. James L. Newman, *The Peopling of Africa: A Geographical Interpretation* (New Haven, CT: Yale University Press, 1995), p. 56. Colin Flight, "The Kintampo Culture and Its Place in the Economic Prehistory of West Africa," in *West African Culture Dynamics: Archaeological and Historical Perspectives*, ed. B. K. Swantz and Raymond E. Dumett (The Hague: Mouton, 1986), p. 219. Jonathan E. Robins, *Oil Palm: A Global History* (Chapel Hill: University of North Carolina Press, 2021), pp. 14–15.

[57] Jan Vansina, *Paths in the Rainforest: Toward a History of Political Tradition in Equatorial Africa* (Madison: University of Wisconsin Press, 1990), p. 49. Philip Curtin et al., *African History* (New York: Longman, [1978] 1991), p. 28.

[58] Rhonda Gonzalez, *Societies, Religion, and History*, p. 33. John M. Janzen, *Ngoma: Discourses of Healing in Central and Southern Africa* (Berkeley: University of California Press, 1992), p. 63.

[59] Vansina, *Paths in the Rainforest*, p. 49. David Lee Schoenbrun, *A Green Place, A Good Place: Agrarian Change, Gender, and Social Identity in the Great Lakes Region to the 15th Century* (Portsmouth, NH: Heinemann, 1998), p. 106.

Western Bantu speakers shared terms for diseases, divination, and healing, as well as the medicines, kaolin, and amulets used in the healing process. Proto-Eastern Bantu speakers (Mashariki) shared words for witches, witch-finding ordeals, divination, medicines, and amulets. They also referred to the dead as *dimu*.[60]

By 2000 BCE, early speakers of Bantu languages had moved to the area where the Kwa and Congo Rivers flow together. By 1500 BCE, Eastern Savanna Bantu speakers had reached the Kasai region of present-day, northeastern Congo. By 1000 BCE, Mashariki speakers had moved even further east to the Great Rift valley.[61] As they moved east and south, they encountered forest-dwelling hunters and gatherers, whom they called Batwa. The Batwa and other hunter-gatherers of the Equatorial Forest are often labeled "Pygmies," a pejorative term in most contexts. Although there may have been some violent encounters, there were strong incentives for Batwa speakers and Bantu speakers to cooperate.[62] From the Batwa, the Bantu-speaking groups learned how to exploit forest animals and plants for food and medicine. The newcomers regarded Batwa as spiritually powerful "owners of the land." They also incorporated Batwa territorial spirits into their religious systems.[63] They relied on Batwa ritual specialists in healing cults and in the rites associated with the installation and maintenance of kingship.[64]

Jan Vansina claims that the early Western Bantu-speaking groups, around 3000 BCE, saw the world as existing beyond that which could be perceived from the five senses. A "real" world included the spirits of heroes, powerful beings who could help people who lived on earth. They used a term referring to something "extinguished" or "lost" (*dimo*), which referred to a distant ancestor who was the subject of ritual libations and sacrifices, often linked to the founding of specific communities. Oral traditions credited these cultural heroes with teaching people how to farm, hunt, make tools or weapons, or

---

[60] Janzen, *Ngoma*, p. 64.

[61] Gonzalez, *Societies, Religion, and History*, p. 33. John Akama, "Historical Evolution of the Gusii," in *Ethnography of the Gusii of Western Kenya: A Vanishing Cultural Heritage*, ed. John S. Akama and Robert Maxson (Lewiston, NY: Edwin Mellen Press, 2005), p. 20.

[62] Robert E. Moise, "'Do Pygmies Have a History? Revisited': The Autochthonous Tradition in the History of Equatorial Africa," in *Hunter-Gatherers of the Congo Basin: Culture, History, and Biology of the Congo Basin*, ed. Barry S. Howlett (Highland Park, NJ: Transaction Publishers, 2014), pp. 91–92.

[63] Catherine Fourshey, Rhonda Gonzalez, and Christine Saidi, *Bantu Africa, 3500 BCE to Present* (New York: Oxford University Press, 2018), p. 13.

[64] Moise, "Do Pygmies Have a History?" p. 93.

perform important rituals. They protected people and, in exchange, they demanded sacrifices, libations, and the construction of shrines.[65]

Fourshey, Gonzalez, and Saidi rely on linguistic evidence to claim that the early Bantu speakers were matrilineal. Both female and male elders exercised authority within the matrilineage. Kairn Klieman claimed that Eastern Bantu terms for "matrilineage" are derived from the word for termite hill and reflect a creation myth describing the first women ancestors emerging from a termite hill. Batwa were often seen as the owners of the termite hills, thus linking them to the creation of humanity. Religious activity focused on the veneration of ancestral and territorial spirits. Territorial spirits included especially well-known ancestors and spirits associated with the earlier inhabitants of the lands they had come to occupy.[66] The supreme being was known in early Bantu languages as Nyambe, a term derived from an earlier Niger-Congo term meaning "to begin."[67] Early Bantu languages also included a term for malevolent power, *bu-logi*, which is often translated as "witchcraft."[68] Rites of passage, associated with menarche for girls and circumcision for boys, appear to have been practiced by Bantu speakers in the second millennium.[69] These rituals marked the passage of children to adulthood. Among Mashariki speakers, male circumcision occurred around the time of puberty. It involved a significant number of boys undergoing the ritual at the same time, and several weeks of ritual seclusion, allowing the boys to be educated about their responsibilities as men in the community as they recovered from the ordeal. Shared terms concerning the entering of the sacred forest and joining in the ritual seclusion of the initiates exist in early Mashariki languages.[70]

As the Bantu-speaking groups moved eastward and broke into several clusters of languages, a similar process was occurring among proto-Ubangi speakers. By 2000 BCE, they had broken into Eastern and Western groups in the area north of the Congo/Zaire River. By 1500 BCE, Eastern Ubangi languages had divided into three distinct branches: proto-Mbomu-Uele,

---

[65] Vansina, *Paths in the Rainforest*, pp. 95–96.
[66] Fourshey et al., *Bantu Africa*, pp. 45–46, 59. Kairn Klieman, *The Pygmies Are Our Compass: Bantu and Batwa in the History of West Central Africa, Early Times to 1900* (Portsmouth, NH: Heinemann, 2003), p. 70.
[67] Fourshey et al., *Bantu Africa*, p. 54. Gonzalez, *Society, Religion, and History*, p. 91.
[68] Gonzalez, *Society, Religion, and History*, p. 56.
[69] Gonzalez, *Society, Religion, and History*, pp. 78, 82.
[70] Gonzalez, *Society, Religion, and History*, pp. 82–83.

pre-Ngbadi, and proto-Zandean.[71] They settled in areas just to the north of the Equatorial forests, continuing to cultivate yams in the well-watered wooded grasslands north of the Ubangi River.[72]

East Africa

As the Saharan region became increasingly arid, people migrated out of the driest areas toward more reliable sources of water along the Mediterranean coast or in the Sahel. This included the movement of people now identified as Nilotics who settled in the south Sudan. By 3300 BCE, some groups continued further south into present-day Uganda, Kenya, and Tanzania. These cattle-herding Nilotic-speaking peoples encountered hunting and gathering communities in the eastern highlands, some of whom spoke Cushitic languages. These southern Cushitic speakers lived in an area that was well-suited to animal husbandry, which they supplemented by cultivating sorghum during the rainy season.[73] Linguistic evidence suggests that these early Cushitic peoples practiced male circumcision.[74] Over centuries of contact, Cushitic speakers and Bantu speakers influenced each other's languages, borrowing words from one another. It would be surprising if they had not influenced one another's systems of thought or ritual practices during the same period.

Two archaeological sites, near Kenya's Lake Turkana, provided evidence of elaborate graves from around 2000 BCE. At Jongole, large stone pillars were erected near burial pits. Mourners left locally made pottery, ostrich eggshell beads, and shells acquired from the East African coast, an indication of long-distance trade during this period. At Namakatuga, also near Lake Turkana, archaeologists uncovered marked burial sites, but there were no grave goods found in the burial pits. According to Turkana oral traditions, the basalt pillars were some of their ancestors who were turned into the stone pillars by a malevolent spirit.[75] A more recent archaeological site, east of Kenya's Lake

---

[71] Douglas E. Sexon, "Linguistic Evidence for the Eastern Spread of Ubangian," in *The Archaeological and Linguistic Reconstruction of African History*, ed. Christopher Ehret and Merrick Posnansky (Berkeley: University of California Press, 1982), p. 68.

[72] Vansina, *Paths in the Rainforest*, p. 65.

[73] Fagan, *People of the Earth*, pp. 288–289. Christopher Ehret, *History and the Testimony of Language* (Berkeley: University of California Press, 2011), p. 187.

[74] Ehret, *History*, p. 211.

[75] Lawrence H. Robbins, "Lake Turkana Archaeology: The Holocene," *Ethnohistory* 53, no. 11 (2006), pp. 71–92.

Turkana, yielded ten burial cairns, which have been dated back to circa 1500 BCE. Worked obsidian objects and goat bones were recovered there. Similar burial cairns were found on the eastern edge of the Rift valley to the south.[76] The presence of goat bones suggests the practice of funerary ceremonies. The presence of obsidian objects suggests the placing of personal objects or tools for the transition to the afterlife. By the end of the second millennium BCE, some groups, known as Elmentaiten, buried their dead under stone cairn near Nakuru, in Kenya's Great Rift valley. Mourners left stone bowls and mortars and pestles in the graves, all essential goods for an afterlife perceived as similar to this life. Kering Cave on the edge of Kenya's Rift valley had similar grave artifacts.[77] East African Nilotic and Cushitic peoples shared concerns about the transition of their deceased kin toward a more beneficent afterlife. The elaborate grave goods accompanying burials were designed to meet that purpose. In sharp contrast to their neighbors in the Great Rift valley, these people placed their dead in the Njoro River Cave, something that appears to have been rare in the region.[78]

Southern Africa

By 3200 BCE, people who practiced elaborate funeral rituals had settled along the Indian Ocean coast of present-day South Africa's Eastern Cape Province. At Tzitzikama, Cold Stream, and at a coastal cave, archaeologists have found painted gravestones, grave goods, and bodies placed in a fetal position, all covered in ocher.[79] These all suggest religious concerns about life after death. Excavations at the Gwisho Springs in central Zambia provide evidence of a hunting and gathering community that settled in this area around 1500 BCE. The Gwisho provide the earliest indications of people whose material culture and diet closely resembled eighteenth- and nineteenth-century San of the Kalahari, Gwisho buried their dead near their campsites. The arrowheads, stone scrapers, pestles, and grinding stones discovered in the graves suggest

---

[76] Peter Robertshaw, "Archaeology in Eastern Africa: Recent Developments and More Dates," *Journal of African History* 25, no. 4 (1984), p. 387.

[77] D. W. Phillipson, *The Late Prehistory of Western and Southern Africa* (New York: Africana Publishing Company, 1977), pp. 76–77.

[78] Graham Connah, *Forgotten Africa: An Introduction to Archaeology* (New York: Routledge, 2004), p. 47.

[79] Merrick Posnansky, "Archaeology, Ritual, and Religion," in *The Historical Study of African Religion*, ed. T. O. Ranger and I. N. Kimambo (Berkeley: University of California Press, 1972), p. 30.

that the Gwisho thought that their dead would need tools to survive in the afterlife. The similarities of material culture have provided the empirical basis for the interpretation of South African rock art by interpolating from more recent San religious practices. This has led scholars such as David Lewis-Williams to interpret rock paintings from the area by focusing on sacred eland and on dancers who appeared to enter a trance state to assume its power. The dancers appropriated the powers of the eland to heal the sick.[80] Images of lines of power emanating from dancers' heads and blood flowing from their noses provide further indications of parallels with later Khoisan concepts of a power generated in ritual dance, known as *N'um*.

Some scholars cite this evidence from rock art to argue for a shared hunter-gatherer culture, centered on trance as a means of access to spiritual power. Religious leaders used this power to heal the sick, ensure fertility, and enhance the success of hunters.[81]

Conclusion

Despite the lack of written texts for most of ancient Africa, it is possible to gather some evidence of religious changes during the second and third millennia. Throughout Africa, from Morocco to its southernmost capes, people carefully buried their dead to protect them against predatory animals or malevolent forces. They sought to equip them with the essential possessions needed for the world to come. In Nubia and Ethiopia, new forms of kingship emerged, governed by rulers who based their power on their religious authority and ritual responsibilities. Their deaths, at least in Nubia, created a crisis requiring massive sacrifices of human beings and the provisioning of the dead with some of their wealth for the arduous journey to the world of the dead. From the Old Kingdom to the religious reforms of Akhenaten, Egyptian religious influences increased in Nubia and, to a lesser extent, in the Ethiopian highlands. As Egyptian influences increased, however, so did Nubian religious influences within Egypt. This raises a serious question about those scholars who insist on the central role of Egypt in the creation of African civilizations.

---

[80] Fagan, *People of the Earth*, pp. 208–210.
[81] John Kinahan, *Namib: The Archaeology of an African Desert* (Woodbridge, UK: James Currey, 2022), pp. 110–117.

Beyond northeast Africa, archaeological and linguistic evidence became our only source of religious history. Both the study of rock paintings and linguistic analysis suggest an importance to certain kinds of animals, but not to others. Perhaps this indicated an association between specific animals and specific clans or the animal-like qualities of particular deities or ritual specialists. Linguistic analysis has also provided evidence of shared concepts of a supreme being, lesser spirits, and ancestors among Bantu-speaking peoples from early in the third millennium. Many communities in Equatorial and East Africa shared concepts of malevolent power, often translated as witchcraft. Linguistic evidence established that these religious traditions, even during this ancient period, were theistic. Many of these traditions included a continuum of spiritual powers that ranged from a supreme being or chief deity to lesser deities and ancestors. Ancestors, who acted on behalf of their living descendants, represented the most personalized and local form of spiritual power.

Both the archaeological and linguistic evidence remains quite incomplete. Large areas, especially in West and Equatorial Africa, have received very limited archaeological work for the ancient period. Similarly, comparative linguistic studies remain quite limited for West Africa, though they are much stronger for Equatorial, East, and southern Africa, which have been studied within the context of the Bantu migrations. As evidence from these sources continues to grow, the history of this formative period will gradually become richer and more certain.

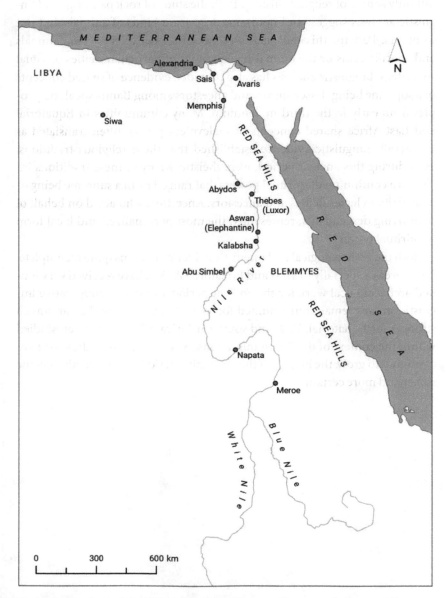

Map 5.1. Egypt and the Nile valley to the Roman Conquest (courtesy of Jonathan Chipman).

5
Egypt and the Nile Valley before the Roman Occupation

This chapter is a study in contrasts. From Ramesside Egypt and its dominance of northeast Africa and the Mediterranean areas of the Middle East to a series of foreign occupations, Egypt retained its hegemonic cultural role in the region (see Map 5.1). However, the Nubian state, strongly influenced by Egyptian political and religious institutions, freed itself from the political control of Egypt and proceeded to conquer it. In doing so, it took on the role of protector of Egypt's religious heritage, especially the worship of the supreme deity, Amun. This chapter examines the religious history of the Nile valley in the last millennium before the beginnings of Christianity in neighboring Palestine. During this period, the Nineteenth Dynasty expanded Egyptian influence into Palestine and Syria and restored Egyptian domination of Nubia. It was also, however, a period of increased military intervention by Middle Eastern empires in the political, economic, and religious affairs of northeastern Africa. First, Assyrian forces occupied most of Egypt and unsuccessfully tried to occupy Nubia. Then, Persian military expeditions conquered Egypt and other northeastern African areas while conducting trade along the Red Sea and Indian Ocean coasts. Egyptian occupation of Palestine and Hebrew migration into Egypt increased Egyptian familiarity with ancient forms of Judaism. The extended Persian domination of Egypt became an important source of Zoroastrian influence, which, in turn, contributed to the ways in which Egypt was influenced both by Greek and early Christian cultures.

Contacts with other literate cultures led to wider variety of written sources to supplement Egyptian and Meroitic texts and archaeological materials. The gradual decline of the power of the Egyptian monarchy also affected the relative importance of different gods within the Egyptian religious tradition. During this period, Nubian religious influences increased within Egypt and Egyptian religion assumed a hegemonic role within Nubian societies. This chapter concludes with Alexander the Great's conquest of Egypt and the establishment of the Ptolemaic Dynasty, which deepened a long period of reciprocal influence between Greeks and Egyptians.

Egypt from the Ramesside Dynasty to the Third Intermediate Period (1320–731 BCE)

With the ascension of Ramesses I in 1320 BCE, the Ramesside Nineteenth Dynasty took over the throne of Egypt. His son Sety, or Sethos, came to power in 1318. As his name implies, he was involved in restoring Seth's place within the Egyptian pantheon. Although sometimes portrayed as evil, Seth was more of a trickster figure, embodying forces of chaos, disorder, and the wilderness, rather than an evil force.[1] Sety patronized a temple at Avaris, dedicated to Seth, that had been established by King Horemheb. Sety emphasized his divine lineage through Seth rather than the more traditional claim of descent through Horus. Sety also restored the cult of Amun-Ra and sought to eradicate any signs of the Atenist religion introduced by Akhenaten. He restored the great temple at Karnak and expanded the temple complex at Abydos, dedicated to Osiris. It included a shrine known as the Oseirion, which was said to be the site where Osiris was buried. That a ruler named after Seth should build a major temple to Osiris suggests that the stark divide between their followers had come to an end. He also established a mortuary temple for his own cult after his death. By establishing it in the temple complex at Abydos, he linked his cult to Osiris.[2] Sethos also restored temples that had been dedicated to other gods that had been defaced during the reign of Akhenaten.[3]

His successor, Ramesses II (1279–1212 BCE), restored the military power and regional influence of the Egyptian empire. Reflecting his acknowledgment of the assistance of the primary Egyptian gods, he named his army's divisions after Amun, Re, Ptah, and Seth.[4] At Abu Simbel, he built a massive temple celebrating Egyptian domination of Nubia, which included towering figures of Ramesses himself and much smaller images of Amun-Ra and of chained Nubian captives heading north into Egypt (see Figures 5.1 and 5.2).

---

[1] Robert Pelton, *The Trickster in West Africa: A Study of Myth, Irony, and Sacred Delight* (Berkeley: University of California Press, 1980). Paul Radin, *The Trickster: A Study in Ancient Indian Mythology* (New York: Greenwood, 1965).

[2] Marc Van De Mieroop, *A History of Ancient Egypt* (Malden, MA: Wiley-Blackwell, 2011), p. 215.

[3] Jacobus van Dijk, "The Amarna Period and the Later New Kingdom (c. 1352–1069 BC)," in *The Oxford History of Ancient Egypt*, ed. Ian Shaw (Oxford: Oxford University Press, 2000), pp. 294–296. Rosalie David, *Religion and Magic in Ancient Egypt* (London: Penguin, 2001), pp. 246–248, 252.

[4] Aidan Dodson, *Monarchs of the Nile*, 2nd ed. (Cairo: American University in Cairo Press, 2000), pp. 126, 142.

Figure 5.1. Ramesses Temple, Abu Simbel, Egypt (photo by Robert M. Baum).

He expanded temples dedicated to Amun and Osiris and built a massive mortuary temple called the Ramesseum across the river from Luxor.[5] It is likely that the biblical Exodus took place during his reign, though there is no specific mention of the flight of the Hebrews from Egypt or the loss of his soldiers. The use of forced labor in the construction of the new cities of Pithon and Ramesses in the Nile delta, described in Exodus, corresponded with Ramesses II's construction of a third Egyptian capital, Pi-Ramesses, in that region.[6] The stele of Ramesses's son Merenptah provides the first written description of the tribes of Israel, who apparently joined a group of "Sea Peoples" allied with Libyans against the Egyptian monarchy. According to the stele, the Hebrews were expelled by Ramesses in retaliation.[7]

Theological texts written during the reign of Ramesses II emphasized the hidden and unknowable nature of Amun-Ra. "'No god knows his true appearance.... No god testifies to him accurately. He is too secret to uncover his

---

[5] Van Dijk, "Amarna Period," p. 299.

[6] A synagogue in Old Cairo was built on the site where a daughter of a pharaoh was said to have found the infant Moses, floating down the Nile in a reed basket. I visited the synagogue in 2000. Jospeh M. Modrzejewski, *The Jews of Egypt: From Ramesses II to Emperor Hadrian* (Princeton, NJ: Princeton University Press, 1995), p. 13. David, *Religion and Magic in Ancient Egypt*, p. 266. Nicolas Grimal, *A History of Ancient Egypt* (Malden, MA: Blackwell, 1994), p. 259.

[7] Françoise Dunand and Christiane Zivi-Coche, *Gods and Men in Egypt: 3000 BCE to 395 CE* (Ithaca, NY: Cornell University Press, 2004), p. 253.

Figure 5.2. Images of enslaved Nubians being taken north into Egypt, Abu Simbel (photo by Robert M. Baum).

awesomeness, he is too great to investigate, too powerful to know."' His face was identified with the sun god, Re, and his body with the creator god, Ptah.[8] A Ramesside-era hymn captures the continued importance of Egypt's solar cults:

> Hail to you, Re.
> When you set in life, After you have joined the horizon of heaven
> You have appeared on the west side as Atum in the sunset
> Having come in your power, none opposing you
> You conquered heaven as Re.
> You received your two heavens in beautiful pleasure
> After clearing away clouds and storms,
> Having descended in the body of your mother, Naunet
> You are greeted by your father, Nun
> The gods of Manu are joyous
> Those in the underworld rejoice

---

[8] Brian Fagan, *Egypt of the Pharaohs* (Washington, DC: National Geographic Society, 2001), p. 186. James Putnam, *Egyptology: An Introduction to the History, Culture, and Art of Ancient Egypt* (New York: Shooting Star Press, 1990), p. 36. Donald B. Redford, *From Slave to Pharaoh: The Black Experience of Ancient Egypt* (Baltimore: The Johns Hopkins University Press, 2004), p. 105.

When they see their lord with broad stride
Amun-Re lord of mankind.[9]

The Ramesside Dynasty ushered in a new emphasis on personal piety that was often described as putting "god in one's heart." Even early in the Eighteenth Dynasty, in the reign of Thuthmosis III, a hymn described Amun as "father and mother, for him who gives into his heart, but he [Amun] turns away from him who passes by his town heedlessly, who is guided by him cannot go astray."[10] In the wake of Akhenaten's reforms and the restoration of a focus on Amun, Egyptian religious structures appeared less stable. Neither pharaohs nor Amun's high priests could reassure ordinary Egyptians who turned increasingly to individual- and family-based religious practice. People seeking forgiveness composed and/or performed psalms and inscribed messages on stelae, seeking absolution and the prevention of divine retribution.[11] By confessing their sins in song or engraved on stelae, worshippers removed the need for the gods to reveal their misdeeds through acts of retribution. The wisdom text, "The Instruction of Amenemope," emphasized a new set of virtues, stressing the importance of righteous behavior and honesty over material success.[12] By this time, boys were circumcised at puberty, as a rite of passage to adult status.[13]

This period was also characterized by a new emphasis on divine assistance in many aspects of life, from surviving illness, to successfully completing business ventures, to a pharaoh seeking military victories. For example, during the battle of Kodesh, in Syria, Ramesses II called on the god Amun-Ra for assistance at a moment when the battle's outcome seemed bleak: "'I found Amun came when I called him, he gave me his hand and I rejoiced. He called from behind as if nearby: 'Forward, I am with you.'"[14] As the gods became more involved in human affairs, oracles gained a new importance, revealing both the will of the gods and of the success of people's plans in many

---

[9] Jan Assmann, *Solar Religion in the New Kingdom: Re, Atum, and the Crisis of Monotheism* (London: Kegan Paul International, 1995), p. 12.

[10] Cited in Jan Assmann, *Mind of Egypt: History and Meaning in the Time of the Pharaohs* (New York: Holt, 1996), pp. 230–231.

[11] Jan Assmann (1995), cited in Emily Teeter, "Change and Continuity in Egyptian Religion in Ramesside Egypt," in *Ramesses III: The Life and Times of Egypt's Last Hero*, ed. Eric H. Cline and David O'Connor (Ann Arbor: University of Michigan Press, 2012), pp. 27, 33, 35.

[12] David, *Religion and Magic in Ancient Egypt*, p. 263.

[13] David, *Religion and Magic in Ancient Egypt*, p. 271.

[14] Cited in Eric H. Cline and David O'Connor, eds., *Thutmose III: A New Biography* (Ann Arbor: University of Michigan Press, 2006), p. 3.

areas of their lives.[15] People seeking advice often wrote out their questions for the oracles. Others relied on oracular dreams in which petitioners spent the night within the temple precincts of the god whose advice they sought. Books of dream interpretation circulated among literate Egyptians during the Ramesside Dynasty.[16] Still others sought to approach the images of the gods when they were taken out of the temples in processions during major religious festivals. David Frankfurter cites an unnamed supplicant who told a deity that he wanted a personal audience "'to tell you some affairs of mine (but) you happened to be concealed in your holy of holies and there was nobody having access to it to send into you.... See you must discard seclusion today and come out in procession in order that you may decide upon the issues."[17] Sometimes the image was seen as responding to questions by the priestly image-bearers who moved forward or backward, indicating a positive or negative response.

Excavations of the workers' and craftsmen's village of Deir el Medina provide a rare glimpse of nonelite religious life in the New Kingdom. Household shrines in artisanal villages included images of Hathor, Taweret, and Bes to protect women in childbirth, and a local deity, Meretsegar, who protected the household and its occupants. The major community shrines included a small temple dedicated to a deified King Amenhotep I, who founded the village; Ramesses II; and Ptah, patron god of craftsmen. Benches in some of these temples provided a place for people to sleep who were seeking healing or a special communication from a god in their dreams.[18]

Ramesses II's son, Khaemwaset, was the most famous of several crown princes, who failed to outlive their long-reigning father. He served as chief priest of Ptah and was involved in the sacrifice of the Apis bulls, while awaiting the opportunity to rule in his own right.[19] Sethnakhte, who was probably a grandson of Ramesses II, founded the Twentieth Dynasty. As his name reflects, he also emphasized the cult of Seth.[20]

---

[15] Van Dijk, "Amarna Period," pp. 312–313.
[16] David, *Religion and Magic in Ancient Egypt*, p. 281.
[17] David Frankfurter, *Religion in Roman Egypt: Assimilation and Resistance* (Princeton, NJ: Princeton University Press, 1998), pp. 145–147.
[18] Leonard H. Lesko, ed., *Pharaoh's Workers: The Villagers of Deir el Medina* (Ithaca, NY: Cornell University Press, 1996), pp. 90–93.
[19] Dodson, *Monarchs of the Nile*, p. 129.
[20] Dodson, *Monarchs of the Nile*, p. 146. John Taylor, "The Third Intermediate Period (1069–664 BC)," in *The Oxford History of Ancient Egypt*, ed. Ian Shaw (Oxford: Oxford University Press, 2000), pp. 396–397.

By the time Ramesses III came to power, in the early twelfth century, the Egyptian monarchy was in sharp decline. Priestly orders particularly associated with the worship of Amun, and the city of Thebes consolidated considerable wealth and power. By the end of the reign of Ramesses III, one-third of Egypt's arable land was owned by priests. Three-quarters of that land was owned directly by the Theban priests of Amun, leading them to wield enormous power in matters of state as well as in the nation's economic life.[21]

The New Kingdom ended with the fall of the Ramesside Nineteenth Dynasty. Ramesses XI was overthrown, and Aenophis, the high priest of Amun, disappeared. The New Kingdom was followed by the Third Intermediate Period, a time of the disruption of central authority and the creation of local principalities. During the Twentieth Dynasty, Amun's priests, most notably Herihor, used a combination of their religious authority and economic clout to become the "military priests" and effective rulers of Upper Egypt, centered on Thebes. Herihor's sons founded the Twenty-First Dynasty, based at the northern city of Sais, but they, too, owed deference to the Amun priests at Thebes. An oracle of Amun, at Karnak, made decisions of matters of state, in the name of Amun. [22]

In 950 BCE, Sheshonk I established the Twenty-Second Dynasty, a royal line of Libyan descent. Sheshonk dominated Lower Egypt and made the delta city of Tanis his capital. To establish their legitimacy, the Libyans emphasized their role as guardians of Ma'at, justice and order, and their relationship to the god, Horus. The oracle of Amun at Abydos blessed Sheshonk's rise from chief of the Meshweh to a king wielding full ritual and political authority.[23] Libyan communities in the western desert, including Siwa, welcomed the Egyptian deities, Isis and Amun. Gabriel Camps suggests that the oracle of Amun drew on the authority of an older god, a deity associated with the cult of the dead at Siwa.[24] Military rulers working with the priests of Amun dominated Upper Egypt and made their capital at Thebes.[25] During the Twenty-Second and Twenty-Third dynasties, the rulers of Libyan descent expanded their rule southward into Upper Egypt.

---

[21] Barbara Watterson, *The Egyptians* (Oxford: Blackwell, 1992), p. 124.
[22] Paul Johnson, *The Civilization of Ancient Egypt* (New York: Atheneum, 1978), pp. 205–208. Grimal, *History of Ancient Egypt*, p. 279. Interview, Cairo, May 25, 2000. Van De Mieroop, *History of Ancient Egypt*, pp. 265–266.
[23] Van De Mieroop, *History of Ancient Egypt*, pp. 271–272.
[24] Gabriel Camps, *Les Berbères: Mémoires et Identité* (Paris: Editions Errance, 1987), p. 159.
[25] Putnam, *Egyptology*, p. 38. Jill Kamil, *Coptic Egypt: History and Guide* (Cairo: American University in Cairo, 1990), pp. 2–3.

Egypt under Its Conquerors

In 730 BCE, Piankhy, the Nubian king, conquered Egypt and established himself as pharaoh. The Nubian Twenty-Fifth Dynasty accelerated a process of cultural exchange in which Egyptians became familiar with Nubian deities and Egyptian deities gained increased followings within Nubia. Piankhy and his successors emphasized their fidelity to Amun and the god's role in choosing them to rule both Egypt and Nubia. In this period the office of High Priest or Prophet of Amun, based at the capital of Thebes, carried significant political and military authority.[26] This office was often a steppingstone to the throne itself. The Twenty-Fifth Dynasty maintained a strict approach to Egyptian religious practice which they had already imposed in Napata.[27]

During this period, women assumed more ritual offices than they had before, especially at Thebes. Both the "god's wife of Amun" and the "chief of the musical troupe" played important roles in the Amun cult. Since the Twenty-First Dynasty, the god's wife was a royal daughter, who was expected to live a celibate life. At times her office was referred to as the Divine Hand, a reference to several creation accounts of the world being created by divine masturbation. In some cases, the god's wife became the prophet of Amun. A resurgent cult of Osiris in a triad with Isis and Horus also enjoyed increasing ritual attention.[28]

In 665 BCE, Assyrian forces, led by King Ashurbanipal, looted the Egyptian capital of Thebes and ended the Nubian Twenty-Fifth Dynasty.[29] Assyrian access to iron weaponry facilitated their conquest of Egypt. Their armies destroyed monuments and temples as their armies advanced into Upper Egypt. Their rule over Egypt was quite short, however, and their religious influence was limited. The Saite Dynasty (Twenty-Sixth), itself of Egyptianized Libyan origin, restored Egyptian independence five years later. In 664 BCE, led by Psamtik I, they drove out the Assyrians and united Upper and Lower Egypt. His daughter was adopted as "God's wife of Amun" at Thebes as a way of assuring the allegiance of the southern districts. The

---

[26] Redford, *From Slave*, pp. 75, 111.
[27] Lionel Casson, "Centuries of Decline," in *Ancient Egyptian Civilization*, ed. Brenda Stalcup (San Diego: Greenhaven Press, 2001), p. 160.
[28] Dodson, *Monarchs of the Nile*, pp. 156, 165, 175. Taylor, "Third," pp. 361–362. David, *Religion and Magic in Ancient Egypt*, p. 306.
[29] Brian Fagan, *People of the Earth: An Introduction to World Prehistory*, 8th ed. (New York: Harper/Collins, 1995), p. 394. Watterson, *Egyptians*, p. 183. Kevin Shillington, *History of Africa*, rev. ed. (New York: St. Martin's Press, 1995), p. 39.

Saites also sponsored the construction of new temples, especially for Isis.[30] During the New Kingdom, Theban priests had established an oracle of Amun at Siwa, but it was expanded under the Libyan rulers of the Twenty-Sixth Dynasty. During this period, Imhotep gained ritual prominence as a son of Ptah, a god associated with wisdom, medicine, writing, and, of course, architecture.[31]

Herodotus visited the Nile valley during the Saite period, though he never traveled south of the Nubian border town of Elephantine. He mentions that Egyptian men were circumcised, a contrast he noted with Greek opposition to such a practice.[32] He provides the earliest description of the practice of infibulation, what was initially known as pharaonic circumcision. This female initiation practice involved the removal of the clitoris and the inner labia and the sewing together of the outer labia. Only a small opening was left so that a woman could urinate or menstruate. This practice, initially restricted to the upper classes, was seen as a way of providing a stable sexual identity, given Egyptian views of a natural human hermaphroditism. According to this theory, the male aspect of the woman resided in the clitoris and the female aspect of the man resided in his foreskin. Removal of the opposite sex part reinforced the dominant sexual characteristics of the individual.[33]

Eventually, in 525 BCE, King Cambyses of Persia, a son of Cyrus the Great, conquered Egypt and ended the longest period of a resurgent, independent Egypt. Cambyses earned the enmity of priestly groups by reducing state subsidies of temples.[34] He dispatched a large military expedition into the Western Desert to capture the Siwa Oasis, home to a major oracle of Amun. In the midst of a desert storm, the expedition disappeared without a trace.[35] Some local priests encouraged Persian interest in Egyptian deities. For example, Wadjohorresnet, a priest from the delta city of Sais, encouraged Cambyses's patronage of the temple of Neith, an important deity of Lower

---

[30] William J. Murnane, "Three Kingdoms and Thirty-Four Dynasties," in *Ancient Egypt*, ed. David P. Silverman (New York: Oxford University Press, 1997), p. 38. Kamil, *Coptic Egypt*, p. 4.

[31] Toby Wilkenson, *Lives of the Ancient Egyptians* (London: Thames and Hudson, 2003), p. 35. Laszlo Torok, *Herodotus in Nubia* (Leiden: Brill, 2014), p. 82.

[32] Herodotus, *The Histories* (London: Penguin, 1972), p. 99.

[33] We find similar views of human hermaphroditism in Dogon and Mande theories of human identity. See Mary N. Wangila, *Female Circumcision: The Interplay of Religion, Culture, and Gender in Kenya* (Maryknoll, NY: Orbis Books, 2007), pp. 99–100. Marcel Griaule, *Conversations with Ogotemmeli* (London: Oxford University Press, 1970).

[34] Watterson, *Egyptians*, p. 180.

[35] B. V. Bovill, *The Golden Trade of the Moors*, 2nd ed. (Oxford: Oxford University Press, 1968), p. 9. Herodotus, *Histories*, p. 164.

Egypt.[36] Darius I built a temple dedicated to Amun, in the Kharga oasis in the Western Desert.[37] Despite such efforts, Egyptians frequently revolted against Persian rule. During this period, a new form of Egyptian language, Demotic, became dominant.[38]

Throughout the period under Persian rule, Egypt experienced its first contacts with Zoroastrianism and its emphasis on conflict dualism, the sustained opposition between forces of good (truth) and forces of evil (the lie). Zoroastrianism also introduced a very different way of looking at the human body. Some Zoroastrians emphasized the ways in which the soul was encased in the flesh, holding it back from achieving its spiritual potential. This opposition between body and soul may have affected later Egyptian receptivity to mind/body dualism in Greek thought of the late first millennium and of their preference for Monophysite Christianity, early in the Common Era.[39]

Jewish religious influences also increased during this period. Persian use of Aramaic as the language of local administration facilitated Jewish participation in administrative and commercial activity.[40] A group of Jewish soldiers settled a garrison island at Elephantine, near present-day Aswan, establishing a more permanent Jewish presence within the territories of Egypt. They found a Hebrew center of worship at Elephantine, built by an earlier group of Jewish settlers, adjacent to a temple dedicated to Khnum. They expanded it into a temple dedicated to their supreme deity whose name was described as Yahu. He was also described as having a female consort, a "queen of the sky," a belief that was not in accordance with Jewish practice in Israel.[41] There were conflicts between the Jewish agents of Persian rule, who rejected the worship of lesser deities and the people of this border area between Egypt and Nubia where the cult of Khnum was deeply entrenched. Particularly offensive to local sensibilities was the Hebrew sacrifice of sheep at the temple in an area dominated by the ram god, Khnum.[42] In 407 BCE,

---

[36] Wilkenson, *Lives*, pp. 306–307.
[37] Courtlandt Canby with Arcadia Kocybala, *A Guide to the Archaeological Sites of Israel, Egypt, and North Africa* (New York: Facts on File, 1990), p. 143.
[38] Van De Mieroop, *History of Ancient Egypt*, pp. 284, 305.
[39] Steven Quirke, *Exploring Religion in Ancient Egypt* (Chichester, UK: Wiley Blackwell, 2015), pp. 2, 17.
[40] Dorothy J. Thompson, *Memphis under the Ptolemies*, 2nd ed. (Princeton, NJ: Princeton University Press, 2012), pp. 78–79.
[41] Françoise Dunand, "Ptolemaic and Roman Egypt," in *Gods and Men in Egypt: 3000 BCE to 395 CE*, ed. F. Dunand and C. Zevi-Coche (Ithaca, NY: Cornell University Press, 2004), pp. 253, 255, 258.
[42] Observant Jews never write out the holiest name of God, which is often abbreviated in written texts. Modrzejewski, *Jews of Egypt*, pp. 22, 26, 39. Alan B. Lloyd suggests that local inhabitants prevailed upon the Persian authorities to destroy the temple. Alan B. Lloyd, "The Late Period,

rebels against Persian rule sacked the Jewish temple.[43] The priests of the Second Temple in Jerusalem were reluctant to allow the Elephantine Temple to be rebuilt once the revolt was suppressed. They claimed there could only be one temple in Jerusalem. Secular authorities in Judea, however, gave permission and the temple was rebuilt.

By the end of the fifth century BCE, Egyptians regained their independence, retaining it for almost a century. In the mid-fourth century BCE, the Persians returned to dominate Egypt until the forces of Alexander the Great occupied the region, in 332 BCE.

Ptolemaic Egypt

After the Macedonian conquest, Alexander had himself crowned as pharaoh at Memphis, performed sacrifices to Egyptian deities, and embraced aspects of Egyptian culture.[44] Alexander visited the Siwa Oasis, in the Western Desert, where he was conducted into the Amun temple's holy of holies and recognized as the divinely chosen ruler of Egypt.[45] Amun's image at this oracular temple was that of a ram, a representation of Amun more like the Nubian than the Egyptian one which characteristically presented Amun in human form.[46] Alexander followed in a tradition that dated back to the time of Herodotus, early in the fifth century, in which Greek settlers equated their gods with those of Egypt. These correspondences were often inexact, however. Thus, Zeus was equated with Amun; Dionysus with Osiris; Aphrodite with Hathor; Demeter with Isis; Hermes with Thoth; Apollo with Horus; and Typhon with Seth.[47] After the death of Alexander, the Ptolemies established a dynasty that dominated Egypt and adjacent areas of Cyrencia and Palestine for nearly

---

664–323 BC," in *Ancient Egypt: A Social History*, ed. R. G. Trigger et al. (Cambridge: Cambridge University Press, 1992), p. 317. Watterson, *Egyptians*, p. 181.

[43] Modrzejewski, *Jews of Egypt*, pp. 40–41.
[44] David O'Connor, "New Kingdom and Third Intermediate Period, 1552–664," in *Ancient Egypt: A Social History*, ed. R. G. Trigger et al. (Cambridge: Cambridge University Press, 1992)," p. 297. Alan B. Lloyd, "The Ptolemaic Period (337–30 BC)," in *The Oxford History of Ancient Egypt*, ed. Ian Shaw (Oxford: Oxford University Press, 2000), pp. 395–396.
[45] Modrzejewski, *Jews of Egypt*, pp. 54, 60. Dunand and Zivi-Coche, *Gods and Men in Egypt*, p. 242.
[46] Herodotus, *Histories*, p. 273.
[47] Mark Smith, *Following Osiris: Perspectives on the Osirian Afterlife from Four Millennia* (Oxford: Oxford University Press, 2017), p. 367. Herodotus, *Histories*, p. 87. Alan K. Bowman, *Egypt after the Pharaohs: From Alexander to the Arab Conquest, 332 BC–AD 642* (Berkeley: University of California Press, 1980), p. 124.

three centuries. Relying on a strong navy, they gained control over several Greek islands and Cyprus. Large numbers of Greek immigrants settled in the new city of Alexandria; smaller groups settled as far south as Elephantine.[48] Ptolemaic rule refocused Egypt's interests from Nubia and the Upper Nile to the Eastern Mediterranean world dominated by Greeks.

The Ptolemaic successors to Alexander the Great sought to create a fusion of Hellenistic and Egyptian religious forms. However, Alexandria was initially maintained as a Greek city, but Egyptian culture reasserted itself as Egyptians were granted permission to settle there. Ptolemy I and Ptolemy II established the great library at Alexandria and called it the Museum, or House of the Muses. Some scholars have estimated that it contained as many as 700,000 texts, which made it the largest library in the ancient world.[49] Oracles had predicted that only rulers who lived in accordance with the ways of the gods would succeed in ruling Egypt. The new rulers established a cult of Alexander himself and eventually extended this to his Ptolemaic successors in order to garner popular support.[50] Ptolemaic emperors chose to portray themselves according to the artistic representations that had previously governed the pharaohs.[51]

Among the Egyptian deities, the Ptolemies were particularly drawn to Isis and Osiris. Isis even had a shrine invoking her healing powers in Athens, within the temple of the healing god, Asclepius.[52] A hymn from the Ptolemaic period celebrated the powers of Isis: " 'I am she who woman called goddess. I ordained that women should be loved by men, brought husband and wife together, and invented marriage. I ordained that women should bear children and that children should love their parents.' "[53] Isis's cult placed new emphasis on her power to heal the sick. As Le Corsu describes her: "She manifested herself especially to the sick during sleep conveying healing treatments and curing in a symbolic fashion those who obey."[54]

---

[48] Bowman, *Egypt after the Pharaohs*, p. 29.
[49] Donald B. Redford, "Egypt and the World Beyond," in *Ancient Egypt*, ed. David P. Silverman (New York: Oxford University Press, 1997), p. 47. Lloyd, "Ptolemaic Period (332–30 BC)," p. 405.
[50] O'Connor, "New Kingdom and Third Intermediate Period," p. 195. Lloyd, "Ptolemaic Period," p. 299, 408.
[51] Canby with Kacybala, *Guide to the Archaeological Sites*, p. 119.
[52] Walter Burkart, *Ancient Mystery Cults* (Cambridge, MA: Harvard University Press, 1987), pp. 6, 15.
[53] Hymn of Isis from Zos, cited in H. Riad with the collaboration of J. Devisse, "Egypt in the Hellenistic Era," in *Ancient Civilizations of Africa, Volume II, UNESCO General History of Africa*, ed. G. Mokhtar (London: Heinemann, 1981), p. 189.
[54] Fraine Le Corsu, *Isis: Mythes et Mystères* (Paris: Société d'Edition "Les Belles Lettres," 1977), p. 53.

They also embraced the growing cult of Imhotep, emphasizing his role as a healer, seeing him as the son of Ptah, and equating him with the Greek god Asclepius. Imhotep received offerings at Ptah's temple at Memphis and at the Asklepion at Saqqara.[55] Some Greeks learned Egyptian Demotic so that they could study Egyptian medical techniques and their healing techniques.[56]

As part of a deliberate campaign to create a Hellenistic-Egyptian religious synthesis, Ptolemy I recruited an Egyptian priest, Manthon, and a Greek priest, Temetheus, to create a new cult. They created a new deity, Serapis, which united aspects of Zeus with the Egyptian deities, Osiris and Apis.[57] Serapis took Egyptian powers over agriculture and fertility, associated with Osiris, and added a healing role associated with the Greek god Asclepius. His portrayal as a bearded male in a Greek style linked him to the Greek supreme being, Zeus. As Françoise Dunand noted: "From the beginning of the third century on, miraculous cures were sought from the god in his sanctuary at Canopus, near Alexandria. Later the practice of incubation to effect a cure became one of the specialties of the temple of Serapis. The faithful would come and spend the night in the Serapeum to obtain a vision and an oracle from the god, and the oracle had to be deciphered by an interpreter of dreams after which the miracle was registered in the archives of the temple."[58] Supplicants also invoked Serapis's authority to enforce family obligations to bury the dead, even allowing relatives to ask Serapis to curse someone who failed to provide proper funerals for close kin.[59] Alexandria's Serapeum was the most well-known of the many temples of Serapis. Serapis's influence grew throughout the Eastern Mediterranean, as far north as the Black Sea and as far south as Nubia.[60]

Ptolemy II Philadelphus followed in the Egyptian tradition of marrying his sister, Arsinoe, whom he later deified. Then he established a temple for her, known as the Arsinoeia. The deified Ptolemy queen was eventually identified as the consort of Ptah.[61] The Ptolemies built new

---

[55] Wilkenson, *Lives*, p. 36. Oleg Berlev, "Bureaucrats," in *The Egyptians*, ed. Sergio Donandoni (Chicago: University of Chicago Press, 1997), p. 95.

[56] Bowman, *Egypt after the Pharaohs*, p. 124.

[57] Thompson, *Memphis under the Ptolemies*, p. 118.

[58] Dunand, "Ptolemaic and Roman Egypt," p. 218. Riad, "Egypt in the Hellenistic Era," p. 188. John B. Stanbaugh, *Sarapis under the Early Ptolemies* (Leiden: Brill, 1972), p. 2.

[59] Jane Rowlandson, ed., *Women and Society in Greek and Roman Egypt: A Sourcebook* (Cambridge: Cambridge University Press, 1987), p. 63.

[60] I visited Alexandria's Serapeum, Ptolemy's Needle, in June 2000. Bowman, *Egypt after the Pharaohs*, p. 175. Riad, "Egypt in the Hellenistic Era," p. 188.

[61] Thompson, *Memphis under the Ptolemies*, p. 218.

temples to Amun, Horus, and Isis from Karnak, to Edfu, and Philae, near Elephantine. They brought back statues of Egyptian gods that had been looted by the Persians and restored them to their original places. The Egyptian state created massive temples in northern Nubia, including Kalabsha, dedicated to the Egyptian/Nubian god Horus-Mandulis, and the older Egyptian gods, Isis and Osiris.[62] As Dorothy Thompson noted: "The progressive pharaohization of the Ptolemies, of their queens, and of their families may be seen as reinforcing the acceptance of immigrant rule among a native population." They developed a particularly close working relationship with the priests of Ptah, based at Memphis. Their relations with Amun's priests at Thebes were far tenser, given this group's historic role as a center of resistance to foreign rulers.[63] Egyptian religious influences manifested themselves even within the multiethnic city of Alexandria. Isis and Osiris had major temples within the metropolitan area. Egyptian beliefs about death and the afterlife were far more developed than those of the Greek newcomers. As Alfred Bowman noted: "Even in the catacombs of Alexandria which might have shown the highest degree of Hellenization, the traditional Egyptian deities preside over the rituals portrayed on the walls of the tomb, the ancient emblems, the sun disk, the uraeus, the feather of Ma'at are present. But the Greek influence is also there strikingly."[64]

There were limits to the Ptolemies' abilities to win over the Egyptian population, which had resisted foreign rule since the time of the Hyksos in the mid-second millennium. Under Ptolemaic rule, by the late second century BCE, a new form of apocalyptic literature began to circulate. The writers of these texts predicted that foreign rulers would be driven out and the early capitol of Memphis would lead the restoration of Egypt's independence. Although the Demotic Egyptian original text was lost, a Greek translation of what became known as *The Oracle of the Potter* remained in circulation, even into the period of Roman domination. "And then the Guardian Spirit will desert the city which they founded and will go to God-fearing Memphis.... That will be the end of our evils when Egypt shall see the foreigners fall like leaves from the branch. The city by the sea [Alexandria] will be a drying place for our fishermen's catch because

---

[62] Fagan, *Egypt*, p. 254. Bowman, *Egypt after the Pharaohs*, pp. 168–169.
[63] Thompson, *Memphis under the Ptolemies*, pp. 117–118.
[64] Bowman, *Egypt after the Pharaohs*, p. 188.

the Guardian Spirit has gone to Memphis, so that passers-by will say 'That was the all-nurturing city in which all the races of mankind live.'"[65] Alexandria, the foreign capital, which faced north toward the Eastern Mediterranean world, would be abandoned by the gods. Memphis which linked Upper and Lower Egypt along the Nile River would return to its rightful place of leadership.

During the Ptolemaic and Roman eras, builders of the new temples commissioned by imperial authorities added a small chapel adjacent to the main temple. These side chapels often focused on the worship of Isis or Hathor and their divine children. During this period, the two goddesses were often equated.[66]

Under Ptolemaic rule, Jewish communities became increasingly influential, especially at the new city of Alexandria and at the border city of Elephantine. The Hellenized Jews of Alexandria, as well as the royal court, wished to be able to read Hebrew Scriptures, so Ptolemy II commissioned the Septuagint, a Greek translation of the Hebrew Bible, prepared by seventy-two scholars of solid legal and moral authority. Egypt's Jewish community saw the translation as useful to those Jews who no longer understood Hebrew and as something that would greatly enhance their ability to proselytize. Egyptian Jews named individuals as "proselytizers" to encourage formal conversions or an intermediate stage of "God-fearers," "individuals who obeyed its basic imperatives and a minimum number of ritual observances."[67]

Cleopatra was the last Ptolemy to rule Egypt. Unlike many of her predecessors, Cleopatra (the seventh with that name) learned the Egyptian language, embraced many aspects of Egyptian religion and culture, and struggled mightily against Rome to preserve Egypt's independence. Ptolemaic rule ended with her defeat at the battle of Actium. Cleopatra committed suicide, and Egypt became a province of the Roman Empire.[68] Ancient Egyptian independence came to an end with Cleopatra's death, but the religious traditions that sustained it continued to attract adherents for centuries into the Common Era.

---

[65] Bowman, *Egypt after the Pharaohs*, p. 31.
[66] Lloyd, "Ptolemaic Period," p. 414. David Peacock, "The Roman Period (30 BC–AD 311)," in *The Oxford History of Ancient Egypt*, ed. Ian Shaw (Oxford: Oxford University Press, 2000), p. 438.
[67] Modrzejewski, *Jews of Egypt*, p. 65. Watterson, *Egyptians*, p. 213. Dunand, "Ptolemaic and Roman Egypt," p. 255.
[68] Putnam, *Egyptology*, p. 38. Peacock, "Roman Period," p. 422.

Nubia

During Egypt's New Kingdom, the pharaohs reasserted their control over northern Nubia, particularly the area from the Third to the First Cataract. They established garrison cities throughout the region, which served as administrative and religious centers of Egyptian domination. Tuthmosis III established the cult of Amun, with an important sanctuary at the sacred mountain of Gebel Barkal, even before the establishment of the Napata kingdom. Traditions developed that Amun originated in the area around Jebel Barkal, which became a major center for his worship. Whether Egyptian deities enjoyed support beyond the Nubian elites of the late second millennium remains uncertain at this time.[69]

Egypt's control over Nubia ended in the tenth century BCE, as instability in Egypt led to the division of the country into small, independent fiefdoms. Freed from Egyptian control, the Nubian kingdom of Kush expanded from al-Kurru, a center for the burial of the earliest members of Nubian royal families.[70] Laszlo Torok claims that the al-Kurru royal burials showed little evidence of Egyptian influence, which he condescendingly suggested was shown by his belief that Nubia "reverted with the withdrawal of Egyptian domination, to some sort of primitive religiosity."[71] By the ninth century BCE, it shifted its capital to Napata, an Egyptian garrison town in the Dongola Reach, a particularly rich agricultural region. Written Egyptian sources provide some detailed descriptions of Nubian religious thought and practice, though the development of Meroitic texts may provide richer materials once they have been more fully deciphered. Literacy in Meroitic language appears to have been widespread, given the prevalence of graffiti written in the language on monuments of this period. Despite extensive Egyptian influence in the Kushite kingdom, Nubian gods remained important. Descriptions of Nubia during what corresponds to the early Third Intermediate Period in Egypt (the eleventh to ninth centuries BCE) became rather scant, as Egyptian influence in the region was at a low ebb.[72]

The Nubian kingdom of Napata was established around 860 BCE and united all of Nubia from Philae/Aswan to the junction of the Blue and White

---

[69] Derek A. Welsby, *The Kingdom of Kush: The Napatan and Meroitic Empires* (Princeton, NJ: Markus Wiener, 1998), p. 72. Taylor, "Third," p. 353. Assmann, *Mind*, p. 318.

[70] Taylor, "Third," p. 353.

[71] Laszlo Torok, *The Kingdom of Kush: Handbook of the Napatan-Meroitic Civilization* (Leiden: Brill, 1997), p. 300.

[72] Torok, *Kingdom of Kush*, p. 300.

Niles. King Kashta began the process of Nubian expansion into Egypt. His son Piankhy became king, in 747 BCE, before defeating Tefnacht of Sais and conquering Memphis during the last half of the eighth century BCE. Piankhy protected the Egyptian temples and paid homage to their gods. According to a text inscribed on a granite stele at Jebel Barkal, Piankhy claimed a close linkage to Amun: "'Hear what I did, more than the ancestors. I am a king, divine emanation, living image of Amun [an aspect of the god of creation] who came forth from the womb, adorned as ruler of whom those greater than him, whose father knew and whose mother recognized, that he would rule'"[73] Kushitic kings were often portrayed wearing uraeus that included ram's horns associated with Amun. Priests sacrificed the royal horses to accompany him into the afterlife. He and his successors ruled Egypt from Napata, from 750 to 660 BCE.[74] After his Egyptian conquests, Piankhy revived the cult of Amun within Nubia. The temples he created in Nubia included images of Amun, in an ithyphallic human form, wearing the double-headed crown of Egyptian royalty topped with a sun disk.[75] His open dedication to Amun as a high god, together with his construction of new temples for him within Egypt and Nubia, helped legitimate his claim to kingship and reassured an Egyptian populace that was uneasy about foreign rulers.[76] Piankhy's brother, Shabako, extended Nubian control over the Nile delta by 696 BCE. Both found the Egyptian emphasis on the close association of kings and major deities valuable for the consolidation of their power within Egypt and in Nubia. However, their successor, Taharqa, was forced to retreat back into Nubia when Assyria invaded Egypt.[77]

Egyptian deities, such as Amun-Ra and Hathor, became popular in Napata, especially because they addressed similar concerns as older Nubian deities.[78] Moreover, some of these deities, including Amun, were specifically

---

[73] Stele at Jebel Barakal, cited in *Horizon History of Africa*, ed. Alvin Josephy (New York: McGraw Hill, 1971), p. 76.

[74] David O'Connor, *Ancient Nubia: Egypt's Rival in Africa* (Philadelphia: Museum of Archaeology and Anthropology, University of Pennsylvania, 1993), p. 71. Dietrich Wildung, *Egyptian Saints: Deification in Ancient Egypt* (New York: New York University Press, 1977), p. 11. Grimal, *History of Ancient Egypt*, p. 335.

[75] Torok, *Kingdom of Kush*, p. 302. Karl-Heinz Preise, "The Napatan Period," in *Africa in Antiquity: The Arts of Ancient Nubia and the Sudan*, ed. Sylvia Hochfield and Elizabeth Riefstahl (New York: Brooklyn Museum of Art, 1978), p. 82.

[76] Welsby, *Kingdom of Kush*, p. 74. E. A. Wallis Budge, *A History of Ethiopia, Nubia, and Abyssinia* (Oosterhuit, The Netherlands: Anthropology, [1928] 1970), pp. 30–32.

[77] Basil Davidson, *African Kingdoms* (New York: Time/Life, 1966), pp. 35–36. Robert O. Collins, *African History: Texts and Readings* (New York: Random House, 1973), p. 231. Welsby, *Kingdom of Kush*, pp. 73–74. David, *Religion and Magic in Ancient Egypt*, p. 304.

[78] Denise M. Doxsey, Rita E. Freed, and Lawrence M. Berman, *MFA Arts of Ancient Nubia* (Boston: Museum of Fine Arts, 2018), pp. 32, 33, 40, 57. Torok, *Herodotus*, p. 85.

linked to local cults. Derek Welsby described a local form of Amun, Amun of Napata, depicted as a ram-headed human carrying a staff and an *ankh*, an Egyptian symbol of life. Amun's temple at Gebel Barkal became a major focus of royal unity.[79] Nubians identified Gebel Barkal as the abode of Amun. The founder of the Kushitic state, Alara, was said to have entered into a covenant with Amun. Meroitic kings claimed that their authority came from this supreme deity. Amun made his wishes known through various types of oracles. Amun's statue could be brought out from his temple to choose the new king.[80] By the time of King Aspelta, Amun was seen as having always been associated with the kings of Kush.[81] Royal princesses often served as musicians at Amun's temples.[82] As in Egypt, priestly offices were often controlled by specific families, resulting in their control of vast estates, including large tracts of arable land and cattle.[83] Isis's temple at Philae, on the northern border of Nubia, enjoyed regular ritual attention from people from Kush, as well as the Blemmyes (Beja) of the Red Sea Hills. A major pilgrimage occurred there around the time of the winter solstice.

The worship of living kings of Napata became a central focus of popular piety. Giant statues of reigning monarchs dominated the plazas outside of major temples, giving ordinary people access to them so that they could serve as intermediaries between the people and their gods. These temples also became centers of local government.[84] Kushitic kings were buried in a tomb which resembled a pyramid, adorned on the interior with inscriptions of Egyptian funerary texts. During this period, for the first time, Kushitic kings were also mummified. Royal burials also included the preparation of small pyramids. In contrast to Egyptian funerary practices, however, Nubians emphasized libations to the dead. Like their northern neighbors, wealthy Napatans relied on *shabtis*, images made of faience, baked clay, serpentine, or other stone, which represented

---

[79] In Egyptian representations of Atum, he was usually portrayed as fully human. J. W. Yellin, "Nubian Religion," in *Ancient Nubia: Africa's Kingdoms on the Nile*, ed. Marjorie Fisher et al. (Cairo: American University at Cairo, 2012), p. 126. Edna R. Russman, "Egypt and the Kushite Dynasty XXV," in *Africa and Africans in Antiquity*, ed. Edwin Yamauchi (East Lansing: Michigan State University, 2001), p. 116.

[80] Torok, *Herodotus*, pp. 87–89.

[81] Torok, *Kingdom of Kush*, p. 219.

[82] Iris Berger, "Women in East and Southern Africa," in *Women in Sub-Saharan Africa: Restoring Women to History*, ed. Iris Berger and E. Francis White (Bloomington: Indiana University Press, 1999), p. 13.

[83] Preise, "Napatan Period," p. 83.

[84] Torok, *Kingdom of Kush*, pp. 312, 317. Peter L. Shinnie, *Meroe: A Civilization of the Sudan* (London: Thames and Hudson, 1967), p. 56.

servants, warriors, or agricultural workers who could serve the deceased in the world to come. At a nonelite level, Nubian practices dominated funerary rituals.[85]

In the fourth century BCE, Nubian rulers moved the kingdom south, near the mouth of the Atbara River, at Meroe. It offered the advantages of distance from the powerful influence of Amun's priesthood at Jebel Barkal. However, Meroe's kings and closest relations continued to be buried at the old capitol at Napata.[86] The "Island of Meroe" was a particularly rich agricultural region, combining the flood plain of the Nile with rain-fed cultivation of sorghum and millet. This new kingdom retained its important role as a supplier of gold, ivory, and captives to their northern neighbors, but it also became an important breeding ground for camels, which were becoming central to trans-Saharan trade. At its peak it controlled the Blue Nile as far south as Sennar, nearly to the Ethiopian Highlands, and the Gezira between the White Nile and the Blue Nile. It was an early center of iron smelting and blacksmithing. Unlike the Egyptians, they had sufficient access to timber to fuel iron smelters on a regular basis. Meroites developed their own form of hieroglyphs and a phonetic alphabet known as Meroitic script, most of which remains undeciphered.[87]

Meroe lessened the role of Egyptian deities and emphasized gods who were directly associated with Nubian traditions.[88] Apedemak was a warrior god who was particularly associated with Meroe. In his temples, artisans portrayed him with a bow and arrows and slaying prisoners of war or as a powerful lion. An inscription describes the god's ability to emit a "flaming breath against his enemies in this his name Great of Power who slays the rebels with (his) strength (?)."[89] In some instances, Apedemak took

---

[85] Visit to the Nubian Collection, Boston Museum of Fine Arts, November 2019. Doxsey et al., *MFA Arts of Ancient Nubia*, p. 112. Welsby, *Kingdom of Kush*, pp. 74–76. Taylor, "Third," p. 356. Kathryn Howley, "Egypt and Nubia," in *Pharaoh's Land and Beyond: Ancient Egypt and Its Neighbors*, ed. Pearce P. Creasman and Richard H. Wilkinson (New York: Oxford University Press, 2017)," p. 226. Torok, *Kingdom of Kush*, pp. 512–514.

[86] Preise, "Napatan Period," p. 77.

[87] As Graham Connah noted, Meroitic language "bears no recognizable relationship to any other language." Graham Connah, *African Civilization: An Archaeological Approach* (Cambridge: Cambridge University Press, 2016), p. 25. Davidson, *African and Magic in Ancient Egypt*, p. 37. Shillington, *History of Africa*, p. 40. O'Connor, *Ancient Nubia*, pp. 71, 77.

[88] Collins, *African*, p. 232. Stanley M. Burstein, "The Kingdom of Meroe," in *Africa and Africans in Antiquity*, ed. Edwin Yamauchi (East Lansing: Michigan State University, 2001), pp. 138, 145.

[89] Hymn to Apedemak, Inscription on the South Wall, Lion Temple at Musawwarat es Sufra. Welsby, *Kingdom of Kush*, p. 77. A. A. Haken, "The Civilization of Napata and Meroe," in *Ancient Civilizations of Africa, Volume II, UNESCO General History of Africa*, ed. G. Mokhtar (London: Heinemann, 1981), p. 318.

on the role of Osiris, appearing as the spouse of Isis and father of Horus. Unlike many of the deities of Egyptian origin, Nubia's Apedemak could be worshipped outside the temple, directly by ordinary people. Other Nubian deities increased their importance as Egyptian influences declined. These included Mash, Arensnuphis, Sebewyemeker, and Iumeker; the latter two were associated with war, hunting, and the desert. Sebewyemeker was particularly associated with the island of Meroe, the region extending south from the Atbara River to the confluence of the Blue Nile and the White Nile. Sebewyemeker was mostly seen as a water god, before ceding that role to the Egyptian god, Amun.[90]

Meroitic attitudes concerning the decline of royal power lend support to some of the ideas associated with divine kingship. As kings aged and showed signs of loss of physical stamina and intellectual acuity, they could be put to death by priests of Amun. Agatharchides, writing in the second century BCE, suggested that Ergamenes (225–220 BCE) opposed both the oracles and priests who sought to remove him and had them executed instead.[91] The sacrifice of prisoners of war to accompany kings into the afterlife appears to have been quite common in Meroe. Horses, camels, and dogs were also sacrificed.[92] Several Meroitic kings were buried in small pyramids, more symmetrical than the Egyptian ones that had been built nearly two thousand years earlier.[93] Ordinary people were buried with clothing, jewelry, food, and drink that they would need in the afterlife. Amulets protected them in their tombs and on their journeys to the land of the dead.[94]

New kings were coronated at Meroe, but they also traveled to Napata and other northern Nubian centers in order to be presented to the gods and to receive emblems of royal authority. Having completed this royal pilgrimage, they returned to Meroe for the completion of the ceremony. The mother of the king, the *kandake*, played an important role in the coronation. She prayed to Horus and Isis to grant her son a long and successful reign.[95]

---

[90] O'Connor, *Ancient Nubia*, p. 79. Yellin, "Nubian Religion," p. 134. Torok, *Kingdom of Kush*, pp. 500, 508. Haken, "Civilization of Napata and Meroe," p. 318.
[91] Welsby, *Kingdom of Kush*, p. 32. Torok, *Kingdom of Kush*, pp. 420–421. Davidson, *African Kingdoms*, p. 37.
[92] Welsby, *Kingdom of Kush*, p. 90. Connah, *African Civilization*, p. 91.
[93] Shillington, *History of Africa*, p. 43.
[94] O'Connor, *Ancient Nubia*, p. 103.
[95] Preise, "Napatan Period," p. 85.

Of the Egyptian gods worshipped in the Kingdom of Meroe, Isis was particularly prominent. Nubian pilgrims regularly paid homage to her at her temple at Philae until well into the Roman period. She had a major temple at Meroe itself and inscriptions to her were found in most major temples throughout Meroitic Kush. Although images of pharaohs nursing at the breast of Isis were common throughout Egypt, in Kush, the queen was also portrayed as being nursed by the goddess.[96] In Meroe, Amun remained the supreme deity, but Osiris, Horus, Mut, and Isis maintained an important presence.[97] In his account of his travels in Nubia, Diodorus described the Nubians (he uses the term "Ethiopians" meaning "burnt faces" in Greek) as particularly pious and the first to worship the gods of Egypt: '"They [Ethiopians] were the first to be taught to honour the gods and to hold sacrifices and festivals and other rites by which men honour the deity; and that in consequence their piety had been published abroad among all men, and it is generally held that the sacrifices practiced among the Ethiopians are those which are most pleasing to heaven."' He refers to a passage in the *Iliad* where Homer describes a Nubian ritual sacrifice and banquet.[98]

By the sixth century BCE, Meroe was smelting iron and making weapons and tools. Meroe's growth as an ironworking center depended on its access to iron itself and to trees which were essential to charcoal manufacture and the smelting process. Given the difficulties of such work and the prevalence of blacksmithing cults in most areas of the early Iron Age, one can assume that this development was accompanied by the development of blacksmithing cults, although we know little about them. The Ptolemy's efforts to create a Greco-Egyptian religious cult of Serapis manifested itself in Meroe as well. A temple of the warrior god Apedemak had a relief of Serapis, suggesting that he was venerated there.[99]

After the Roman conquest of Egypt, they made a brief attempt to occupy Nubia. However, by 24 BCE Roman forces were compelled to withdraw from Lower Nubia. Meroitic forces occupied Aswan and destroyed Roman statues at the temple complex at Philae.[100]

---

[96] Welsby, *Kingdom of Kush*, pp. 75–76. Yellin, "Nubian Religion," p. 133. Connah, *African Civilization*, p. 86.
[97] O'Connor, *Ancient Nubia*, p. 79. Herodotus, *Histories*, p. 96.
[98] Diodorus, cited in Frank M. Snowden Jr., *Blacks in Antiquity: Ethiopians in the Greco-Roman Experience* (Cambridge, MA: Harvard University Press, 1971), p. 146.
[99] Welsby, *Kingdom of Kush*, p. 182.
[100] Welsby, *Kingdom of Kush*, p. 68.

Conclusion

This chapter examined a period from the height of Egypt's power and influence in the Nineteenth Dynasty, to a series of invasions and the loss of independent rule. During the Ramesside period of the late second millennium, Egyptian leaders focused on the eradication of the memory of Akhenaten and of his religious reforms, destroying Amarna and all temples to Aten. Throughout the latter part of the New Kingdom and the Third Intermediate Period, Amun occupied the role as supreme deity. During this period, Egyptians also expanded the empire into Nubia and into the eastern Mediterranean under the divine patronage of Amun-Re. This was followed by a series of foreign dynasties: Libyans, Nubians, Assyrians, Persians, and Greeks. Each group of conquerors introduced some of their own deities and religious concepts. Most of them, once they settled in Egypt, however, were strongly influenced by Egyptian religious practices. This was especially true in regard to the sacred authority of Egypt's rulers. Although exposed to the limited incorporation of foreign deities brought by their conquerors, Egyptians remained focused on long-standing Egyptian gods and their cults. Persians and Greeks were also drawn to Egyptian views of the resurrection of the dead and to Egyptians views of the afterlife.[101] The Greeks sought to link their gods to those they encountered in Egypt, by giving them the names of what they considered their Greek equivalents.

Each conquering nation sought to rule in the name of Egyptian deities as well as their own. Libyans sought the blessing of Seth, who was associated with the desert. Beginning with Piankhy, Nubians sought the blessings of Amun to legitimate their rule. This continued under Alexander the Great, who sought the blessings of Amun's oracle at Siwa, as well as during the reign of his Ptolemaic successors. The Greek rulers of Egypt became convinced that the most effective way of controlling Egypt was to embrace Egyptian deities and styles of worship, especially the continually blurred boundary between king and gods. To bolster their authority, they created a new deity, Serapis, drawing on both Greek and Egyptian traditions, whose cult grew throughout the Hellenistic world.

Throughout this period, Nubia itself welcomed major Egyptian gods associated with fertility and wealth, while incorporating Amun in a Nubian form.

---

[101] Frank J. Yurco, "Mother and Child Imagery in Egypt and Its Influence in Christianity," in *Egypt in Africa*, ed. Theodore Celenko (Indianapolis: Indianapolis Museum of Art, 1996), p. 43.

Their Amun was in the image of a ram which became identified with Gebel Barkel, near Napata. Nubian kings became identified with Amun. They continued to worship Nubian deities and encouraged their growing influences among their Egyptian neighbors to the north. Intermarriage was common, especially in Upper Egypt. The Island of Philae, near the First Cataract, became a shared religious site for sedentary Egyptians and Nubians, and the desert nomads of the Red Sea Hills Nubians had a profound impact in Egypt during the first millennium BCE. Nubian rulers of Egypt embraced the cult of Amun, even though the Egyptians were less focused on it. They introduced Nubian gods into Egypt, while receiving deities from ancient and Hellenistic Egypt, incorporating them into a Nubian system of religious practice. Shortly after the Greek occupation of Egypt, however, the center of the Nubian kingdom was shifted south to Meroe in the better watered and wooded areas near the confluence of the Atbara and Nile Rivers. This area was able to support a burgeoning iron industry and the growth of trade to the south.

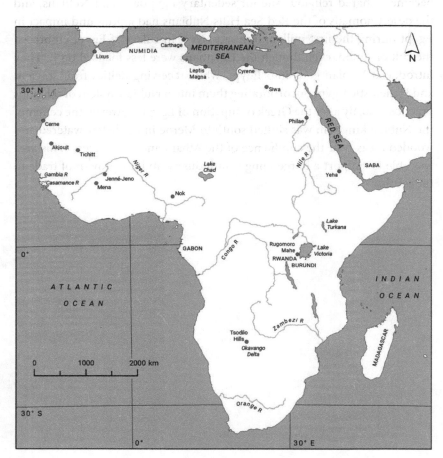

Map 6.1. Africa before the Common Era (courtesy of Jonathan Chipman).

6

Beyond the Nile Basin

African Religious History from 1300 BCE to the Dawn of the Common Era

Beyond the Nile valley, Africa experienced a time of increased trade across the Sahara and along the East African coast throughout the last millennium before the Common Era (see Map 6.1). Growing commercial interaction carried South and Southwest Asian and Mediterranean influences into the heartlands of West, Equatorial, and East Africa. Less well known, however, was that these trade routes also served as conduits for West African, Equatorial, and East African influences into adjacent regions. Phoenician expeditions led to the establishment of the Carthaginian Empire centered in present-day Tunisia and explorations along the northwest African coast. Sabean (Yemenite) cultures played an increasingly important role in the coastal areas of Eritrea and Somalia as well as the Ethiopian Highlands. South and Southeast Asian traders brought new food crops and new cultural and linguistic influences to Madagascar and southeastern Africa. This allowed coastal settlements and the interior's Interlacustrine region to increase in population. The continued migration and diversification of Bantu-speaking peoples dominated the history of Equatorial, East, and southern Africa throughout this period. Furthermore, the spread of iron technologies in West and East Africa led to significant changes in religious practices and concepts of spiritual power. Religious changes were influenced by environmental and economic changes throughout the continent.

In contrast to north and northeast Africa, most of Africa does not have an abundance of written sources or excavated archaeological sites before the Common Era. Written sources are limited to where people from the Arabian Peninsula or the Mediterranean traveled. They rarely learned local languages nor did they focus on the religious practices of the countries they traversed. Archaeological sites have been most extensively explored in areas focused on the origins of humanity or on Iron Age settlements, but to a far lesser extent than for northeast Africa. Excavated sites become more readily available for the Common Era.

Ethiopia/Eritrea

Prior to the last millennium BCE, the Ethiopian and Eritrean highlands were occupied by Cushitic-speaking farmers and herders. According to the *Kebra Nagast* (*Glory of the Kings*), said to have been written sometime between the fourth and sixth century CE, Ethiopia's first monarchs were the ancestors of the Queen of Sheba, also known as Makeda.[1] Following this Ethiopian epic, the earliest known monarch was Za Besi Angabo, who established his authority in 1370 BCE. According to the *Kebra Nagast*, Angabo promised to kill a tyrannical snake or dragon named Waynaba or Waimolo, who ruled the area, but only if the people made Angabo king. Waynaba exacted tribute of a young girl each year, suggesting that it may have been a sacrifice in a local snake cult. Angabo buried an iron object, laden with destructive power, along a road that the creature, Waimolo, would travel to get to the capitol of Axum. His iron object killed Waimolo, enabling Angabo to assume the kingship.[2] Three centuries later, Za Sebado, the grandfather of Makeda, assumed the throne, ruling from 1076 to 1026 BCE.

Makeda was the second child of Sebado's daughter, who had married the chief minister. Makeda was born in 1020 and became the ruler in 1005. She inherited a prosperous kingdom that was engaged in trade along the Red Sea corridor as far north as Egypt, Israel, and Syria.[3] According to Ethiopian and Hebrew traditions, she spent several years at King Solomon's court in Jerusalem after learning of his extraordinary wisdom and culture. Solomon convinced her to give up the worship of the sun and the moon and focus on the God of Israel. These same traditions suggest that Solomon wanted to marry her, but she felt an obligation to return home to her royal duties. Nevertheless, using his wits and the determination of someone who was constantly looking for new liaisons, Solomon was able to prevail upon the young Makeda. Solomon gave her many presents and his blessings, including a ring to be given to what he hoped would be their son. According to the *Kebra Nagast*, Solomon and Sheba went for a walk just before her departure:

---

[1] The oldest known copy of the *Kebra Nagast* dates from the fourteenth century. Both Yemenite and Ethiopian traditions claim to be the original Saba or Sheba and, hence, heirs to the Solomonic tradition. Given that most historians trace the origins of the royal tradition in and around Axum to Yemenite immigrants, it is possible that both Sabean and Ethiopian traditions are connected to the account of Solomon and Sheba. Joseph E. Harris, ed., *Pillars in Ethiopian History, The William Leo Hansberry African History Notebook*, Vol. I (Washington, DC: Howard University Press, 1974), p. 39.

[2] E. A. Wallace Budge, *A History of Ethiopia, Nubia, and Abyssinia* (Oosterhout, The Netherlands: Anthropological Publications, 1970), pp. 143–144. Stuart Munro-Hay, *Axum: An African Civilization of Late Antiquity* (Edinburgh: Edinburgh University Press, 1991), p. 12.

[3] First Kings, *The Hebrew Bible*, chapter 10.

When they had gone a certain distance he wished to speak alone with Queen Magda [Makeda]. He took from his finger a ring. He gave it to her and said: "Take this ring and keep it as a token of my love. If thou shouldst ever bear a child this ring will be the sign of recognition. If it should be a son send him to me.... While I was sleeping by thy side, I had a vision. The sun which before my eyes was shining upon Israel, moved away. It went and soared above Ethiopia. It remained there. Who knows but that thy country may be blessed because of thee. Above all keep the truth which I have brought thee. Worship God.[4]

She returned home and gave birth to a boy, Ebna Hakim, meaning "son of the wise man." According to these traditions, their son, who took on the royal name, Menelik, traveled to Jerusalem to meet his father. Solomon's knowledge of the precariousness of Middle East politics of his era led him to secretly include the Ark of the Covenant with his other gifts.[5] He also sent some Levite priests to accompany Menelik back to Ethiopia, where they served as religious advisors. When Sheba died around 955, their son, under the name Menelik I, became king of Axum.[6]

An alternative tradition suggests that the Queen of Sheba, known as Belkis, came from Yemen and that the Sabean monarchy was descended from Solomon and Sheba. Some Sabeans, however, settled in Ethiopia which would allow both for the possibility that the Queen of Sheba was from present-day Yemen and that the Ethiopian monarchs were her lineal descendants.[7]

Sabeans began to establish farming communities in the area, as early as 1000 BCE. They intermarried with the local populace known as Ona. Ona settlements on the Asmara Plain of present-day Eritrea remained outside of Sabean control throughout the period from 800 to 400 BCE. Unfortunately, we know very

---

[4] *Kebra Nagast*, cited in *Horizon History of Africa*, ed. Alvin Josephy (New York: McGraw Hill, 1971), p. 79.
[5] This tradition has been the basis for the maintenance of a church in Axum which is said to house the original Ark of the Covenant on its grounds. Only its most immediate caretakers are allowed to see it. It is seen as the justification that the Solomonic line continued in Ethiopia through the reign of King Haile Selassie. It is also the reason for the existence of a model of the Ark, the Tabot, being placed in all Ethiopian Orthodox churches. I visited this church in Axum in 2012. I was not permitted to approach the building that was said to house the Ark, though I did read the commentary on display in a museum on the church grounds.
[6] Harris, *Pillars in Ethiopian History*, pp. 39–49. Steven Kaplan, *The Beta Israel (Falasha) in Ethiopia: From Earliest Times to the Twentieth Century* (New York: New York University Press, 1992), pp. 22–23.
[7] Jack Phillips, "Punt and Aksum: Egypt and the Horn of Africa," *Journal of African History* 38 (1997), pp. 441–442.

little about their religious ideas or practices.[8] Their Southern Semitic languages changed to incorporate central Cushitic vocabulary and grammatical forms producing a new language cluster, *Ethio*-Semitic.[9] These people came with a form of writing, known as Sabean script. They prospered in the Ethiopian highlands which were similar ecologically to the highlands of southwestern Arabia. Both areas produced incense which they used in religious rituals and sold north to the densely populated areas of Egypt and the Middle East. They seem to have brought a moon cult with them to their new homes. When iron production began in Ethiopia remains unclear, but it may have been as early as the initial influx from Yemen.[10] They also brought a sophisticated knowledge of irrigation that was essential for farming in a relatively arid area.

By 600 BCE, Sabean immigrants to Ethiopia had established agricultural communities in rich valley farmlands. They may have been part of an early highland state known as D'MT or Daamat which had its own written language, initially very close to Sabean. Yeha was one of the most important settlements, located near Adowa and the Eritrean/Ethiopian border. A major temple dominated the town, a rectangular structure made of sandstone blocks. Carved images of Ibexes decorated some of the walls. Outside were three stone slabs, inscribed with Sabean script. Inside was a large stone incense burner inscribed with an image of the moon. Nearby were a series of stone columns, at a place called Grat Beal Gebri, that were strikingly similar to columns at the temple of the moon goddess at Marib, the capitol of the Sabean kingdom of Yemen.[11] Crescent-shaped altars complete with incense burners also resembled those found at temples of that moon goddess. However, pottery found at Yeha closely resembled Nubian styles, suggesting the possibilities of trade between Napata and Yeha.[12] Excavations at Matara, near Kaskase, yielded statues of female ancestors, also similar to those at

---

[8] Peter R. Schmidt, *Historical Archaeology: Representation, Social Memory, and Oral Traditions* (Lanham, MD: Altamira Press, 2006), pp. 260–261, Rodolfo Fattovich, "Aksum and the Habasha: State and Ethnicity in Ancient Northern Ethiopia and Eritrea," Working Papers in African Studies #278 (Boston: Boston University African Studies Center, 2000), p. 12.

[9] James L. Newman, *The Peopling of Africa: A Geographical Interpretation* (New Haven, CT: Yale University Press, 1995), p. 89. Rodolfo Fattovich, "The Development of Ancient States in the Northern Horn of Africa, c. 3000 BC–AD 1000: An Archaeological Outline," *Journal of World History* 22 (2010), pp. 121–122.

[10] David W. Phillipson, *Ancient Ethiopia, Aksum: Its Antecedents and Its Successors* (London: British Museum Press, 1998), pp. 41–44. Kaplan, *Beta*, p. 16. Graham Connah, *African Civilization: An Archaeological Perspective* (Cambridge: Cambridge University Press, 2016), p. 126.

[11] I visited the ruins in Yeha in July 2012. Phillipson, *Ancient Ethiopia*, pp. 44–47. Connah, *African Civilization*, p. 121.

[12] Incense burners and other ritual objects from these sites are on display at the National Museum of Ethiopia, Addis Ababa. Phillips, "Punt," p. 443. George Hatke, *Aksum and Nubia: Warfare, Commerce, and Political Fictions in Ancient Northeast Africa* (New York: New York University Press, 2013), p, 26.

Marib. Some of these may have been used to ensure fertility, but translations of the Sabean texts are quite ambiguous.[13] Matara's female figures, with large breasts and hips, gathered from grave sites in the early first millennium, underscore the importance of women's life-giving powers. Other objects found in graves from this period include incense burners, pots, and foods, which could have been used to perform rituals or were placed there for the deceased's use in entering the afterlife.[14]

Written texts for the sixth century BCE, in the Yemenite language of Sabean, mention a number of deities. Some of them corresponded with deities from the Middle East: Astar, the Sabean form of the goddess Astarte, associated with the morning star, Venus; and Almaqh, a moon god, who was her consort. The reason the Sabean moon goddess was transformed into a male deity in the Ethiopian highlands remains unclear. The Yeha temple was probably dedicated to Almaqh, who was the most widely worshipped deity in the highland region. Solar goddesses Dat Himyam (the summer sun) and Dat Ba'dari (the winter sun) had important altars dedicated to them at the Yeha temple and other early sites in northern Ethiopia.[15]

Herodotus claims that the Ethiopians practiced both male and female genital cutting. Since that time, many Ethiopians, regardless of religious affiliation, have practiced infibulation, the most radical form of female genital cutting, involving the removal of the clitoris and inner labia, and the sewing together of the outer labia, leaving only a small opening to allow for urination and menstruation.[16] Both Ethiopian Christians and Muslims continue to practice infibulation.

By the beginning of the third century BCE, the old Sabean-inspired political system had broken down. During this period, a new political power developed, centered on the town of Punt. Increasingly, historians have placed the ancient land of Punt in the Eritrean highlands and adjacent coastal areas, to the north of the Sabean settlements of northern Ethiopia. Since the Old Kingdom, Egyptians had traded with Punt for incense, ivory, and gold. In the third century, Ptolemy II established an Egyptian port, Philadelphus, at

---

[13] H. de Contenson, "Pre-Aksumite Culture," in *Ancient Civilizations of Africa, Volume II of UNESCO General History of Africa*, ed. G. Mokhtar (London: Heinemann, 1981), pp. 347–351.

[14] Visit to exhibits at the National Museum of Ethiopia, July 12, 2012.

[15] De Contenson, "Pre-Aksumite Culture," pp. 352–353. Yuri M. Kobishanov, Joseph W. Milds and Loraine T. Kapitharoff, *Axum* (University Park: Pennsylvania State University Press, 1979), p. 224. Kathryn A. Bard and Rudolfo Fattovich, "Processes of State Formation in Egypt and Ethiopia," in *Africa and Africans in Antiquity*, ed. Edwin Yamauchi (East Lansing: Michigan State University, 2001), p. 281. Connah, *African Civilization*, p. 126.

[16] Mary N. Wangila, *Female Circumcision: The Interplay of Religion, Culture, and Gender in Kenya* (Maryknoll, NY: Orbis Books, 2007), pp. 99–100.

the site of the modern Red Sea port of Adulis. It became a source of Greco-Egyptian influence in the region.[17] Although little is known about Punt's religious practices, the Egyptian god Bes, who protected the harmony of the home and facilitated the safe delivery of babies, originated in Punt. It is also reported that the people of Punt worshipped the Egyptian goddess Hathor, associated with motherhood and female sexuality.[18]

A little north of Punt, Blemmyes (Beja) cattle, sheep, and goat-herding communities settled in the Red Sea Hills. They raided adjacent communities in Nubia and in the Ethiopian highlands, while maintaining their political independence. Although little is known about their religious practices during this period, the Blemmyes engaged in regular pilgrimages to the temple of Isis at Philae, at the First Cataract of the Nile River. This suggests that Blemmye religious practices were significantly influenced by Egyptian religious traditions.

North Africa

The North African coast, west of the Nile valley, was inhabited by people known as Libyans or Berbers. The latter term came from the Greek word for "barbarian," which is said to have come from the Greek idea that the speech of barbarians sounded like the bleating of sheep.[19] Those whom the Greeks called Berbers called themselves various forms of the term "Azamagh," meaning "free-born."[20] Ancient Azamagh religion was firmly rooted in agrarian communities of cattle, sheep, and goat herders who also practiced farming where water supplies were sufficiently stable. In the Maghreb, rain rituals played a prominent role in their religious activity. Rain itself, wells, and springs all possessed a sacred quality associated with their ability to sustain life. Springs and grottoes were often associated with water spirits or other spiritual beings. North Africans in coastal Algeria particularly worshipped the god Ifru, linked to a grotto in the coastal hills near present-day Constantine.[21] As part of Azamagh funerals, ritual specialists smeared a

---

[17] Kobishanov et al., *Axum*, p. 25. De Contenson, "Pre-Aksumite Culture," p. 343. Bard and Fattovich, "Processes of State Formation," p. 281.

[18] Joyce Tyldesley, *Hatchepsut: The Female Pharaoh* (London: Viking, 1996), pp. 144, 147. Edda Bresciani, "Foreigners," in *The Egyptians*, ed. Sergio Donadoni (Chicago: University of Chicago Press, 1997), pp. 231, 239.

[19] Reuben G. Bullard, "The Berbers of the Maghreb and Ancient Carthage," in *Africa and Africans in Antiquity*, ed. Edwin Yamauchi (East Lansing: Michigan State University, 2001), pp. 183, 188.

[20] Philip C. Naylor, *North Africa: A History from Antiquity to the Present* (Austin: University of Texas Press, 2009), p. 4.

[21] Marcel Bénabou, *La Résistance africaine à la romanization* (Paris: Maspero, 1976), pp. 292–296.

red paste, made of ocher, on the deceased's body. It was a way of restoring the vitality of the deceased for the afterlife.[22]

Further east, celestial deities associated with the sun and the moon played an important role in Libyan religious practice.[23] Libyan cattle and sheep-herding communities frequently raided Egyptian farming villages but were eventually incorporated as mercenaries in the Egyptian army. Under Ramesses III, in the twelfth century, Libyans received land to settle on in the Western delta region of Lower Egypt. Early in the first millennium, two successive Libyan dynasties ruled over Egypt.[24] Libyan rulers sought out the temple of Seth because of Seth's association with the "red" desert lands on both sides of the Nile valley.

Greek immigrants established coastal settlements in Cyrencia by 631 BCE.[25] They founded the city of Cyrene, a good port with a permanent water supply, including a spring they named for Apollo. Temples of Apollo, Zeus, and Artemis dominated the community.[26] When the local population, known as Gilgimani, granted Greek settlers land to colonize, they gave them land belonging to a rival group, the Asbystai. They also kept the Greeks away from their primary ritual center at Irasa. Southwest of Cyrene, in a grotto at Slonta, worshippers performed rituals that were probably linked to fertility, given the presence of statues and rock carvings of men with erect penises and women with large breasts.[27] By the sixth century, the Cyrencian Greeks had established a monarchical system, although their kings primarily exercised a religious authority.[28] One of their primary exports was an herb used in healing rituals, known as silphium.[29] With the establishment of Ptolemaic rule in Egypt, new cults spread into Cyrencia. These included the cults of the Ptolemaic kings, older cults of Osiris and Isis, and the Greco-Egyptian cult of Serapis.[30] Egyptian amulets also became widely used.

---

[22] Bénabou, *La Résistance africaine*, p. 282.
[23] Gabriel Camps, *Les Berbères: Mémoire et Identité* (Paris: Editions Errance, 1982), p. 148.
[24] Hamid Zayed, "Egypt's Relations with the Rest of Africa," in *Ancient Civilizations of Africa, Volume II of UNESCO General History of Africa*, ed. G. Mokhtar (London: Heinemann, 1981), pp. 139–140. Herodotus, *The Histories* (London: Penguin, 1972), p. 270.
[25] Jamil M. Abun-Nasr, *A History of the Maghreb* (Cambridge: Cambridge University Press, Second Edition, 1975), p. 16.
[26] Donald White, "An Archaeological Survey of the Cyrencian and Mamanican Regions of Northeast Africa," in *Africa and Africans in Antiquity*, ed. Edwin Yamauchi (East Lansing: Michigan State University, 2001), p. 218. Courtlandt Canby with Arcadia Kocybala, *A Guide to the Archaeological Sites of Israel, Egypt, and North Africa* (New York: Facts on File, 1990).
[27] Canby and Kocybala, *Guide to the Archaeological Sites*, p. 208.
[28] R. C. C. Law, "North Africa in the Period of Phoenician and Greek Colonization, c. 800 to 325 BC," in *The Cambridge History of Africa, Volume II, From 500 BC to AD 1050*, ed. J. D. Fage (Cambridge: Cambridge University Press, 1978), pp. 107, 112.
[29] Canby and Kocybala, *Guide to the Archaeological Sites*, pp. 186, 198.
[30] Zayed, "Egypt's Relations with the Rest of Africa," p. 203. Law, "North," p. 115.

Phoenician traders began to settle along the North African coast as earlier as 1100 BCE, beginning with the port of Lixus (Larashe) along Morocco's Atlantic coast. They established the city of Carthage in 814 BCE, after fleeing increasing pressure from the Assyrians on the Phoenician city of Tyre.[31] Phoenician sources claim that a princess named Elisa fled the city after her brother, the king, executed her husband. She eventually founded Carthage. Readers of Virgil's Roman epic, the *Aeneid*, know her better as Dido.[32] The rich agricultural lands of the Mediterranean coast produced large crops of wheat and barley, often with the use of enslaved Libyans and Berbers who worked on huge estates. The Phoenicians introduced a variety of fruit trees, including olives, as well as grapes. By 500 BCE, Carthage had developed extensive farming communities which relied on slave labor brought in from West Africa. Some Berber communities paid tribute to Carthage and sold their agricultural produce within Carthaginian markets.[33]

The Carthaginians brought with them many aspects of Phoenician religion, including Melqart, a war god and patron deity of Tyre. Although Melqart had a temple at Carthage, Carthaginians regularly sent delegations to the senior shrine at Tyre, at least for the most important rituals. Melqart was seen as a god who periodically died and was resurrected through rituals performed by a priest who was known as the "awakener of the god."[34] Only men could enter his temple at Carthage. As Egyptian influence increased, Melqart became identified with Horus. With growing Hellenistic influence, he was also identified with Herakles.[35] Mourners often left protective amulets associated with Melqart in the graves of the dead. They also left utensils for food and drink in the tombs, suggesting the dead would need them in the afterlife. These amulets, placed by the head, took the form of a long-handled hatchet-razor. The Phoenician god of healing, Eshmoun, had the largest temple in Carthage.[36]

The Carthaginians also worshipped Baal and his consort, the goddess Tanit. Accompanying the rise of agriculture, Tanit gained increasing importance as a goddess of the fertility of the land.[37] She probably originated among

---

[31] Abun-Nasr, *History of the Maghreb*, pp. 13–15. Connah, *African Civilization*, p. 46. Rolfe Humphries, *The Aeneid of Virgil: A Verse Translation* (New York: Scribner's, 1951), pp. 87–88.

[32] Serge Lancel, *Carthage: A History* (Oxford: Blackwell, 1997), pp. 23–32. David Soren, "An Ancient Overview," in *Carthage: A Mosaic of Ancient Tunisia*, ed. Aiche Ben, Ahmad Ben Khadari, and David Soren (New York: The American Museum of Natural History, 1987), p. 46.

[33] Newman, *Peopling of Africa*, p. 64. A. G. Hopkins, *An Economic History of West Africa* (New York: Columbia University Press, 1973), p. 79.

[34] Dexter Hoyas, *The Carthaginians* (London: Routledge, 2010), p. 99.

[35] Lancel, *Carthage*, pp. 193, 197, 205, 209.

[36] Lancel, *Carthage*, p. 216. Sora, *Carthage*, p. 45.

[37] Abun-Nasr, *History of the Maghreb*, pp. 21–22. Michael Brett and Elizabeth Fentress, *The Berbers* (Malden, MA: Blackwell, 1997), pp. 34–35. Connah, *African Civilization*, p. 63. Hoyas, *Carthaginians*, p. 99.

the Amazagh communities near Carthage.[38] Both Baal and Tanit received sacrifices of children, sometimes offered by their parents to protect them from major harm or to advance an important initiative. Paul Mackendrick described a stele, dated between the early fourth century and the late third century BCE, which included the image of a "priest carrying in the crook of his arm an infant for sacrifice."[39] Child sacrifice had been common practice in Phoenicia prior to the settlement of Carthage.[40] Sacrificed children were cremated, and their ashes were placed in urns marked with the insignia of the god who received the offering. Thousands of these urns have been excavated from special cemeteries known as *tophet*.[41] The sacrificed children had to appear happy so '"the parents played with them so that they would die laughing for the salvation of themselves, the city, and their family."'[42] In 310 BCE, two hundred children of the nobility were sacrificed to avert an invasion by Sicilian Greeks.[43] Baal, often addressed as Baal Hammon, was equated with the Egyptian Amun, the Greek Kronos, and the Roman Jupiter. As B. H. Warmington noted, Greek observers equated Baal with Kronos rather than Zeus because Kronos was a "cruel tyrant who devoured his own children, a trait which recalled the human sacrifices at Carthage."[44] In Carthage, Amun was revered, but in his Nubian form with a ram's head.[45] Although the high priests, the Ras Kohenim, were male, both women and men served as priests of Baal Hammon and Tanit. Women also became "prophetesses" who consulted oracles of the gods on behalf of clients.[46] Carthaginians used protective amulets, as well as various kinds of love medicines that would aid the insecure in courtship. Some parents would tell their unruly children of a dangerous creature of the night who would steal away young people who were not careful.[47]

Phoenician ships explored the West African coast as far south as the Mauritanian coastal port of Cerne. Cerne became a major market center where Carthaginians purchased goods from West Africa's Sahel region,

---

[38] Soren, *Carthage*, p. 44.

[39] Paul MacKendrick, *The North African Stones Speak* (Chapel Hill: University of North Carolina Press, 1980), p. 8. Hoyas, *Carthaginians*, p. 100.

[40] The Genesis account of Abraham's willingness to sacrifice his first son and God's substitution of a ram could be interpreted as an ancient Hebrew rejection of this Canaanite and Phoenician practice.

[41] Margaret Mills, "Native North African Christian Spiritualties," in *African Spiritualties: Forms, Meanings, and Expressions*, ed. Jacob Olupona (New York: Crossroad, 2000), pp. 353–354. Soren, *Carthage*, pp. 40–41.

[42] Aline Rousselle quoted in Mills, "Native North African Christian Spiritualties," p. 355.

[43] Hoyas, *Carthaginians*, p. 101.

[44] B. H. Warmington, *Carthage*, rev. ed. (New York: Praeger, 1969), p. 148.

[45] C. G. Lapeyre and A. Pellegrin, *Carthage Punique (813–146 avant J. C.)* (Paris: Payot, 1942), pp. 134, 147.

[46] Lapeyre and Pellegrin, *Carthage Punique*, p. 143.

[47] Soren, *Carthage*, pp. 22, 46.

including gold and ivory.[48] This was the site where the alleged "silent trade" took place, where goods of the seafaring group were placed on the shore and a suitable amount of gold was placed alongside it. Carthaginians developed trans-Saharan trade routes, as well, relying on oxen and horses, chariots and carts to reach as far south as West Africa's Sahel.[49] Sadly, few written sources from Carthaginian authors have been located, despite the wide use of Punic language in written form. Many of these texts were destroyed when Rome destroyed the city. Most existing written sources reflect the perspectives of their archrivals, the Romans.[50] Still recorded names of Carthaginian provide evidence of the veneration of important deities. Thus, one finds Abdeshmoun (servant or slave of Eshmoun), Abdelmelqart (servant or slave of Melqart), Holdiat (sister of Allat, the goddess), and, the most famous Carthaginian, Hannibaal (who has Baal's favor).[51]

Carthage governed itself without royal authority, a form of aristocratic republic dominated by a council of elders.[52] The Carthaginian state supported public religious life, including the building of temples for Melqart, Baal, and Tanit.[53] Commercial and diplomatic contacts made Carthage a major place for the meeting of cultures. Egyptian amulets of Anubis, the jackal god associated with death and mummification, and Bes, the androgynous dwarf deity linked to domestic harmony, were widely used as protective talisman in Carthaginian society. Scarab amulets associated with Egypt's supreme deity, Amun, were found in many Carthaginian graves.[54] From Leptis Magnus, Carthaginian merchants purchased enslaved West Africans who had been forcibly transported across the Sahara by way of the Fezzan.[55] We do not know if these West Africans introduced their own spirit cults into the growing diversity of North African cultures, though we know they did during the Islamic period. Jewish refugees from the fall of Israel and Judah settled on the Tunisian island of Djerba by the sixth century BCE.[56]

---

[48] Kevin Shillington, *A History of Africa*, 2nd ed. (New York: St. Martin's Press, 1995), p. 45. Frank M. Snowden Jr, *Blacks in Antiquity: Ethiopians in the Greco-Roman Experience* (Cambridge, MA: Harvard University Press, 1971), p. 106. Herodotus, *Histories*, p. 270.
[49] Hopkins, *An Economic History of West*, p. 79. R. M. Wainwright, "The Carthaginian Period," in *Ancient Civilizations of Africa, Volume II of UNESCO General History of Africa*, ed. G. Mokhtar (London: Heinemann, 1981), p. 446.
[50] André N. Chouraqui, *Between East and West: A History of the Jews of North Africa* (Philadelphia: The Jewish Publication Society of America, 1968), p. 6.
[51] François Décret, *Carthage ou l'empire de la Mer* (Paris: Édition du Seuil, 1977), p. 130.
[52] Lancel, *Carthage*, p. 116.
[53] Lancel, *Carthage*, p. 193.
[54] Lapeyre and Pellegrin, *Carthage Punique*, p. 151. Lancel, *Carthage*, p. 68.
[55] Canby and Korybala, *Guide to the Archaeological Sites*, p. 203.
[56] Donald G. McNeil Jr., "Tunisian Jews at Blast Site: A Stalwart Remnant," *New York Times*, April 15, 2002.

Small Berber kingdoms dominated the coastal areas west of Carthage. The kingdom of Numidia, centered on the present-day city of Oran, was ruled by a dynasty founded by Massinissa (ruled 202–148 BCE). He lived in a palace and was described as follows: "Although he was raised in the tradition of the Berbers—indeed his mother had become a popular prophetess—he knew the refined culture of Carthage, where he perhaps spent some of his early years." Massinissa married a woman from a leading Carthaginian family. Their children received a Greek education. This suggests that coastal Berbers were strongly influenced both by Carthaginians and Greeks. His mother, a Berber prophetess, was quite influential, but it remains unclear whether she served as an oracle, diviner, or a prophetic spokesperson for a deity.[57] Carthaginian cults of Baal-Hammon and Tanit spread widely in Berber communities.[58] Numidian Berbers also used amulets to invoke the power of spirits to protect themselves against misfortune.[59] Funeral cults associated with the kings of Numidia and Mauretania remained important until after the Roman Conquest.[60]

Carthage fought three major wars against its major competitor in the central Mediterranean, the Roman Republic. In the final campaign, Romans destroyed the city. With the Roman occupation of Carthage, Tripolitania, and the Algerian littoral, some Berber communities abandoned the coastal areas and moved south to oases in the Sahara. During the third and second century BCE, these groups sought to evade the imposition of Roman cults over their religious lives, preferring the practice of Berber religious traditions. Some of their concerns are reflected in Libyan written inscriptions in the rock art of the central Sahara.[61] Carthaginian and Roman sources describe Berber communities as focused on a number of local deities that were not linked to Punic, Roman, Egyptian, or Greek pantheons. Sacred spaces included springs, grottos, unusual stones and trees, and mountain summits. They also focused on the veneration of ancestors who were seen as closely linked to the fertility of the land and to the welfare of the living. They had a sense of a divine judgement after death, focusing on the moral acts that deceased persons had performed throughout their lives.[62]

---

[57] Stuart Schaer, "The Barbary Coast," in *The Horizon History of Africa*, ed. A. M. Josephy (New York: McGraw Hill, 1971), p. 106.
[58] Mills, "Native North African Christian Spiritualties," p. 303.
[59] Schaer, "The Barbary Coast," p. 107. Camps, *Les Berbères*, p. 114.
[60] Camps, *Les Berbères*, p. 162.
[61] Paul Huard, "Introduction et diffusion du fer au Tchad," *Journal of African History* VII, no. 3 (1966), p. 384.
[62] Brett and Fentress, *Berbers*, p. 35. Bernard Rosenberger, "Des Origines aux Almoravides," in *Histoire du Maroc*, ed. Jean Brignon et al. (Casablanca: Librairie Nationale, 1967), p. 15.

In the Cyrencian oasis community of Augila, Berber communities engaged in trade along a route stretching south toward the Fezzan and Lake Chad, as well as a route that connected Tripoli and Lepcis with the western Egyptian oasis community of Siwa. The Roman commentator, Pomponius Mela, described Augila as people who "'consider the spirits of their ancestors gods, they swear by these and consult them as oracles and, having made their requests, treat the dreams of those who sleep in their tombs as responses.'"[63] Similar burial tumuli and chapels have been found in a wide area extending from the mountains of the Tunisian/Algerian borderlands to the coastal areas of Mauritania. The size of these tumuli varied with economic wealth and social status. It appears that these, too, were places where ritual specialists would sleep to receive dreams from those buried there, which would enable them to prophesy the future. Divination that relied on dreams played a central role in ancient Berber religious practices. The remains of a temple at Slonta, in the Cyrencian Mountains, emphasized the links of cults of the dead and fertility rituals. Decorations of the temple included disembodied heads as well as images of humans that stressed their procreative powers.[64]

The Sahara

By the beginning of the first millennium BCE, Saharan Berbers were working with copper and bronze and buying copper ore from mines from southern Mauritania to Niger. Along the hills of southern Mauritania, Tichitt became a center of copper smelting and long-distance trade, reaching its peak of influence in the early first millennium BCE.[65] The towns of Agades, Azelik, and Akjoujt were centers of copper smelting and the manufacture of copper and bronze tools. They traded these items to neighboring peoples in the Sahara and the Sahel.[66] Presumably, this new occupation was protected by new types of spirit cults associated with guilds of copper smiths.

[63] Herodotus described similar phenomena nearly five hundred years earlier. Herodotus, *Histories*, p. 271. Brett and Fentress, *Berbers*, p. 35.
[64] Brett and Fentress, *Berbers*, p. 35. Gabriel Camps, "Funerary Monuments with Attached Chapels from Northern Sahara," *African Archaeological Review* IV (1986), pp. 151–154. Rosenberger, "Des Origines aux Almoravides," p. 15.
[65] Kevin C. MacDonald, "A View from the South: Sub-Saharan Evidence for Contacts Between North Africa, Mauritania, and the Niger, 1000 BC–AD 700, in *Money, Trade, and Trade Routes in Pre-Islamic North Africa*, ed. Amelia Dawler and Elizabeth K. Galvin (London: British Museum Press, 2011), pp. 72–93.
[66] Shillington, *History of Africa*, p. 37. Eugenia Herbert, *Red Gold of Africa: Copper in Pre-Colonial History and Culture*, (Madison: University of Wisconsin Press, 1984). Camps, *Les Berbères*, p. 83.

No later than the early fifth century, people known as Garamantes developed an urban culture in the Fezzan region of the central Sahara, including the mountain areas of Tassili and Air. Its economic prosperity was built on its role in long-distance trade and a technologically sophisticated agricultural system, based on intensive oasis farming. They served as commercial intermediaries between West Africa's Sahel region and the Carthaginian and Greek settlements along the North African coast. To Herodotus, however, they were the ultimate barbarians, based on what he thought was the strange sound of their language. He never visited the Garamantes homeland, however. Gabriel Camps identifies the Garamantes as Berbers.[67] The Garamantes buried their dead under stone tumuli. They built altars and offering tables adjacent to the tumuli in order to perform funeral rituals and rituals to honor their ancestors.[68]

A people identified as Gétules were also Berbers, but they were nomadic herders, living between the Fezzan and the Mediterranean coast. They did not develop a centralized state, even though in other ways they closely resembled the Garamantes. Their religious system emphasized funerary cults and included altar and chapels dedicated to the ancestors.[69]

At the beginning of the first millennium, the Mena region, west of the Niger Bend, had a fairly stable water supply capable of supporting the farming of fonio and other grains. Excavations at Kolima, in the late ninth century, reveal sacrifices of small oxen and offerings of fonio grain associated with ritual sites dedicated to local deities.[70] At the end of the first millennium BCE, camel caravans carried salt from mines in the central Sahara and horses and high-value artisanal goods from the coast south to the Sahel. From the Sahel, Berber merchants carried gold, ivory, kola, and slaves north toward the Mediterranean coast. Along the southern edge of the Sahara, ancestors of the Sarrakholé in the area of Dat Tichitt began to develop towns, including Walata and Mema.[71]

---

[67] David J. Mattingly, "The Garamantes of Fazzan: An Early City State with Trans-Atlantic Connection," in *Money, Trade, and Trade Routes in Pre-Islamic North Africa*, ed. Amelia Dawler and Elizabeth Galan (London: British Museum Press, 2011), p. 49. David J. Mattingly, "The African Way of Death: Burial Rituals Beyond the Roman Empire," in *Mortuary Landscapes of North Africa*, ed. David L. Stone and Lea M. Stirling (Toronto: University of Toronto Press, 2007), pp. 138–140. Hopkins, *An Economic History of West Africa*, p. 79.
[68] Mattingly, "African Way of Death," pp. 140, 160.
[69] Camps, *Berbères*, p. 85.
[70] Shoichiro Takezawa, Mamadou Cissé, and Hirolaka Ode, "Mema in the History of West Africa," *Journal of African Studies* 66 (2005), pp. 31–46.
[71] Michael A. Gomez, *African Dominion: A New History of Empire in Early and Medieval West Africa* (Princeton, NJ: Princeton University Press, 2018), p. 31.

West Africa

In a provocative essay, Roderick McIntosh has argued that Sudanic and Sahelian oral traditions often contain perceptions of ancient environmental relationships between various ethnic groups and the ways they developed relationships to the land.[72] Agriculture expanded within West Africa's savannah grasslands and in irrigable land within the Sahel. By the fifth century BCE, farmers in the Niger, Gambia, and Casamance River valleys had domesticated a form of swamp rice known as *Oryza glaberrima*. At the same time, they developed iron smelting and worked with iron tools, which enabled them to clear mangrove swamps in coastal areas and swamp plants of the inland delta of the Niger River.[73] In the fifth century BCE, ancestors of the Sarrakholé founded what may have been the oldest town in the Sahel, Dia/Deghe. In the third century, migrant farmers from Dia Daghe established the community of Jenné-Jeno, which became an important trade center for several hundred years.[74] Towns in the Middle Niger, however, developed in unusual ways, based on clusters of town quarters associated with specific occupational groups such as blacksmiths and other skilled craftsmen and their differing relationships to the environment.[75] McIntosh provides the example of the Nono or Marka rice farmers who asked Bozo fishing communities for land to settle on and create rice paddies in the inland delta of the Niger River.[76] I presume that each of these occupational clusters had specific spirit cults associated with their crafts, which provided protection and guidance for members of the guild. Similar patterns of a southern migration of ironworking farmers developed further east in southern Niger during the same period.

By 1000 BCE, farmers from the Sudanic region began to penetrate the forests of the Upper Guinea Coast, armed with more sophisticated tools that enabled them to clear patches of forest land and practice small-scale farming operations. They grew yams and supplemented them with grains of the Sudanic region, including millet and sorghum. According to Daniel

---

[72] Roderick J. McIntosh, "The Pulse Model: Genesis and Accommodation of Specialization in the Middle Niger," *Journal of African History* 34, no. 2 (1993), p. 181.

[73] Olga Linares d'y Sapir, "Shell Middens of Lower Casamance and Problems of Diola Protohistory," *West African Journal of Archaeology* I (1971), pp. 33, 36.

[74] Brian M. Fagan, *People of the Earth: An Introduction to World Prehistory* (New York: Harper/Collins, 1995), p. 399. McIntosh, "Pulse Model," p. 187. Gomez, *African Dominion*, pp. 15–16.

[75] McIntosh, "Pulse Model," p. 190

[76] McIntosh, "Pulse Model," pp. 187–190.

F. McCall, these farmers focused their religious attention on an earth goddess cult and invoked lesser spirits associated with specific crops and economic activities such as farming and hunting.[77]

People in the central Sudanic region of present-day Burkina Faso began smelting and forging iron by the eighth century.[78] Iron smelting and blacksmithing technologies were known in central Nigeria as early as the seventh century BCE. Some of the earliest iron workers were associated with the Nok culture. The town of Taruqa with its fifteen operating iron smelters became the center of Nok blacksmithing. Nok communities included some of West Africa's earliest smelters of iron and creators of striking works of art and ritual, the Nok terra cotta. These were images both of humans and animals that may have had a religious significance. One of these images appears to be that of a priest holding a knife in one hand and an animal to be sacrificed in the other.[79] According to archaeologist Thurstan Shaw: "The terra cottas are probably best interpreted as altars belonging to a cult concerned with the fertility of the land." The shrines were often established near agricultural fields. Since Nok farmers relied on shifting agriculture, new fields required new shrines. Old shrines were left near the old fields to be washed away in the torrential rains of the wet season.[80] Some of the figurines had been found in or on top of graves, suggesting links to ancestor veneration.[81] Art historians see a clear artistic and, quite possibly, a religious influence on early Yoruba and Edo cultures associated with Ife and Benin City.[82]

Ancestors of the Igbo and other southeastern Nigerian ethnic groups adopted iron-smelting techniques by the fifth century and expanded yam cultivation in the forested savannah. Blacksmiths often assumed roles as wood sculptors, diviners, healers, buriers of the dead, surgeons, and circumcisers. This reflected their control of the transformative power of fire

---

[77] Daniel F. McCall, "Mother Earth: The Great Goddess of West Africa," in *Mother Worship: Themes and Variations*, ed. James L. Preston (Chapel Hill: The University of North Carolina Press), p. 313.

[78] "Ancient Ferrous Metallurgy Sites of Burkina Faso," UNESCO World Heritage Sites, http://whc.unesco.org.

[79] Gert Chesi and Gerhard Merzeder, eds., *The Nok Culture: Art in Nigeria 2500 Years Ago* (Munich: Prestal, 2006), p. 33.

[80] Thurstan Shaw, *Nigeria: Its Archaeology and Early History* (London: Thames and Hudson, 1978), p. 82.

[81] J. F. Jemkur, *Aspects of the Nok Culture* (Zaria: Ahmadu Bello University, 1991), p. 44.

[82] Shillington, *History of Africa*, p. 47. Wai Andah, "West Africa before the Seventh Century," in *Ancient Civilizations of Africa, Volume II of UNESCO General History of Africa*, ed. G. Mokhtar (London: Heinemann, 1981), p. 611. Newman, *Peopling of Africa*, p. 107. Martin Hall, *Farmers, Kings, and Traders: The People of Southern Africa, 200–1860* (Chicago: University of Chicago Press, 1990), p. 28

and their mastery of metal tools. Their wives often worked as potters and, in some cases, performed female excision.[83]

Fertility goddesses associated with agriculture and human fertility became important during this era.[84] Terra cotta images of men with enormous penises, almost as large as the rest of their bodies, and prominent testicles suggest a relationship to male fertility cults. That these penises are depicted as circumcised demonstrates a knowledge of the practice within Nok communities.[85] Other examples of terra cotta figures suggest physical ailments, ranging from prolapsed hemorrhoids to Bell's palsy. Bernard Fagg suggests that Nok healers used these objects in rituals, offering animal sacrifices and palm wine libations to appease the spirit causing the affliction. The spirit would leave the patient and dwell in the terra cotta object.[86] Along the coast of Lower Guinea, farmers concentrated on such tree production of kola and oil palms as well as black-eyed peas, coco-yams, and plantains.[87] Both kola and palm wine acquired important ritual uses and became central to West African concepts of hospitality.

Eastern Sudan and Upper Nile Regions

This area was connected to the Kingdom of Meroe, through trade. Merchants of Meroe purchased ivory and slaves in exchange for iron and horses in the region. In the northwestern portion of present-day Central African Republic, a cluster of stone megaliths, approximately 2,500 years old, have been found. Although most commentators on the site see it as a ritual center, they remain uncertain about its specific uses. Peter Wotzka describes the possibilities: "Interpretation of the megaliths as cult places, territorial markers, burial places for important group members." One archaeologist thought that it was a site for rites of passage, from childhood to adulthood, for girls and boys. Still others suggested that it was used for rain rituals. The multiple possibilities of the functions of these intentionally placed clusters

---

[83] Terry Childs and Eugenia Herbert, "Metallurgy and Its Consequences," in *African Archaeology*, ed. Ann B. Stahl (Malden, MA: Blackwell, 2005), p. 287.

[84] John N. Oriji, *Political Organization in Nigeria Since the Late Stone Age: A History of the Igbo People* (New York: Palgrave/Macmillan, 2011), pp. 35–36.

[85] Chesi and Merzeder, *Nok Culture*, pp. 96–97.

[86] Bernard Fagg, *Nok Terracottas* (Lagos: Ethnographies for the National Museum, 1977), pp. 31–32.

[87] Newman, *Peopling of Africa*, p. 120.

of megaliths, illustrates the difficulty of interpreting such archaeological evidence without the assistance of written or oral testimony about their use.[88]

Equatorial

Western Bantu-speaking communities moved south into the Equatorial forests of southern Cameroun and Gabon by the late second millennium These communities shared a concept of spirit heroes (*dimo*), powerful beings who had once lived on earth. One of the terms used by these groups linked these spirits to the idea of a supreme being, Modimo, may have initially referred to a particularly powerful ancestor. This term *dimo* came from an early Western Bantu term meaning "to get lost" or 'to become exhausted,' referring to ancestors whose memories had been lost until they manifested a power after they died, which then became a part of an oral tradition.[89] Not surprisingly, they also shared a term meaning "to cure" or "to divine" the nature and identity of witches and witches' attacks. They also used related terms for witches themselves.[90] As they moved south and east within the Equatorial region, they carried with them detailed knowledge of the manufacture of palm oil, palm wine, and related products, as well as the many other uses of West Africa's oil palm trees. Palm oil offered an extraordinarily rich source of food oil, whereas palm wine played an important role in social interactions and religious rituals, where it served as a sacramental beverage.[91]

Around 950 BCE, eastern Bantu languages diverged between a northern Zairean cluster and a southern group which included KiKongo and most of the languages of present-day Gabon.[92] Among the southwestern Bantu-speaking groups near the mouth of the Congo River, the term *simbi* took on a different meaning than it had in East Africa. Along the coast of Congo/northern Angola, *simbi* were linked to the Batwa as the first inhabitants, "the owners of the earth," and female fertility.[93] They were linked to specific

---

[88] Peter Wotzka, "Central African Neolithics," in *Encyclopedia of Prehistory*, Vol. I (New York: Kluwer Academic, 2007), p. 52.
[89] Jan Vansina, *Paths in the Rainforest: Toward a History of Political Tradition in Equatorial Africa* (Madison: University of Wisconsin Press, 1990), pp. 95, 297.
[90] Vansina, *Paths in the Rainforest*, pp. 21, 97.
[91] Jonathan E. Robins, *Oil Palm: A Global History* (Chapel Hill: University of North Carolina Press, 2021), p. 15.
[92] Vansina, *Paths in the Rainforest*, p. 52.
[93] Catherine Symone Fourshey, Rhonda M. Gonzalez, and Christine Saidi, *Bantu Africa: 3500 BCE to Present* (New York: Oxford University Press, 2017), p. 49.

territories within which they could exercise particular forms of spiritual power.[94] As Batwa faced pressure to enter into the newcomers' farming communities, they retained their status as first inhabitants, as "owners of the land." Often politically marginalized, they retained powerful roles linked to the fertility of the land and the initiation of chiefs.[95]

The proto-Njila linguistic group diverged from other Bantu languages in coastal areas of Equatorial Africa during the first century BCE. The proto-Njila languages shared common root words for "witchcraft" and "to bewitch," suggesting that some kind of malevolent behaviors had been considered important to these linguistic communities. They also shared the term *ganga*, which refers to a religious specialist and the medicines and amulets that they produced.[96]

East Africa

Until the beginning of the first millennium, the coastal areas of East Africa were dominated by hunter/fisher/gatherer communities which had developed a short-distance maritime trading tradition. Cushitic-speaking groups—ancestors of the Oromo and Somali who herded livestock—were probably the first to build small, permanent villages.[97] With time this local Indian Ocean trade expanded, linking coastal areas to the older trade networks of the Red Sea and the Arabian Sea, as far east as the Persian Gulf and western India.[98] Greek, Egyptian, and Arab traders referred to this region as Azania.

During the first millennium BCE, East Africa was dominated by the increasing interaction of eastern Savanna Bantu-speaking immigrants with earlier Cushitic-speaking communities. The new groups in the Rift valley continued to grow yams, but they expanded their agricultural

---

[94] Vansina, *Paths in the Rainforest*, p. 97. Kairn A. Klieman, "*The Pygmies Were Our Compass*": *Bantu and Batwa in the History of West Central Africa, Early Times to c. 1900* (Portsmouth, NH: Heinemann, 2003), pp. 145–146.

[95] Vansina, *Paths in the Rainforest*, p. 65.

[96] Jan Vansina, *How Societies Are Born: West Central Africa before 1600* (Charlottesville: University of Virginia Press, 2004), p. 51.

[97] John Middleton, *The World of the Swahili: An African Civilization* (New Haven, CT: Yale University Press, 1992), p. 12.

[98] Thomas N. Huffman, *Handbook to the Iron Age: The Archaeology of Pre-Colonial Farming Societies in Southern Africa* (Scottsville, South Africa: University of Kwa-Zulu/Natal Press, 2017), p. 75. Colin Breen and Paul J. Lane, "Archaeological Approaches to East Africa's Changing Seascapes," *Journal of World Archaeology* 35 (2003), pp. 473–475.

activities to incorporate grassland crops such as sorghum and millet and added the herding of sheep and cattle.[99] Among the Mashariki (Eastern Bantu) speakers, including the proto-Sabi, male elders initiated boys in a circumcision ritual that involved a prolonged ritual seclusion during which they were taught about their religious and social responsibilities as men. During this period, they developed lifelong bonds with their fellow initiates that were forged during their shared ordeal. Age sets formed by boys initiated together were recognized as important religious and social groups in these societies.[100]

Girls received two types of initiation, both at the individual level. At menarche, women taught girls what they needed to know about their transition to adulthood, a ritual known as *nyamkungwi* in proto-Mashariki. A second stage of female initiation occurred in many of these communities during the latter stages of pregnancy or in the maternity house during labor and shortly after birth. Cushitic influences led to the introduction of clitoridectomy as a part of initiation rituals among some Bantu-speaking communities.[101] A new term for the supreme being which, Christine Saidi claims, stressed her feminine aspects, became common during this period.[102] During this period, Kaskazi speakers revered a new type of spirit described as a spirit of the dead or of young women going through female initiation. Early in the first millennium, some Kaskazi speakers embraced a new term for the supreme being, Mulungu, who was seen as the source of life. The new term emphasized the deity's role in providing order to the world and serving as an example of proper human behavior. By the fourth century BCE, some Kaskazi speakers, under Southern Cushitic influence, began to associate Mulungu with the sun.[103]

By the ninth century BCE, peoples practicing funeral cremation settled around Lake Nakuru and the Njoro River of western Kenya. Mourners

---

[99] Christine Saidi, *Women's Authority and Society in Early East-Central Africa* (Rochester: University of Rochester Press, 2010), p. 61.

[100] Christopher Ehret, *An African Classical Age: Eastern and Southern Africa in World History, 1000 BC to 400 AD* (Charlottesville: University Press of Virginia, 1998), p. 155. Philip Curtin, Steven Feierman, Leonard Thompson, and Jan Vansina, *African History* (London: Longman, 1978), p. 123.

[101] Iris Berger, "Women in East and Southern Africa," in *Women in Sub-Saharan Africa: Restoring Women's History*, ed. Iris Berger and E. Frances White (Bloomington: Indiana University Press, 1999), p. 16.

[102] Saidi, *Women*, pp. 62–64.

[103] Fourshey et al., *Bantu Africa*, p. 49, 55. Rhonda Gonzalez, *Societies, Religion, and History: Central East Tanzanians and the World They Created, c. 200 BCE to 1800 CE* (New York: Columbia University Press, 2009), p. 92. Ehret, *African Classical*, pp. 166–157.

left tools, beads, and jewelry covered in ocher.[104] During the third century BCE, what is known as the Highland Savanna culture spread throughout the grasslands of northern Tanzania and southern Kenya. Excavations at Ngorongoro Crater reveal internments in rocky crevices on hillsides with grave goods, including palettes used to grind ocher, obsidian blades, and stone bowls. In many areas, ocher was linked to blood and fertility, and figured prominently in mortuary and other rituals.[105]

Southern Nilotics moved into northwestern Kenya by the beginning of the first millennium. By 800 BCE, after prolonged interaction with Southern Cushitic-speaking communities around Lake Turkana, the new Southern Nilotic group increasingly began to identify divinity with the sun. They also incorporated ideas about dangerous and unpredictable lesser spirits. Linguistic analysis suggests these changes were a result of Southern Cushitic influences.[106] By 300 BCE, they had influenced Southern Kaskazi speakers, around Lake Victoria, to adopt this solar deity as the supreme being.[107]

During this period, Southern Nilotes moved southwestward from near Lake Turkana to the highland area east of Lake Victoria. They entered the region with a working knowledge of iron smelting and forging, grain cultivation, and the herding of cattle and goats.[108] Groups identified with the Elmenteitan culture cremated their dead but also left grave goods—palettes, knives, and bowls—that were strikingly similar to those of the Highland Savanna Groups.[109] Their descendants may have included the Kalenjin of western Kenya. Those who remained in the Lake Turkana area built what was considered to be the oldest ethnoarchaeological megalith complex in Africa. This was associated with the Turkana Turwell culture. Most likely, this complex had religious significance, given its focus on the movement of the sun and the planets. Its precise meaning, however, remains unclear.[110] Archaeologists claim that these communities, around 350 BCE, erected stone

---

[104] David Leakey, *Excavations at the Njoro River Cave: Stone Age Cremated Burials in Kenya Colony* (Oxford: Clarendon, 1956), pp. 2, 74.
[105] Stanley H. Ambrose, "Archaeological and Linguistic Reconstruction of History in East Africa," in *The Archaeological and Linguistic Reconstruction of African History*, ed. Christopher Ehret and Merrick Posnansky (Berkeley: University of California, 1982). Ehret, *African Classical*, p. 164.
[106] Christopher Ehret, *History and the Testimony of Language* (Berkeley: University of California Press, 2011), pp. 31–32.
[107] Fourshey et al., *Bantu Africa*, pp. 55, 87.
[108] Shillington, *History of Africa*, p. 119.
[109] Ambrose, "Archaeological and Linguistic Reconstruction," pp. 127–128, 141.
[110] Ambrose, "Archaeological and Linguistic Reconstruction," pp. 121, 126. Peter R. Schmidt, *Iron Technology in East Africa: Symbolism, Science, and Archaeology* (Bloomington: Indiana University Press, 1997), pp. 14, 239–241.

monuments above the graves of their male dead, but not females. These stones were marked with specific animal images, possibly linked to a social organization based on clans. Turkana oral traditions suggest these stone pillars were punishment for ancient diners who mocked a malevolent spirit.[111]

In the Interlacustrine region, evidence of iron-smelting technologies in Rwanda and Burundi suggests the existence of blacksmithing craftsmen as early as the late second millennium BCE. Archaeological research reveals the role of herbal bundles to protect smelters against attacks by witches. The smelters themselves were often built on the site of old termite hills. The linkage of Great Lakes Bantu term for "matrilineage" and "termite hill" may help explain the linkage of smelting furnaces to female power.[112] As the smelter was being constructed, smelters dug a small hole where herbal medicines, iron slag, and charcoal were buried—all designed to ensure the efficacy of the smelting process from attacks by witches or other malevolent powers.[113]

Eastern Bantu or Mashariki speakers, including the ancestors of the present-day Buhaya, were smelting iron by the middle of the first millennium. In Buhaya, archaeologists have found evidence for a spirit shrine, Kaiija (Place of the Iron Forge), linked to blacksmiths at Rugomora Mahe, the ruins of King Rugomora's palace, east of Lake Victoria. The shrine and smelting precede the royal palace by over a millennium. Peter Schmidt describes it as a "ritual center for economically and politically powerful iron workers," which can be dated back to the middle of the first millennium BCE.[114] The shrine itself was linked to a large tree, near the west bank of Lake Victoria. Oral traditions confirm the ritual link to blacksmithing work in close proximity to the shrine. Both Peter Schmidt and Felix Chami attribute the rise of population density in the Great Lakes Region, degradation of local forests, and a series of political and religious changes to this concentration of iron smelting.[115] Iris Berger

---

[111] Lawrence H. Robbins, "Lake Turkana Archaeology: The Holocene," *Ethnohistory* 53, no. 1 (2006), pp. 84–87.
[112] Fourshey et al., *Bantu Africa*, p. 62.
[113] Schmidt, *Iron*, pp. 238, 240–241, 244–245.
[114] This shrine was eventually associated with Abacwezi spirits around 1000 CE and with the Bahaya King Rugomora in the seventeenth century. Peter R. Schmidt, *Community-Based Heritage in Africa: Unveiling Local Research and Development Initiatives* (New York: Routledge, 2017), pp. 15–16. Newman, *Peopling of Africa*, p. 160. Schmidt, *Iron*, p. 14. Schmidt, *Historical Archaeology*, p. 136.
[115] Peter R. Schmidt, "Archaeological Views on a History of Landscape Change in East Africa," *Journal of African History* 38, no. 3 (1997), p. 395. Schmidt, "Archaeology of Listening: Listening and Waiting: Excavating Later." Eugenia W. Herbert, *Iron, Gender, and Power: Rituals of Transformation in African Societies* (Bloomington: Indiana University Press, 1993), pp. 145–148. Felix Chami, *The Tanzanian Coast in the First Millennium AD* (Uppsala: Studies in African Archaeology, 1994), p. 43.

claims that the environmental disruptions and growing scarcity of natural resources also contributed to a greater emphasis on patrilineal descent and patriarchal authority.[116]

Schmidt argues that the ancestors of the Buhaya have sustained a high degree of cultural continuity and settlement patterns for over two millennia.[117] Rulers in this area trace the origins of their power back to lineages descending from chiefs of ironworking clans in the early Iron Age. Spirit mediums, the *kumandwa*, most of whom were women, associated with these deities and/or ancestors, also trace the origins of their authority to these early Iron Age chieftaincies and blacksmith clans, several centuries before the Common Era.[118] David Schoenbrun claims that the term *kumandwa* was derived from the Great Lakes Bantu word for one who was "seized in the head by a spirit and consecrated to it."[119] The spirit medium's relationship to these spirits, known as Bacwezi, remains elusive, though the Nyango clan of the Kyawintwara Kingdom claims to be their direct descendants.[120] Whether they were an actual dynasty, cultural heroes/rulers, or regarded entirely as divine is unclear. How long these spirits, such as Mugashi, the Buhaya god of rain, thunder, and lightning; or Irun, the god of iron smelting, have been worshipped is also unclear.[121] Offerings of banana seeds and cowry shells at shrines of Mugashi suggest that his cult gained importance after the rise of the Indian Ocean trade in the first millennium. Accompanying the smelting process were an elaborate set of restrictions on sexual relations by smelters with their spouses, the prohibition of menstruating women from being present at the smelt, and, in some cases, the prohibition of women altogether. Schmidt clearly demonstrates the smelting process's close relationship to issues of fertility and reproduction.[122] Slag by-products of the smelting process were used as protective amulets in many Interlacustrine communities. Smelters went to great lengths to protect their materials from destructive use from malevolent individuals such as witches.[123]

Linguistic evidence suggests that these Bantu-speaking ironworking groups learned to work with iron from central Sudanic speakers who practiced

---

[116] Berger, "Women," p. 15.
[117] Schmidt, *Historical Archaeology*, pp. 7, 62. Iris Berger, *Religion and Resistance: East African Kingdoms in the Precolonial Period* (Tervuren: Musée Royale de l'Afrique Centrale, 1981), p. 16.
[118] Schmidt, *Iron*, p. 30. Schmidt, *Historical Archaeology*, pp. 11–119. Berger, *Religion*, pp. 36, 45, 89.
[119] David Schoenbrun, *A Green Place, A Good Place: Agrarian Change, Gender, and Social Identity in the Great Lakes Region to the Fifteenth Century* (Portsmouth, NH: Heinemann, 1998), p. 112.
[120] Schmidt, *Iron*, p. 74.
[121] John Roscoe, *The Bakitara or Banyoro* (Cambridge: Cambridge University Press, 1923), p. 21.
[122] Schmidt, *Iron*, pp. 60. Schmidt, *Historical Archaeology*, p. 40. Berger, *Religion*, pp. 29, 32–33, 94.
[123] Schmidt, *Iron*, p. 197.

a mixed pastoral and farm economy.[124] These are the earliest known blacksmith shrines in East Africa. It appears that the blacksmiths associated with the ancestors of the Buhaya enjoyed an enormous prestige based on their ability to control fire and to transform iron into tools and weapons. Their religious importance and the sense of spiritual power associated with their craft were comparable to their economic importance in these Interlacustrine societies.[125]

Southern Africa

To the north and west of Lake Malawi, people called Kafula and Batwa dominated the area before the arrival of Bantu-speaking groups. They maintained a series of rain shrines in the hills west of the Lake.[126] Proto-Sabi speakers moved into the Copperbelt region of present-day Zambia early in the first millennium BCE. Their rituals included elaborate girls' puberty rituals held at menarche and a second ritual in the seclusion of a birthing house. Male initiation continued in the Copperbelt communities, often including a lengthy period of seclusion during which the social ties between members of an age set developed as lifelong bonds. During the first millennium, some of the hunter-gatherers of South Africa acquired cattle and goats from the newly arriving Bantu-speaking communities. This led to a division of Khoisan groups, between those who retained their focus on hunting and gathering and those who added animal husbandry to their means of sustenance. These divisions would have been reflected in the types of ritual activities practiced by each group. The various caves found in the Tsodilo Hills, northwest of the Okavango delta, which had been covered in rock art, may have been used as ritual sites by early Iron Ages groups that settled in the area.[127]

Many of the Bantu-speaking groups who settled in the eastern portion of southern Africa spoke languages from the Kusi cluster of languages that developed out of Mashariki languages of East Africa during the last millennium before the Common Era.[128]

---

[124] Schmidt, "Archaeological," p. 396. SAA, digitaleditions.sheridan.com//publication/?t = 440506&article-id2886.

[125] For comparative perspectives on the religious, economic, and social importance of blacksmiths, see Patrick R. McNaughton, *The Mande Blacksmiths: Knowledge, Power, and Art of West Africa* (Bloomington: Indiana University Press, 1988). Herbert, *Iron, Gender, and Power*.

[126] Matthew Schoffeleers, *Rivers of Blood: The Genesis of a Martyr Cult: In Southern Malawi, c. A. D 1600* (Madison: University of Wisconsin Press, 1992), p. 26.

[127] Sheila Coulson, Sigrid Staurset, and Nick Walter, "Ritualized Behaviour in the Middle Stone Age: Evidence from Rhino Cave, Tsodilo Hills, Botswana," *PaleoArchaeology* (2011), p. 23.

[128] Gonzalez, *Societies, Religion, and History*, p. 47.

Conclusion

This chapter illustrates the disparity of evidence available in regard to the different regions of Africa and their religious history. The Ethiopian highlands and the North African littoral benefit from significant numbers of written sources in Sabean, Ge'ez, Egyptian, Punic, and Greek languages. Relatively rich archaeological sources also provide evidence of a religious history in these areas as well as the Saharan region. Sub-Saharan Africa suffers from a lack of written sources and archaeological investigations. Linguistic analysis offers scholars the deepest insights into the religious ideas and practices for the first millennial period, but primarily in the areas most affected by the Bantu migrations: Equatorial, East, and southern Africa. The religious history of West Africa during this period remains particularly opaque.

Much of what we know at this stage of historical inquiry reflects the migration of Middle Eastern peoples into the northern and northeastern areas of Africa. There is strong evidence of Yemenite/Sabean religious influence in the development of the Ethiopian highlands, in the area of Yeha and the early kingdom of D'mt. Traditions from southwestern Arabia and/or Ethiopia provide a link of early regional kingdoms to the influence of the Solomonic kingdom of Israel, through the Queen of Sheba. Similarly, the Phoenician settlement of Carthage provides insights into the transplantation of a Semitic religion into North Africa and its interaction with Berber religious traditions already established in the region. Nubian and Puntian religious cults became influential in Egypt, however.

In East and West Africa, the beginnings of iron smelting and blacksmithing gave rise to ironworking religious cults, linked to the fertility of the land and the marginalization of women from this technology. The increasing emphasis on agriculture may have contributed to a growing emphasis on earth goddesses, particularly in West Africa. Linguistic studies provide evidence of a widening range of concepts of the supreme being and of lesser spirits. They also provide indications of the growing importance of rites of passage for both boys and girls and the growing social significance of age sets as a source of cross-cutting allegiances that helped build communities beyond the lineages. These age sets, associated with rites of passage from childhood to adulthood, created institutions that supported forms of social cohesion beyond the limits of kinship. This opened the way for new types of political organization based on shared territories and interests rather than clans and lineages.

7

Egyptian Religious Traditions under Foreign Domination

From the Roman Conquest to the Arab Conquest

With Egypt's defeat at the Battle of Actium and Cleopatra's suicide, Egypt began nearly two millennia of foreign domination. Roman rule differed from that of the Ptolemies because Egypt was reduced to the position of a province within an empire. Its Roman rulers never made Egypt the center of their realm. Roman governors did not embrace Egyptian religion and culture to the extent that the Ptolemies had done. The removal of state support of Egyptian temple cults and the loss of lands leased out to peasant farmers who worked for the priestly classes deprived temples of economic power. Still, Egyptian religion continued to thrive, often at a more popular level, and in sustained interaction with Greek, Roman, and other Mediterranean religious movements of the early Common Era. During the first two centuries of the Roman occupation, Egyptian religious traditions retained their dominant position and their vitality as they continued to influence the religious practices of both their Nubian and Eastern Mediterranean neighbors. In these first two centuries, Judaism was a stronger foreign influence in Egypt than its newer offspring, Christianity. Jewish influence, particularly in the increasingly turbulent atmosphere of Alexandria, resulted in a xenophobic backlash, where frustration with foreign rule was manifested against another marginalized group.

During the third and fourth centuries, Christianity became increasingly influential. By the middle of the fourth century, it had become the dominant religion in Egypt's many urban areas and an increasing presence in the countryside. Alexandria became a center of Christian theological studies and debates. It also became centrally involved in many of the religious schisms that threatened the unity of the Christian tradition. Egyptian Christians were particularly drawn to what became known as the Monophysite tradition, an understanding of the nature of Christ that rejected the idea that he had a separate and distinctly human nature. Other Egyptians embraced the teachings of an Alexandrine priest named Arius who rejected the divinity of Christ in favor of the idea that he was a perfect, but not divine messenger of God, who had been created by God the Father in historical time. As these divergent traditions took root in the rich spiritual soils of Egypt, church leaders increasingly turned their attention against the persistence of Egyptian and Greek religious practices. By the fifth, sixth, and early seventh centuries, when Egypt passed to Byzantine control, Christianity had gained a clear dominance. Many areas of Egyptian religion persisted, however, from the continued veneration of Egyptian deities to the heavy reliance on amulets, spiritual healing, and dream revelations to deal with the vicissitudes of daily life. During this period, Christian leaders, such as Bishops Shenoute and Theophilus, denounced the continuation of "pagan" practices and incited mobs to destroy Egyptian temples and Hellenistic centers of learning and ritual. These included the Great Library and the Serapeum of Alexandria. It was Egyptian Christians who first developed the traditions of Christian hermits, most notably Saint Antony of the Desert, and the monastic orders that became increasingly influential as Christianity entered its medieval phase.

This chapter focuses on the sustained interaction among Egyptian religious traditions, already influenced by Greek and Nubian religious practices; with various religious traditions developing in the Eastern Mediterranean world, including Rabbinic Judaism, early Christianity, and Zoroastrian-influenced religious movements. Although Christianity gradually deepened its influence in the religious life of Roman Egypt, older traditions persisted through most of the period up to the Arab Conquest in the seventh century. These other traditions influenced the newly hegemonic Christianity in a variety of ways, ranging from creating a receptivity to forms of Christianity less influential in other areas of the Christian world, to the persistence of popular religious practices within a Christian-dominated culture.

Given the enormous extant literature on early Church history, on doctrinal schisms, and on Patristics, this chapter will focus primarily on the sustained interaction between Egyptian religious traditions and the growing ascendency of Christianity. It will focus on issues of conversion and the continued religious influence of highly complex Egyptian/Hellenistic religious traditions that dominated the religious life of early Roman Egypt. Rather than offer yet another interpretation of the writings of Clement of Alexandria, Arius, Athanasius, or Origen, it will explore the reasons that

Egypt became a center of so many different interpretations and practices of early Christianity, looking for explanations in the rich religious history of Egypt itself, as Egyptians sought to preserve their identity during this long period of foreign domination.

The Early Roman Period

The Romans were less successful than previous conquerors in legitimating their rule through the support of religious authorities. Even though they provided state support for the completion of temples at places such as Dendera, Edfu, Esna, and Philae, begun by the Ptolemies, and constructed new temples throughout their Egyptian domains, the Romans did not rule from Egypt itself.[1] Nor did they seek the blessings of Amun or other deities for their governance or their presence in the land of Egypt (see Figure 7.1). As part of their imperial rule, they constructed temples dedicated to the Roman emperor, such as the temple of Augustus at Philae that was built in 15 BCE.[2] Imperial Rome imposed heavy taxes which fell primarily on the lower classes. When people resisted, Roman officials held the unmummified bodies of the recent dead as hostages for the unpaid taxes, having learned the importance that Egyptians placed on proper burial of their dead. They confiscated lands owned by the temples, which had supported the religious work of priests and made them powerful political and economic players in Egyptian society. Instead, Roman authorities rented out these lands as an imperial revenue source. They required that all Egyptian temple priests report to a Roman-appointed High Priest, based in Alexandria.[3] Roman rulers also tried to control Egyptian consultation of oracles, especially when they discovered that some of the consultations had political dimensions.[4] Most of these initiatives were bitterly resented by Egyptians of all economic classes.[5]

---

[1] Roger S. Bagnall, *Egypt in Late Antiquity* (Princeton, NJ: Princeton University Press, 1993), p. 262.

[2] Françoise Dunand and Christine Zivi-Coche, *God and Men in Egypt: 3000 BCE to 395 CE* (Ithaca, NY: Cornell University Press, 2004), p. 256.

[3] Jill Kamil, *Coptic Egypt: History and Guide*, rev. ed. (Cairo: American University in Cairo Press, 1990), pp. 14–16. Bagnall, *Egypt in Late Antiquity*, p. 262. Lois M. Farag, "The Early Church Period (42–642): The Spread and Defense of the Christian Faith under Roman Rule," in *The Coptic Christian Heritage: History, Faith, and Culture*, ed. Lois M. Farag (London: Routledge, 2014), pp. 23–24.

[4] David Frankfurter, *Religion in Roman Egypt: Assimilation and Resistance* (Princeton, NJ: Princeton University Press, 1995), p. 26.

[5] S. Donadoni, "Egypt under Roman Domination," in *Ancient Civilizations of Africa, Volume II of UNESCO General History of Africa*, ed. G. Mokhtar (London: Heinemann, 1981), pp. 212–213.

188   ANCIENT AFRICAN RELIGIONS

Figure 7.1. Falcon image associated with the god Horus, Edfu, Egypt (photo by Robert M. Baum).

A series of revolts against Roman authorities in 155 and 192 were organized by traditional priests.[6]

Farming communities in the Nile Valley and in the Western desert oases continued to build new temples for the goddess Isis. She became increasingly associated with the fertility of the land, sexuality, and the joys of drinking wine.[7] Her influence spread throughout the Roman Empire as a goddess of marriage and maternal fertility, linked to a cluster of Egyptian mystery cults with Osiris and Serapis. Isis was also linked to the Hellenistic goddess, Demeter, and was invoked to ensure the Nile floods, something that had previously been associated with the Egyptian god, Hapy.[8] As Christianity became influential, Egyptian Christians associated the mother goddess Isis and the Virgin Mary, introducing similar forms of representation and ritual supplication as a focus of the new religion.[9]

---

[6] Farag, "Early," p. 24.
[7] Frankfurter, *Religion*, p. 38.
[8] Jane Rowlandson, ed., *Women and Society in Greek and Roman Egypt: A Sourcebook* (Cambridge: Cambridge University Press, 1987), p. 62.
[9] Frank J. Yurco, "Mother and Child Imagery in Egypt and Its Influence on Christianity," in *Egypt in Africa*, ed. Theodore Celenko (Indianapolis: Indianapolis Museum of Art, 1996), p. 44.

In the early 170s, during the reign of the philosopher emperor Marcus Aurelius, grievances stemming from a lack of imperial deference to Egyptian deities and its restrictions on public support of Egyptian temples increased dramatically. Disaffected cattlemen (*boukoloi*) in the Nile Delta joined a revolt led by an Egyptian priest, Isidor, who claimed mystical powers as he united his followers into a highly effective, popular revolt. His opponents among the Roman and Greek inhabitants of Alexandria accused him of performing a human sacrifice on a Roman centurion, swearing an oath on his entrails, and inviting his followers to feast on what remained.[10]

Practitioners of Egyptian religion used other means to protect their traditions. For example, priests at Egyptian temples used the Demotic language as a way of protecting their rituals from Greek or Roman interference. By the middle of the second century, temples were the only area where Demotic was still dominant.[11] At Esna, priests developed a new cosmogonic myth, focused on one of the older Egyptian goddesses, Neith. She was depicted as a "sexless great cow who was a part of Nun, the watery chaos, and who created thirty other gods by mainly naming them, in Ptah/Memphis theology fashion. She also created her son Re and the great snake god Apophis."[12]

In some ways, Roman religious systems were quite open to Egyptian influences. The Isis cult, especially, gained influence throughout the Roman world. Emperor Caligula built a temple to Isis in Rome. Amun's cult, especially his oracle at Siwa, received notice as far north as Greek settlements on the Black Sea in the second century. The Egyptian-Greek deity, Serapis, was also widely worshipped. His temple was rebuilt and expanded by imperial mandate in 130. Tacitus described the continuing importance of Serapis in Roman Egypt:

> The god himself, many supposed to be Aesculepius, because he offers healing to sick bodies; some to be Osiris, the most ancient deity these people have; a large number to be Jupiter, on the grounds that his capabilities

---

[10] Donadoni, "Egypt under Roman Domination," p. 213. Katherine Blouin, *Triangular Landscapes: Environment, Society, and the State in the Nile Delta under Roman Rule* (Oxford Scholarship on Line, 2014), p. 283.

[11] Walter Burkert, *Ancient Mystery Cults* (Cambridge, MA: Harvard University Press, 1987), pp. 6–15. David Peacock, "The Roman Period (30 BC–AD 395)," in *The Oxford History of Ancient Egypt*, ed. Ian Shaw (Oxford: Oxford University Press, 2000), p. 438.

[12] Simon Najovits, *Egypt: Trunk of the Tree, Volume I, The Contexts* (New York: Algora Press, 2003), p. 115.

extend to all things; and a great many, to be Dis Pater, drawing this conclusion either by the attributes which appear with him, or through abstruse conjectures.[13]

Both Isis and Serapis were seen as a source of healing powers.[14] Imhotep, the Old Kingdom's architect of the Saqqara Pyramid, became a deity who received ritual attention as a god of healing and fertility. Childless women and couples without a son invoked the assistance of Imhotep through ritual offerings.[15] A hymn to Imhotep dates to the reign of Emperor Claudius in the mid-first century:

> Veneration of Imhotep. Praise to you. O god, borne a god, divine offspring of Ptah, engendered in Memphis, august child, son of Kheranduankh... who restores what is destroyed everywhere in the temples, of perfect intelligence, who calculates everything, skillful like Toth, the great... who attenuates famine, skillful in his words, experienced with the divine writings, who gives life to the people and protects the pregnant, who gets the sterile with child, who gives a son to everyone who implores it, who protects the child, who regenerates the age of all who serve god, who soothes illness.

Greeks in Egypt identified Imhotep with their god of healing, Asclepius.[16] Conversely, Greek and Roman representations of their deities through painted portraits were adopted by Egyptian religionists to portray the gods for their household shrines.[17]

Christianity, Egyptian Religion, and Roman Persecution

Egyptians claimed a connection to the beginnings of Christianity dating back to traditions that Joseph and Mary fled with their newborn son, Jesus,

---

[13] Tacitus, *Histoire*, quoted in John B. Stanbaugh, *Sarapis under the Early Ptolemies* (Leiden: Brill, 1972), p. 3. Alan K. Bowman, *Egypt after the Pharaohs: From Alexander to the Arab Conquest, 332 BC–A.D. 642* (Berkeley: University of California Press, 1986), p. 143.

[14] Bagnall, *Egypt in Late Antiquity*, p. 251. Robin Lane Fox, *Pagans and Christians* (New York: Alfred A. Knopf, 1986), pp. 201–202.

[15] Rowlandson, *Women and Society*, p. 64.

[16] Hymn to Imhotep cited in Dietrich Wildung, *Egyptian Saints: Deification in Pharaonic Egypt* (New York: New York University Press, 1977), pp. 55, 76.

[17] Frankfurter, *Religion*, p. 135.

to Egypt. They escaped the edicts of the Roman-appointed king of Palestine, Herod the Great, who had ordered the death of all newborn Hebrew males. Jesus and his parents traveled from the Nile Delta to the Middle Egyptian city of Asyut and back. Many miracles are attributed to the infant Jesus, ranging from creating freshwater springs to stopping a boulder from capsizing the boat in which they were traveling. Egyptian Christians carefully marked out the family's route across the Nile delta, into the Western Desert, and into Middle Egypt. Wherever they sought shelter for the night, Christians eventually built a church.[18] In many ways, this resembles the travels of Isis and Nephthys as they gathered the severed body parts of the god Osiris, after Seth had butchered him. Wherever they found a body part, Egyptians built a shrine to Osiris.

Egyptians trace the origins of Egyptian Christianity to Saint Mark, author of the oldest known gospel, who was said to be of Libyan origin. Some of the first converts were members of Alexandria's large Jewish community.[19] The first Egyptian convert to Christianity was said to be a Jewish shoemaker named Anianus.[20] We know very little about the first century of Christianity in Egypt, perhaps because it was dangerous to be a Christian or possess written documents that would prove one's religious identify to Roman authorities.

Information about the still persecuted Christian community becomes more accessible in the late second century. Poor people, heavily taxed under Roman rule, were especially drawn to the Christian movement. In 180, Pantaenus established a center of Christian theological debate known as the Catechetical School of Alexandria, one of the first such institutions in the history of Christianity. Pantaenus was succeeded as the head of the school by Clement of Alexandria (c. 150–215).[21] Raised in a Hellenistic home, Clement studied Greek philosophy before converting to Christianity

---

[18] When I visited Egypt in 2000, Egyptian Christians had carefully marked out the flight of the Holy Family in commemoration of the 2000th anniversary of Joseph, Mary, and Jesus's escape to Egypt. It has become a pilgrimage route. I visited one such church in Old Cairo, immediately adjacent to a Jewish synagogue constructed on the alleged site where pharaoh's daughter found the infant Moses in a reed basket on the Nile. I was told about the imprint of Jesus's hand on a boulder perched above the Nile as well. Matthew 2:13–21. Acts 2:10. Lois M. Faraq, "The Early Christian Period: The Spread and Defense of the Christian Faith under Roman Rule," in *The Coptic Christian Heritage: History, Faith, and Culture*, ed. Lois M. Faraq (London: Routledge, 2014), p. 23.
[19] Kamil, *Coptic Egypt*, p. 18. Bagnall, *Egypt in Late Antiquity*, p. 278.
[20] Barbara Watterson, *The Egyptians* (Oxford: Blackwell, 1997), p. 227. W. H. C. Frend, "The Christian Period in Mediterranean Africa, circa A.D. 200–788," in *Cambridge History of Africa, Volume II 500 BC to A.D. 1050*, ed. John Fage (Cambridge: Cambridge University Press, 1975), p. 416.
[21] Elizabeth Isichei, *History of African Christianity* (Grand Rapids, MI: Eerdmans, 1995), p. 20.

and seeking out the mentorship of Pantaenus. Clement was in regular contact with Christian communities in Palestine and Syria. During the anti-Christian persecutions of Emperor Septimius Severus, he fled from Alexandria and sought refuge in Syria.[22] As early as the last decades of the second century, Egyptian scholars translated the Psalms and some New Testament writings from Greek into Coptic, a new form of Egyptian language, closely associated with Egyptian religious expression beyond Greek or Roman control.[23] By the end of the second century, there were forty bishoprics in Lower Egypt.

Born in 185, Origen became one of the leading Christian theorists of the third century. His Roman father was executed in 202, during the persecution of Christians under Emperor Septimus Severus. Origen's mother was Egyptian. Her non-Roman status extended to her son, making them lower priorities of the anti-Christian state. The year before he lost his father, Origen became a student at Alexandria's Catechetical School, eventually joining the faculty and remaining there for the last twenty-eight years of his life.[24] He advocated the idea that God loved everyone unconditionally: "in the end, even the devil would be saved because of the love of God."[25] In 249, Origen was arrested and tortured, during the Decian persecution. He died in 254.[26]

Roman persecutions of Egyptian Christians continued throughout the third century. Emperor Decius, who only ruled from 249 until 251, ordered everyone to make ritual offerings of incense or other items for the imperial cults and to produce certificates attesting to their fulfillment of these obligations. People who refused were suspected of being Christians and could become subject to arrest and torture. Some Christians submitted documents, falsely attesting to having made the required offerings. However, as Eusebius of Caesarea described them, some Christians of Thebes received "sentences of death with joy and laughter and gladness; so that they sang and sent up songs of thanksgiving to the God of the Universe even to the very

---

[22] Elizabeth Clark, "Clement of Alexandria," in *The Encyclopedia of Religion*, 2nd ed., Vol. 3, ed. Lindsay Jones (Detroit: Thomson/Gale, 2005), pp. 1822–1823.
[23] Aziz Suryal Atica and Mark N. Swanson, "Coptic Church," in *The Encyclopedia of Religion*, 2nd ed., Vol. 3, ed. Lindsay Jones (Detroit: Thomson/Gale, 2005), pp. 1979–1983.
[24] Kamil, *Coptic Egypt*, p. 21.
[25] Elias K. Bongmba, "Christianity in North Africa," in *The Routledge Companion to Christianity in Africa*, ed. Elisa Bongmba (New York: Routledge, 2016), p. 31. Isichei, *History of African Christianity*, p. 22.
[26] Elaine Pagels, *The Origin of Satan: How Christians Demonized Jews, Pagans, and Heretics* (New York: Random House, 1996), pp. 135–138. Rosalie David, *Religion and Magic in Ancient Egypt* (London: Penguin, 1997), p. 341.

last breath."[27] Bishop Dionysius wrote a letter describing the death of Saint Apollonia, in 249, at the hands of an angry mob in Alexandria. This elderly deaconess was "repeatedly struck in the face, her teeth being knocked out; then a bonfire was set and her tormentors threatened to burn her alive if she did not renounce her faith. She uttered a short prayer, walked into the flames, and was consumed."[28]

Diocletian renewed the persecution of Christians shortly after he became emperor. In 297, he required all military officers and administrative personnel to offer sacrifices to the emperor or lose their positions. Imperial authorities equated refusals to offer sacrifices with political disloyalty, so many Christians were killed. Egyptians rebelled against his favoritism toward Latin over Greek, which was more widely spoken in Egypt. Diocletian identified Christians as the group most committed to the maintenance of Greek language, which was linked to the Septuagint and the New Testament. In 303, Diocletian ordered the destruction of Christian religious texts, the dismissal of Christians from imperial service, and the confiscation of their property. Among the Christian martyrs was a woman named Dimiana, who had established a convent when she was just fifteen. She and forty other nuns were tortured and beheaded.[29] Along with his persecution of Christians, however, Diocletian encouraged the practice of Egyptian religion.

The persecutions continued under Emperor Maximentius. According to hagiographies, Catherine of Alexandria was a learned young woman from a wealthy home. She protested the persistence of what she termed "idol worship" in a letter to the emperor. He ordered her to debate the virtues of Christianity and the various traditions of Alexandria with fifty Alexandrine philosophers. She won the debate. He put the fifty philosophers to death and announced that he wanted to marry her. She rejected the offer. He had her beaten and then imprisoned her both for refusing to marry him and to abandon Christianity. While in jail, it is said that a dove brought her food and that she had a vision of Jesus. After being tortured, she was put to death. Her body was carried off to Mount Sinai, where her tomb is a place of pilgrimage at St. Catherine's monastery.[30]

---

[27] Eusebius of Caesarea, quoted in Kamil, *Coptic Egypt*, pp. 23–24. Donadoni, "Egypt under Roman Domination," p. 217.

[28] Donald Attwater, *The Penguin Dictionary of Saints*, 2nd ed. (Harmondsworth, UK: Penguin,1983) p. 49.

[29] Kamil, *Coptic Egypt*, pp. 25–26. Lois M. Farag, "The Early Church Period (42–642): The Spread and Defense of the Christian Faith under Roman Rule," in *The Coptic Christian Heritage: History, Faith and Culture*, ed. Lois M. Farag (London: Routledge, 2014), p. 27.

[30] Attwater, *Penguin Dictionary of Saints*, pp. 77–78.

During the first century of the Common Era, Alexandria's Jewish community had grown to become the largest Jewish community in the Mediterranean world. It prospered through work in commerce and administration. Relying on the Greek translation of the Hebrew Bible and ready access to Greek texts, the Jewish community produced important theologians and philosophers, most notably Philo of Alexandria, who lived from approximately 20 BCE to 50 CE. He produced many texts that were important in Hellenistic philosophical circles, among Jews, and eventually among Christian philosophers and theologians. Philo seemed to work entirely within Hellenistic and Jewish contexts; there were few Egyptian influences.[31] Tensions developed among Jews, Greeks, and Egyptians in Alexandria, where each community thought of the others as collaborators with Rome.[32] Emperor Hadrian violently suppressed a revolt by Jews in Alexandria and other urban areas, decimating the Jewish community that had played a central role in shaping Judaism's transition from a temple-focused religion to a diasporic and decentralized tradition.[33] As anti-Jewish sentiment gained a new prominence in Roman Egypt, Jews were identified with the dangerous god, Seth, or, as the Greeks called him, Typhon.[34] The Roman governor, Tiberius, closed the Jewish temple of Onias, which had been a religious center for several centuries.[35]

Although some early Christians had withdrawn from the world in favor of communities of faith awaiting the second coming of Christ, some Egyptian Christians withdrew to avoid imperial persecution and the corruption of Roman-dominated society. In the latter half of the third century, Saint Paul of Thebes (248–343) and Saint Antony of the Desert (251–356) helped to establish the hermetic tradition. They retreated into the desert mountains east of the Nile valley, living alone in caves, though they received food from and provided instructions to faithful neighbors and pilgrims. They met for the first time shortly before Paul's death.[36] Many of these monks earned reputations as healers of the sick and as exorcists of demons.[37] Antony started

---

[31] David Winston, "Introduction," in *Philo of Alexandria: Contemplative Life, the Giants, and Selections* (New York: Paulist Press, 1981), pp. 1–4.
[32] M. Stern, "The Period of the Second Temple," in *A History of the Jewish People*, ed. H. H. Ben-Sasson (Cambridge, MA: Harvard University Press, 1975), pp. 368–369.
[33] Bagnall, *Egypt in Late Antiquity*, p. 276.
[34] Frankfurter, *Religion*, p. 112.
[35] Stern, "The Period of the Second Temple," pp. 368–369.
[36] Paul of Thebes is regarded as a saint by Catholic and Orthodox Churches, though most question the historicity of the hagiographic account by Saint Jerome. Attwater, *Penguin Dictionary of Saints*, p. 260. Kamil, *Coptic Egypt*, p. 25.
[37] Bagnall, *Egypt in Late Antiquity*, p. 273.

out in solitary meditations in Lower Egypt, subjecting himself to many spiritual and physical challenges and overcoming both threats and temptations of the Devil and a host of demons.[38] He eventually gathered others pursuing the solitary spiritual path and created a contemplative community that still placed an emphasis on solitary meditation. He spent the last forty years of his life living in a cave on Mount Kolzim, near the Red Sea, where it meets the Gulf of Suez. Athanasius spent time with Antony when he was removed from his role as Patriarch in the controversies over Arianism. Based in part on his experiences with Antony, Athanasius wrote a study, *The Life of Saint Antony*, which has become a major text in the study of the Desert Fathers, an Egyptian Christian tradition that influenced asceticism throughout the Christian world.[39] At least according to Athanasius, Saint Anthony described a deranged and defeated Satan as "a little black boy from Ethiopia [who was] black of mind."[40] This was one of the earliest overt Christian associations of blackness and evil. Saint John the Egyptian followed in the tradition of Paul and Antony. He was born in Lycopolis (Asyut) circa 304, where he was a carpenter. He eventually renounced worldly pursuits and became a hermit on a nearby mountain. He was known for his asceticism and piety but also for his ability to predict the future. Even Emperor Theodosius consulted him on several occasions.[41]

As the Diocletian persecutions subsided, a new form of religious community developed in Egypt. Saint Pachom was born to non-Christian parents at Esna, just as the persecutions began. His biographers describe Pachom's parents as devotees of a deity associated with the Nile flood, making an offering of river fish to ensure an adequate flood.[42] Pachom served in the Roman army. He ran afoul of his commanders, was imprisoned briefly, and was converted to Christianity, by Christians whose piety and altruism impressed him. After being released from the army, he was baptized and served a rural community for several years.[43] Then he studied with a rigorous ascetic, Palomen, who died from excessive fasting. Pachom had a vision that he and some of his followers should establish their own religious community

---

[38] Athanasius of Alexandria, *The Life of Saint Antony*, trans. Tim Vivian and Apostolus Athanassakis (Kalamazoo: Cistercian Publications, 2003).
[39] Attwater, *Penguin Dictionary of Saints*, p. 47.
[40] Cited in Diarmaid MacCulloch, *Christianity: The First Three Thousand Years* (New York: Viking, 2018), p. 205.
[41] Attwater, *Penguin Dictionary of Saints*, p. 188.
[42] Frankfurter, *Religion*, p. 62.
[43] Philip Rousseau, *Pachomius: The Making of a Community in Fourth Century Egypt* (Berkeley: University of California Press, 1985), p. 58.

Figure 7.2. Monastery of St. Simeon, seventh century, west of Aswan, Egypt (photo by Robert M. Baum).

at the Upper Egyptian town of Akhmin. He attracted the attention of many of the hermits in the hills of Upper Egypt, gathered them together in a walled and isolated community, which strove for economic self-sufficiency as well as a life centered on pious actions. He established farm fields, bakeries, wine presses, and strict discipline for all members of the community. Pachom's sister established a similar community for women.[44] Another female ascetic, Thalis, founded twelve convents in Antinoe.[45] Their highly disciplined communities of men or women focused on prayer, piety, and productive labor (see Figure 7.2). Pachom had a strong influence on Saint Basil and Saint Benedict and their creation of European monastic orders.

Before the Common Era, intercultural contacts and conquests often resulted in the incorporation of new deities and ritual practices from these groups. In some cases, this involved initiation into specific ritual communities. For example, Isis became linked to Asclepius and Imhotep in relation to healing and was more closely associated with Demeter regarding

---

[44] Kamil, *Coptic Egypt*, pp. 26–28. Attwater, *Penguin Dictionary of Saints*, p. 255. Rousseau, *Pachomius*, pp. 59, 99.

[45] Elise Boulding, *The Underside of History: A View of Women through Time* (London: Sage, 1990), p. 324.

fertility. A third- or fourth-century ritual designed to ensure the sexual fidelity of a woman was done by piercing a clay doll with needles and attaching a scroll that invoked Persephone, Hermes, Ereshkigal, and Anubis. The first two were Greek, the third was Mesopotamian, and the fourth was Egyptian, but all were invoked in this ritual.[46]

In most cases, however, religious change did not involve conversion—that is, the process of entering into a new religious tradition—altogether. This did occur in terms of the growth of Judaism in Berber communities, discussed in Chapter 6, and may have occurred on an individual basis in Alexandria, Elephantine, and other Egyptian communities. Before the spread of Christianity, the acceptance of an entirely new religious tradition was quite rare. However, Christians modelled their ideas of conversion on the Pauline narrative of a Hellenized Jew, Saul, who actively persecuted the followers of Jesus. On his way to Damascus to continue this persecution, he was struck by a lightning bolt, fell off his donkey, and heard a voice calling out "Why dost thou persecute me?" He underwent a sudden and powerful conversion to embrace the new religious movement, changed his name to Paul, and became the most important apostle of what became Christianity.

This idea of conversion as a profound and sudden event has influenced generations of theorists who sought to explain conversion. This is especially true of Arthur Darby Nock, who wrote on conversion to Christianity in the ancient world. His definition of conversion draws directly on the Pauline model: "By conversion we mean the reorientation of the soul of an individual, his deliberate turning from indifference or from an earlier form of piety to another, a turning which a consciousness that a great change is involved, that the old was wrong, and the new is right."[47] This transformative conversion experience is historically quite rare but does appear to explain the willingness to die among converted martyrs during the Roman persecution. More commonly, however, conversion from "pagan" traditions involved the acceptance of a new source of religious authority but did not involve a rejection of older traditions. Shirley Jackson Case, a contemporary of Nock's, did not share his view of conversion in the ancient world. She points out that embracing new deities "had long been in vogue in the Roman Empire. He could easily be persuaded to seek divine aid from a new source.... But

---

[46] Rowlandson, *Women and Society*, p. 69.
[47] Arthur Darby Nock, *Conversion: The Old and the New in Religion from Alexander the Great to Augustine of Hippo* (London: Oxford University Press, 1933), p. 7. For a critique of Nock in an African context, see Robert M. Baum, "The Emergence of a Diola Christianity," *Africa* 60 (1990).

the notion that on allying himself with a new divine protector he must immediately renounce allegiance to all others was an entirely novel idea for the average Gentile. From this point of view, the more friends one could have among the divine powers, the happier was one's lot."[48] As David Frankfurter points out, Nock's narrow view of conversion was quite rare in ancient Egypt. Pharaonic and Ptolemaic ideas and practices continued to influence the receptivity and expression of Egyptian forms of Christianity.[49] Especially in Philae and the western oases, Egyptian religion coexisted with Christianity until the end of the fifth century.[50]

Conversion is not a single event, but the beginning of a long process in which converts embrace a new religious teaching and a new source of authoritative interpretation, but older ways do not disappear. This was particularly the case in ancient Egypt, where people had long shared an openness to new forms of religious teachings from neighboring communities. Initially, converts often saw Christian concepts as a new source of authoritative knowledge but continued to draw insights from older Egyptian or Hellenistic sources. Converts heard and assimilated these new teachings according to the categories of experience and understanding that they brought to the encounter from their older traditions. Conversion initiates an ongoing internal debate between old and new religious traditions.[51] Rarely does it result in a rejection of all prior beliefs or practices.

During this early period of Christianity in Egypt, Gnostic traditions became important. Gnosticism enjoyed considerable support among Egyptian Christians until the late fourth century. They did not form separate churches but were deeply suspicious of ecclesiastical hierarchies. They emphasized the transcendence and absolute "otherness" of God and the corrupt nature of the flesh.[52] Gnostics sought a special, hidden knowledge of God and the ultimate order of the cosmos. According to Geoffrey Parrinder, Gnostics envisioned Christ "as a divine emanation who came bringing gnosis, but he was not properly human and did not die, either becoming a spirit who lived in the human Jesus for a while or merely a phantom human appearance."[53]

---

[48] Shirley Jackson Case, *Jesus through the Centuries* (Chicago: University of Chicago Press, 1932), pp. 112–113.
[49] Frankfurter, *Religion*, p. 17.
[50] Frankfurter, *Religion*, p. 19.
[51] For a more detailed discussion of issues of conversion in Africa, see Robin Horton, "African Conversion," *Africa* 41 (1971). Robin Horton, "On the Rationality of Conversion," *Africa* 45 (1975). Baum, "Emergence of a Diola Christianity."
[52] MacCulloch, *Christianity*, p. 125.
[53] Geoffrey Parrinder, *Religion in Africa* (Baltimore: Penguin Books, 1969), p. 105.

This Christological view influenced the development of Monophysite interpretations which became dominant in Egypt and throughout northeast Africa. Gnostics stressed the importance of personal experience of mysteries of the universe. Women played a central role in this tradition.[54] These texts, manuscripts largely from the fourth century, included several noncanonical gospels. They emphasized two theories: "the nation of dualism which implies the condemnation and rejection of matter, an opposition between the transcendent God and creation, which could only be the work of an interior demiurge; and the nation of *sophia*, wisdom, an emanation of the supreme God, a portion of which is in every being, fallen into matter. Sophia aspires to renascent to God and unite with him."[55] This approach is emphasized in the Gospel of Philip: " 'You have seen the spirit, you have become the spirit. You have seen Christ, you have become Christ.' "[56] One of the largest collections of Gnostic texts ever found, however, was hidden away in Upper Egypt, in a place called Nag Hammadi.[57] Once Christianity became the official religion of the Roman Empire and gained the ability to persecute dissident groups, Gnostic texts were systematically destroyed.

Egyptian Religious Life under Christian Hegemony

In the midst of an armed struggle against an alternate claimant to the throne, Constantine had a vision or a dream in which he was told to paint Christian symbols on the shields of his soldiers before the battle of Milvian Bridge. After his decisive victory and coronation as emperor, Constantine issued the Edict of Milan, which ended the persecution of Christians throughout the Roman Empire. Constantine did not, however, formally become a Christian by receiving the sacrament of baptism until he was on his death bed. It appears that the conversion of Constantine was a gradual process, not just a sudden vision in which he renounced old practices.[58]

---

[54] Karen Jo Torjesen, *When Women Were Priests: Women's Leadership in the Early Church and the Scandal of Their Subordination in the Rise of Christianity* (San Francisco: Harper/San Francisco, 1995), p. 100. Isichei, *History of African Christianity*, pp. 18–19.

[55] Françoise Dunand, *Gods and Men in Egypt: 3000 BCE to 395 CE* (Ithaca, NY: Cornell University Press, 2004), p. 261.

[56] Cited in Dunand, *Gods and Men in Egypt*, p. 261.

[57] These texts were discovered by shepherds in 1945. In some cases, they provide the only available copies of texts that had previously been known by their mention in critiques by more orthodox Christian writers. See Elaine Pagels, *The Gnostic Gospels* (New York: Vintage, 1989).

[58] Frankfurter, *Religion*, p. 17.

Even though the establishment of Christianity as the official religion of the Roman Empire did not occur until 395, under Emperor Theodosius I, imperial authorities shifted strongly against the practice of Egyptian religion during Constantine's reign.

In 330, Macedonius, the Roman governor at Philae, was deeply troubled by the persecution of Christians in this Nubian border town that was a center of Egyptian temples and "pagan" practices. Macedonius reported what he witnessed to Athanasius, the bishop of Alexandria, who responded by appointing Macedonius as the first bishop at Philae. According to traditions written down in the ninth century, Macedonius destroyed a falcon statue associated with the temple of Horus. He pretended to have come to perform a sacrifice. Instead, he cut off the falcon statue's head. The incident ultimately led to the conversion of the priest of Horus.[59]

In 359, still well before Theodosius, the oracle of Bes at Abydos was closed by imperial edict.[60] In 385, a Praetorian Prefect prohibited sacrifices to Zeus throughout Egypt.[61] In 391, Bishop Theophilus attempted to transform a temple of Dionysus into a church. Riots broke out. The Christians gained the upper hand and destroyed Alexandria's Serapeum.[62] Once he assumed the throne, Theodosius ordered the closing of most Egyptian temples.[63] Throughout the fourth century, however, Egyptian religious practices enjoyed broad community support. Temple rituals persisted, including divination performed by temple priests. A Syrian visitor to Alexandria described what he heard about the vitality of Egyptian religious practices. "'[Here the people are] eminently reverent toward the gods. At no other place are the mysteries of the gods thus celebrated as they were from ancient times through today.... For truly there we know that the gods have lived and still live.'"[64] At the Isis temple of Canopus, near Alexandria, pilgrims would sleep at the shrine and report their dreams to a priest who would interpret them.[65] For example, a philosopher named Asclepiodotes of Alexandria visited the oracle of Isis, at Menouthis, together with his wife.

---

[59] James E. Goehning, "Imagining Macedonius, the First Bishop of Philae," in *Christianity and Monasticism in Aswan and Nubia*, ed. Gawdat Gabra and Hany N. Takla (Cairo: American University in Cairo Press, 2013), pp. 12–13.
[60] Mark Smith, *Following Osiris* (Oxford: Oxford University Press, 2017), p. 528.
[61] Bowman, *Egypt After*, p. 192
[62] Cyril Aldred, *The Egyptians*, 3rd ed. (London: Thames and Hudson, 1998), p. 14.
[63] David, *Religion and Magic in Ancient Egypt*, p. 342. Farug, "Early," p. 25.
[64] Frankfurter, *Religion*, p. 19.
[65] Frankfurter, *Religion*, pp. 40–41. Fraire Le Corsu, *Isis: Mythes et Mystères* (Paris: Société d'Editions "Les Belles Lettres," 1977), p. 53.

He stayed some time in Menouthis and offered a considerable number of sacrifices to the demons. But it was to no avail. The sterility of his wife persisted nonetheless, having believed that he saw in a dream Isis lying beside him he heard it declared by those who interpreted dreams there and who served the demon expressed in Isis, that he ought to join himself to the idol of that goddess, then to have sex with his wife—that thus, a child would be born to him.[66]

Theodosius's attempts to close rural temples were thwarted by the continued adherence of rural communities to the worship of Egyptian deities.[67] In 386, the imperially appointed High Priest of Egypt still had to be someone "'who has not withdrawn from the cult of the temples, by his observance of Christianity.'"[68] Libanius cautioned Emperor Theodosius against any precipitous actions against rural temples:

Temples are the soul of the countryside: they mark the beginning of the settlement, and have been passed down through many generations to the men of today. In them the farming communities rest their hopes for husbands, wives, children, for their oxen and the soil they sow and plant. An estate that has suffered [a temple's defilement/ demolition] has lost the inspiration of the peasantry together with their hopes, for they believe that their labour will be in vain once they are robbed of the gods who direct their labours to their due end.[69]

Furthermore, these rural temples were centers of local intellectual life. Since imperial authorities moved initially against urban temples, rural ones became increasingly important for the practice of Egyptian religion. Local shrines of Horus, Isis, Sobek, and other gods proliferated as imperial support of major temples was withdrawn.[70] New prophetic teachers emerged in the late fourth century, speaking for the gods to systematize religious belief systems in opposition to the new religions of Christianity and Manichaeism.[71] The cult of Isis persisted into the fifth century, attracting women concerned about their fertility and their ability to carry a pregnancy to term. In the

---

[66] Frankfurter, *Religion*, p. 164.
[67] Frankfurter, *Religion*, p. 23.
[68] Codex Theodosius, quoted in Frankfurter, *Religion*, p. 24.
[69] Libanius, cited in Frankfurter, *Religion*, p. 28.
[70] Frankfurter, *Religion*, pp. 98–99.
[71] Frankfurter, *Religion*, pp. 30, 32.

western desert oases of Kharga and Dakhla, people established temples for Seth, the patron deity of the wilderness, of the red desert lands.[72]

However, the end of persecutions and the ability of the empire to enforce orthodoxy opened it up to religious schisms and to the persecutions of other Christian groups that had fallen out of favor. For nearly a century and a half, Alexandria had been a center of Christian learning and theological debates, but increasingly in the fourth century, emperors intervened in these debates, wielding their authority in support of what they regarded as "orthodoxy."

Early in the fourth century, an Alexandrine priest named Arius was troubled by the idea of the oneness of God the Father and God the Son. He decided that, since there was a time when the Son was created, he was a historic figure, and not divine. In *The Thalia* [The Festivities], Arius set out his basic criticism of Trinitarian thought. Only excerpts taken from its rebuttal by Bishop Alexander of Alexandria still exist, since Arius's original writing was destroyed.

> The Unbegun appointed the Son to be Beginning of things begotten,
> and bore him as his own Son, his in this case giving birth.
> He has nothing proper to God in his essential property,
> for neither is he equal nor yet consubstantial with him.

Arius offers a brief suggestion that God the Father, gave birth to the Son.

> To sum up, God exists ineffable to the Son,
> for he is to himself what he is, that is unutterable,
> so that none of things said ... will the Son
> know how to express comprehensively, for it is impossible for him
> to explore the Father, who exists by himself.
> For the Son himself does not know his own essence;
> for being Son he truly came to be at his Father's will. ...
> For clearly for what has a beginning to encompass,
> by thought or apprehension, the one who is unbegun is impossible.[73]

---

[72] Frankfurter, *Religion*, p. 113.
[73] Arius, *The Thalia*, excerpt in Bart D. Ehrman and Andrew S. Jacobs, eds., *Christianity in Late Antiquity, 300-450 CE: A Reader* (New York: Oxford University Press, 2004), p. 159.

He was opposed by the Church establishment led by Alexander, the Patriarch of Alexandria. Bishop Melitius of Lycopolis (Asyut) agreed with Alexander but took advantage of the controversy to ordain priests on his own in Upper Egypt, a reaction against Lower Egypt's control over church affairs.

Arius's teachings were sufficiently popular that Constantine called representatives of the churches to assemble in the Council of Nicaea in 325. Alexander and his deacon, Athanasius, as well as Arius attended. The adoption of the Nicene Creed was a victory for Alexander, Athanasius, and the doctrine that the Son was fully divine and fully human, "of one essence with the Father." Athanasius wrote several texts concerning the Arian position, emphasizing the importance of the Logos (the Word) becoming incarnate and restore the possibility of humanity gaining eternal life.[74] Arius was condemned as a heretic, defrocked, banished, and his writings destroyed. Still his teachings continued to be influential, especially in the oases of the western desert.[75] When Constantine's successor, Constantius, became interested in Arian doctrine, he forced Athanasius out of the Patriarchy of Alexandria. Athanasius sought refuge with Saint Antony in the eastern desert. Athanasius was recalled whenever the emperors lost interest in Arianism and returned to exile with other desert hermits whenever Arianism regained influence.[76] Arius's teachings, however, remained extremely important to the Libyan Church, to the Germanic tribes, and to the Vandals, who eventually conquered large areas of North Africa.[77]

When Theodosius proclaimed Christianity as the official religion of the empire, he embraced Roman Catholic understandings of that doctrine and equated the continued worship of "pagan" cults with treasonous acts. After Theodosius's death, the Roman Empire was divided between East and West. Egypt fell into the Eastern Empire and the primacy of the Patriarch of Constantinople. Theophilus, who served as Patriarch of Alexandria at this time, encouraged attacks on Egyptian and Greek temples, including the Serapeum and its famous statue of Serapis. Many temples were converted into churches or monasteries.[78] Theophilus was said to have ordered the melting

---

[74] Charles Kannengiesser, "The Spiritual Message of the Church Fathers," in *Christian Spirituality: Origins to the Twelfth Century*, ed. Bernard McGinn, John Meyendorff, and Jean LeClerq (New York: Crossroads, 1987), pp. 63–64.

[75] Kamil, *Coptic Egypt*, pp. 30–32.

[76] Kamil, *Coptic Egypt*, p. 34. Attwater, *Penguin Dictionary of Saints*, p. 50.

[77] Thomas C. Oden, *Early Libyan Christianity: Uncovering a North African Tradition* (Downers Grove, IL: Intervarsity Press, 2011), p. 206.

[78] Kamil, *Coptic Egypt*, pp. 35–36. Oden, *Early Libyan Christianity*, p. 178.

down of statues of the gods for use as kitchen utensils for the Alexandrine Church. He was succeeded as Patriarch, by his nephew Cyril of Alexandria, who continued his confrontational ways, both against non-Christians and against schismatics within the Christian movement. He called for the expulsion of Jews from Alexandria and incited mobs to attack Egyptian and Greek temples and the priests and scholars associated with them. One of the victims of these attacks was the Hellenistic philosopher Hypatia, who died at the age of thirty. She was a Neo-Platonist who taught many of the more philosophically inclined Christians, including Bishop Synesius of Cyrene.[79] She was accused of fomenting discord between the Roman governor and Bishop Cyril of Alexandria. A mob dragged her to the Kaiserion Church, formerly a temple to Caesar Augustus. There they stripped her naked, tore her limb from limb, and burnt her remains.[80]

In the mid-fifth century, Bishop Shenoute of Atripe was particularly outspoken against the persistence of "pagan" beliefs and practices, which he often equated with Satanism. He criticized Egyptian Christians who continued to pray toward the west, which was historically associated with the land of the dead.[81] In a sermon entitled "The Lord Thundered," he attacked them:

> Accursed be he who worships or pours out (libations) or makes sacrifices to any creature [*krisma*] whether in the sky or on the earth or under water! Woe upon those who will worship the sun and the moon and the whole army [*stratia*] of heaven, putting their hearts in them as gods, when they are not gods.... Woe upon those who will worship wood and stone or anything made by man's handiwork (with) wood and stone (molded by putting) clay inside them.... Consider your foolishness, O pagans who serve and worship (things) that have no power to move whatsoever.[82]

Shenoute led attacks on "pagan" worshippers' homes, including the home of a man named Gesius who kept a hidden room filled with images of Egyptian gods.[83] Bishop Shenoute expressed particular concern regarding

---

[79] For a discussion of Saint Cyril of Alexandria, see Attwater, *Penguin Dictionary of Saints*, pp. 98–99. For an extensive discussion of the life and teachings of Bishop Synesius, see Oden, *Early Libyan Christianity*, pp. 158–169, 180, and 153–211. Boulding, *Underside of History*, p. 334.

[80] Rowlandson, *Women and Society*, pp. 74–75.

[81] David Frankfurter, *Christianizing Egypt: Syncretism and Local Worlds in Late Antiquity* (Princeton, NJ: Princeton University Press, 2018), p. 13.

[82] Bishop Shenoute, cited in Frankfurter, *Religion*, p. 78.

[83] Frankfurter, *Christianizing*, pp. 13, 46.

his fellow Christians, who, in times of severe illness, suffering, or calamity, turned to Egyptian gods and performed rituals seeking their assistance.[84] He went on to establish monastic communities in the Eastern Desert which may have housed as many as 2,000 monks and 1,800 nuns.[85]

Christian writers began to demonize religious practitioners whom they identified as "pagans." A fifth-century text, *The Life of Moses of Abydos*, describes Moses's combat against an Egyptian god (described as a demon) who inflicts illness and suffering on Christians. Moses exorcises the spirit, but in a long, arduous night is first tempted, and then cursed and threatened.[86] A Coptic text usually attributed to Bishop Dioscurus of Alexandria, in 451, celebrates the miracles attributed to Bishop Macarius of Tkow (who died in 451) and illustrates this process. According to the text, *A Panegyric on Macarius, Bishop of Tkow Attributed to Dioscurus of Alexandria*, Macarius confronted worshippers of the god Kothos who maintained images of the god in niches in their own homes. A local Christian priest complained to Macarius, accusing the "pagans" of "murdering Christian children and pouring their blood out at the altar of Kothos. Afterwards, they would remove the intestines of the slaughtered children and use them to string the lyres which they played when singing hymns to the god and, also, when looking for buried treasure."[87] Macarius and three other men confronted the "pagans," only to be seized and prepared for sacrifice. Fourteen monks, led by Besa (a follower of Bishop Shenoute), tried to rescue them. According to the text, God broke down the doors and freed them, before destroying the temple where they had been detained. Then the oppressed Christians of the village rose up and threw the priest of Kothos and his primary statue into a fire. Some 360 images of Kothos were destroyed. Some "pagans" converted because they had witnessed the miraculous destruction of the temple. Others gathered their possessions and their images of the gods and fled into the desert.[88] This narrative portrays "pagans" as savage and celebrates the triumph of the Christians. Its description of "pagans" was remarkably similar to blood libels against Jews in Medieval and Modern Europe. During this period, the New Testament was translated into Coptic

---

[84] Frankfurter, *Christianizing*, p. 69.
[85] Boulding, *Underside of History*, p. 325.
[86] Frankfurter, *Christianizing*, p. 55.
[87] The text probably was written in the sixth century. Cited in Mark Smith, *Following*, p. 439. See Frankfurter, *Christianizing*, p. 78.
[88] Mark Smith, *Following*, p. 440.

and included some portions of the book of Revelations which are not found in the Orthodox or Latin texts.[89]

During the period when Christianity coexisted with what they liked to call paganism, Egyptian and Greek priests performed rituals to propitiate particular deities on behalf of their communities and to expiate specific polluting conduct. Christians placed a strong emphasis on the spiritual origins of disease and relied on priests, monks, and nuns to heal the sick.[90] In some cases, Christians built churches on the sites of pagan temples. The old temple at Menouthis was converted to a church, where Christian pilgrims sought healing in the name of Christian saints. Living saints and holy men and women healed the sick, protected crops from animal pests, brought water to dry wells, and even mediated land and water disputes. For example, the female saint/prophet Piamoun was "hailed in her village for resolving an irrigation dispute during the Nile's inundation and for protecting her village from marauders.[91] The saints appeared to supplicants in dreams, either curing them immediately or by prescribing a healing regime.[92] This closely paralleled the incubation rituals of non-Christian deities in Egypt and North Africa. As recently as the seventh century, miraculous healings, particularly associated with eye disorders, were reported at a church built on the site of the temple of Isis at Canopis.

Popular religion, which was not specific either to Christians or pagans, including astrology and the making of amulets, which were peripheral to both traditions, offered predictive and protective strategies in uncertain times.[93] Here, too, Christian and older traditions continued well into the seventh century. David Frankfurter cites the example of a papyrus describing an amulet from the seventh century, illustrating the persistence of Egyptian influence in the ways that Christians invoked protective powers.

> Jesus Horus [the son of Is]is went upon a mountain in order to rest. He [performed his] music, [set] his nets, and captured a falcon . . . [He] cut it without a knife, cooked it without fire and [ate] it without salt . . . He

---

[89] Kamil, *Coptic Egypt*, p. 35.
[90] Bagnall, *Egypt in Late Antiquity*, p. 273.
[91] Frankfurter, *Christianizing*, p. 90.
[92] Dominic Montserrat, "Pilgrims to the Shrines of SS Cyrus and John at Menouthis in Late Antiquity," in *Pilgrimage and Holy Space in Late Antique Egypt*, ed. David Frankfurter (Leiden: Brill, 1998), p. 271. Frankfurter, *Religion*, p. 47. Frankfurter, *Christianizing*, pp. 132–134. Le Corsu, *Isis: Mythes et Mystères*, p. 53.
[93] Bagnall, *Egypt in Late Antiquity*, p. 274.

had pain and the area around his navel [hurt him] and he wept with loud weeping, saying "Today, I am bringing my [mother] Isis to me. I went as messenger spirit ... so that I may attend my mother, Isis. [The Spirit] went upon the mountain of Heliopolis and found his mother Isis wearing an iron crown and stoking a copper oven.... Let every sickness and every difficulty and every power that is in the belly of N, child of N, stop at this moment! I am the one who calls, the lord Jesus is the one who grants healing![94]

At least in this text, Jesus is equated with Horus, the son of Osiris and Isis.

Since the fifth century, most Egyptian Christians favored the Monophysite understanding of the nature of Christ, insisting that Jesus had only one, indivisible, and divine nature. His human aspect was inseparable and indistinct from his divinity. The Council of Chalcedon was convened in 451 in order to suppress Monophysite doctrine and establish Byzantine Orthodox control over the Egyptian Church. Emperor Justinian's persecution of the Monophysites in the mid-sixth century led to the formal separation of the Egyptian Church from Constantinople. The Egyptian or Coptic Church retained the practice of pharaonic circumcision. A minority, known as Melkites, remained loyal to the Byzantine emperor and his Church. The Monophysites named their own Patriarch of Alexandria, who lived at a monastery in Wadi Natrun.[95] During this period, popular forms of Christianity developed, centered on the role of Christian oracles.[96] Although these oracles were Christian, they addressed religious concerns that occupied a prominent place in Egyptian and Hellenistic religious practice.

In Lower Nubia, Emperor Diocletian decided to withdraw Roman forces in the third century. Along this turbulent southern border, he encouraged the settlement of the Nobatae, who had previously dominated some of the western oases. The Nobataes and the eastern desert people, the Blemmyes, would enter Roman territory at Philae to worship and engage in ritual processions in honor of Isis. These rituals continued into the sixth century when they were suppressed. Around 535, the Byzantine Emperor Justinian ordered one of his generals to close the temple, which had become the last major temple complex of "pagan" Egyptian religion.[97]

---

[94] Papyrus cited in Frankfurter, *Christianizing*, pp. 1–2.
[95] Kamil, *Coptic Egypt*, p. 39. Donadoni, "Egypt under Roman Domination," p. 220.
[96] Frankfurter, *Religion*, p.32.
[97] J. LeClant, "The Empire of Kush: Napata and Meroe," in *Ancient Civilizations of Africa, Volume II of UNESCO General History of Africa*, ed. G. Mokhtar (London: Heinemann, 1981), pp. 294–295.

Conclusion

During the first six centuries of the Common Era, Egypt occupied a central place in the struggle between "pagans" and Christians. From the time of the Roman Conquest in 30 BCE, Egyptians sought to sustain their religious traditions in major temples, local shrines, and family ritual sites. Religious leaders emphasized the similarities of Hellenistic and Egyptian traditions while spreading the worship of Isis, Osiris, Amun, and the Hellenistic-Egyptian deity Serapis throughout the Mediterranean world. During most of the first and second century of Roman rule, Egyptian concerns focused on containing foreign influences from imperial cults and Jewish immigrants, particularly in Alexandria. As Christianity became more influential, this concern for the vitality of Egyptian religion shifted to an effort to contain the new religion. Egyptian religion remained a separate and distinct tradition until the sixth century.

Significant Egyptian interest in Christianity had developed toward the end of the second century. The first Christian converts in Egypt seem to have been concentrated among the Jews of Alexandria, but it quickly spread to the Egyptian population, which felt the heavy burden of a Roman regime that made little effort to accommodate Egyptian norms of assimilating foreign rulers. Alexandria became one of the major centers of Christian thought and debates about the core doctrines of the new tradition. The Catechetical School of Alexandria, founded by Pantaenus, and directed for many years by Clement and Origen, became a center of debate about the core beliefs and practices of the early Church.

Christian refusal to participate in the imperial cults was seen by Roman authorities as a sign of disloyalty and brought intense periods of persecution against them. Christians demanded a different kind of commitment from those seeking to join the movement. It was no longer sufficient to welcome new deities, new forms of rituals, or concepts and incorporating them within a religious system that had long been open to new religious ideas and practices. Christians expected a type of conversion embodied in the example of Paul of Tarsus or of the many martyrs in the first centuries of Christianity. Many converts opened themselves to a new source of religious teaching but did not necessarily reject older beliefs and practices. Thus, many Christians continued to seek out Egyptian rituals related to harvests, fertility, and healing. Egyptian religion coexisted with Christianity for several centuries. The guardians of Christian orthodoxy, however, used their access to imperial authorities to impede what they considered pagan practices. They circulated miraculous accounts of Christian defiance of traditional religious leaders whom they often described in demonic terms.

Egyptian Christians had a profound effect on Christian practice throughout the Mediterranean world. Not only did the cult of Isis influence the representation of the Virgin Mary, but theological debates in Alexandria and its hinterland shaped Christian thought and the ways that people sought to live in a Christian way. Origen emphasized the totality of God's love. Arius emphasized the incommensurate natures of an uncreated God and the created Jesus. Anthony of the Desert and Pachomius shaped the development of the hermetic and monastic traditions throughout the Christian world. In the fifth century these debates resulted in the development of a new branch of Christendom, strongly associated with Egyptian identity and the primacy of the Patriarch of Alexandria. They rejected the consensus of church councils sponsored by Rome and Constantinople in favor of a new understanding of Jesus. Egyptian Monophysites emphasized the united essence of Jesus which was entirely divine. This understanding of Christology drove them to proselytize in Axum and the Ethiopian highlands, as well as the Nubian kingdoms of the Upper Nile, Nobatea, Makuria, and Alwa. These missions were successful. For nearly one thousand years, Monophysites dominated Nubian Christian societies. Ethiopia's embrace of Monophysite traditions became central to the Ethiopian monarchy, which lasted until the late twentieth century.

Even in the early seventh century, however, Egyptian religious influences continued to manifest themselves. Churches built on the site of temples dedicated to Isis or other deities continued to serve as centers for healing rituals. The techniques of incubation, the seeking of religious instruction and healing methods, through dreams at temples or churches had originated before the Christian era but persisted in the healing practice of the various Christian traditions found in Egypt. Saints replaced Hellenistic and Egyptian gods in providing counsel to pilgrims. The iconography of the cult of Isis, as well as her example of selfless devotion to her son strongly influenced Christian veneration of "the mother of God." Long-standing practices of male circumcision and female excision persisted within Egyptian forms of Christianity despite the rejection of these practices in most of the Mediterranean Christian world.

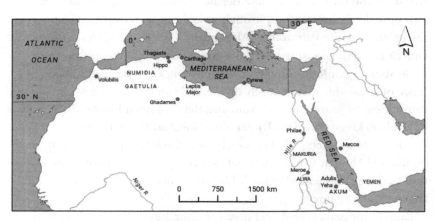

Map 8.1. North and northeast Africa to the Hijra, 622 CE (courtesy of Jonathan Chipman).

8
North and Northeast Africa in the Age of Roman and Byzantine Domination

From the First Century BCE to the Lesser Hijra

This chapter focuses on three distinct geographical areas: North Africa, Nubia, and the Horn of northeast Africa (see Map 8.1). In each area, African religious traditions interacted with Christianity brought by missionaries from neighboring countries which were still in the process of becoming predominantly Christian societies. Although they share a relatively rich supply of written and archaeological sources, they are a study in contrast. Amazigh (Berber) populations of North Africa had begun to develop their own kingdoms in response to Carthaginian efforts to expand their control over the region. During this period, Amazigh sought to play off the Romans against the Carthaginians until Rome occupied the region. The Amazigh accepted both Punic and Egyptian deities and rituals, while introducing some of their own practices to their more urban neighbors. Since the third century, Christianity became increasingly influential, producing such Christian thinkers as Tertullian and Augustin, many of whom came from Amazigh backgrounds, though they wrote in Latin. In the third century and the early fourth century, Roman persecution deeply divided North African Christians, between those who compromised their beliefs to survive and those who shouldered the burden of harassment, even martyrdom. As Roman authority declined, Vandals and other groups conquered the North African littoral, establishing more localized states, and embracing what had been labelled by the Latin and Byzantine churches as the Arian Heresy.

During this same period, the Upper Nile, from the Gezira to Philae, was dominated by the kingdom of Meroe, a state that prospered through its control of riverain trade and iron smelting. This was an area that welcomed Egyptian deities, including Amun, but incorporated them into a distinctly Meroitic religious system. In the mid-fourth century, King Ezana, the newly Christian king of Axum, defeated Meroe in a war. It never recovered. In the sixth century, a new group identified as Noba conquered Meroe and established a series of small Nubian kingdoms: Makuria, Alwa, and Nobatia. Shortly after their creation, the Noba converted to Monophysite Christianity, providing a basis for religious unity and allowing them to successfully resist Islamic conquest for half a millennium.

Finally, in the Horn of Africa, the kingdom of Axum slowly developed into a centralized state in the waning centuries before the Common Era. Ethiopians built an empire that dominated the coastal areas of present-day Eritrea and the Ethiopian highlands, focused on an elaborate royal funerary cult, marked by massive and spectacular carved stelae. In the fourth century, a young man from Syria converted the Axumite king to Christianity, beginning a tradition of a monarchy and a national identity closely associated with Monophysite Christianity and with royal descent through Solomon and Sheba. Here, too, Christianity played a central role in sustaining the state. An undercurrent of identification with Jewish traditions, however, reemerged, manifesting itself in the practice of male circumcision, the prohibition on the consumption of pork, and the centrality of fast days. Early in the seventh century, Axum was the first African state to encounter a new religion that became Islam, even before Muhammad's *hijra* to Medina.

North Africa

Roman North Africa played a vital role in the imperial economy as an important source of wheat and other grains, olives, and grapes. Roman administration divided the region into five provinces, from west to east: Mauretania, Numidia, Africa, Proconsulari, and Libya. It was also a region in which Berber, Punic, Egyptian, Greek, and Roman deities coexisted. Adherents of each tradition influenced the others' ritual practices and the beliefs that accompanied them. During this period, North Africans also experienced their first contacts with Christianity.[1] Eventually, North Africa produced many of the Church Fathers who played an important role in the development of Christian thought in both the Western and Eastern traditions. It also produced many of the Christian martyrs, both women and men, some of whom died at the hands of Roman authorities. However, some died as a result

---

[1] Robin Lane Fox, *Pagans and Christians* (New York: Alfred A. Knopf, 1989), pp. 274–275.

of conflicts between different Christian groups. North Africans seriously considered many of the theological and socio-religious movements that failed to gain the imprimatur of "orthodoxy" from Rome or Constantinople. It also produced defenders of what became orthodoxy, such as Tertullian and Augustine. Finally, North Africans provided the first Latin translation of the New Testament.[2]

In Numidia and Mauretania, a Berber king, named Juba II, was able to preserve some degree of independence from Roman sovereignty. He had received a Greek education in Italy and wrote dozens of scholarly essays. He married Cleopatra Sabine, the daughter of Antony and Cleopatra, who introduced Serapis and Isis into the kingdom. During this period, Serapis became associated with the Punic god Baal Hammon and Isis with the goddess Tanit.[3] Dream-seeking pilgrims continued to seek healing and other insights at the tombs of family members. In 40 BCE, Emperor Caligula executed King Ptolemy, annexed the kingdom of Mauretania, and made it a province of the Roman Empire.[4]

Cyrencia's close connections to Palestine and Egypt made it the first area of North Africa to be influenced by the Christian message. Jewish communities had established themselves throughout the region, well before the spread of Christianity. Jewish Cyrencians often returned to Jerusalem for major festivals. Members of this Jewish community appeared in the New Testament narratives, most notably Simeon the Cyrene, who was forced by Roman centurions to carry Jesus's cross on the way to his crucifixion. Some Gnostic and Islamic traditions suggest that it was Simeon, rather than Jesus, who was crucified, as Jesus was carried up to Heaven. The book of Acts described a permanent Cyrenaic Jewish community in Jerusalem at the time of Jesus.[5]

After the destruction of the Second Temple, in 68 CE, the Jewish community of Libya increased dramatically. Synagogues were built in the major Libyan and Tunisian towns in the early Roman era. Archaeological

---

[2] Margaret Mills, "Native North African Spiritualities," in *African Spirituality*, ed. Jacob Olupona (New York: Crossroad, 2000), p. 353.

[3] Reuben G. Bulllard, "The Berbers of the Maghreb and Ancient Carthage," in *Africa and Africans in Antiquity*, ed. Edwin Yamauchi (East Lansing: Michigan State University, 2001), p. 197. Garry Wills, *Saint Augustine* (New York: Penguin, 1999), p. 6.

[4] Bernard Rosenberger, "Des Origines aux Almoravides," in *Histoire du Maroc*, ed. Jean Brignon et al. (Casablanca: Librairie Nationale, 1967), p. 29.

[5] Thomas C. Oden, *Early Libyan Christianity: Uncovering a North African Tradition* (Downers Grove, IL: Intervarsity Press, 2011), p. 78.

evidence of synagogues has been found as far west as Tangiers (Tingis) in present-day Morocco. At the city of Volubilis (fourth century) in the Roman province of Mauretania, archaeologists found an oil lamp attached to a menorah.[6] In 115, a man named Loukias (Lukeus) Andias claimed to be the long-awaited Jewish messiah. His followers in Cyrene joined a revolt against Roman rule. In the process, they attacked and destroyed temples dedicated to Roman, Greek and Egyptian deities, including Pluto, Apollo, Artemis, Demeter, Hecate, and Isis. Roman legions brutally suppressed the revolt and inflicted heavy casualties. Many Jews fled to Alexandria, where they also faced violent reprisals, often at the hands of Cyrencian "pagans" who had fled the Jewish revolutionaries.[7] Other Jews moved away from the North African coast and settled among Berber communities that had preserved their autonomy. Several Berber communities embraced Judaism, especially nomadic communities in the Aures Mountains and the western Maghreb.[8]

Through the mid-second century, the provinces of Numidia and Gaetulia, along the northern coast of Tunisia and Algeria, remained largely unaffected by Christianity. Worship of Baal-Hammon, a deity forged from Carthaginian and Egyptian sources, became important to Berber communities.[9] Numidian rulers venerated their ancestors, who were closely linked to the fertility and the well-being of their domains. Both royal and commoner ancestors could assist their living descendants with the challenges of daily life and in planning for future events. A Roman commentator, Pomponius Mela, described Numidians as people who "consider the spirits gods, they swear by these and consult them as oracles, and, having made their requests, treat the dreams of those who sleep in their tombs as responses."[10] The seeking of oracular dreams at temples or shrines was known as incubation. Under Roman rule, however, worship of gods became central. In the second century, the temple

---

[6] Site visit to Volubilis, December 2022. Rosenberger, "Des Origines aux Almoravides," p. 44.

[7] Oden, *Early Libyan Christianity*, p. 214. Françoise Dunand and Christine Zivi-Coche, *God and Men in Egypt: 3000 BCE to 395 CE* (Ithaca, NY: Cornell University Press, 2004), p. 208. See www.Livius.org, "Roman-Jewish Wars, "Articles on Ancient History."

[8] André Chouraqui, *Between East and West: A History of the Jews of North Africa* (Philadelphia: Jewish Publication Society, 1968), pp. 13, 219.

[9] A. Mahjoubi, "The Roman and Post-Roman Period in North Africa," in *Ancient Civilizations in Africa, Volume II of UNESCO General History of Africa*, ed. G. Mokhtar (London: Heinemann, 1981), p. 496.

[10] Pomonious Mela, cited in Michael Brett and Elizabeth Fentress, *The Berbers* (Malden, MA: Blackwell, 1997), p. 35.

complex at the provincial town of Thugga included a temple dedicated to Frugifer, the town's tutelary deity, and Liban Pater, the Punic god of wine.[11] The cult of Asclepius became increasingly important in coastal areas of present-day Algeria and Tunisia, building on the Punic cult of Eshmoun. It focused on healing. Strict rules of purity required all participants to abstain from sexual relations or the eating of pork or beans, for three days prior to any ritual.[12]

During this period the writer Apuleius grew up in the provincial town of Madauros, where his father was mayor. He probably grew up speaking Punic, was educated in Greek schools, and was a devotee of the goddess Isis.[13] In his writings, Christianity seems to be more of an object of ridicule than a threat to the complexity of "pagan" religious practice in Roman Carthage.[14] After Apuleius married an older woman, her sons accused him of practicing sorcery to win her affections and gain control of her estate. This suggests that suspicions of sorcery and the manufacture of love medicines were common in this period. Apuleius wrote *The Apologia* in his defense and was acquitted by the Roman Proconsul.[15] Libyans also continued their practice of local traditions, focused on temples where funerary and fertility rituals took place. Here, too, supplicants came to the temples to sleep in the hope of oracular dreams in which they could learn how to heal an illness or how to address other problems in life.[16] Soldiers stationed in the area commissioned the building of temples to Mithra, a deity of Persian origin, especially venerated by Roman centurions.[17]

The earliest specific reference to Christians in the Carthage area was the *Acts of the Scillitan Martyrs*. As the name suggests, it describes the trial of twelve African men and women in the year 180. They were executed because they refused to renounce their Christian faith and sacrifice to the Roman gods. Margaret Mills describes them as "African Christians with native names from a small town near Carthage." As they were taken

---

[11] Paul MacKendrick, *The North African Stones Speak* (Chapel Hill: University of North Carolina Press, 1980), p. 67.
[12] MacKendrick, *North African Stones Speak*, p. 71.
[13] Jack Lindsay, "Introduction," to Apuleius, *The Golden Ass* (Bloomington: Indiana University Press, [1932] (1975), pp. 5–7, 21.
[14] Apuleius, *Golden Ass*, pp. 55–59.
[15] B. B. Osborn, "Introduction" to *The Golden Ass of Lucius Apuleius* (London: The Abbey Library, [n.d.] 1669), p. x.
[16] Brett and Fentress, *Berbers*, p. 35.
[17] Courtlandt Canby, with Arcadia Kocybala, *A Guide to the Archaeological Sites of Israel, Egypt, and North Africa* (New York: Facts on File, 1990), p. 254.

to be beheaded, they called out "Thanks be to God," which became the final words of many Christian martyrs in the years before the Edict of Toleration, in 315.[18]

By the last decades of the second century, Libya was playing a central role in early Church history and the history of the Roman Empire. Three families from Leptis Magna assumed powerful roles. In 193, Septimius Severus founded a new dynasty of Roman emperors that ruled the empire for over forty years. At Leptis, Severus became involved with the Hellenistic cult of Serapis, a practice that he continued as emperor. He patronized the worship of Roman deities and the restoration of their temples. Christians endured persecution during his reign. In 202, Septimius Severus prohibited Roman subjects from converting to Christianity or Judaism, both of which he saw as threats to imperial authority.[19] During the same period, Pope Victor served as Bishop of Rome, becoming the first African head of the Roman Catholic Church. He sought to establish a shared Sunday for the celebration of Easter and encouraged the transition from a Greek to a Latin mass.

Finally, Quintus Septimius Florens Tertullianus, born into a wealthy family, also came from Leptis Magna during this period. After a rigorous Latin education, he became a teacher, working in a school where staff made offerings to Minerva, the Roman goddess of wisdom. As he continued his study of law and theology, Tertullian formalized the concept of the trinity and became one of early Christendom's leading theologians.[20] He also supported the idea "that the human soul is transmitted by parents to their children and is therefore inescapably associated with continuing human sin."[21] This idea marked a clear departure from North African and Egyptian concepts of the body. Tertullian harshly condemned any cooperation with what he considered "paganism": "Tertullian's most stringent demands for purity forbid his fellow Christians from serving in the army, in the civil service, or even in schools. To Tertullian, Christians should not earn their livings producing anything that might indirectly minister to idolatry. Tertullian's concept of the Christian life was first and foremost a

---

[18] Mills, "Native North African Spiritualities," p. 352. Harvey Sindone, *Drums of Redemption: An Introduction to African Christianity* (Westport, CT: Praeger, 1999), p. 8.
[19] Diarmaid MacCulloch, *Christianity: The First Three Thousand Years* (New York: Viking, 2010), p. 72.
[20] Oden, *Early Libyan Christianity*, pp. 106–107. Fox, *Pagans and Christians*, p. 83.
[21] MacCulloch, *Christianity*, p. 145.

battle with the devil."[22] He was deeply troubled by what he alleged was the continuation of child sacrifice by Punic speakers in the region.[23]

He eventually became sympathetic to the Montanist movement, which stressed the importance of ongoing revelation from the Holy Spirit. In his essay, "On the Soul," Tertullian described an unnamed African woman who communicated with God and with angels, had visions, preached sermons, and healed the sick. "We have now amongst us a sister whose lot it has been to be favoured with sundry gifts of revelation, which she experiences in the spirit by ecstatic vision amidst the sacred rite of the Lord's day in the Church. She converses with angels and sometimes even with the Lord; she both hears and sees mysterious communication; some men's hearts she understands and to those in need she distributes remedies."[24] With Tertullian's support, women assumed prophetic roles in the Christian movement in the third century.[25] The Montanist movement did not become schismatic within the early church. Its teachings, however, commanded significant support among North African Christians.[26]

By the beginning of the third century, North African Christians had a well-defined vision of both the catechumenate, which could last several years, and the formal conversion process. The North African Christians recognized the need for concerted study and socialization in order to fully understand the new faith and to undertake a decisive break with the multilayered traditions of North African paganism. Church leaders interrogated catechumens about their beliefs and commitments, and exorcised the devil and what they considered to be devilish "paganism." The church leaders laid their hands on the catechumenates to heal them, and the candidates were fed salt. Only then could they enter into formal catechumenate status.[27]

Although Christianity did not become important in most of North Africa until the third century, it quickly assumed a central role. The fertility

---

[22] Henry Chadwick, *The Early Church* (Harmondsworth, UK: Penguin, [1967] 1982), pp. 91–92.
[23] Dexter Hoyas, *The Carthaginians* (London: Routledge, 2010), p. 101.
[24] Tertullian, *A Treatise on the Soul*, trans. Peter Holmes, Christian Apologetics and Resource Ministry.
[25] Karen Jo Torjesen, *When Women Were Priests: Women's Leadership in the Early Church and the Scandal of Their Subordination in the Rise of Christianity* (San Francisco: Harpers San Francisco, 1995), pp. 29–31. Sindone, *Drums of Redemption*, p. 9.
[26] Mills, "Native North African Spiritualities," p. 357.
[27] Thomas M. Finn, "'It Happened One Saturday Night': Ritual and Conversion in Augustine's North Africa," *Journal of the American Academy of Religion* LVIII, no. 4 (1990), pp. 590–592.

and healing cults of Tanit and Isis found new modes of expression in the veneration of the Virgin Mary. Representations of Isis as a grieving woman influenced the portrayal of Mary, grieving over her deceased son.[28] In 203, saints Perpetua and Felicity were publicly martyred in a Carthaginian arena.[29] Saint Cyprian became a Christian around 246, and then a bishop two years later. During the Decian persecutions, Cyprian went into hiding but continued to guide his diocese. When the persecutions eased, he advocated allowing apostatized Christians back into the Church, as did Pope Cornelius. The persecutions resumed under Emperor Valerian and, in 258, Cyprian was ordered to recant. He refused to do so and was beheaded.[30]

As recently as the fifth century, people in the province of Africa (western Tunisia and the eastern part of Algeria) still spoke the Punic language. This demonstrated the persistent influence of Carthaginian culture. Saint Augustine, who was born in the region, described Punic speakers in his diocese.[31] Augustine complained about the persistence of Berber religious practices, especially the idea that divinity could best be sensed in the rugged areas of the Atlas Mountains. Pliny the Elder also complained about Berber nocturnal rituals in grottoes lit by fires and accompanied by the music of flutes.[32] Further west, in the Canary Islands, sacred rock formations were the subject of pilgrimages. Various springs in the Atlas Mountains and their foothills were associated with healing spirits who received ritual supplications at local shrines. Ritual baths performed in the nude were considered part of the healing process throughout the Maghreb. These, too, were denounced by Augustine.[33] Pilgrims made offerings of milk and butter accompanied by prayers sung in solemn hymns. In the course of the ritual, supplicants would travel down to the sea where they would pray for rain.[34] Local magistrates performed rituals for municipal deities, offering up rams in prayers for community well-being.[35] Roman religious practices continued

---

[28] Gabriel Camps, *Les Berbères: Mémoires et Identité* (Paris: Editions Errance, 1987), p. 113.
[29] Elizabeth Isechei, *History of Christianity in Africa* (Grand Rapids, MI: Eerdmans, 1995), pp. 34–35.
[30] Donald Attwater, *The Penguin Dictionary of Saints* (Harmondsworth, UK: Penguin, 1983), pp. 96–97.
[31] Reuben G. Bullard, "The Berbers of the Maghreb and Ancient Carthage," in *Africa and Africans in Antiquity*, ed. Edwin Yamauchi (East Lansing: Michigan State University, 2001), p. 197.
[32] Camps, *Les Berbères*, p. 145.
[33] Camps, *Les Berbères*, pp. 146–147.
[34] Camps, *Les Berbères*, p. 145.
[35] Camps, *Les Berbères*, p. 165.

throughout the fourth century. The city of Volubulis in Roman Mauretania had a large temple dedicated to Jupiter, Juno, and Minerva, a Roman trinity that may have facilitated the adoption of the Christian one. An altar for animal sacrifice was installed in front of the temple (see Figures 8.1 and 8.2).[36]

During the first decade of the fourth century, persecution of Christians resumed under Emperor Diocletian. He mandated that every adult must make offerings to the Imperial cult. This could be as little as an offering of incense, but failure to do so could lead one to be suspected of being a Christian. In 304, a Numidian Christian woman named Crispina was one of those who refused to make the offering. She was from a wealthy family and had several children. The Roman Proconsul, Anulinus, had her arrested and ordered her to renounce her Christian faith, but she refused. So he had her executed.[37] She is considered a martyred saint of the Catholic Church. Some church leaders, however, renounced their faith and surrendered religious texts to Roman authorities who destroyed them.

Though he only converted on his death bed, Constantine stopped the persecution of Christians. Those who had suffered for their faith objected to the restoration of those Church leaders who had renounced their faith under duress. During the fourth century, the Donatist Church challenged Roman civil and ecclesiastical authorities, and this helped the dissenters garner widespread support in North Africa, especially in areas with relatively few Latin speakers. They opposed imperial interference in matters of religion.[38] As Bishop Donatus, whose name was given to the entire movement, was quoted as demanding: "'What does the emperor have to do with the Church?'"[39] Donatists in North Africa appointed bishops who rejected the authority of the Catholic Church and who ordained their own clergy. They stressed the purity of the Church and denounced those who had surrendered scriptures and other church documents to the Roman authorities during the Diocletian persecutions. Peter Brown noted that "The Church had to survive in its full holiness. It was a 'true vine', and like a vine it had to be drastically pruned. It could only survive as pure if unworthy bishops were excluded, for the guilt of the bishop automatically

---

[36] Site visit, Volubilis, December 2022.
[37] Attwater, *The Penguin Dictionary of Saints*, p. 94. MacKendrick, *North African Stones Speak*, p. 262.
[38] Elias Bongmba, "Christianity in North Africa," in *The Routledge Companion to Christianity in Africa*, ed. E. Bongmba (New York: Routledge, 2016), p. 36.
[39] Quoted in Brent D. Shaw, *Sacred Violence: African Christians and Sectarian Hatred in the Age of Augustine* (Cambridge: Cambridge University Press, 2011), p. 490.

Figure 8.1. Roman sacrificial altar by a Christian church, Volubilis, Morocco (photo by Robert M. Baum).

rendered ineffective the prayers by which he baptized and ordained."[40] They saw themselves as the true Church and repudiated the corruption they associated with the Roman church.

[40] Brown, *Augustine*, p. 20.

Figure 8.2. Menorah oil lamp, Volubilis, Morocco (photo by Robert M. Baum).

Donatism also had a social dimension, rejecting the elitism of a Roman-oriented clergy and the growing opulence of the fourth-century church. They marshalled the grievances of North African rural communities who resented the tax policies of the Roman administration and its favoritism toward Catholic officials. At Djebel Edogh, a poor and rugged region, Donatist dissidents attacked and killed a number of Catholic priests. Groups of young men who gathered at shrines of Christian martyrs (*cellae*) became known as Circumcellions. They formed gangs that used violence to advance the Donatist cause.[41] Circumcellions sought out martyrdom, not only by risking their lives in violent confrontations, but in a willingness to commit suicide to advance their cause. They considered Catholic clergy and the wealthy classes who supported them as a threat to the purity of the Christian movement. The Donatists enjoyed strong support among the Berbers in the mountainous areas south of the coastal plain.[42] In many areas of North Africa, Donatist churches enjoyed the support of a majority of local Christians in the late fourth century. The Catholic Church only regained a hegemonic position in the fifth century, though Donatist influence persisted into the seventh century.[43]

The newly ascendant Christians did more than quarrel among themselves. They turned the power of imperial authority against people they identified as "pagans." Christian leaders worked to suppress festivals dedicated to Berber, Punic, Egyptian, Greek, and Roman deities and destroyed their temples.[44] A law adopted in 399 "contained specific measures calling for the official physical dismantling of sacred images in public temples and shrines."[45] In some cases, they leveled the temples so they could build churches on the sites; in other cases they remodeled the temples and transformed them into Christian houses of worship. In 407, Roman authorities suppressed payments of public funds to all temples in Carthage. In 415, local authorities confiscated all lands associated with the temples.[46] Christians destroyed temples and statues, often provoking resistance from people who still found these rituals meaningful. During the late fourth century, in Carthage itself, statues of gods were hidden away in a subterranean room and covered by a mosaic to keep Christians from destroying them.[47]

---

[41] Brent D. Shaw, "Who Were the Circumcellions?" in *Vandals, Romans, and Berbers: New Perspectives on Late Antique North Africa*, ed. A. H. Merrills (New York: Routledge, 2016), pp. 228–229, 236–237.

[42] Peter Brown, *Augustine of Hippo* (Berkeley: University of California Press, 1967), pp. 139–140, 194. Elizabeth Isichei, *A History of the Church in Africa: From Antiquity to the Present* (Grand Rapids, MI: Eerdmans, 1995), p. 36. Shaw, "Who Were the Circumcellions?" p. 227.

[43] Mills, "Native North African Spiritualities," pp. 358–360.

[44] Brown, *Augustine*, p. 280.

[45] Shaw, *Sacred Violence*, p. 211.

[46] Shaw, *Sacred Violence*, pp. 222–223.

[47] Gareth Sears, *Late Roman African Urbanism: Continuity and Transformation in the City* (Oxford: Archaeopress, 2007), pp. 42–43. Shaw, *Sacred Violence*, pp. 248–249.

In many ways the life of Saint Augustine paralleled the religious transformations of the coastal regions of the Roman Maghreb. Saint Augustine was born in Thagaste, Numidia (Algeria), in 354, to a Christian mother named Monica and a "pagan" Numidian father, who was a landowner and minor Roman official.[48] Her name referred to a Berber deity named Mon, whose main sanctuary was at the nearby town of Thibilis.[49] After a long period of resisting Christianity, pursuing a career in letters, and becoming involved with Manichaeanism, Augustine became a Christian. He eventually became the Bishop of Hippo, along the north coast of Tunisia, and went on to become one of the most important theologians in Catholic Church history. He wrote his most famous work, *The Confessions*, at age forty-three, shortly after being named bishop. He described his religious journey, including his reluctance to convert to Christianity and accept the discipline of life according to Christian mores. His mother, also canonized, sought to influence her son's spiritual journey. Her devotions included popular North African practices of having meals in cemeteries to honor the ancestors and Christian martyrs, something eventually discouraged by the Church hierarchy. A series of dreams convinced Monica that her son would eventually find his way to the Christian path.[50]

As an adolescent, Augustine rebelled against the constraints of provincial Numidian life, stealing pears from a farm. He joined a group of young men who challenged local authority. Augustine discovered the appeal of sexual activity and the pleasures of the world. He had a long-term relationship with a woman he described as unsuitable for marriage, because of class differences, but he did have a child with her. He does not name her in the *Confessions*. Still, he remained interested in learning—rhetoric, literature, and philosophy—seeking to reconcile his love of worldly activity with his pursuit of knowledge. He rejected astrology, seeing it as irrational, as well as the use of magic to win competitions or advance one's career, both frequently resorted to in the pluralistic environment of Roman Numidia.[51] During his intellectual quest, he became influenced by Manichaeanism and its opposition of Good and Evil, the Spirit and the Material. He met with a Manichean bishop, named Faustus, whose eloquence and knowledge

---

[48] R. S. Pine-Coffin, "Introduction," Saint Augustine, *Confessions* (Harmondsworth, UK: Penguin, 1970), pp. 13, 19
[49] Wills, *Saint Augustine*, p. 2.
[50] Brown, *Augustine of Hippo*, pp. 29–30.
[51] Augustine, *Confessions*, pp. 72–73.

enticed him in a way that he likened to a "decoy of the devil."⁵² Augustine's critics, however, mocked his poor command of Greek language. One of them, Julian of Eclanum, dismissed him as "'what passes for a philosopher among Africans.'"⁵³

Augustine modified the process of preparing for baptism, introducing a several-weeks-long rite of passage for catechumens before they entered into the Christian community. It began fifteen days before Easter. Like his North African predecessors, Augustine saw exorcism as an essential part of transforming potential Christians into a part of what he called the *corpus mysticum Christi*. The exorcism included the laying on of hands and the removal of all diabolic forces. Augustinian baptisms were by immersion, which was followed by the initiates' first communion. A second communion followed as part of the Easter mass.⁵⁴

In 410, shortly after the capture of Rome by Alaric the Goth, Augustine wrote *The City of God*, in which he reflected on the religious significance of an increasingly turbulent world. He focused on the celestial world as the only perfectible one. These more westerly Church Fathers wrote in Latin, reflecting the lesser impact of Hellenization in the Maghreb.⁵⁵ By 420, most people in the Maghrebian coastal region, where Augustine served as bishop, had embraced Christianity.⁵⁶

In 429, Vandal armies crossed the Mediterranean and established a series of states in the Roman provinces of Mauretania and Numidia. King Geiseric led 80,000 soldiers and their families and settled in the coastal regions from Tangier as far east as Carthage, which they made their capitol. Initially, Berber communities welcomed them as liberators from Roman rule.⁵⁷

Despite the popularity of the teachings of Arius in Egypt and Libya, the Maghreb did not accept Arian doctrines until the mid-fifth century, when they were introduced by the Vandals. The Vandals had accepted his teachings in Germany, before they moved south into Iberia and North Africa.⁵⁸ Vandal Arianism differed from Arius's initial teachings in Egypt, however. Ufilias, a missionary to the Goths described Jesus as "'a creature like man ... exalted

---

⁵² Augustine, *Confessions*, p. 92.
⁵³ Julian of Eclanum, cited in Wills, *Saint Augustine*, p. xi.
⁵⁴ Finn, "It Happened One Saturday Night," pp. 591–594.
⁵⁵ Philip Curtin et al. *African History* (London: Longman, [1978] 1991), p. 62. Attwater, *Penguin Dictionary of Saints*, pp. 52–53.
⁵⁶ Serge Lancel, *Saint Augustine* (London: SCM Press, 2002), p. 306.
⁵⁷ Walter Pohl, "The Vandals: Fragments of a Narrative," in *Vandals, Romans, and Berbers: New Perspectives on Late Antique North Africa*, ed. A. H. Merrills (New York: Routledge, 2016), pp. 38–43.
⁵⁸ Curtin et al., *African History*, p. 62.

above man by the design and will of the Father, not by virtue of his own essence.'"[59] Geiseric sought to broaden his support by favoring the Arian Church over the Catholic Church. He went as far as to require adherence to Arian doctrines to hold government office. His son Huneric closed many Catholic churches in his North African territories.[60] Despite such actions, Vandals attempted to reconcile the Arian and Catholic traditions. For example, in 515, King Thrashmund convened a meeting of Catholic and Arian religious leaders, at Carthage. The meeting was unsuccessful. One of the Catholic delegates, Bishop Fulgentius of Ruspe, was such an effective speaker against Arianism that the king had him exiled to Sardinia, to keep him from challenging North Africa's Arian church. The Vandal king Geiseric deported Catholic clergy and seized church treasures.[61]

When the Byzantines returned to North Africa, in 533, they quickly drove the Vandals from power. The Berbers continued their resistance for another fifteen years. At least until the mid-sixth century, Berber communities beyond the control of the Byzantines, near the Sahara, continued to worship the Carthaginian deity Baal-Hammon.[62] In 534, the newly restored Byzantine authorities expropriated "pagan" and Jewish places of worship, as well as Arian and Donatist churches. They made it a capital offense for Jews and Christians to intermarry.[63] Once in control, the Byzantines sent missionaries south from North Africa, to convert Garamantes and Tuareg to Christianity. In 568, the Saharan communities of Audjila and Ghadames embraced Christianity.[64]

Religious traditions associated with North African communities persisted into the sixth century. They also influenced Christian expressions of their religious tradition, including the influence of goddess worship on the veneration of the Virgin Mary and her artistic representation. Adherents of North African traditions clashed with increasingly powerful Christian groups. As Christians assumed a hegemonic position in North Africa, however, Christians struggled against one another over doctrinal differences, often violently, with Donatists and Arians from local communities opposed

---

[59] G. A. A. Scott, quoted in C. J. Speel II, "The Disappearance of Christianity from North Africa in the Wake of Islam," *Church History* V. XXIX, no. 4 (1960), p. 384.
[60] Pohl, "Vandals," p. 44.
[61] Speel, "Disappearance of Christianity," p. 386.
[62] Isichei, History of the Church in Africa, p. 42.
[63] Chouriqui, *Between East and West*, pp. 26–27.
[64] R. C. C. Law, "The Garamantes and Trans-Saharan Enterprise in Classical Times," *Journal of African History* VIII, no. 2 (1967), p. 199.

to Christian groups based in Rome and Constantinople. As most North Africans embraced Christianity, they continued to see religious life as integrally involved in their struggle to maintain their autonomy from the powers on the northern side of the Mediterranean.

Nubia

After repelling the forces of Emperor Augustus, in 20 BCE, Meroe signed a peace treaty with Rome which established peaceful and profitable relations with its powerful northern neighbor.[65] Meroe's rulers remained suspicious of Roman influence, however. Until the sixth century, Nubia remained a center for the continuation of adherence to Egyptian and Nubian religious traditions. Well after the establishment of Christianity as Rome's official religion, cults of Isis and Amun continued to attract significant followings in Nubia. Nubian deities like Mandulis received frequent attention at pilgrimage sites at Kalabsha, Thalmis, and the island of Philae in the frontier zone between Upper Egypt and Lower Nubia. Emperor Diocletian expanded the temple complex at Philae and allowed Blemmye and Nobatean priests to perform rituals there.[66] Mandulis became associated with the Hellenistic deity Aion (Eternal Time or Fate) and drew Egyptian pilgrims into lower Nubia. Aion had become associated with the increasingly important mystery cults that were attracting participants throughout the Eastern Mediterranean world.[67]

As Christianity gained a widespread following in Egypt, in the third century, Meroe resisted the new religion. Its rulers preferred to practice a Meroitic tradition which had accepted a number of Egyptian deities, such as Amun and Isis. Nubia became the center of this Egyptian/Nubian religious practice, first against Romanization and, then again, after Christianity had become the dominant tradition in Egypt. Still, some Christian refugees moved south into Nubia, during the third century, to escape Roman persecution of the new religion. Beginning in the fourth century, however, members of persecuted Christian sects joined them, seeking

---

[65] Stanley M. Burstein, "The Kingdom of Meroe," in *Africa and Africans in Antiquity*, ed. Edwin M. Yamauchi (East Lansing: Michigan State University, 2001), p. 135.
[66] Procopius of Caesaria, *History*, Fordham Internet Ancient History Sourcebook: Egypt, c. 550 CE.
[67] David Frankfurter, *Religion in Roman Egypt: Assimilation and Resistance* (Princeton, NJ: Princeton University Press, 1998), pp. 35, 109.

a place where they could practice their interpretations of Christianity free of Roman or Byzantine interference. Christian merchants also made their way south during this period.[68]

The rise of Axum in the Ethiopian highlands undercut Meroe's trading position along the Red Sea and curtailed its access to the Indian Ocean. Deforestation resulting from a high demand for charcoal undermined the iron industry. These factors led to a sharp economic decline for the Meroitic kingdom.[69] King Ezana's destruction of the city of Meroe in 350 seriously weakened the Nubian state. Motivated by his recent conversion to Christianity, Ezana destroyed statues and temples dedicated to Meroitic gods.[70] Lavish burials of Meroe's kings seemed to have ceased during this period, suggesting a sharp decline in royal prestige and wealth.[71] By the fifth century, Christianity was rapidly growing among the urban poor within the kingdom of Meroe.[72]

Shortly thereafter, the Ballana dynasty took control of Meroe. They also had little interest in Christianity and continued Meroitic practices of more elaborate royal burials.[73] A new ethnic group moved east into the Nile Valley and established three Nubian kingdoms: Makuria and Nobatia centered on the old territory of Napata and the Dongola Reach; and Alwa on the territories around the Meroitic capital. In 539, Emperor Justinian abrogated the treaty which guaranteed Nubian and Blemmye access to pilgrimage sites at Philae.[74] A few years later, in 549, a Monophysite missionary named Julian, sent by Empress Theodora, a staunch Monophysite, converted the Nobatean king,s. Makuria was converted to the Melkite (Orthodox) Church in 576. Alwa was officially converted in the Monophysite tradition, by Longinus. By 600, all three kingdoms had become officially Christian.[75] Even though they had resisted Christian

---

[68] Roland Werner, William Anderson, and Andrea Wheeler, *Day of Devastation, Day of Contentment: The History of the Sudanese Church across 2,000 Years* (Nairobi: Paches Publications, 2001), pp. 27–28.
[69] Kevin Shillington, *A History of Africa* (New York: St. Martin's Press, 1995), pp. 44–45.
[70] Ezana, "The Destruction of Kush," in *African History: Texts and Readings*, ed. Robert O'Collins (New York: Random House, 1973), pp. 257–268.
[71] George Hatke, *Aksum and Nubia: Warfare, Commerce, and Political Fictions in Ancient Northeast Africa* (New York: New York University Press, 2013), p. 143.
[72] W. H. C. Frend, "The Christian Period in Mediterranean Africa, c. A/D. 200 to 708," in *Cambridge History of Africa Volume II*, ed. J. D. Fage (Cambridge: Cambridge University Press, 1975), p. 447.
[73] Isichei, *History of the Church in Africa*, p. 30.
[74] Frend, "Christian Period in Mediterranean Africa," p. 447.
[75] William Y. Adams, *Nubia: Corridor to Africa* (Princeton, NJ: Princeton University Press, 1972), p. 443. Curtin et al., *African History*, p. 63. Leclant, "The Empire of Kush," p. 295.

missionaries from Egypt and Axum for several hundred years, once they embraced Christianity, it became central to their national identity and facilitated their resistance to Arab invaders beginning in the late seventh century.

The Blemmyes, ancestors of the Beja of northern Sudan, inhabited the hill country between Nubia and the Red Sea and herded livestock. Relying on the mobility provided by camels, they often raided the more sedentary communities of the Nile valley. They negotiated the right to perform pilgrimages to the temple of Isis at Philae, an island that alternated between the control of Rome and Meroe. Blemmye priests served in these temples. They even built a shrine for one of the Blemmye deities on the island. From the fourth century, some of Philae's priests were Hellenized Blemmyes, literate in Greek, Demotic, hieroglyphics and Meroitic. In the fifth century, Blemmyes created their own state along the Nile, with their capital at Kalabibas, home of a major temple of the god, Mandulis.[76] They continued to perform rituals there until the sixth century when the Byzantine emperor, Justinian, ordered it closed.[77] In 538, Romans and Nubians joined forces to defeat the Blemmyes, who swore an oath, to maintain peaceful relations, on an image of their patron deity.[78]

The Horn of Africa

Little is known about the founding of the kingdom of Axum, but it gained ascendancy over the former domains of D'MT in northeastern Ethiopia and Eritrea before the beginning of the Common Era. The first-century navigator's guide, *The Periplus of the Erythraean Sea*, described Axum's port of Adulis as the Northeastern African center of the ivory trade.[79] By the third century, however, Axum had become the dominant power in the Ethiopian highlands, the adjacent coastal areas, and occasionally exerted control over Yemen, in southwestern Arabia. During this period, Mani, the founder of Manicheanism, described the Axumite kingdom as one of the

---

[76] Derek A. Welsby, *The Medieval Kingdoms of Nubia: Pagans, Christians, and Muslims along the Middle Nile* (London: British Museum Press, 2002), pp, 16–19, 119.
[77] LeClant, "Empire of Kush," p. 295. Frankfurter, *Religion*, p. 105. Welsby, *Medieval*, p. 19.
[78] Frend, "Christian Period in Mediterranean Africa," p. 447.
[79] Wilfred H. Schoff, translator, *The Periplus of the Erythraean Sea* (New York: Longman, 1912). Shillington, *History of Africa*, p. 69. Jack Phillips, "Punt and Aksum: Egypt and the Horn of Africa," *Journal of African History* 38 (1997), p. 441.

major world civilizations.[80] The kingdom of Axum actively engaged with trade with the Romans and as far east as India, while maintaining their political and religious independence. Through long-standing commercial activities along the Red Sea, Axumites had become familiar with Judaism. Beginning in the first century, kings of Axum created enormous, engraved stelae marking their graves and communicating their achievements. One of the stele has an inscription about Mahrem, the patron god of the Axumite kings, who Greek observers equated with their war god, Ares.[81] The sheer number of them, nearly two hundred, suggests that wealthy Axumites also had stelae commissioned The largest of the stelae was over one hundred feet high and was carved to resemble a nine-story building (see Figure 8.3). Early Axumites worshipped other deities besides Mahrem: Astar (the morning star, Venus), Almaqah (the moon, primary god of the Sabeans), Nuru (the god of the dawn), Hakyas (an aspect of the moon), Dhat Hunya (an aspect of the sun, linked to summer), and Dhat Ba'eoli (an aspect of the sun associated with winter). A stele erected in the second century included an image of Almaqah.[82]

Beja (Blemmyes) and Agauw groups were less influenced by South Arabian and other Semitic traditions, but preserved their independence from Rome, Axum, and the Nubian kingdoms. Within their religious systems, spiritual beings were more associated with unusual trees, prominent rock formations, mountains, rivers, lakes, and springs. They had less of a focus on celestial deities than the Axumites had in their religious traditions.[83] The Blemmyes continued to conduct pilgrimages to the Isis shrine at Philae until Emperor Justinian closed it down in the sixth century.

Christianity came to Axum in the fourth century, brought by young men from Tyre, in Lebanon. According to a contemporary account by Ruffinus, two young men accompanied a Tyrean philosopher named Meropius to the Axumite court. The philosopher was killed, perhaps by pirates, but his young

---

[80] Anene Ejikeme, "Ezana (Ahola)," in *Holy People of the World: A Cross-Cultural Encyclopedia*, Vol. I, ed. Phyllis G. Jestice (Santa Barbara, CA: ABC-Clio, 2004), p. 267. James L. Newman, *The Peopling of Africa: A Geographic Interpretation* (New Haven, CT: Yale University Press, 1995), p. 91.

[81] Y. M. Kobishanov, "Aksum: Political System, Economics, and Culture, First to Fourth Century," in *Ancient Civilizations in Africa, Volume II of UNESCO General History of Africa*, ed. G. Mokhtar (London: Heinemann, 1981), p. 307. Stuart Munro-Hay, *Aksum: An African Civilization in Late Antiquity* (Edinburgh: Edinburgh University Press, 1991), p. 159.

[82] Munro-Hay, *Aksum*, pp. 196, 203. Yuri M. Kobishanov, *Axum* (University Park: The Pennsylvania State University Press, 1979), pp. 49, 224.

[83] Tekele Tsadik Makarim, "Christian Aksum," in *Ancient Civilizations of Africa, Volume 2, UNESCO General History of Africa*, ed. G. Mokhtar (London: Heinemann, 1981), p. 401.

Figure 8.3. Stele, Axum, Ethiopia, with the Church of Mary Our Lady of Zion in the background (photo by Robert M. Baum).

protégés, Frumentius and Aedesius, found positions at the Axumite Court. Frumentius convinced King Ella Amida to allow Greek merchants to open chapels in Axum, and he began to proselytize on his own. After the death of Ella Amida, Frumentius tutored the future king while Ezana's mother served as regent. When Ezana assumed the throne, Frumentius returned to the Mediterranean region and stopped in Egypt where he asked Bishop Athanasius to send missionaries to Axum. Athanasius appointed Frumentius as Bishop of Ethiopia and sent him back to expand his mission.[84] According to Ruffinus, Athanasius asked Frumentius "'What other man shall we find in whom the Spirit of God, as in thee, can accomplish these things.'"[85] Frumentius converted Ezana, though not before the king had conducted military campaigns against the Beja, where he thanked Axumite deities. As a mark of his acceptance of Christianity, Ezana had the cross engraved on Axumite coins. He was the first Christian ruler to mint coinage with Christian symbols.[86] His commemorative stele, marking his capture of Meroe, c. 350, offered thanks to the "Lord of Heaven," and described himself as a "servant of Christ." Earlier such stelae had offered thanks to the deities of Axum, including Mahrem and Astarte.[87] During this period, Axum developed its own language, Ge'ez, the liturgical language of the Ethiopian church and the precursor of Amharic and Tigrinya.[88]

The Axumite Church developed with a strong tie to Egypt and the Patriarch of Alexandria. These connections led the Ethiopian Church to accept the majoritarian tendency within Egyptian Christianity, associated with a Monophysite understanding of the nature of Christ. The Patriarch of Alexandria, the head of the Monophysite Church, appointed the Abuna, the head of the Axumite Church. However, long-standing contact with Israelite

---

[84] Attwater, *Penguin Dictionary of Saints*, p. 141. Steven Kaplan, *The Beta Israel (Falasha) in Ethiopia: From Earliest Times to the Twentieth Century* (New York: New York University, 1992), p. 34. Isichei, *History of the Church in Africa*, pp. 32–33.

[85] Ruffinus quoted in Munro-Hay, *Aksum*, p. 203.

[86] Ejikeme, "Ezana (Ahola)," p. 267. Joseph Harris, ed., *The William Leo Hansberry African History Notebooks* (Washington, DC: Howard University Press, 1974), p. 67. Stanley Burstein, ed., *Ancient African Civilization: Kush and Axum* (Princeton, NJ: Markus Wiener, 2009), pp. 107–108.

[87] Cited in Munro-Hay, *Aksum*, p. 229. Robert W July, *A History of the African People*, 4th ed. (Prospect Heights, IL: Waveland, 1992), p. 39. Hatke, *Aksum and Nubia*, p. 123. P. L. Shinnie, "The Nilotic Sudan and Ethiopia, c. 660 BC to AD 600," in *The Cambridge History of Africa, Volume II, From c. 500 BC to AD 1050*, ed. J. D. Fage (Cambridge: Cambridge University Press, 1978), p. 260.

[88] Shillington, *History of Africa*, p. 70. Kathryn A. Bard and Rudolfo Fattovich, "Processes of State Formation in Egypt and Ethiopia," in *Africa and Africans in Antiquity*, ed. Edwin Yamauchi (East Lansing: Michigan State University, 2001), p. 242. David W. Phillipson, *Ancient Ethiopia: Axum, Its Antecedents and Successors* (London: British Museum Press, 1998), pp. 51, 95, 113.

traditions led Ethiopian Christians to adopt the Jewish prohibition on the consumption of pork and to incorporate the practice of male circumcision and fasting days. They also included models of the Ark of the Covenant (tabot) in their churches, a reminder of the claim that it was brought to Axum by Menelik I, the son of Solomon and Sheba. These practices mark just a few of the distinctive aspects of Ethiopian Christianity.[89] Initially, however, Christianity was centered on Ezana's court. It spread very slowly in rural areas, where Ezana continued to present himself as a worshipper of astral deities.[90]

In the mid-fifth century, a second wave of evangelization swept through Ethiopia, bringing Christianity out of the capital into the rural areas. Christian dissenters from Egypt, mainly Monophysites, sought refuge in Axum. Among them were a group that became known as the Nine Saints, whose activities are recorded in the Ge'ez text the *Gadle Tsadkan, The Acts of the Saints*. They taught and built churches in small towns such as Yeha and Debra Damo.[91] By the sixth century, much of the New Testament was translated into Ge'ez, in a work known as the Garima Gospel. It was attributed to Abba Garima, one of the Nine Saints. At Yeha, they transformed the ancient temple into a church dedicated to the hermit saint, Abba Atse.[92] At Metera, a center of ancient Axumite religion, armed resistance to the spread of Christianity led to the killing of several of the "saintly" hermits.[93] By the sixth century, dioceses had been established and Ethiopia had become a Christian kingdom. At the Red Sea port of Adulis, there was a Monophysite bishop by the name of Moses, who traveled to India to meet with fellow Monophysites.[94] At Beta Semati, archaeologists have found the ruins of a cathedral, with three naves, elaborately decorated with marble imported from the Maghreb or Spain, as well as elaborate window fittings. At Adulis, several church sites have been found, suggesting that it was more than a major trading port on the route from Egypt to India, but a center of early Christianity.[95]

---

[89] Kaplan, *Beta Israel*, p. 19.
[90] Kaplan, *Beta Israel*, pp. 34–35. Frend, "Christian," p. 446.
[91] Phillipson, *Ancient Ethiopia*, pp. 64, 112. Harold Marcus, *A History of Ethiopia* (Berkeley: University of California Press, 1994), p. 8.
[92] Francis Anfray, *Les Anciens Ethiopiens: Siècles de l'histoire* (Paris: Armand Colin, 1990), p. 17. Bairu Tafla, "The Establishment of the Ethiopian Church," *Tarikh* 2 (1967), special issue on "Early African Christianity," p. 32.
[93] Tafla, "Establishment of the Ethiopian Church," p. 32.
[94] Y. M. Kobishchanov, "On the Problem of Sea Voyages of Ancient Africans in the Indian Ocean," *Journal of African History* VI, no. 2 (1965), pp. 138–139.
[95] Jason Urbanus, "Africa's Merchant Kings," *Archaeology* July/August 2023.

In 525, led by King Elia Asbeha (Kaleb), Axum conquered the Himyarite kingdom in Yemen, bringing an end to the seventy-five-year reign of a Jewish monarch, Dhu Nuwas. Axum dominated the region until 570, the year of Muhammad's birth at Mecca.[96] In 560, the Axumite governor of Yemen tried unsuccessfully to expand his domains northward to Mecca, to gain control of the important trade routes linking the Hijaz to most of Arabia. Axumite control ended with the Persian invasion of Yemen.[97] Axum's embrace of Christianity led to an exodus of Jews from the capital to the mountainous areas near Lake Tana. They converted Agauw-speaking communities in the Semien Mountains. Their descendants became the Bet Israel, the Ethiopian Jews.[98] Kaleb eventually abdicated in order to become a monk at Debre Damo. His son succeeded him as king of Axum.[99]

When the Islamic movement was facing increasingly intense persecution in Mecca, the prophet Muhammad sent some of his most devout followers to seek asylum at the court of the Axumite king. In 615, a small group sought the Axumite king's protection. In 616, a second group of over one hundred people led by Ja'far, Ali's brother and Muhammad's cousin, came to Axum.[100] Included in these early "hijra" were Muhammad's daughter Ruqayyah and her husband, Uthman (who eventually became the Third Caliph).[101] The anti-Muslim faction at Mecca pursued them and urged the king to send these malcontents back to Mecca. According to tradition, the leader of the Muslim party asked if he could read some of the texts that had been revealed to Muhammad. He read from Sura Miriam, in which the Angel Djibril (Gabriel) spoke to Mary and revealed her destiny. It focused on her fear of bearing a child out of wedlock in a Palestinian society that often responded violently against unwed mothers. When he finished reading, the king of Axum was in tears and said, "What you believe is what I believe. You may have asylum here for as long as you need it." He gave them a gift of land, which is still held as a *waqf*, a philanthropic trust, on behalf of the Muslim community, near Axum. There were Muslims in Axum before there were Muslims in Medina, welcomed by a Christian monarch who recognized

---

[96] Karen Armstrong, *Muhammad: Biography of a Prophet* (New York: HarperCollins, 1992), pp. 6, 67. Kaplan, *Beta Israel*, pp. 37–39. Hatke, *Aksum and Nubia*, p. 43. July, *History of the African People*, p. 39.
[97] Armstrong, *Muhammad*, pp. 122–123.
[98] Newman, *Peopling of Africa*, p. 93. Kaplan, *Beta Israel*, p. 39.
[99] M. Mengistu, guide to Asum Stelae Field, July 21, 2012.
[100] Munro-Hay, *Aksum*, pp. 56, 58. Kobishanov, *Axum*, pp. 111–112.
[101] David Robinson, *Muslim Societies in African History* (Cambridge: Cambridge University Press, 2004), p. 111.

that these two Abrahamic religions were intimately connected to one another. In 628, as Muslim control of the Hijaz strengthened, most of the exiles returned home.[102] Umm Habiba, who had accompanied her husband from Mecca to Axum, returned alone after her husband converted to Christianity and decided to remain there. Ethiopia's Christian king provided her with a dowry so that when she returned to the Hijaz she could marry the prophet Muhammad.[103]

Conclusion

In North Africa, Nubia, and Ethiopia, what Christian commentators labelled as "pagan" religion dominated both royal courts and homes of the lower classes. Each of these local traditions continued to adapt to political, economic, and social changes. Adherents of North African traditions associated with Berbers and Libyans welcomed new religious cults and practitioners introduced by Carthaginians, Greeks, and Egyptians. Similarly, Nubians welcomed Egyptian cults of Amun and Isis into their religious practice. In Axum, religious practices drew on local Agauw practices and the traditions associated with Sabeans who had immigrated into the region.

Beginning in the late second century, Christianity became an important influence, initially in North Africa, then in the Ethiopian highlands, and finally in the Nubian kingdoms of the Upper Nile. In the last decades of the second century, small Christian communities emerged in Cyrencia and Carthage. Among these early Christians was the theologian Tertullian, who developed the concept of the Trinity that became a central article of faith for Catholic and Orthodox Christians. North Africans continued the worship of deities and ritual practices associated with local traditions. Practices like incubation remained central to the religious practices of people in need of healing or other forms of spiritual assistance. This practice found its ways into rituals performed at North African Christian saints' tombs. Still, adherents of the new religious tradition expected a firm renunciation of prior religious practices and traditions.

The introduction of Christianity, particularly in North Africa, generated new sources of religious tensions within the already pluralistic community

---

[102] Robinson, *Muslim Societies*, p. 111.
[103] Robinson, *Muslim Societies*, p. 111.

labelled as "pagan." Initially Romans persecuted Christians, producing a long list of church martyrs. By the late fourth century, with the establishment of Christianity as the official religion, persecution was redirected against people who worshipped the gods associated with the peoples of North Africa. Pagans were subjected to violent harassment; their temples were closed, destroyed, or converted into churches. In the fifth century, new religious struggles among Donatists, Arians, and Catholics were added to these conflicts. Increasing economic stratification and divisions between pro-Roman factions exacerbated these religious conflicts. What remained throughout this period was the imperial demand that local people accept the religious authority of the State. This was an assertion that many North and Northeast Africans refused to accept.

North Africans were particularly drawn to the Donatist strand of Christianity, which became a means to challenge Christian elites in the urban areas and to assume a distinctive North African Christian identity in opposition to Rome. However, Nubians and Ethiopians favored Monophysite Christian traditions and remained in close contact with the Egyptian churches. This, too, may have served as a way of asserting religious independence from the two concentrations of church authority in Rome and Constantinople.

In Ethiopia, Christianity found fertile ground in an area already influenced by Jewish traditions. Ezana, the first Christian ruler of Axum, was converted by Frumentius and patronized Christianity at court. However, he continued to patronize traditional Ethiopian religious cults in the rural areas where Christianity grew more slowly. Like the conversion of Constantine, Ezana's conversion was more cautious than the dramatic Pauline model of conversion often associated with these monarchs. Seven years before the Hijra of 622, a small group of Muslims established a small, but permanent presence in Ethiopia.

In Nubia, the kingdom of Meroe resisted Christianity until it was conquered by Axum. After the fall of Meroe and the rise of the three Nubian kingdoms of Nobatea, Makuria, and Alwa, Christian missions from Egypt were welcomed. Christianity spread quite rapidly in the area, and it became a source of political and cultural unity, which enabled them to preserve their independence after the Arab conquest of Egypt and North Africa.

At the time of the Hijra, North and northeast Africa had become predominantly Christian, but with strong influences from older Berber, Egyptian, and Punic traditions. Jewish communities continued to exert influences in

North Africa, Egypt, and Ethiopia. Tensions persisted, however, between various Christian communities and the polities associated with each of them. Some Berber communities embraced Judaism as a way of asserting their desire to maintain their independence from Byzantium's Orthodoxy and from the Catholic Church's Bishop of Rome. Many people in North and northeast Africa embraced Monophysite or other minority interpretations of Christianity for similar reasons.

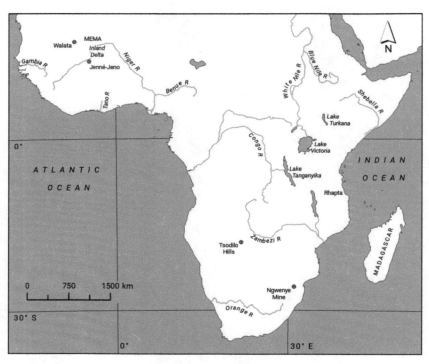

Map 9.1. Africa before the Hijra (courtesy of Jonathan Chipman).

9
The Sahara and the South

African Religious History from the Beginnings of the Common Era to the First Hijra

This chapter explores the history of African religions from the Sahara south to the capes of southern Africa (see Map 9.1). It explores these areas before either Christianity or Islam became a factor in the subcontinent's history. This period marked the beginning of urbanization south of the Sahara. The focus of this chapter is on the growth of ancestor cults, territorial cults, and changing ideas of the supreme being, as well as the relationship between religious authorities and the increasing complexity of African state formation. Male and female initiation rituals simultaneously instructed young people about their responsibilities as adults and as members of a religious community. It also created a series of cross-cutting social groups that transcended kinship ties and fostered the creation of wider political allegiances.

Most of West Africa and the Interlacustrine region of East Africa had developed a working knowledge of the smelting of and working with iron by 250 BCE. Southern Africa's use of iron technology came somewhat later. The Ngwane mine area in present-day Eswatini did not develop blacksmithing activities until the fifth century of the Common Era.[1] Blacksmithing cults and the inclusion of iron and blacksmiths in African creation myths spread with the diffusion of iron technology.[2] This also generated a new source of religious authority, independent of royal and ancestral cult structures.

Once again, contemporary written sources are extremely limited for most of sub-Saharan Africa during the first centuries of the Common Era. Most written sources come from travelers and merchants visiting the East African coast, who rarely commented on the religious lives of the people they

---

[1] Philip Curtin, Steve Feierman, Jan Vansina, and Leonard Thompson, *African History* (London: Longman, [1978] 1991), p. 24.

[2] John Middleton, *The World of the Swahili: An African Mercantile Civilization* (New Haven, CT: Yale University Press, 1992), pp. 12, 36.

encountered. Archaeological and linguistic evidence, however, increases significantly for this period.

East Africa

By the beginning of the first century of the Common Era, Bantu-speaking groups expanded into the coastal areas of East Africa, where they encountered hunter-gatherer groups and Cushitic-speaking herding communities. Cushitic speakers are seen as the source of the practice of male circumcision practices within the region. This is based on the Cushitic origin of the terms used to describe this rite of passage. Cushitic speakers also introduced their neighbors to cattle-keeping practices in areas that were free of tsetse fly and the African sleeping sickness which they spread.[3] Greek and Arab traders frequented the area, trading as far south as the port of Rhapta, near the original homeland of the Swahili, a place called Shingiwayo. Bantu-speaking people had established communities along the coast by the beginning of the Common Era. By the beginning of the second century, they were smelting and working with iron in coastal settlements as far south as northern Mozambique.[4] They forged iron tools for clearing land, farming, fishing, boatbuilding, and warfare. By the sixth century, Proto-Sabaki speakers settled along the coast from the Shabella River in present-day Somalia to the Tana River in present-day Kenya. They worked with iron, herded cattle, and farmed sorghum and millet.[5] These coastal settlements were increasingly linked to Indian Ocean trade networks. Archaeologists even found Chinese beads in the ruins of communities built at the beginning of the Common Era.[6]

About two thousand years ago, southern Nilotic communities expanded south and eastward from the area between the Nile River and Lake Turkana. Their reliance on male circumcision as a rite of passage facilitated the creation of male age sets composed of boys who experienced the ordeals and teachings together through their initiation camps. The close ties forged among coinitiates lasted throughout their lives, aiding the development of interlineage relationships that facilitated the growth of larger political and

---

[3] J. E. G. Sutton, "East Africa before the Seventh Century," in *Ancient Civilizations of Africa, Volume II, UNESCO General History of Africa*, ed. G. Mokhtar (London: Heinemann, 1981), pp. 579–580.

[4] Chaparukha M. Kusimba, *The Rise and Fall of Swahili States* (Walnut Creek, CA: Altamira Press, 1999), pp. 90–91. Felix Chami, *The Tanzanian Coast in the First Millennium AD* (Uppsala: Studies in African Archaeology, 1994), pp. 43–44.

[5] Kusimba, *The Rise and Fall of Swahili States*, p. 80.

[6] Chami, *Tanzanian*, p. 46.

social groups. They created military units that were able to mobilize warriors beyond the lineage to conquer and defend territories taken from Cushitic-speaking and other early inhabitants of northern Kenya and Uganda.[7] The Nilotic groups entered the region already possessing skills as herders of cattle, sheep, and goats, but they may have learned new techniques from their Cushitic-speaking predecessors.[8]

Bantu-speaking farming groups in the Interlacustrine region continued to interact with Cushitic-speaking peoples who were more focused on cattle and goat herding. Contact with Cushitic grain farmers encouraged Bantu speakers to expand the range of farming activities from a reliance on root crops. As a result, Great Lakes Bantu speakers developed a mixed economy, especially in tsetse-fly-free uplands and in more arid areas of the region.[9] By the beginning of the Common Era, the Great Lakes Bantu language had developed five distinct linguistic groups: Luhyia, East Nyanza, Western Lakes, pre-Ru-Gongu, and West Nyanza.[10] Within the region, goat herders provided the animals needed for ritual sacrifice at lineage shrines and in connection with funeral ceremonies. This essential role as producers of animals for ritual purposes and for sustenance enhanced their social standing within their communities. Their better access to protein, through regular access to meat and dairy, reinforced the tendency to see them as military and political leaders. This had implications for future social and religious stratification. Their dual dependency on herding associated with men and farming associated with women underscored the importance of female and male spiritual powers and ritual organizations.[11]

David Schoenbrun suggests that Great Lakes Bantu speakers' religions changed as well. Based on linguistic analysis, he claims that there was a growing divergence among healers, diviners, and those subject to spirit possession, on the one hand, and the office of chief, on the other. As they settled in the Interlacustrine region, with its more variable rainfall, new specialists focused on rain-making rituals for the communities they served.[12]

---

[7] Curtin et al., *African History*, p. 124.
[8] Sutton, "East Africa before the Seventh Century," p. 586.
[9] Tsetse flies carry African sleeping sickness, which is particularly dangerous for most varieties of cattle. David L. Schoenbrun, "We Are What We Eat: Ancient Agriculture between the Great Lakes," *Journal of African History* 34, no. 1 (1994), pp. 1–17.
[10] Schoenbrun, "We Are What We Eat," p. 18.
[11] Iris Berger, "Women in Eastern and Southern Africa," in *Women in Sub-Saharan Africa: Restoring Women's History*, ed. Iris Berger and E. Frances White (Bloomington: Indiana University Press, 1999), p. 16.
[12] David Schoenbrun, "A Narrative of People and Forests between the Great Lakes, ca. 1000 BC and ca. 1500 AD" (Boston: Boston University African Studies Center, # 194, 1995), pp. 2–3.

During the first century of the Common Era, Bantu-speaking ironworking communities expanded, especially along the western shore of Lake Victoria. They encountered Cushitic-speaking groups living in the Karagwe Depression and borrowed sorghum-growing and cattle-herding techniques from them. These Bantu-speaking newcomers prospered in the area, using iron tools for growing sorghum and root crops and for fishing and hunting. Iron smelting's demand for firewood led to widespread deforestation and the dispersal of these groups. By the seventh century, iron production in the area had ceased.[13] Ironworking then expanded along the eastern shore of Lake Tanganyika, presumably accompanied by new blacksmith and smelter cults.[14]

Still shrouded in uncertainty are some of the key places and spirits of the early Common Era. How early was the kingdom of Kitara that figures so prominently in the oral traditions describing the region's formative history? Similarly, what was the relationship of Abacwezi spirits to actual rulers of the earliest kingdoms, and did their veneration for them predate these kingdoms? Sutton describes certain "Chwezi" spirits as having "a common Bantu root, suggesting that the particular spirit or the concept behind it may have a history much older than that of the kingdom and even their antecedents." Okot P'Bitek suggests that they belong to a period, before all dynasties, when the gods roamed the earth and humans could marry them. Oral traditions describe the Abacwezi spirits as imprinting themselves on the hills and lakes of the region.[15]

Some scholars, such as P'Bitek and Sutton, describe an Abacwezi era of culture heroes, extending well beyond the longest genealogies, a time of the first ancestors. Peter Schmidt suggests that the worship of the Abacwezi spirits goes back to the earliest iron smelters around 500 BCE. Schmidt contends that the displacement of Abacwezi blacksmiths from political authority in places like Buhaya may explain the determined opposition of Abacwezi spirit mediums to subsequent royal dynasties and eventually to colonial powers. In oral traditions concerning the Abacwezi, they are often contrasted with later rulers, such as the Ababito, who privileged the occupation of cattle herding

---

[13] Peter R. Schmidt, "Archaeological Views on a History of Landscape Change in East Africa," *Journal of African History* 38 (1997), pp. 377–401.
[14] Bertram B. B. Mapunde, "Fipa Iron Technology and Their Impact on Social History," in *East African Archaeology: Foragers, Potters, Smiths, and Traders and Archaeology*, ed. Chapurukho M. Kusimba and Sibel B. Kusimba (Philadelphia: Museum of Archaeology, 2003), p. 21.
[15] Sutton, "East Africa before the Seventh Century."

and imposed new hierarchical structures in their domains, going back to the period just before the Common Era.[16]

The Abacwezi spirits' links to early iron tools and anvils are also found on more recent shrines of these spirits.[17]

Mashariki-speaking groups who had practiced male circumcision in a wide area from Tanzania to Zimbabwe abandoned the practice around the fifth century. However, they did continue the male initiation schools, without the surgery. Words for the initiation shelters used by boys persist throughout the area.[18] Why male circumcision was abandoned or why this major shift in male initiation practice occurred remains uncertain at this time.

Madagascar

During the last few centuries before the Common Era, Bantu-speaking Africans established farming communities on the western side of Madagascar. Vérin suggests that these Bantu-speaking settlers introduced a snake cult which became associated with royal authority in a series of small, regional kingdoms. These immigrants also introduced cattle herding to the island.[19] In the second century, the island of Madagascar was colonized by Malayan sailors who introduced bananas and cocoyams to the island. These crops prospered in the forests of Madagascar, providing higher yields than the root crops that had been previously grown. They eventually spread to other well-watered areas in East Africa.[20] The sailors settled

---

[16] Iris Berger, *Religion and Resistance: East African Kingdoms in the Precolonial Period* (Tervuren: Musée Royale de l'Afrique Centrale, 1981), p. 32. Peter R. Schmidt, *Historical Archaeology: Representation, Social Memory, and Oral Traditions* (Lanham, MD: Altamira Press, 2006), p. 119.

[17] J. E. G. Sutton, "The Antecedents of the Interlacustrine Kingdoms," *Journal of African History* 34, no. 1 (1994), pp. 39, 42. Iris Berger, "Deities, Dynasties, and Oral History: The History and Legend of the Abacwezi," in *The African Past Speaks: Essays on Oral Tradition and History*, ed. Jospeh C. Miller (Folkstone, UK: Dawson, 1980), p. 76. Peter R. Schmidt, *Iron Technology in East Africa: Symbolism, Science, and Archaeology* (Bloomington: Indiana University Press, 1997), p. 198.

[18] Rhonda Gonzalez, *Societies, Religion, and History: Central East Tanzanians and the World They Created, c. 200 BCE to 1800 CE* (New York: Columbia University Press, 2009), pp. 157–159.

[19] P. Vérin, "Madagascar," in *Ancient Civilizations of Africa, Volume II, UNESCO General History of Africa*, ed. G. Mokhtar (London: Heinemann, 1981), p. 697.

[20] Jan Vansina, *Paths in the Rainforest: Toward a History of Political Tradition in Equatorial Africa* (Madison: University of Wisconsin Press, 1990). Kevin Shillington, *A History of Africa* (New York: St. Martin's Press, 1995), p. 55.

on the island, introducing their language and intermarrying with the earlier inhabitants. The Malagasy language originated in South East Asia, though it did receive some African influences. Pollen studies document the presence of South East Asian food crops by the fourth century. These included taro, bananas, Asian rice (*Oryza sativa*), and coconuts. Sumatran immigrants introduced the practice of terracing for rice cultivation. No archaeological evidence of buildings, settlements, or shrines has been found, however, prior to the early ninth century.[21]

Southern Africa

The southern Africa region experienced three major waves of Bantu-speaking migration. They gradually displaced and/or intermarried with the earlier inhabitants, Batwa- and Khoisan-speaking peoples. The newcomers introduced farming and herding into the region.[22] The initial settlement of agriculturalists was limited to areas with permanent access to water. Hunter-gatherers were able to preserve their independence during this period.[23] Bantu-speaking herders often adopted Khoisan ritual centers, such as the Tsodilo Hills, which enjoyed a spiritual authority derived from their association with the area's first inhabitants. Speakers of early Khoisan languages had covered many of the rock surfaces of the hills with art depicting dances and other rites. Some drawings depict dancers in positions that could be interpreted as trance, sometimes with rays emanating from their heads. Scholars have interpreted these rays in light of more contemporary knowledge of Khoi-San concepts of a spiritual power called *!Num*.[24] As the region became more arid, rain rituals assumed greater importance.[25] By the seventh century the newcomers had established a settlement called Divuyu, on

---

[21] Mark Horton and John Middleton, *The Swahili: The Social Landscape of a Mercantile Society* (Oxford: Routledge, 2000), p. 27. Vansina, *Paths in the Rainforest*, p. 61.

[22] Matthew Schofeleers, *River of Blood: The Genesis of a Martyr Cult in Southern Malawi, circa 1600* (Madison: University of Wisconsin Press, 1992), p. 26.

[23] John Parkington and Simon Hall, "The Appearance of Food Production in Southern Africa 1000 to 2000 Years Ago," in *The Cambridge History of South Africa, Volume I, From Early Trade to 1885*, ed. Carolyn Hamilton, Bernard K. Mbenga, and Robert Ross (Cambridge: Cambridge University Press, 2010), p. 96.

[24] J. David Lewis-Williams, *The Rock Art of South Africa* (Cambridge: Cambridge University Press, 1983), pp. 21–22.

[25] John Kinahan, *Namib: The Archaeology of an African Desert* (Woodbridge, UK: James Currey, 2022), p. 190.

Tsodilo's Female Hill, where they raised sheep, goats, and cattle. They also smelted iron and engaged in long-distance trade.[26]

Bantu speakers also brought knowledge of ironworking technologies as they moved south. Ngoni speakers in present-day Eswatini were smelting iron by the fourth century. Zimbabweans were smelting iron by the fifth century, while Zambians were mining copper in the same period.[27] In the Copper Belt region of Zambia and Congo, Proto-Sabi and Proto-Botawe-speaking agriculturalists abandoned elaborate male initiation rituals focused on circumcision during this period. The reason for this change in male rites of passage remains unclear. However, female initiation remained central, perhaps increasing in importance during the first millennium. According to Christine Saidi, these rites became the focus of these matrilineal societies, creating social bonds between coinitiates that transcended lineage groups. They also expanded the importance of a second female initiation rite associated with the birth of a woman's first child. At this time, female elders (the *bumba*) decided if her husband had performed sufficient work for her matrilineage to allow them to settle in her community or to send them to settle in the village of his matrilineage.[28]

During the first seven centuries of the Common Era, Bantu-speaking communities developed symbiotic relationships with the peoples they encountered as they entered the region. Economic ties centered on Khoisan-speaking groups trading game meats and hides for iron tools and implements as well as grain and other agricultural products. Even though there is some disdain for the Khoisan, Bantu speakers accorded them a certain spiritual prestige as "owners of the land." These first inhabitants were seen as powerful practitioners of healing and malevolent medicines, who had special access to the supreme being. The Khoisan were valued as rainmakers, especially by the early Nguni settlers along the South African Indian Ocean coastal areas. Their special powers earned them a valued place in a region where Bantu speakers were becoming increasingly dominant.[29]

---

[26] Edwin N. Wilmsen, *Land Filled with Flies: A Political Economy of the Kalahari* (Chicago: University of Chicago Press, 1989).

[27] James L. Newman, *The Peopling of Africa: A Geographic Interpretation* (New Haven, CT: Yale University Press, 1995), p. 148. Shillington, *History of Africa*, p. 57. Roland Oliver and Brian Fagan, *Africa in the Iron Age: c. 500 BC to AD 1400* (Cambridge: Cambridge University Press, 1975), pp. 98–99, 107.

[28] Christine Saidi, *Women's Authority in Early East Central Africa* (Rochester: University of Rochester Press, 2010), pp. 63–64.

[29] Parkington and Hall, "Appearance of Food Production," p. 97.

Equatorial Africa

Archaeological and linguistic sources provide most of the evidence for this period of Equatorial African history. This includes the people inhabiting the current BaKongo area who were working with iron by the first century of the Common Era.[30] Pierre de Maret excavated a series of caves in the region, which included Neolithic materials deposited in their innermost recesses. He thinks that the KiKongo names for some of the caves indicate their long-standing use as fertility shrines. He claims that one of the caves, "Secret of the Country," contained "an ancient chtonian divinity related to a fertility cult."[31] This may have reflected the earlier inhabitants' control of the transitional zones between coastal plain and interior plateau, and wooded savannah and equatorial rain forest.

In the southeastern Congo, Proto-Sabi-speaking peoples adopted a new term for their supreme being, Leza. The name "Leza" emphasized a concept of a "God who nurtures." Rather than a more distant source of life-giving energy, Leza was seen not only as a beginner of creation, but one who cared about and assisted the creation of life. Glottochronological analysis suggests that this shift occurred around 500 CE.[32]

In the Western-Bantu-speaking areas north of the Zaire (Congo) River, small political units, usually little more than a thousand people, became increasingly important in the fifth century. These groups were led by "big men" and included members of a shared matrilineage, as well as hunter-gatherer client groups These hunter-gatherer clients retained a special spiritual power as "owners of the soil," as first inhabitants. Hunter-gatherer groups, such as the Batwa, retained important roles in performing rituals associated with healing, fertility, and the power of kings. Their independence was compromised, however, as Bantu-speaking groups were able to increase their agricultural production. This was closely associated with the spread of banana production, which generated the kind of economic surpluses that could support occupational specializations. With increased agricultural surpluses, big men sought to control the circulation of women through bridewealth transactions, which allowed them to provide women to male clients. Eastern Sudanic speakers in

---

[30] Shillington, *History of Africa*, p. 57.

[31] Pierre de Maret, "Archaeological and Other Prehistoric Evidence of Traditional African Religious Expression," in *Religion in Africa: Experience and Expression*, ed. Thomas D. Blakey, Walter E. A. van Beek, and Dennis Thomson (London: James Currey, 1995), p. 187.

[32] Fourshey et al., *Bantu Africa: 3500 BCE to Present* (New York: Oxford University Press, 2017), pp. 30–31.

this region developed alternative marriage patterns to resist this new source of centralized authority by emphasizing reciprocal marriages in which siblings married siblings of another family, thereby keeping bridewealth within families and eliminating costly gifts that could be controlled by local patrons.[33] Increasingly, kings and big men exercised new powers to make power objects (*Nkisi*) and medicines which protected both individuals and the community-at-large. They were also able to negotiate with local spirits on behalf of the community.[34]

Ironworking communities in southeastern Gabon did their own smelting. They built smelters which included upright *tuyeres* (ventilation pipes) filled with kaolin, a white clay said to symbolize male semen.[35] This underscored the importance of male control of the smelting process. BaKongo oral traditions link copper and ironworking to the earliest chiefs and kings through the prominent display of copper and iron implements at royal shrines.[36] As in the case of the Dogon, oral traditions stressed the importance of ironworking lineages and their religious communities.

During this period, Equatorial Africa experienced a dramatic expansion in agricultural production associated with the spread of banana cultivation and the increasing availability of iron tools. This economic growth facilitated greater occupational specialization in the overlapping spheres of political and religious life.

West Africa

West Africa commercial and interstate contacts tended to focus on the region's river valleys and the oases of the Sahara, connecting people of various ecological and social systems. The region was linked to North Africa by camel caravans since the first century.[37] Urban settlements grew along these

---

[33] Jan Vansina, "Reconstructing the Past," in *African Reflections: Art from Northern Zaire*, ed. Enid Schildkrout and Curtis Keim (Seattle: University of Washington Press, 1990), p. 77.

[34] Vansina, *Paths in the Rainforest*, p. 146. Robert E. Moise, "'Do Pygmies Have a History?' Revisited: The Autochthonous Tradition in the History of Equatorial Africa," in *Hunter-Gatherers of the Congo Basin: Culture, History and Biology of the Congo Basin*, ed. Barry S. Howlett (Highland Park, NJ: Transaction Publishers, 2014), pp. 93–94.

[35] Peter R. Schmidt, "Reading Gender in the Ancient Iron Technology of Africa," in *Gender in African Prehistory*, ed. Susan Kent (Walnut Creek, CA: Altamira, 1998), p. 166.

[36] Michael S. Bisson, "Pre-Colonial Copper Metallurgy: Socio-political Content," in *Ancient African Metallurgies: The Sociocultural Content*, ed. Joseph O. Vogel (Walnut Creek, CA: Altamira Press, 2001), p. 131.

[37] Shillington, *History of Africa*, p. 46.

trade routes, especially in the Niger valley. In the mountainous region known as the Ahoggar, a woman ruled over one of these small trading states. In the fourth century, she combined her political authority with the authority derived from her status as a "holy woman." According to Tuareg oral traditions, her name was Tin Hinran, a woman from present-day Morocco, claimed as the "ancestress of the Tuareg." Her tomb revealed her considerable wealth in silver and gold jewelry, as well as precious stones and a gold coin stamped with the image of Emperor Constantine.[38]

On the inland delta of the Niger River, the Bozo ethnic group were considered the first inhabitants and enjoyed prestige as "masters of water." They retained the rights to perform rituals for the local spirits before the planting of rice. This continued even after they were incorporated in Bamana-dominated city-states in the middle of the first millennium.[39] This included Jenné-Jenno, which was situated on higher ground and escaped all but the most serious floods. Perhaps, in response to flooding issues, people in the town buried their dead in large pottery urns. Jenné-Jenno gradually developed several dozen satellite communities based on occupational and/or ethnic groups.[40] Presumably, each of these communities had its own lineage and occupationally related shrines. These included blacksmiths and coppersmiths, each of which included guild shrines.[41] Smelters at Jenné-Jenno included images of females on the walls of their furnaces and serpents on pots found at the sites. These features were not merely decorative, but may have indicated a ritual significance to the smelting process, akin to the creation of life.[42] Adria LaViolette reports archaeological evidence that Jenné-Jenno's blacksmiths maintained shrines related to iron production and the procurement of rain.[43] Creation accounts from Proto-Mande- and Dogon-speaking groups began to stress the importance of blacksmiths as the

---

[38] P. Salama, "The Sahara in Classical Antiquity," in *Ancient Civilizations of Africa, Volume II, UNESCO General History of Africa*, ed. G. Mokhtar (London: Heinemann, 1981), p. 521. Henri Lhote, *Les Touaregs du Hoggar (Ahoggar)* (Paris: Payot, 1955), p. 88.

[39] Roderick J. McIntosh, *Ancient Middle Niger Urbanism and the Self-organizing Landscape* (Cambridge: Cambridge University Press, 2005), p. 112. Peter Garlake, *Early Art and Archaeology of Africa* (Oxford: Oxford University Press, 2002), p. 97.

[40] Roderick McIntosh, "The Pulse Model: Genesis and Accommodation of Specialization in the Middle Niger," *Journal of African History* (1993), pp. 182, 188.

[41] Michael A. Gomez, *African Dominion: A New History of Empire in Early and Medieval West Africa* (Princeton, NJ: Princeton University Press, 2018), p. 17.

[42] McIntosh, *Ancient*, p. 155.

[43] Adria LaViolette, *Ethno-Archaeology in Jenné, Mali* (Oxford: Oxford University Press, 2000), p. 78.

senior lineage of the community. Sacred oral traditions of the Dogon of Mali and Burkina Faso describe the theft of fire from celestial beings known as Nummo. As the first ancestors descended to the earth in what is described as a celestial granary, the blacksmith was the first to emerge. He set up his forge at the edge of the primal field. The rhythm of his hammering at the forge spread the fertilizing word, which allowed the Dogon to create an ordered sacred space where they could settle.[44]

In the last two hundred years before the Common Era, groups of Saharan farmers moved south into the Sahelian and Sudanic regions and established towns such as Mema and Walata. They engaged in long-distance trade, animal husbandry, and copper smelting, along with farming.[45] The first three centuries of the Common Era were a time of abundant rainfall in the West African Sahel and the Sahara, which facilitated commercial relations and agricultural expansion.[46]

In the fifth century, the ancestors of the Sarakhollé (Soninké) moved north from the Upper Niger River valley and established what became known as Ghana or Wagadu, in southeastern Mauritania. It dominated the trade of the western Sahara. Merchants based in Ghanaian towns purchased salt, artisanal goods, and horses. They sold gold, ivory, and enslaved persons from the Sudanic region further south. A member of the Diabé clan, named Magha, established the town of Kumbi Saleh, which became the capitol of Wagadu or Ghana.[47] Its king served as the ritual leader of the kingdom, drawing on the power of royal ancestor cults. Its wealth depended, according to traders, on rituals performed for a spirit who appeared in the form of a snake. It was said to demand the annual sacrifice of the prettiest, still unmarried woman in the kingdom.[48] In turn, the snake, known as Bida, assured the stability and the prosperity of the town, providing it with adequate rainfall and access to significant gold mines. Eventually, a powerful maker of medicines and amulets fell in love with a woman selected for sacrifice. He killed the serpent in order to save her. As Bida was dying, he was said to have cursed the entire kingdom,

---

[44] Marcel Griaule, *Conversations with Ogotemmeli* (Oxford: Oxford University Press, 1965).
[45] Gomez, *African Dominion*, p. 37.
[46] McIntosh, *Ancient*, p. 197.
[47] Sixeau Daouda Koné, *Le Peuplement ancien en Basse Guinée: XIIe- XIX siècles* (Paris: L'Harmattan, 2015), p. 25.
[48] Gomez, *African Dominion*, pp. 31–32. Susan Keech McIntosh, "Reconceptualising Early Ghana," *Canadian Journal of African Studies* 42, no. 2–3, p. 368.

claiming it would become an arid and impoverished wasteland.[49] An area known as the Valley of the Serpent, an area rich in Neolithic archaeological sites, recalls the travels of this snake on its journey to Kumbi Saleh.[50] According to oral traditions from the Jenné-Jenno, a local spirit protected the town from floods as long as they sacrificed a virgin by burying her alive in the foundation of a building. This annual sacrifice eventually was replaced by offerings of terra cotta figurines to the spirit. Both traditions suggest a long-standing concern with territorial spirits and human sacrifices, particularly of women, throughout the region. These traditions also suggest the importance of female chastity and physical beauty.[51]

Along the middle reaches of the Gambia River, sedentary farmers constructed dozens of stone circles, carved from locally quarried laterite rock. Although their exact significance remains unclear, many of them were burial sites.[52] Further south, along the Upper Guinea coast, the increasing availability of iron and iron tools facilitated the clearing of mangrove swamps and other low-lying areas for swamp rice cultivation. The growing dependence of farmers on blacksmiths enhanced the spiritual prestige of these masters of fire. Their guild shrines ensured their exclusive control of ironworking.

A similar expansion of access to iron and iron tools allowed for greater use of slash-and-burn techniques for clearing land and planting crops in the forested areas of lower Guinea. By the beginning of the Common Era, ancestors of the Igbo began to migrate southeast from the Niger-Benue confluence into the present-day Igbo homeland. They brought iron technologies with them along with a knowledge of the cultivation of yams and cocoyams. Their religious system focused on the earth goddess, Ala, who was closely associated with fertility of the land, livestock, and people.[53]

---

[49] Werner Gillan, *A Short History of African Art* (New York: Facts on File Publications, 1984), pp. 93–94. Robyn d'Avignon, *A Ritual Geology: Gold and Subterranean Knowledge in Savanna West Africa* (Durham, NC: Duke University Press, 2022), pp. 65–66.

[50] McIntosh, *Ancient*, p. 49. In the eleventh century, Al-Bakri described a snake cult and idol worship among a people he called Zafqu in this area. Al-Bakri is cited in *Corpus of Early Arabic Sources for West African History*, ed. Nehemia Levtzion and J. F. P. Hopkins (Cambridge: Cambridge University Press, 1981), p. 78.

[51] Gillan, *Short History of African Art*, pp. 94–95.

[52] UNESCO World Heritage Sites, "Stone Circles of Senegambia," who.unesco.org/en/list/1226.

[53] John N. Oriji, *Political Organization in Nigeria Since the Late Stone Age: A History of the Igbo People* (New York: Palgrave/Macmillan, 2011), pp. 5, 35–36, 41.

Conclusion

Throughout sub-Saharan Africa, during the early centuries of the Common Era, African states expanded their abilities to smelt and forge iron. This allowed people to establish clusters of blacksmith-related cults and the intensification of farming. Increased availability of iron tools eased the task of clearing potential agricultural land, facilitating an increase in arable land. It also allowed the availability of iron weaponry readily controlled by emerging chieftaincies. Cosmogonic myths and other sacred traditions began to include important roles for blacksmiths in the act of creation. Chieftaincies became increasingly important, legitimated in part by their own lineage shrines and, especially in Equatorial and East Africa, with the shrines of chiefly clients who enjoyed a special deference as first inhabitants of the polity. In the Interlacustrine region, oral traditions blurred the distinction between cultural heroes who introduced both religious and technical practices, descendants of the oldest chiefly lineages who continued to communicate with spirit mediums.

Continued migration of Bantu-speaking groups into eastern and southern Africa led to extensive intermarriage with and linguistic borrowings from Khoi-San-speaking groups. These population movements also spread animal husbandry and farming into the better watered regions of southern Africa and the incorporation of Khoi-San ritual sites into increasingly dominant Bantu-speaking communities. South East Asian immigrants to Madagascar and their interaction with already established Bantu-speaking communities and with people settled on the East African mainland yielded a variety of new foodstuffs and new religious influences within eastern Africa. In West Africa, the expansion of trans-Saharan trade led to the development of urban agglomerations in the Sahel region and the increasingly importance of royal cults that protected their land and the people who lived within its borders. Similar to the early Ethiopian account of Angabo slaying the snake/dragon king, the Western Sahelian snake traditions of a snake that supported the rulers of Ghana played an important role in the establishment of West African kingdoms. The expansion of West African agricultural production into the Guinean forest regions may have contributed to the rise of earth goddess cults, such as the Igbo earth goddess, Ala.

During these first centuries of the Common Era, blacksmith lineages became increasingly important throughout sub-Saharan Africa. Blacksmiths often assumed additional roles as the religiously important manufacturers of amulets, the performers of male circumcision and other operations, and the practitioners of divination. Their wives shaped and fired pottery used regularly in both domestic and ritual contexts. Communities regarded blacksmiths as "masters of fire" who could wield their powers for the common good or for hidden and private purposes.[54] During this period some blacksmiths assumed the positions of royalty; others performed vital ritual roles in the coronation of kings.

---

[54] S. Terry Childs and Eugenia W. Herbert, "Metallurgy and Its Consequences," in *African Archaeology: A Cultural Introduction*, ed. Ann Stoler (Malden, MA: Blackwell, 2005), pp. 287–288.

10
Conclusion

Many years ago, a religious studies acquisitions editor approached me about writing a short, single-volume history of African religions. I accepted the invitation quickly, but prematurely, since I was still in the early stages of my career as a historian of African religions. I insisted that I include Egypt and North Africa as an integral part of the book, and I proposed that we include both the Atlantic and Indian Ocean diasporas. Initially, I thought that I would include four chapters in a twenty-chapter work on the origins of African religions and ancient African religions, before moving on to the areas where I had done most of my work, the early modern and modern periods of African history. In looking at this early period, I realized that there were many detailed archaeological works on specific sites and local areas. However, there were few attempts to apply them to a regional or continent-wide perspective, especially regarding religious change. There were also detailed studies examining the spread of Bantu languages, but far fewer on other language groups. Where such linguistic studies existed, a careful scholar could discern shifts in terminology for supreme beings, various kinds of lesser spirits, ancestors, kinship terminology, rites of passage, and guild-based technologies, such as ironworking. Word lists could not always indicate the significance of word shifts for the practitioners of the religious traditions, however. For northern and northeastern Africa, there were written texts dating as far back as the late fourth millennium BCE. Oral traditions became increasingly valuable as the study approached the Common Era. Some of these initially oral traditions had been written down during the ancient period and incorporated into sacred texts or commentaries.

Together, these kinds of evidence produced a pattern of specialized studies with few attempts to address the broader range of religious changes prior to the growth of Christianity and Islam. I realized that to do justice to the writing of a history of the world's second largest continent, currently home to over one billion people, I would have to work out the detailed history of African religions before a more synthetic text could be written. This volume is the first part of that research. It constitutes the first continent-wide study focused primarily on the history of indigenous African religions. I began with the earliest manifestations of what could be considered religious behavior and concluded with the arrival of the first persecuted Muslims who fled from Mecca and sought asylum at the court of the Christian king of Axum. In the last millennium before the Common Era similar written documents became available for northwestern Africa as well. Focusing initially on the earliest evidence of intentional burials, this study builds to the creation of ritual sites and sanctuaries, rock art and other symbolic expressions of religious ideas and practices, and the changes associated with the Neolithic Revolution. The ancient empires of Egypt, Nubia, and Ethiopia provide us with our earliest written documents, with an increasingly rich documentation of religious change in northeast Africa throughout the ancient period. For most of the continent throughout the period of this study, however, archaeological and linguistic evidence offer our primary insights into the religious history of ancient Africa.

This study focuses on indigenous African religions—that is, on religious ideas and practices that originated on the African continent and remain closely linked to specific communities' sense of group identity and cohesiveness. It also looks at ancient Christianity and Judaism, and the very first contacts with Muslims in Ethiopia. One should keep in mind, however, that these were not the first practitioners of outside religions who sought to spread their cults and practices. The Hyksos and Phoenicians of the Eastern Mediterranean coast introduced new deities and ritual practices into Egypt and northern Africa. So did the Greeks and Romans. Sabeans of Southwest Arabia also introduced important religious traditions that helped to shape the distinctive culture of Ethiopia. Further south, merchants and settlers from Southeast Asia introduced new plant crops, languages, and religious practices to the Indian Ocean islands, especially Madagascar. It should not be assumed that these influences from external powers were imposed on passive African societies. African religious cults from Egypt and Nubia were embraced by many North Africans and, eventually, throughout the Roman Empire before the achievement of Christian hegemony. Even then, African religious traditions not only endured, but continued to influence those religious communities of the Mediterranean world with whom they had contact.

I am aware that this work challenges basic assumptions that are shared by outside commentators in the West, the Middle East, and the Indian Ocean worlds: that Africa has neither its own history nor what could be considered to be integrated systems of religious thought and practice. In a major study of the representation of Africa, Valentin Mudimbe has traced the persistence of these images of Africa as a place outside of history and without religion as far back as the ancient Greeks. These images were alive and well when he wrote *The Invention of Africa*.[1] In the West this image of Africa endured because of the reasons that Europeans came to Africa, initially to gain access to Africa's abundant natural resources and to find a sea route to more lucrative markets in southern and southeastern Asia, and then to exploit the labor of African people through the Atlantic slave trade. Denying Africa's own history and the religious thought and practices that forged African religious traditions became a highly effective method for legitimating the Atlantic slave trade. By the late nineteenth century, similar arguments were made to legitimate the partition, conquest, and colonization of the African continent. In some quarters, it continues to fuel the nostalgia some people feel about the good old days when they were recognized for shouldering the "white man's burden."

I am also aware, however, that issues of sources have contributed to the problem. Both history and religious studies, as academic disciplines, privilege written materials, archival sources, and scriptural texts. These were in short supply for most of Africa before colonization and the spread of Islam and Christianity. There also remained a certain scholarly suspicion of oral traditions as historical and religious sources, despite the fact that many sacred texts were not far removed from the oral traditions that inspired them. Persistently, critics of oral traditions have underestimated the diversity of African communities, reinforcing a tendency to overlook the different "schools" or interpretations of oral traditions in ways that bear more than a passing resemblance to different "schools" of history or in other scholarly endeavors.[2] They also fail to recognize the greater capacity of memory in those societies that are not dependent on written methods for preserving information.

The time pressures and systems of funding research have also proven to be obstacles. Dissertation researchers sent by leading Western universities have conducted much of the primary research in the fields of African history and in the study of African religions. Graduate students were expected, in a year or two overseas, to conduct archival and field research, learn appropriate African languages, and amass sufficient data to produce a doctoral

---

[1] Valentin Mudimbe, *The Invention of Africa* (Bloomington: Indiana University Press, 1988), p. 177.
[2] Jan Vansina, *Oral Tradition as History* (Madison: University of Wisconsin Press, 1985), p. 120.

dissertation. Community elders, both oral historians and religious leaders, found this rush to research profoundly disturbing. Given the close association of religious knowledge and power, African religious education often emphasized how what was taught affected the sense of personhood of the people involved. Were they receiving the power associated with what they were learning in a socially and ethically responsible way? Students who wanted to learn about religious traditions had to prove themselves to their would-be teachers. Foreign researchers, often associated with the nations or broader cultures of the colonial powers, on a fixed and limited time schedule, often failed to meet that test. Consequently, they were told what elders tell outsiders, the uninitiated, and children—that is, the people who did not have the right to know—a simplified account. What was often left out was the historical dimension, which acknowledged that some practices followed in the past had been abandoned and that other practices were relatively recent additions. Such simple presentations were often recorded by researchers as grist for their dissertations, even commenting on how little depth there was to the African religions being presented. Rarely did they realize that such simple lessons were quite intentional, a presentation of a religious system to people who had not yet demonstrated their ability to handle the power that comes from learning the esoteric knowledge in a responsible way that would not expose their traditions to ill-founded criticism or commentaries or lead to an abuse of the power that such knowledge bestows.

Throughout my academic career, I have been intrigued by the dynamism of what have often been labeled as traditional societies. The term itself, preferable to older terms like "primitive," conjures up an image of rigid and unchanging ideas and practices.[3] This was contrasted with the West, which was portrayed as change-oriented, always ready to critique existing theories or beliefs. Historians of religion constructed the category of indigenous religions, which they saw as unchanging and unreflective, and which they contrasted with another category, world religions, seen as historically situated and engaged in critical reflection. These contrasts are overstated. A willingness to critique existing beliefs and practices, an awareness of alternatives, and a sense of their advantages and their disadvantages are deeply rooted in many traditional societies. Structures of innovation were

---

[3] Yves Person, "Pour une histoire des religions africaines," in *L'Invention religieuse en Afrique: Histoire et religion en Afrique Noire*, ed. Jean-Pierre Chrétien (Paris: Karthala, 1993), p. 14.

embedded in many African systems of thought and religious practice. They were not celebrated, however. Newer beliefs and practices confronted the challenges of establishing their authority within a preexisting system. As in the case of traditionalism in many sects of world religions, knowledge of innovation is left to those able to handle the uncertainties of such challenges to established practice.

So what have we learned about the history of religions in ancient Africa? First of all, we know that much work still needs to be done, particularly in the areas of archaeology and linguistic analysis. Important archaeological sites have yet to be excavated or even identified. The rich linguistic explorations of the Bantu languages need to be extended to other branches of the Niger-Congo language family, to Afro-Asiatic and Khoisan language families as well. Meroitic texts need to be more fully understood and, hopefully, a variety of written sources may still come to light.

Based on existing evidence, however, we can develop a history of African religions. At the present time, no evidence has been found that the earliest hominids, Ardipithecus and Australopithecus, conducted activities that could be considered religious. African religious history begins with the emergence of the genus *Homo*, even before the emergence of *Homo sapiens*. According to recent research in South Africa, *Homo naledi*, a species that lived from two million to about 250,000 years ago, went to great lengths to discretely deposit the remains of their friends and relatives in largely inaccessible caves, suggesting a concern for the well-being of the dead and the need to preserve their bodies for their ultimate fates. Although we cannot say with certainty that such concerns were "religious," it is quite clear that their thoughts transcended the limits of mundane existence.

With the emergence of *Homo sapiens*, the earliest evidence of what could be considered religious was also focused on burial practices. Mourners decorated the dead with red ocher and buried them in a careful and deliberate way. By 78,000 BCE, signs of intentional burials, using soils brought from different places covering human remains, provided clear evidence of *Homo sapiens* concerns for the welfare of the dead. Shortly after the discovery of an early grave in coastal Kenya, and decorations of ritual objects, like bars of ocher which were often used in marking of dead bodies, a growing sense of aesthetic expression emerged, reflecting both symbolic and religious thought. Repeated patterns of burial in which bodies were placed facing the rising or setting sun suggest that there were early links between the cycle of life and death and the movements of the sun.

In the past twenty-five years, archaeological discoveries in the Tsodilo Hills of northwestern Botswana have led some scholars to claim the existence of ceremonial sites that can be dated back 70,000 years to a carved image of a snake inside a cave where rituals may have taken place. Although this finding is strongly contested by some archaeologists concerning the dating of this ritual site, the discovery of decorated ocher bars, the intentional burials of the dead, and the depositing of grave goods provide strong evidence of religious thought and practice by 70,000 BCE. These data challenge cognitive scientists' claims that early humans did not develop the cognitive capacity for religious, aesthetic, or scientific thought until 60,000 years ago.

From a period beginning around 30,000 years ago, rock art depicts dancing activities in the Saharan and southern African regions, which may have religious significance. The dancers themselves, together with what appears to be bleeding from their noses and the depiction of what have been suggested are lines of power emanating from their heads, may indicate ecstatic ritual activity. Images that combine animal and human characteristics indicate both a human capacity for symbolic representation and the possibility of spiritually significant visionary experience. Rock art that focused on women's and men's genitalia, on sexual intercourse, or fellatio performed on humans by wild animals suggests the artists' concerns with human fertility.

With the Neolithic Revolution, evidence for an African religious history becomes more abundant. Increasing tendencies to remain in settled communities contributed to the construction of more lasting buildings and, hence, more lasting archaeological remains. Pressures for greater cooperation and the development of storable food surpluses allowed for occupational specialization and the emergence of government and priesthoods. The Nile valley provides early evidence of deliberate burials associated with the Badarian culture of the fifth millennium BCE. Badarians placed their graves at some distance from their homes, with the bodies facing to the west, the direction which later Egyptians identified as the abode of the dead. Offerings of grain and bread and the sacrifice of animals may have been done to provide food for the deceased in the afterlife.

At the beginning of the fourth millennium BCE, Amratian graves in Middle Egypt contained figurines with prominent breasts and pubic areas, as well as ithyphallic men. These reflected growing concerns about human fertility. Toward the end of the fourth millennium BCE, there were indications that gods like Horus were already being worshipped. The new kingdom of Lower Egypt enjoyed the protection of the cobra goddess, Wadjyt. A vulture goddess, Nekhbet, played a similar role in Upper Egypt. Even before the unification of Egypt, many of the major deities were already receiving cultic attentions. Various texts available from the late fourth millennium BCE provide the earliest evidence of the worship of deities within the African continent.

Archaeological evidence yields similar patterns in the Nubian region of the Upper Nile. By 10,000 BCE, elaborate grave goods and carved figurines indicate that Nubians, too, were concerned that their dead have the necessary assistance of tools and servants for their journey into the afterlife. By 3300 BCE, Nubian graves contained copper goods and representations of a falcon god, which may have protected local rulers. Saharan rock and burial sites reveal the presence of cattle and the possible existence of a cattle cult by the fifth millennium BCE. In the vast region from the Sahara to the Sahel, graves have been found with bodies deliberately placed facing west, the direction of the setting sun. This suggests links between the rising and setting sun and cycles of birth and death. Rock paintings found in the Atlas Mountains of northeast Africa, dated to the fourth millennium BCE, suggest the existence of a ram deity that could have influenced the iconography of the Amun cult of pharaonic Egypt.

Linguistic sources provide evidence of Proto-Bantu language, spoken in the fourth millennium, which already contained words for a supreme being, Nyambe, and for lesser spirits. Both linguistic and archaeological evidence suggest the existence of rites of male initiation, including circumcision, and the existence of age sets that played an important role in early social structures.

By the fourth millennium BCE, African religions had begun to differentiate themselves. Throughout the continent, people left evidence of their concerns about the proper care of the dead, both in sedentary communities and among nomadic groups. By the end of the fourth millennium, sedentary communities manifested a growing distinction between the graves of the rich and powerful and the poor and marginalized. Concepts of deities emerged in the Nile valley and in the Benue/Cross River regions of West Africa where Bantu languages were spoken. Distinctions between spiritual beings tied to the land and ancestral spirits linked to specific families became increasingly important in Bantu-speaking communities.

During the third and second millennium BCE, written sources and richer archaeological evidence allowed scholars to trace the development of competing cosmogonic myths in ancient Egypt. Each of these traditions emphasized different relations between humanity and their gods. They also focused on different deities as creators. These divergent traditions coexisted throughout the period of ancient Egyptian independence. Previously dominant myths fell out of favor, while others became ascendant, reflecting the increasing or declining influences of certain deities and certain provinces within Egyptian society. Egyptian deities also gained wide acceptance in Nubia and Punt in northeast Africa and influenced Libyan, Carthaginian, and other North African religious traditions. Egyptian society proved adept at incorporating Nubian and Eastern Mediterranean deities while adopting them within Egyptian traditions of religious practice. Despite the frequency of foreign occupations of Egypt during the last millennium before the Common Era, these new rulers found it advantageous to accept the close association of the monarchs of Egypt with the major deities and systems of temple patronage. The Ptolemies went so far as to try to create a Hellenistic/Egyptian religious cult, of Serapis, to unite Egyptian and Greek citizens of their empire.

Innovations in Egyptian religious life, however, were not limited to changing creation myths and new deities gaining adherents. Scholarly attention has focused more on the rich archaeological and textual sources concerning the preservation of the dead, concepts of judgment, and the journey into the afterlife. In the course of Egyptian history, tombs of royalty grew from simple rock cairns to more elaborate *mastabas*, to the pyramids, the largest tombs known in the history of humanity, all by the end of the Old Kingdom. By the Middle of the New Kingdom, however, ideas of eternal life had been extended beyond the nobility to commoners, whose journeys to the afterlife also had to be protected. Ideas of *ma'at*, of justice in this life and in the afterlife, became increasingly important for all Egyptians. Powerful images of the goddess Ma'at weighing the souls of the dead before determining their fates influenced not only Egyptian ideas of morality and justice but became powerful symbols of the judicial process in Western civilization.

During the New Kingdom, the pharaoh Amenhotep IV attempted to reform Egyptian religious practice by focusing exclusively on the manifestations of the sun's rays, Aten. Although textual sources do not allow us to gain insight into the religious experiences that led up to his decision, we do know that he was something of a solitary individual who had not been groomed to become king. Only the death of his older brother opened a path for him to ascend the throne. He outlawed the ritual supplication of the previous supreme deity, Amun-Ra, which was closely associated with the powerful priests based at Memphis. He moved his capital and ritual center to Akhetaten, changed his name to Akhenaten, gave new ritual responsibilities to his wife, Nefertiti, and consolidated religious life under the direct control of the monarchy. His decisions to eliminate festivals of other gods and his reluctance to develop elaborate mythic traditions about Aten led to the decline and eventual abandonment of this religious reform. His emphasis on the oneness of the Aten and that it was the god of all peoples influenced later Egyptian understandings of the role of the gods, even though they abandoned his movement toward monotheism. By the end of the New Kingdom, Akhenaten's religious reforms had been suppressed. They may have lived on, however, in the readiness of Nubian peoples to embrace a universality they associated with Amun-Ra. Akhenaten's stress on the one god, Aten, may have reinforced the monotheistic teachings of a young Hebrew, raised at court during the early Ramesside Dynasty, a young man named Moses.

During the three millennia before the Common Era, archaeological and linguistic sources provide much of the evidence of a religious history outside the Nile valley. Much of the sources concern burial practices, including the ritual sacrifices and offerings that accompanied the burial of the dead, and the direction in which the deceased was placed in the grave. Figurines found in graves, with exaggerated breasts or hips on women or ithyphallic portrayals of men, suggest concerns about fertility even while people observed rituals to ensure the proper treatment of the dead.

In northeast Africa, Cushitic- and Semitic-speaking groups forged a complex social and religious tradition in the highlands of present-day Eritrea and Ethiopia. The earliest Ethiopian state may have focused its religious concerns on a snake cult, which was eventually overcome in the establishment of the D'MT state. Strong Sabean influences from southwest Arabia contributed celestial deities associated with the sun and the moon and may have introduced the tradition of the Queen of Sheba who played such a prominent role in the development of the Ethiopian monarchy. Further west, communities known as Imazighen (better known as Berbers) venerated spirits associated with unusual rock formations and springs. Rock art from the Tassili and Hoggar regions of the Saharan suggests the importance of ritual dance and its use in seeking visionary trance experience. In West Africa, during this period, agricultural activities dramatically increased. In the Niger, Gambia, and Casamance River valleys, new labor-intensive forms of wet-rice agriculture developed, along with various types of spirit cults to ensure the fertility of land and crops and the reliable supply of labor.

Because of the richness of linguistic studies, Equatorial and East Africa provide the clearest evidence of religious change in sub-Saharan Africa. As Bantu-speaking peoples moved east and south throughout these regions, new vocabulary developed which suggested changes in concepts of a supreme being, territorial spirits, and spirits associated with the hunter-gatherer first inhabitants of the land who were incorporated into the new farming communities. Both male and female initiation became important for the socialization of young people and the establishment of social and religious organizations that transcended the limitations of lineal descent.

Like Egypt, North Africa experienced a series of invasions by people from across the Mediterranean, beginning with Phoenicians and Greeks and concluding with Romans and Vandals. Each brought new religious cults which were incorporated into North African religious systems focused on a sacred landscape. As Phoenicians established Carthage, they also established new religious cults associated with Baal and Melqart. Eventually, Baal became associated with the Egyptian god, Amun, which was already influential in North Africa. The goddess Tanit was identified as the wife of Baal-Amun and may have been of Libyan origin. Greek communities established themselves in Cyrencia, introducing their gods Apollo, Artemis, and Asclepius, but they eventually embraced the Hellenistic deity of Serapis. Further west, small Berber kingdoms retained their independence. Such rulers as Massinissa respected the important role of women prophets, such as his mother in Berber traditions, while incorporating Carthaginian and Roman cults and religious practices.

Further south, in the West African savannahs, blacksmiths became increasingly important, playing a vital role in the forging of farm implements and weapons to support the growing towns of the West African Sahel. Accompanying this increased role of blacksmiths, new guild shrines in separate neighborhoods of the growing towns played an important role in religious life. This is supported by the increasingly prominent role of blacksmiths in the oral traditions and creation myths of West African communities. By the fifth century BCE, these blacksmithing traditions had become important in the Nok culture of central Nigeria. In this area, new manufacturing techniques of terracotta figurines played an important role in the growth of healing and fertility cults. These traditions influenced newer cultures of people who settled along the Lower Guinea Coast. East Africa's Interlacustrine region experienced a similar expansion of the role of blacksmiths who became important religious leaders and chiefs.

Memories of their roles persist in the important role of the Abacwezi spirits and their spirit mediums, who continue to play a central role in this region.

During the Common Era, Egypt, North Africa, and Ethiopia entered into a long and sustained interaction with the Abrahamic religious traditions, of Judaism and Christianity, as well as the continued influence of Greek and Roman religious practices. During the early centuries of the Common Era, North and northeastern African religious practices drew on local traditions and the religious practices of prior conquerors. When the Romans conquered Egypt and North Africa, they kept them as dependent provinces. They did not grant them autonomous political power or religious authority. Instead, they cut off state subsidies to Egyptian temples and placed major religious practices under the control of Roman officials. Christianity was viewed with suspicion both by Roman authorities and practitioners of local religious traditions. By the end of the second century, however, Christianity had made significant inroads in Alexandria, which quickly became a major center of Christian thought, even while remaining a center of Hellenized Egyptian and Jewish communities.

By the fourth century, Christianity had become an important force in Egypt, North Africa, and Ethiopia. The harsh persecutions of Christians in Egypt and North Africa became less common by 315 when Emperor Constantine issued his Edict of Toleration. By the end of the century, however, the Roman state used its authority to persecute "pagans," cutting off state support of temples and eventually closing them. Nevertheless, North African and Egyptian traditions surrounding healing and fertility, the mysteries of Isis, the reliance on dreams and visions to resolve spiritual challenges to health, all persisted, even within a hegemonic Christianity. North Africans and Egyptians played important roles in the development of Christian orthodoxy, particularly Tertullian's clear articulation of the doctrine of the Trinity. They played an important role in the development of the ermetic and monastic traditions that became important throughout the Christian world. They also kept alive interpretations of Christian doctrine, most notably the Arian and Monophysite traditions that failed to win the support of Rome or Constantinople. Less constructively, Christians of North and northeast Africa entered into harsh conflicts with traditionalists, even accusing "pagans" of using Christian blood in their rituals, an accusation that later Christians made against Jews. They also entered into bitter and violent with fellow Christians over doctrinal distinctions concerning such issues as the nature of Christ and the position of people who recanted in the face of Roman persecution after that persecution had ended.

Further south, the Nobatae conquerors of the kingdom of Meroe embraced a Monophysite form of Christianity, tying them to the Patriarch of Alexandria, but using their new faith as a unifying tradition that helped them sustain their independence after the Arab conquest of Egypt. In Ethiopia, the Axumite monarchy embraced Christianity in the fourth century, while adding long-standing traditions of the Queen of Sheba, to produce a distinctly Ethiopian form of the religious tradition. In the seventh century, the Ethiopian Christian monarch welcomed Muslim refugees who sought asylum at his court because of the severity of Meccan persecution of the new religious tradition. The Ethiopian king recognized what the two faiths had in common and granted them a permanent gift of Ethiopian land, nearly a decade before there were any Muslims in the holy city of Medina.

In East Africa and Equatorial Africa during the Common Era, some communities developed new concepts of the supreme being which emphasized a nurturing role alongside the deity's continuing role as the primary force for creation. Blacksmiths continued to play important roles in both the economic and religious life of their communities. In the Interlacustrine Region, the spirits of ancestral chiefs of blacksmith clans gained ritual prominence as Abacwezi spirits. Age sets created during rites of passage became important sources of interlineage unity that was central to both political and religious organization. Age sets facilitated the development of regional spirit cults and state formation.

In this summary of the ancient history of African religions, it has become clear that Africa is not a laboratory for non-Africans to view the religious activities of their ancestors. Each African religion has its own distinct history, even if the sources remain problematic. African religious traditions have changed dramatically over time, sometimes as a result of internal social change, sometimes as a result of environmental shifts or migrations, sometimes as a result of contacts with other religious communities. Evidence for these histories can be found in the archaeological record, through linguistic studies, and, where available, oral traditions and written texts. "Traditional" societies often do not celebrate the major changes in their religious traditions. This stems from a concern about the idea of innovation standing in opposition to the authority of ancestors and traditions. Knowledge of such changes must be safeguarded for those who can understand their significance. Religious innovation is one of religion's greatest mysteries. Africa has had a history as long as Africa has had human beings to create it. Africans have had religious concerns as long as they have pondered the ultimate destiny of deceased relatives and friends. This work draws on a broad range of research methods applied to communities all over the continent. Using these studies, this book crosses a threshold bringing scholarly perspectives to build a history of African religions.

Bibliography

Published Sources

Abu Bakar, A. "Pharaonic Egypt." In *Ancient Civilizations of Africa, Volume II of UNESCO General History of Africa*, edited by G. Mokhtar. London: Heinemann, (1981), pp. 84–111.

Abun-Nasr, Jamil M. *A History of the Maghreb*. 2nd ed. Cambridge: Cambridge University Press, 1975.

Adams, William Y. *Nubian Corridors to Africa*. Princeton, NJ: Princeton University Press, 1977.

Akama, John. "Historical Evolution of the Gusii." In *Ethnography of the Gusii of Western Kenya: A Vanishing Cultural Heritage*, edited by John S. Akama and Robert Maxson. Lewiston, NY: Edwin Mellen Press, 2005.

Aldred, Cyril. *The Egyptians*. 3rd ed. London: Thames and Hudson, 1998.

Ambrose, Stanley. "Archaeological and Linguistic Reconstruction of History in East Africa." In *The Archaeological and Linguistic Reconstruction of African History*, edited by Christopher Ehret and Merrick Posnansky. Berkeley: University of California, 1982, pp. 104–157.

Ambrose, Stanley. "East African Neolithic." In *Encyclopedia of Prehistory, Volume I, Africa*, edited by Peter N. Peregrine and Melvin Ember. New York: Kluwer, 2001, pp. 97–109.

"Ancient Ferrous Metallurgy Sites of Burkina Faco." UNESCO World Heritage Sites. http://whc.unesco.org, 2019.

Andah, B. Wai. "West Africa before the Seventh Century." In *Ancient Civilizations of Africa, Volume II, UNESCO General History of Africa*, edited by G. Mokhtar. Paris: UNESCO, 1981, pp. 593–620.

Andrews, Carol. *The Ancient Egyptian Book of the Dead*. Austin: University of Texas Press, 1995.

Anfray, Francis. *Les Anciens Ethiopiens: Siècles de l'histoire*. Paris: Armand Coiln, 1990.

Apter, Andrew. *Black Critics and Kings: The Hermeneutics of Power in Yoruba Society*. Chicago: University of Chicago Press, 1992.

Arens, W. *The Man-Eating Myth: Anthropology and Anthropophagy*. New York: Oxford University Press, 1979.

Aristotle. *Politics*. Edited by Louise Ropes Loomis. New York: Walter Black, 1942.

Arkell, A. J. *The Prehistory of the Nile Valley*. Leiden: Brill, 1975.

Armstrong, Karen. *Muhammad: Biography of a Prophet*. New York: HarperCollins, 1992.

Asad, Talal. *Genealogies of Religion: Discipline and Reasons of Power in Christianity and Islam*. Baltimore: Johns Hopkins University Press, 1993.

Asante, Molefi Kete. *Kemet, Afrocentricity and Knowledge*. Trenton, NJ: Africa World Press, 1990.

Assmann, Jan. *The Mind of Egypt: History and Meanings in the Time of the Pharaohs*. New York: Holt, 1996.

Assmann, Jan. *Moses the Egyptian: The Memory of Egypt in Western Monotheism*. Cambridge, MA: Harvard University Press, 1997.

Assmann, Jan. *The Search for God in Ancient Egypt*. Ithaca, NY: Cornell University Press, 2001.

Assmann, Jan. *Solar Religion in the New Kingdom: Re, Atum, and the Crisis of Monotheism*. London: Kegan, Paul International, 1995.

Athanasius of Alexandria. *The Life of Saint Antony*. Translated by Tim Vivian and Apostolus Athanassakis, Kalamazoo: Cistercian Publications, 2003.

Atica, Aziz Suryal, and Mark N. Swanson. "Coptic Church." In *The Encyclopedia of Religion*, Vol. 3, edited by Lindsay Jones. Detroit, MI: Thomson/Gale, 2005, pp. 1979–1983.

Attwater, Donald. *The Penguin Dictionary of Saints.* 2nd ed. Harmondsworth, UK: Penguin, 1983.
Augustine. *Confessions.* Harmondsworth, UK: Penguin, 1970.
Bagnall, Roger S. *Egypt in Late Antiquity.* Princeton, NJ: Princeton University Press, 1993.
Bailey, Susan. "Circumcision and Male Initiation in Africa." In *Egypt in Africa,* edited by Theodore Celenko. Indianapolis: Indianapolis Museum of Art, 1996.
Baines, John, "Society, Morality, and Religious Practice." In *Religion in Ancient Egypt: Gods, Myths, and Personal Practice,* edited by Byron E. Shafer. Ithaca, NY: Cornell University Press, 1991, pp. 123–200.
Baird, Bill. "Strange Earths: Ancient Mining in Swaziland." *The Edinburgh Geologist* 12, no. 42.
Bard, Kathryn A., and Rodolfo Fattovich. "Processes of State Formation in Egypt and Ethiopia." In *Africa and Africans in Antiquity,* edited by Edwin Yamauchi. East Lansing: Michigan State University, 2001, pp. 276–290.
Bauer, Dan, and John Hinnant. "Normal and Revolutionary Divination: A Kuhnian Approach to African Traditional Thought." In *Explorations in African Traditional Thought,* edited by Ivan Karp and Charles Bird. Washington, DC: Smithsonian, 1980, pp. 213–236.
Baum, Robert M. "The Emergence of a Diola Christianity." *Africa* 60 (1990), pp. 370–398.
Baum, Robert M. "The Forgotten South: African Religions in World Religions Textbooks." *Religious Studies Review* 21 (January 6, 2006), pp. 27–30.
Baum, Robert M." From a Boy Not Seeking a Wife to a Man Discussing Prophetic Women: A Male Fieldworker among Diola Women in Senegal, 1974–2005." *Men and Masculinities* 11 (2008), pp. 154–163.
Baum, Robert M. "Indigenous Religions." In *A Concise Introduction to World Religions,* 2nd ed., edited by Willard G. Oxtoby and Alan F. Segal. Toronto: Oxford University Press, 2007, pp. 10–50.
Baum, Robert M. "Secrecy, Shrines, and Memory: Diola Oral Traditions and the Slave Trade in Senegal." In *Activating the Past: History and Memory in the Black Atlantic World,* edited by Andrew Apter and Robin Derby. New Castle upon Tyne: Cambridge Scholars Press, 2010, pp. 139–155.
Baum, Robert M. "Setting out on the Awasena Path: Conducting Field Research in Diola Communities in Senegal." *Mande Studies* 20 (2018), pp. 61–70.
Baum, Robert M. *Shrines of the Slave Trade: Diola Religion and Society in Pre-Colonial Senegambia.* New York: Oxford University Press, 1999.
Baum, Robert M. *West Africa's Women of God: Alinesitoué and the Diola Prophetic Tradition.* Bloomington: Indiana University Press, 2016.
Beidelman, T. O. *Moral Imagination in Kaguru Modes of Thought.* Bloomington: Indiana University Press, 1986.
Beidelman, T. O. "Myth, Legend, and Oral History: A Kaguru Traditional Text." *Anthropos* 70 (1970), pp. 74–97.
Bénabou, Marcel. *La Résistance africaine à la romanization.* Paris: Maspero, 1976.
Ben-Jochannan, Yosef. *African Origins of the Major Western Religions.* Baltimore: Black Classics Press, (1970) 1991.
Berger, Iris. "Deities, Dynasties, and Oral History: The History and Legend of the Abacwezi." In *The African Past Speaks: Essays on Oral Tradition and History,* edited by Joseph C. Miller. Folkestone, UK: Dawson, 1980, pp. 61–81.
Berger, Iris. *Religion and Resistance: East African Kingdoms in the Precolonial Period.* Tervuren: Musée Royale de l'Afrique Central, 1981.
Berger, Iris, and E. Francis White. *Women in Sub-Saharan Africa: Restoring Women to History.* Bloomington: Indiana University Press, 1999.
Berger, Lee R., John Hawks, Paul H. G. M. Dirks, Marine Eliot, and Eric Roberts. "Homo Naledi and Pleistocene Human Evolution in Subequatorial Africa." eLIfe, May 9, 2017.
Berlev, Oleg. "Bureaucrats." In *The Egyptians,* edited by Sergio Donadoni. Chicago: University of Chicago Press, 1997, pp. 87–120.

Berman, Lawrence W. "Overview of Amenhotep III." In *Amenhotep III: Perspectives on His Reign*, edited by David O'Connor and Eric H. Cline. Ann Arbor: University of Michigan Press, 2001, pp. 1–26.
Bernal, Martin. *Black Athena: The Afroasiatic Roots of Western Civilization*. New Brunswick, NJ: Rutgers University Press, 1987.
The Bible. Cambridge New American Standard Bible. Cambridge: Cambridge University Press, 1977.
Bisson, Michael S. "Pre-Colonial Copper Metallurgy: Socio-Political Content." In *Ancient African Metallurgies: The Sociocultural Content*, edited by Joseph O. Vogel. Walnut Creek, CA: Altamira Press, 2001, pp. 83–146.
Blouin, Katherine. *Triangular Landscapes: Environment, Society, and the State in the Nile Delta under Roman Rule*. Oxford Scholarship on Line, 2014.
Bockie, Simon. *Death and the Invisible World: In Kongo Belief*. Berkeley: University of California Press, 1993.
Bongmba, Elias K. "Christianity in North Africa." In *The Routledge Companion to Christianity in Africa*, edited by Elias Bongmba. New York: Routledge, 2016, pp. 25–44.
Boulding, Elise. *The Underside of History: A View of Women through Time*. Vol. I. London: Sage, 1992.
Bourgeois, Arthur P. "Masking in Sub-Saharan Africa." In *Egypt in Africa*, edited by Theodore Celenko. Indianapolis: Indianapolis Museum of Art, 1996.
Bovill, B. V. *The Golden Trade of the Moors*. 2nd ed. Oxford: Oxford University Press, 1968.
Bowman, Alan K. *Egypt after the Pharaohs: From Alexander to the Arab Conquest, 332 BC–AD 642*. Berkeley: University of California Press, 1980.
Brady, Alisa, and Peter Robertshaw. "The Glacial Maximum in Tropical Africa, 22,000–12,000 BP." In *The World of 18,000 BP, Vol. Two, Low Latitudes*, edited by Clive Gamble and Olga Soffer. London: Hyman, 1990, pp. 120–121.
Breen, Colin, and Paul J. Lane. "Archaeological Approaches to East Africa's Changing Seascapes." *Journal of World Archaeology* 35 (2003), pp. 469–489.
Brenner, Louis. "Religious Discourses in and About Africa." In *Discourse and Its Disguises: The Interpretation of African Oral Texts*, edited by Karin Barber and P. F. de Moraes-Farias. Birmingham: Centre for West African Studies, University of Birmingham, 1989, pp. 87–105.
Bresciani, Eddi. "Foreigners." In *The Egyptians*, edited by Sergio Donadoni. Chicago: University of Chicago Press, 1997, pp. 221–254.
Brett, Michael, and Elizabeth Fentress. *The Berbers*. Malden, MA: Blackwell, 1997.
Brewer, Douglas J. *Ancient Egypt: Foundations of a Civilisation*. Harlow, UK: Pearson, Longman, 2005.
Brook, George A., L. Bruce Railsback, Alec C. Campbell, Lawrence H. Robbins, Michael L. Murphy, Greg Hodgins, and Joseph McHugh. "Radiocarbon Ages for Coatings on Cupules Ground in Quartzite Bedrock at Rhino Cave in the Kalahari Desert of Botswana, and Their Paleoclimatic Significance." *Geoarchaeology: An International Journal* 26, no. 1 (2011).
Brown, Peter. *Augustine of Hippo: A Biography*. Berkeley: University of California Press, 1967.
Budge, E. A. Wallis. *Egyptian Magic*. New York: Dover Books, (1903) 1971.
Budge, E. A. Wallis. *The Gods of Ancient Egypt*. Vol. I. New York: Dover Books, 1969.
Budge, E. A. Wallis. *A History of Ethiopia, Nubia, & Abyssinia*. Oosterhout, The Netherlands: Anthropological Publications, (1928) 1970.
Bullard, Reuben G. "The Berbers of the Maghreb and Ancient Carthage." In *Africa and Africans in Antiquity*, edited by Edwin Yamauchi. East Lansing: Michigan State University, 2001, pp. 180–209.
Burkert, Walter. *Ancient Mystery Cults*. Cambridge, MA: Harvard University Press, 1987.
Burridge, Kenelm. *New Heavens, New Earth: A Study of Millenarian Activities*. Oxford: Basil Blackwell, 1969.
Burstein, Stanley M. "The Kingdom of Meroe." In *Africa and Africans in Antiquity*, edited by Edwin Yamauchi. East Lansing: Michigan State University, 2001, pp. 132–158.

Callender, Gae. "The Middle Kingdom Renaissance (c. 2055-1669 BC)" in Ian Shaw, *Oxford History of Ancient Egypt*, Oxford: Oxford University Press, 2000, pp. 148-183.
Campbell, Alec, Larry Robbins, and Michael Taylor, eds. *Tsodilo Hills: Copper Bracelet of the Kalahari*. East Lansing: Michigan State University Press, 2010.
Camps, Gabriel. "Funerary Monuments with Attached Chapels from Northern Sahara." *African Archaeological Review* IV (1986), pp. 151-164.
Camps, Gabriel. *Les Berbères: Mémoires et identité*. Paris: Editions Errance, 1987.
Canby, Courtlandt, with Arcadia Kocybala. *A Guide to the Archaeological Sites of Israel, Egypt, and North Africa*. New York: Facts on File, 1990.
Carmody, Denise, and John Carmody. *Original Visions: The Religions of Oral Practices*. New York: Macmillan, 1993.
Carter, Howard. *The Tomb of Tutankhamun*. New York: E. P. Dutton, (1954) 1972.
Case, Shirley Jackson. *Jesus through the Centuries*. Chicago: University of Chicago Press, 1932.
Chadwick, Henry. *The Early Church*. Harmondsworth, UK: Penguin (1967) 1982.
Chami, Felix A. "Diffusion in the Studies of the African Past: Reflections from New Archaeological Findings." *African Archaeological Review* 24 (2007), pp. 1-14.
Chami, Felix A. *The Tanzanian Coast in the First Millennium AD*. Uppsala: Studies in African Archaeology, 1994.
Chesi, Gert, and Gerhard Merzeder, eds. *The Nok Culture: Art in Nigeria 2500 Years Ago*. Munich: Prestal, 2006.
Chidester, David. *Savage Systems: Colonialism and Comparative Religion in Southern Africa*. Charlottesville: University Press of Virginia, 1996.
Childs, Terry, and Eugenia Herbert. "Metallurgy and Its Consequences." In *African Archaeology*, edited by Ann B. Stahl. Malden, MA: Blackwell, 2005, pp 276-300.
Chinweizu. *The West and the Rest of Us: White Slavers, Black Slavers, and the African Elite*. New York: Vantage Press, 1970.
Chouraqui, André. *Between East and West: A History of the Jews of North Africa*. Philadelphia: The Jewish Publication Society of America, 1968,
Clark, J. Desmond, Patrick Carter, Dianne Gilford-Gonzalez, and Andrew Smith. "The Adrar Bous Cow and African Cattle." In *Adrar Bous: Archaeology of a Central Saharan Granite Ring Complex in Niger*, edited by Desmond Clark et al. Tervuren: Royal Museum for Central Africa, 2008, pp. 355-368.
Clark, Elizabeth. "Clement of Alexandria." In *The Encyclopedia of Religion*, Vol. 3, 2nd ed., edited by Lindsay Jones. Detroit, MI: Thomson/Gale, 2005, pp. 1822-1824.
Clark, R. T. Rundle. *Myth and Symbol in Ancient Egypt*. London: Thames and Hudson, (1959) 1991.
Clarke, Peter B. *West African Islam*. London: Arnold, 1982.
Cline, Eric H., and David O'Connor, eds. *Thutmose III: A New Biography*, Ann Arbor: University of Michigan Press, 2006.
Coakley, George A. "The Mining Industry of Swaziland." *United States Geological Survey* 27, no. 1 (2000).
Cohen, William D. *The French Encounter with Africans*. Bloomington: Indiana University Press, 1980.
Collins, Robert O. *African History: Texts and Readings*. New York: Random House, 1973.
Connah, Graham. *African Civilizations: An Archaeological Perspective*. 2nd ed. Cambridge: Cambridge University Press, 2001.
Connah, Graham. *Forgotten Africa: An Introduction to Archaeology*. New York: Routledge, 2004
Connerton, Paul. *How Societies Remember*. Cambridge: Cambridge University Press, 1989.
Cornelius, Izak. "From Bes to Baal: Religious Interaction Between Egypt and the East." In *Pharaoh's Land and Beyond: Ancient Egypt and Its Neighbors*, edited by Pearce P. Creasman and Richard H. Williams. New York: Oxford University Press, 2017, pp. 209-218.
Coulson, David. Trust for African Rock Art. Nairobi, n.d. www.Africanrockart.org.

Coulson, David, and Alec Campbell. *African Rock Art: Paintings and Engravings on Stone.* New York: Harry Abrams, 2000.

Coulson, Sheila. "The Secret of the Rhino Cave." In *Dangerous and Divine: The Secret of the Serpent*, edited by Wouter Welling. Amsterdam: KITNair, Afrika Museum, 2012, pp. 120–125.

Coulson, Sheila, Philip Segadika, and Nick Walker. "Ritual in the Hunter-Gatherer/Early Pastoralist Period: Evidence from Tsodilo Hills, Botswana." *African Archaeological Review* 33, no. 2 (2016), pp. 205–222.

Coulson, Sheila, Sigrid Staurset, and Nick Walker. "Ritualized Behaviour in the Middle Stone Age: Evidence from the Rhino Cave, Tsodilo Hills, Botswana." *Paleoanthropology* (2011), pp. 18–61.

Cox, James. *From Primitive to Indigenous: The Academic Study of Indigenous Religions.* Aldershot, UK: Ashgate, 2007.

Craemer, W. J., Jan Vansina, and R. Fox. "Religious Movements in Central Africa." *Comparative Studies in Society and History* 18 (1976), pp. 458–475.

Curtin, Philip. *The Image of Africa.* Madison: University of Wisconsin Press, 1964.

Curtin, Philip, Steven Feierman, Leonard Thompson, and Jan Vansina. *African History.* New York: Longman, (1978) 1991.

Danquah, J. B. *The Akan Concept of God: A Fragment of Gold Coast Ethics and Religion.* London: Cass, 1966.

Dark, K. R. *Theoretical Archaeology.* Ithaca, NY: Cornell University Press, 1995.

David, Rosalie. *Religion and Magic in Ancient Egypt.* London: Penguin, 2002.

Davidson, Basil. *African Kingdoms.* New York: Time/Life, 1966.

Davies, Vivian, and Renée Friedman. *Egypt Uncovered.* New York: Stewart, Tabori, and Chang, 1998.

D'Avignon, Robyn. *A Ritual Geology: Gold and Subterranean Knowledge in Savanna West Africa.* Durham, NC: Duke University Press, 2022.

DeBono, F. "Prehistory in the Nile Valley." In *Methodology and African Prehistory, Vol. I, UNESCO General History of Africa*, edited by J. Ki-Zerbo. London: Heinemann, 1982, pp. 634–655.

De Brosses, Charles. "On the Worship of Fetish Gods: Or Parallel of the Ancient Religions of Egypt with the Present Religions of Nigrita (1760)." In *The Returns of Fetishism: Charles de Brosses and the Afterlife of an Idea*, edited by Rosalind C. Morris and David H. Leonard. Chicago: University of Chicago Press, 2017.

De Contenson, H. "Pre-Aksumite Culture." In *Ancient Civilizations of Africa, Volume II of UNESCO General History of Africa*, edited by G. Mokhtar. London: Heinemann, 1981, pp. 341–361.

Décret, François. *Carthage ou l'empire de la Mer.* Paris: Edition du Seuil, 1977.

De Heusch, Luc. *Le Roi Ivre ou l'origine de l'état.* Paris: Gallimard, 1972.

De Maret, Pierre. "Archaeological & Other Prehistoric Evidence of Traditional African Religious Expression." In *Religion in Africa*, edited by Thomas D. Blakely, Walter E. A. van Beek, and Dennis L. Thomson. London: James Currey, 1994, pp. 182–195.

Des Songes, J. "The Proto-Berbers." In *Ancient Civilizations of Africa, Volume II UNESCO General History of Africa*, edited by G. Mokhtar. London: Heinemann, 1981, pp. 423–440.

D'Errico, Francesco, and Christopher S. Henshilwood. "The Origin of Symbolically Mediated Behavior: From Antagonistic Scenarios to a Unified Research Strategy." In *Homo Symbolicus: The Dawn of Languages, Imagination, and Spirituality*, edited by Christopher Henshilwood and Francesco d'Errico. Philadelphia: John Benjamin, 2011, pp. 49–74.

Derricourt, Robin. *Inventing Africa: History, Archaeology, and Ideas.* London: Pluto Press, 2011.

Desroches-Noblecourt, Christiane. *Life and Death of a Pharaoh: Tutankhamen.* London: George Rainbird Limited, 1963.

Diop, Cheikh Anta. *Egypte Ancienne et Afrique Noir.* Dakar: IFAN, 1989.

Diop, Cheikh Anta. "Histoire primitive d'humanité: Evolution du monde noir." *Bulletin de l'IFAN*, Tome XXIV, Ser B #3& 4 (1962), pp. 3–13.

Diop, Cheikh Anta. "The Origins of Ancient Egyptians." In *Ancient Civilizations of Africa, Volume II, UNESCO General History of Africa*, edited by G. Mokhtar. London: Heinemann, 1981, pp. 27–57.

Dirks, Paul H. G. M., John Hawks, Patrick S. Randolph, Quincy Marina Elliott, Charles M. Musiba, Steve E. Churchill, Lee R. Berger, Eric M. Roberts, and Jon D. Kramers. "Geological and Taphonomic Context for the New Hominin Species Homo Naledi from the Dinaledi Chamber, South Africa." *eLife*, September 10, 2015.

Dodson, Aidan. *Amarna Sunrise: Egypt from Golden Age to Age of Heresy*. Cairo: American University in Cairo, 2014.

Dodson, Aidan. *Amarna Sunset: Nefertiti, Tutankhamun, Ay, Horemheb, and the Egyptian Counter Reformation*. Cairo: American University in Cairo Press, 2009.

Dodson, Aidan. *Monarchs of the Nile*. Cairo: American University in Cairo Press, 2000.

Donadoni, S. "Egypt Under Roman Domination." In *Ancient Civilizations of Africa, Volume II of UNESCO General History of Africa*, edited by G. Mokhtar. London: Heinemann, 1981, pp. 208–225.

Doxey, Denise Rita E. Freed, and Lawrence M. Berman. *MFA Highlights of Ancient Nubia*. Boston: Museum of Fine Arts Publications, 2018.

Dunand, Françoise, and Christiane Zivi-Coche. *Gods and Men in Egypt, 3000 BCE to 395 CE*. Ithaca, NY: Cornell University Press, 2004.

Durkheim, Emile. *The Elementary Forms of Religious Life*. New York: The Free Press, (1915) 1965.

Edwards, David. "African Perspectives on Death, Burial, and Mortuary Archaeology." In *The Oxford Handbook of the Archaeology of Death and Burial*, edited by Sarah Tarlow and Liv Nilsson Slutz. Oxford: Oxford University Press, 2013, pp. 209–226.

Ego, Renaud. *San: Art rupestre d'Afrique Australe*. Paris: Société Nouvelle d'Adam Biro, 2006.

Ehret, Christopher. *An African Classical Age: Eastern and Southern Africa in World History, 1,000 BC to AD 400*. Charlottesville: University Press of Virginia, 1998.

Ehret, Christopher. *History and the Testimony of Language*. Berkeley: University of California Press, 2011.

Ehrman, Bart D., and Andrew S. Jacobs, eds. *Christianity in Late Antiquity, 300–450 CE: A Reader*. New York: Oxford University Press, 2004.

Eisenstadt, S. N. "Introduction: The Axial Age Breakthrough: Their Characteristics and Origins." In *The Origins and Diversity of Axial Age Civilizations*, edited by S. N. Eisenstadt. Albany: State University Press of New York, 1986, pp. 1–25.

Ejikeme, Anene. "Ezana (Ahola)." In *Holy People of the World: A Cross-Cultural Encyclopedia*, edited by Phyllis G. Jestice, Vol. I. Santa Barbara, CA: ABC-Clio, 2004, pp. 266–267.

Eliade, Mircea. *History of Religions*. 3 vols. Chicago: University of Chicago Press, 1978.

Eliade, Mircea. *Patterns of Religion*. New York: New American Library, (1968) 1974.

Eliade, Mircea. *The Quest: History and Meaning in Religion*. Chicago: University of Chicago Press, 1984 (1969).

Emery, W. B. *Archaic Egypt*. Harmondsworth, UK: Penguin, 1967.

Encyclopedia Britannica. "Homo Habilis." 2018: https://www.britannica.com/topic/Homohabilis.

Evans-Pritchard, E.E. *Nuer Religion*. Oxford: Oxford University Press, (1956) 1974.

Evans-Pritchard, E.E. *Theories of Primitive Religion*. London: Oxford University Press, (1965) 1984.

Fabunmi, Chief (Dr.). *An Anthology of Historical Notes on Ife City*. Lagos: John West Publishing, 1985.

Fagan, Brian M. *Egypt of the Pharaohs*. Washington, DC: National Geographic, 2002.

Fagan, Brian M. *People of the Earth: An Introduction to World Prehistory*. New York: Harper/Collins, 1995.

Fagg, Bernard. *Nok Terracottas.* Lagos: Ethnographies for the National Museum, 1977.
Farag, Lois M. "The Early Christian Period (42–642): The Spread and Defense of the Christian Faith under Roman Rule." In *The Coptic Christian Heritage: History, Faith and Culture*, edited by Lois M. Farag. London: Routledge, 2014, pp. 23–38.
Fattovich, Rodolfo. "Aksum and the Habasha: State and Ethnicity in Ancient Northern Ethiopia and Eritrea." Working Papers in African Studies #278. Boston: Boston University African Studies Center, 2000.
Fattovich, Rodolfo. "At the Periphery of Empire: The Gash Delta." In *Egypt and Africa: Nubia from Prehistory to Islam*, edited by W.V. Davies. London: British Museum Press, 1987, pp. 40–47.
Fattovich, Rodolfo. "The Development of Ancient States in the Northern Horn of Africa, 3000 BC to 1000 AD." *Journal of World Prehistory* 23 (2010), pp. 145–175.
Fernandez, James. *Bwiti: An Ethnography of the Religious Imagination in Africa.* Princeton, NJ: Princeton University Press, 1982.
Fields, Edda J. "'Before 'Baga': Settlement Chronologies of the Coastal Rio Nunez Region, Earliest Times to 1000 CE." *International Journal of African Historical Studies* 32 (2004), pp. 229–253.
Finn, Thomas M. "'It Happened One Saturday Night': Ritual and Conversion in Augustine's North Africa." *Journal of the American Academy of Religion* LVIII, no. 4 (1990), pp. 589–616.
Fisher, Marjorie M., Peter Lacovera, Sahiman Ikrem, and Sue d'Auna, eds. *Ancient Nubia: African Kingdoms of the Nile.* Cairo: American University in Cairo, 2012.
Fletcher, Joann. *The Egyptian "Book of Living and Dying:" The Illustrated Guide to Ancient Egyptian Wisdom.* London: Duncan Baird Publishers, 2002.
Flight, Colin. "The Kintampo Culture and its Place in the Economic Prehistory of West Africa." In *West African Culture Dynamics: Archaeological and Historical Perspectives*, edited by B. K. Swantz and Raymond Durnett. The Hague: Mouton, 1986, pp. 91–100.
Fogelin, Lars. "Delegitimating Religion: The Archaeology of Religion as Archaeology." In *Belief in the Past: Theoretical Approaches to the Archaeology of Religion*, edited by D. S. Whitley and K. Hays-Gilpin. Walnut Creek, CA: Left Coast Press, 2017, pp. 129–141.
Folorunsa, Caleb A. "Views of Ancient Egypt from a West African Perspective." In *Ancient Egypt in Africa*, edited by David O'Connor and Andrew Reid. London: UCL Press, 2002, pp. 77–92.
Fourshey, Catherine Symone, Rhonda M. Gonzalez, and Christine Saidi. *Bantu Africa: 3500 BCE to Present.* New York: Oxford University Press, 2017.
Fox, Robin Lane. *Pagans and Christians.* New York: Alfred A. Knopf, 1986.
Frankfort, Henri. *Ancient Egyptian Gods.* New York: Harper and Row, (1948) 1961.
Frankfurter, David. *Christianizing Egypt: Syncretism and Local Worlds in Late Antiquity.* Princeton, NJ: Princeton University Press, 2018.
Frankfurter, David. *Religion in Roman Egypt: Assimilation and Resistance.* Princeton, NJ: Princeton University Press, 1998.
Frazer, James. *The Golden Bough.* New York: Macmillan, 1935.
Frend. W. H. C. "The Christian Period in Mediterranean Africa, circa A.D. 200–788." In *Cambridge History of Africa, Volume II 500 BC to AD 1050*, edited by John Fage. Cambridge: Cambridge University Press, 1975, pp. 410–489.
Freud, Sigmund. *Moses and Monotheism.* New York: Knopf, 1959.
Friedman, Renée. "Herakonpolis." In *Before the Pyramids: The Origins of Egyptian Civilization*, edited by Emily Teeter. Chicago: Oriental Institute of the University of Chicago, 2011.
Gardiner, Sir Alan. *The Admonitions of an Egyptian Sage: From a Hieratic Papyrus in Leiden.* Leipzig: T. C. Hinrichsasche, 1909.
Gardiner, Sir Alan. *Egypt of the Pharaohs.* London: Oxford University Press, 1961.
Garlake, Peter. *Early Art and Architecture of Africa.* Oxford: Oxford University Press, 2002.
Gatto, Maria Carmela. "The Nubian Pastoral Culture as Link between Egypt and Africa: A View from the Archaeological Record." In *Egypt in Its African Context: Proceedings of the*

Conference Held at the Manchester Museum, University of Manchester, 2-4 October 2009, edited by Karen Exell, pp. 21-29. Oxford: Archaeopress, 2011.

Geertz, Clifford. "Religion as a Cultural System." In *The Interpretation of Cultures*, ed. Clifford Geertz. New York: Basic Books, 1973, pp. 87-25.

Gillan, Werner. *A Short History of African Art.* New York: Facts on File Publishing, 1984.

Goehring, James E. "Imagining Macedonius, The First Bishop of Philae." In *Christianity and Monasticism in Aswan and Nubia*, edited by Gawdat Gbra and Hany N. Takla. Cairo: American University in Cairo Press, 2013, pp. 9-20.

Gomez, Michael A. *African Dominion: A New History of Empire in Early and Medieval West Africa*. Princeton, NJ: Princeton University Press, 2018.

Gonzalez, Rhonda. *Societies, Religion, and History: Central East Tanzanians and the World They Created, c. 200 BCE to 1800 CE.* New York: Columbia University Press, 2009.

Goody, Jack. *The Domestication of the Savage Mind.* Cambridge: Cambridge University Press, (1986) 1987.

Goody, Jack. *The Interface between the Written and the Oral.* Cambridge: Cambridge University Press, 1987.

Goody, Jack, and Ian Watt. "The Consequences of Literacy." In *Literacy in Traditional Societies*, ed. Jack Goody. Cambridge: Cambridge University Press, 1975, pp. 27-68.

Greenberg, Joseph. *The Languages of Africa.* Bloomington: Indiana University Press, 1966.

Griaule, Marcel. *Conversations with Ogotemmeli.* London: Oxford University Press, 1970.

Grimal, Nicolas. *A History of Ancient Egypt.* Malden, MA: Blackwell, (1992) 2008.

Grove, C. P. *The Planting of Christianity in Africa.* Volume One. London: Lutterworth Press, (1946) 1954, pp. 1-100.

Guenther, Mathias. *Tricksters and Trancers: Bushman Religion and Society.* Bloomington: Indiana University Press, 1999.

Hakem, A. A. "The Civilization of Napata and Meroe." In *Ancient Civilizations of Africa, Volume II of UNESCO General History of Africa*, edited by G. Mokhtar. London: Heinemann, 1981, pp. 298-325.

Halbwachs, Maurice. *The Collective Memory.* New York: Harper, 1980.

Hall, Martin. *Farmers, Kings, and Traders: The People of Southern Africa 200-1860.* Chicago: University of Chicago Press, 1990.

Hansberry, William. *Pillars in Ethiopian History: The Willim Leo Hansberry African History Notebook.* Vol. I. Edited by Joseph E. Harris. Washington, DC: Howard University Press, 1974.

Hardwerk, Brian. "Python Cave Reveals Oldest Human Ritual, Scientists Suggest." *National Geographic News*, December 22, 2006.

Harig, Ben. "Administration: Temple Administration." In *The Oxford Encyclopedia of Ancient Egypt*, edited by Donald B. Redford. Vol. 1. Oxford: Oxford University Press, 2001, pp. 20-23.

Harrington, Nicole. *Living with the Dead: Ancestors, Worship, and Mortuary Ritual in Ancient Egypt.* Oxford: Oxbow Books, 2010.

Harvey, Graham. *Animism: Respecting the Living World.* London: Hurst and Company, 2017.

Harvey, Stephen P. "Interpreting Punt: Geographic, Cultural, and Artistic Landscapes." In *Mysterious Lands: Encountering Ancient Egypt*, edited by David O'Connor and Stephen Quirke. London: UCL Press, 2003, pp. 81-91.

Hassan, Fekri. "The Predynastic of Egypt: Africa's Prelude to Civilization." In *Egypt in Africa*, edited by Theodore Celenko. Indianapolis: Indianapolis Museum of Art, 1996.

Hassan, Fekri. "Primeval Goddess to Divine Kingship: The Mythogenesis of Power in the Early Egyptian State." In *The Followers of Horus: Studies Dedicated to Michael Allen Hoffman, 1944-1996*, edited by Renée Friedman and Barbara Adam. Oxford: Oxbow Books, 1997, pp. 307-322.

Hatke, George. *Aksum and Nubia: Warfare, Commerce, and Political Fictions in Ancient Northeast Africa.* New York: New York University Press, 2013.

Hawkes, Jacquetta. *Prehistory* Volume I, Part One, *History of Mankind: Culture and Development*. New York: New American Library, 1963.

Hayes, William C. *The Scepter of Egypt: A Background for the Study of the Egyptian Antiquities in the Metropolitan Museum of Art, Part I, From the Earliest Times to the End of the Middle Kingdom*. New York: Henry N. Abrams, 1953.

Hegel, Georg F. *The Philosophy of History*. New York: Dover, 1956.

Hendrickx, Stan, and Pierre Vermeersch. "Prehistory: From the Paleolithic to the Badarian Culture (c. 70,000–4000 BC) in *The Oxford History of Ancient Egypt*, edited by Ian Shaw. Oxford: Oxford University Press, 2000, pp. 17–43.

Henshilwood, Christopher Stuart. *Holocene Prehistory of the Southern Cape, South Africa: Excavations at Blombos Cave and the Blombos Pontein Nature Reserve*. Cambridge: Cambridge Monographs in African Archaeology #75, 2008.

Herbert, Eugenia. *Iron, Gender, and Power: Rituals of Transformation in African Societies*. Bloomington: Indiana University Pres, 1993.

Herbert, Eugenia. *Red Gold of Africa: Copper in Precolonial History and Culture*. Madison: University of Wisconsin Press, 1984.

Herodotus. *The Histories*. London: Penguin, 1972.

Hiskett, Mervyn. *The Development of Islam in West Africa*. London: Longman, 1984.

Hoffman, Michael A. *Egypt before the Pharaohs: The Prehistoric Foundations of Egyptian Civilization*. New York: Knopf, 1979.

Hoffmeyer, James K. *Akhenaten and the Origins of Monotheism*. Oxford: Oxford University Press, 2015.

Hollis, Susan T. "Isis." In *Encyclopedia of Women and World Religion*, Vol. 2, edited by Serinity Young. New York: Macmillan Reference, 1999, pp. 487–488.

Hollis, Susan T. "Neith." In *Encyclopedia of Women and World Religion*, Vol. 2, edited by Serinity Young. New York: Macmillan Reference, 1999, pp. 714–715.

Hopkins, A. G. *An Economic History of West Africa*. New York: Columbia University Press, 1987.

Horton, Mark, and John Middleton. *The Swahili: The Social Landscape of a Mercantile Society*. Oxford: Routledge, 2000.

Horton, Robin. "A Hundred Years of Change in Kalabari Religion." In *Black Africa: Their Peoples and Their Cultures Today*, edited by John Middleton. New York: Macmillan, 1970, pp. 192–211.

Horton, Robin. "African Conversion." *Africa* 41 (1971), pp. 85–108.

Horton, Robin. "African Traditional Thought and Western Science." In *Patterns of Thought in Africa and the West*, edited by Robin Horton. Cambridge: Cambridge University Press, pp. 197–258.

Horton, Robin. "On the Rationality of Conversion." *Africa* 45 (1975), pp. 219–238, 373–399.

Howley, Kathryn. "Egypt and Nubia." In *Pharaoh's Land and Beyond: Ancient Egypt and Its Neighbors*, edited by Pearce Paul Creasman and Richard H. Wilkinson. New York: Oxford University Press, 2017.

Hoyas, Dexter. *The Carthaginians*. London: Routledge, 2010, pp. 219–228.

Huard, Paul. "Introduction et diffusion du fer au Tchad," *Journal of African History* VII, no. 3 (1966), pp. 377–404.

Huffman, Thomas N. *Handbook to the Iron Age: The Archaeology of Pre-Colonial Farming Societies in Southern Africa*. Scottsville, South Africa: University of Kwa-Zulu/Natal Press, 2017.

Humphries, Rolfe. *The Aeneid of Virgil: A Verse Translation*. New York: Scribner's, 1951.

Idowu, E. Bolaji. *African Traditional Religions*. London: SCM Press, 1971.

Idowu, E. Bolaji. *Olodumare: God in Yoruba Religion*. New York: Wazobia Press, (1962) 1994.

Isichei, Elizabeth. *A History of the Church in Africa: From Antiquity to the Present*. Grand Rapids, MI: Eerdmans, 1995.

Isichei, Elizabeth. *The Religious Traditions of Africa: A History*. Westport, CT: Greenwood, 2004.

James, E. G. *The Ancient Gods: The History and Diffusion in the Ancient Near East and the Mediterranean.* New York: Capricorn Books, 1964.

Janzen, John M. *Ngoma: Discourses of Healing in Central and Southern Africa.* Berkeley: University of California Press, 1992.

Jemkur, J. F. *Aspects of the Nok Culture.* Zaria: Ahmadu Bello University, 1991.

Jiménez, Ana I. Navajas. "The Predynastic Bas primigenius as a Royal Image of Territory, Boundaries, and Power in an African Context." In *Egypt in Its African Context: Proceedings of the Conference Held at the Manchester Museum, University of Manchester, 2–4 October 2009*, edited by Karen Exell. Oxford: Archaeopress, 2011.

Johnson, Douglas. *Nuer Prophets: A History of Prophecy from the Upper Nile in the Nineteenth and Twentieth Centuries.* Oxford: Clarendon Press, 1994.

Johnson, Paul. *The Civilization of Ancient Egypt.* New York: Atheneum, 1978.

Johnson, Reverend Samuel. *History of the Yoruba from Earliest Times to the Beginning of the British Protectorate.* Lagos: CMS Bookstore, 1921.

Johnson, W. Raymond. "Akhenaten in Nubia." In *Ancient Nubia: African Kingdoms of the Nile*, edited by Marjorie Fisher et al. Cairo: American University in Cairo, 2012, pp. 92–107.

Josephy, Alvin, ed. *Horizon History of Africa.* New York: McGraw Hill, 1971.

July, Robert W. *A History of the African People.* 4th ed. Prospect Heights, IL: Waveland Press, 1992.

Kamil, Jill. *Coptic Egypt: History and Guide.* Cairo: American University in Cairo, 1990.

Kannengiesser, Charles. "The Spiritual Message of the Church Fathers." In *Christian Spirituality: Origins to the Twelfth Century*, edited by Bernard McGinn, John Meyendorff, and Jean LeClerq. New York: Crossroads, 1987, pp. 61–88.

Kaplan, Steven. *The Beta Israel (Falashas) in Ethiopia: From Earliest Times to the Twentieth Century*, New York: New York University Press, 1992.

Kemp, Barry J. "Old Kingdom, Middle Kingdom, and Second Intermediate Period in Egypt." In *Cambridge History of Africa*, Vol. I, edited by J. Desmond Clark, pp. 658–769.

Kemp, Barry J. *The City of Akhenaten and Nefertiti: Amarna and Its People.* London: Thames and Hudson, 2012.

Kendall, Timothy. "Sudan's Kingdom of Kush." *National Geographic* 178, no. 5, 1990, pp. 96–125.

Kinahan, John. *Namib: The Archaeology of an African Desert.* Woodbridge, UK: James Currey, 2022.

Klieman, Kairn. *"The Pygmies Were Our Compass": Bantu and Batwa in the History of West Central Africa, Early Times to c. 1900.* Portsmouth, NH: Heinemann, 2003.

Kobishanov, Y. M. "Aksum: Political System, Economics, and Culture, First to Fourth Century." In *Ancient Civilizations of Africa, Volume Two, UNESCO General History of Africa*, edited by G. Mokhtar. London: Heinemann, 1981, pp. 381–408.

Kobishanov, Y. M. "On the Problem of Sea Voyages of Ancient Africans in the Indian Ocean." *Journal of African History* VI, no. 2 (1965), pp. 137–141.

Kobishanov, Yuri M., Joseph W. Milds, and Loraine T. Kapitharoff. *Axum.* University Park: Pennsylvania State University Press, 1979.

Koné Sixeau Daouda. *Le Peuplement ancien en Basse Guinée: XIIe-XIX siècles.* Paris: L'Harmattan, 2015.

Kozloff, Arielle P. *Amenhotep III: Egypt's Radiant Pharaoh.* Cambridge: Cambridge University Press, 2012.

Kuhn, Thomas. *The Structure of Scientific Revolutions.* 2nd ed. Chicago: University of Chicago Press, 1970.

Kusimba, Chaparuka. *The Rise and Fall of Swahili States.* Walnut Creek, CA: Altamira Press, 1999.

Lancel, Serge. *Carthage: A History.* Oxford: Blackwell, 1997.

Lancel, Serge. *Saint Augustine.* London: SCM Press, 2002.

Lane, Peter. "Barbarian Tribes and Unrevealing Gyrations: The Changing Role of Ethnographic Imagination in African Archaeology." In *African Archaeology*, edited by Ann Stahl. Malden, MA: Blackwell, 2015, pp. 24–54.
Lapeyre, C. G., and A. Pellegrin. *Carthage Punique (813–146 avant J.C)*. Paris: Payot, 1942.
La Violette, Adria. *Ethno-Archaeology in Jenné, Mali*. Oxford: Oxford University Press. 2000.
Law, Robin. "The Garamantes and Trans-Saharan Enterprise in Classical Times." *Journal of African History* VIII, no. 2 (1967), pp. 181–200.
Law, Robin. "The 'Hamitic Hypothesis' in Indigenous West African Thought." *History in Africa: A Journal of Method*, Vol. 36, 2009, pp. 293–314.
Law, Robin. "North Africa in the Period of Phoenician and Greek Colonization, c. 800 to 325 BC." In *The Cambridge History of Africa, Volume II, From 500 BC to AD 1050*, edited by J. D. Fage. Cambridge: Cambridge University Press, 1978, pp. 87–147.
Leakey, David. *Excavations at the Njoro River Cave: Stone Age Cremated Burials in Kenya Colony*. Oxford: Clarendon, 1956.
LeClant, J. "The Empire of Kush: Napata and Meroe." In *Ancient Civilizations of Africa, Volume II, UNESCO General History of Africa*, edited by G. Mokhtar. London: Heinemann, 1981, pp. 278–297.
Le Corsu, France. *Isis: Mythes et Mystères*. Paris: Société D'Edition 'Les Belles Lettres, 1977.
Lefkowitz, Miriam. *Not Out of Africa: How Afro-centrism Became an Excuse to Teach Myth as History*. New York: New Republic and Basic Books, 1997.
Le Quellec, Jean-Loic. *Rock Art in Africa: Myth and Legend*. Paris: Flammarion, 2004.
Leroi-Gouhan, André. *Les religions de la préhistoire*. Paris: Presses Universitaires de France, (1964) 1990.
Lesko, Barbara. "Ancient Egyptian Religion." In *Encyclopedia of Women and Religion*, Vol. 1, edited by Serinity Young. New York: Macmillan, 1999, pp. 32–35.
Lesko, Barbara. *The Great Goddesses of Egypt*. Norman: University of Oklahoma Press, 1999.
Lesko, Leonard. "Ancient Egyptian Cosmologies and Cosmogonies." In *Religion in Ancient Egypt: Gods, Myths, and Ancient Practice*, edited by Byron E. Shafer et al. Ithaca, NY: Cornell University Press, 1991, pp. 88–122.
Lesko, Leonard. "Egyptian Religion: An Overview." In *Encyclopedia of Religion*, Vol. 4, edited by Lindsay Jones. Detroit, MI: Thomson/Gage, 2005, pp. 2702–2717.
Lesko, Leonard. *Pharaoh's Workers: The Villagers of Deir el Medina*. Ithaca, NY: Cornell University Press, 1996.
Levi-Strauss, Claude. *The Raw and the Cooked*. New York: Octagon Books, 1969.
Levi-Strauss, Claude. *The Savage Mind*. Chicago: University of Chicago Press, 1966.
Levtzion, Nehemia. *Ancient Ghana and Mali*. London: Metheun, 1973.
Levtzion, Nehemia, and J. F. P. Hopkins, eds. *Corpus of Early Arabic Sources for West African History*. Cambridge: Cambridge University Press, 1981.
Levtzion, Nehemia, and Randall Pouwels, eds. *History of Islam in Africa*. Athens: Ohio University Press, 2000.
Lewis-Williams, J. David. *The Rock Art of Southern Africa*. Cambridge: Cambridge University Press, 1983.
Lewis-Williams, J. David. *San Rock Art*. Athens: Ohio University Press, 2013.
Lewis-Williams, David, and Sam Challis. *Deciphering Ancient Minds: The Mystery of San Bushman Rock Art*. London: Thames and Hudson, 2011.
Lewis-Williams, David, and Thomas Dawson. *Images of Power: Understanding Bushman Rock Art*. Johannesburg: Southern Book Publishers, 1989.
Lewis-Williams, J. D., and T. A. Dawson. *San Spirituality: Roots, Expressions and Social Consequences*. Cape Town: Double Story, 2003.
Lhote, Henri. *Les Touaregs du Hoggar (Ahoggar)*. Paris: Payot, 1955.
Lienhardt, Godfrey. *Divinity and Experience: The Religion of the Dinka*. Oxford: Oxford University Press, 1961.

278 BIBLIOGRAPHY

Linares d'y Sapir, Olga. "Shell Middens of Lower Casamance and Problems of Diola Protohistory." *West African Journal of Archaeology* I (1971), pp. 33, 36.
Lindsay, Jack. "Introduction." Apuleius, *The Golden Ass.* Bloomington: Indiana University Press, (1932) 1975.
Litell, David. "Late Pleistocene/Early Holocene Maghreb." In *The Encyclopedia of Prehistory, Vol. 1, Africa,* edited by Peter N. Peregrine and Melvin Ember. New York: Kluwer Academic, 2001, pp. 129–149.
Livius.org. "Roman-Jewish Wars." Articles on Ancient History, 2020, pp. 129–149.
Lloyd, Alan B. "The Late Period, 664-323 BC." In *Ancient Egypt: A Social History,* edited by R. G. Trigger et al. Cambridge: Cambridge University Press, 1992, pp. 279–318.
Lloyd, Alan B. "The Ptolemaic Period (337–30 BC)." In *Oxford History of Ancient Egypt,* edited by Ian Shaw. Oxford: Oxford University Press, 2000, pp. 388–413.
Longman, Timothy. *Christianity and Genocide in Rwanda.* Cambridge: Cambridge University Press, 2010.
MacCulloch, Diarmaid. *Christianity: The First Three Thousand Years.* New York: Viking, 2018.
MacDonald, Kevin C. "A View from the South: Sub-Saharan Evidence for Contacts Between North Africa, Mauritania, and the Niger, 1000 BC–A.D. 700." In *Money, Trade, and Trade Routes in Pre-Islamic North Africa,* edited by Amelia Dowler and Elizabeth Galvin. London: British Museum Press, 2011, pp. 72–82.
MacGaffey, Wyatt. "African History, Anthropology, and the Rationality of Natives." *History in Africa* 5 (1978), pp. 101–120.
MacGaffey, Wyatt. *Religion and Society in Central Africa: The BaKongo of Lower Zaire.* Chicago: University of Chicago Press, 1986.
MacKendrick, Paul. *The North African Stones Speak.* Chapel Hill: University of North Carolina Press, 1980.
Mahjoubi, A. "The Roman and Post-Roman Period in North Africa." In *Ancient Civilizations of Africa, Volume II UNESCO General History of Africa,* edited by G. Mokhtar. London: Heinemann, 1981, pp. 465–512.
Mekouria, Tekele Tsadik. "Christian Aksum." In *Ancient Civilizations of Africa, Volume II UNESCO General History of Africa,* edited by G. Mokhtar. London: Heinemann, 1981, pp. 401–422.
Malek, Jaromir. "The Old Kingdom (c.2686–2125 BC), *The Oxford History of Ancient Egypt,* edited by Ian Shaw. Oxford: Oxford University Press, 2000, pp. 89–117.
Mapunde, Bertram B. B. "Fipa Iron Technology and Their Impact on Social History." In *East African Archaeology: Foragers, Potters, Smiths, and Traders and Archaeology,* edited by Chaparuka Kusimba and Sibel B. Kusimba. Philadelphia: Museum of Art, 2003, pp. 71–86.
Marcus, Harold. *A History of Ethiopia.* Berkeley: University of California Press, 1994.
Marcus, Joyce. "Rethinking Ritual." In *The Archaeology of Ritual,* edited by Evangelos Kyrickidis. Berkeley: University of California Press, 2007, pp. 43–76.
Marean, Curtis, and Zelelan Assefa. "The Middle and Upper Pleistocene African Record for the Biological and Behavioral Origins of Modern Humans." In *African Archaeology: A Critical Introduction,* edited by Ann Brower Stahl. Malden, MA: Blackwell 2012, pp. 93–129.
Marshal, Fiona, and T. Eildebrand. "Cattle before Crops: The Beginning of Food Production in Africa." *Journal of World Prehistory* 11 (2002), pp. 49–103.
Martinon-Torres, Maria, Michael Francesco d'Errico, and D. Petraglia. "Earliest Known Human Burial in Africa." *Nature* 593 (May 5, 2021), pp. 95–100.
Masson, John. "Apollo 11 Cave in Southwest Namibia: Some Observations on the Site and Its Rock Art." *The South African Archaeological Bulletin* 61, no. 183 (2006), pp. 76–89.
Masuzawa, Tomoko. "World Religions." In *The Encyclopedia of Religion,* 2nd ed., edited by Lindsay Jones, Vol. 14, 9800–9804. Detroit, MI: Thomson/Gale, 2005.
Matory, J. Lorand. *The Fetish Revisited: Marx, Freud, and the Gods Black People Made.* Durham, NC: Duke University Press, 2007.

Mattingly, David J. "The African Way of Death: Burial Rituals beyond the Roman Empire." In *Mortuary Landscapes of North Africa*, edited by David L. Stone and Lea M. Stirling. Toronto: University of Toronto Press, 2007, pp. 138-163.

Mattingly, David J. "The Garamantes of Fezzan: An Early City State with Trans-Atlantic Connection." In *Money, Trade, and Trade Routes in Pre-Islamic North Africa*, edited by Amelia Dawler and Elizabeth Galen.Toronto: University of Toronto Press, 2007, pp. 49-60.

Mbiti, John. *African Religions and Philosophy*. 2nd ed. Oxford: Heinemann, 1990.

Mbiti, John. *Concepts of God in Africa*. New York: Praeger, 1976.

McCall, Daniel F. "Mother Earth: The Great Goddess of West Africa." In *Mother Worship: Themes and Variations*, edited by James L. Preston. Chapel Hill: The University of North Carolina Press, 1982, pp. 304-323.

McIntosh, Roderick J. *Ancient Middle Niger Urbanism and the Self-Organizing Landscape*. Cambridge: Cambridge University Press, 2005.

McIntosh, Roderick J. "The Pulse Model: Genesis and Accommodation of Specialization in the Middle Niger." *Journal of African History* 34, no. 2 (1982), pp. 181-220.

McIntosh, Susan Keech. "The Holocene Prehistory of West Africa." In *Themes in West African History*, edited by Emmanuel K Akyeampong. Oxford: James Currey, 2006, pp. 11-32.

McIntosh, Susan Keech. "Reconceptualizing Early Ghana." *Canadian Journal of African Studies* 42, no. 2-3 (2008), pp. 347-373.

McNally, Michael D. "Native American Site Visits in the Context of Service Learning." *Spotlight on Teaching*. American Academy of Religion, October 2004.

McNaughton, Patrick. *The Mande Blacksmiths: Knowledge, Power, and Art of West Africa*. Bloomington: Indiana University Press, 1988.

McNeill, Donald G. Jr. "Tunisian Jews at Blast Site: A Stalwart Remnant." *New York Times*, April 15, 2002.

McNeill, William, and Jean W. Sedlar, eds. *The Ancient Near East*. New York: Oxford University Press, 1968.

Mertz, Barbara. *Red Land Black Land: Daily Life in Ancient Egypt*. New York: Dodd, Mead, and Company, 1978.

Mertz, Barbara. *Temples, Tombs, and Hieroglyphs: A Popular History of Ancient Egypt*. New York: HarperCollins, 2007.

Midant-Reynes, Beatrix. *The Prehistory of Egypt: From the First Egyptians to the First Pharaohs*. Oxford: Blackwell, 2000.

Middleton, John. *The World of the Swahili: An African Civilization*. New Haven, CT: Yale University Press, 1992.

Mills, Margaret. "Native North African Spiritualities." In *African Spiritualities: Forms, Meanings, and Expressions*, edited by Jacob Olupona. New York: Crossroad, 2000, pp. 350-377.

Mitchell, Peter. *The Archaeology of Southern Africa*. Cambridge: Cambridge University Press, 2002.

Mithen, Steve. *After the Ice: A Global Human History, 2,000-5,000 BC*. London: Weidenfeld and Nicholson, 2003.

Mithen, Steve. *The Prehistory of the Mind: The Cognitive Origins of Art, Religion, and Science*. London: Thames and Hudson, 1998.

Modrzejewski, Joseph M. *The Jews of Egypt: From Ramesses II to Emperor Hadrian*. Princeton, NJ: Princeton University Press, 1995.

Moise, Robert E. "'Do Pygmies Have a History? Revisited': The Autochthonous Tradition in the History of Equatorial Africa." In *Hunter-Gatherers of the Congo Basin: Culture, History and Biology of the Congo Basin*, edited by Barry S. Howlett Highland Park, NJ: Transaction Publishers, 2014, pp. 86-117.

Mokhtar, G. "Introduction." In *Ancient Civilizations of Africa, Volume II, UNESCO General History of Africa*, edited by G. Mokhtar. London: Heinemann, 1981, pp. 1-26.

Montserrat, Dominic. "Pilgrims to the Shrines of SS Cyrus and John at Menouthis in Late Antiquity." In *Pilgrimage and Holy Space in Late Antique Egypt*, edited by David S. Frankfurter. Leiden: Brill, 1998, pp. 257–279.
Monteil, Vincent. *L'Islam Noir*. Paris: Edition du Seuil, 1971.
Morris, Brian. *Anthropological Studies of Religion: An Introductory Text*. Cambridge: Cambridge University Press, (1987) 1998.
Mudimbe, Valentin. *The Invention of Africa: Gnosis, Philosophy, and the Order of Knowledge*. Bloomington: Indiana University Press, 1988.
Munro-Hay, Stuart. *Axum: An African Civilization of Late Antiquity*. Edinburgh: Edinburgh University Press, 1991.
Murnane, William, ed. *Texts from the Amarna Period in Egypt*. Atlanta: Scholars Press, 1995.
Murnane, William. "Three Kingdoms and Thirty-Four Dynasties." In *Ancient Egypt*, edited by David P. Silverman. New York: Oxford University Press, 1997, pp. 26–39.
Muzzolini, Alfred. "La 'Neolithisation' du nord de l'Afrique." In *Neolithisations: Proche et Moyen Orient, Méditerranée orientale, nord de l'Afrique, Europe méridionnale, Chine, Amérique du Sud*, edited by Olivier Aurenche and Jacques Cauvin. Lyon: CNRS, 1989, pp. 145–186.
Muzzolini, Alfred. "L'Art rupestre préhistorique des massifs centraux Saharan." Oxford: Cambridge Manuscripts in African Archaeological Research, 1986.
Najovits, Simson. *Egypt, The Trunk of the Tree, Vol I: The Contexts*. New York: Algora Publishing Company, 2003.
Nash, G., Coulson, S.,Staurset, S., Ulyott, J.S., Babutsi, M., Hopkinson, L, and Smith, M.P. "Provenancing of Silcrete Raw Materials Indicates Long-Distance Transport to Tsodilo Hills, Botswana, during the Middle Stone Age." *Journal of Human Evolution* 64 (2013), pp. 280–288.
Naylor, Philip C. *North Africa: A History from Antiquity to the Present*. Austin: University of Texas Press, 2009.
Newman, James L. *The Peopling of Africa: A Geographical Interpretation*. New Haven, CT: Yale University Press, 1995.
Niane, D. T. *Soundiata: An Epic of Old Mali*. London: Longman, 2006.
Nielsen, Niels, Normin Hein, Frank Reynolds, Alan L. Mioller, Samuel Karf, Alice C. Cowan, Paul McLean, Grace Burford, John Y. Fenton, Laura Grillo, Elizabeth Leeper, Robert K.C. Forman. *Religions of the World*. 3rd ed. New York: St. Martin's Press, 1993, pp. 1–79.
Nock, Arthur Darby. *Conversion: The Old and the New in Religion from Alexander the Great to Augustine of Hippo*. London: Oxford University Press, 1933.
Nurse, Derek. "The Contributions of Linguistics to the Study of History in Africa." *Journal of African History* 38 (1997), pp. 359–391.
Nutt, Amy Ellis. "Scholars Identify New Human Ancestor." *Washington Post*, September 11, 2015.
Obenga, Théophile. *Ancient Egypt & Black Africa: A Student's Handbook for the Study of Ancient Egypt in Philosophy, Linguistics, &Gender Relations*. London: Karnak House, 1992.
O'Connor, David. *Abydos: Egypt's First Pharaohs and the Cult of Osiris*. London: Thames and Hudson, 2012.
O'Connor, David. *Ancient Nubia: Egypt's Rival in Africa*. Philadelphia: Museum of Archaeology and Anthropology, University of Pennsylvania, 1993.
O'Connor, David. "New Kingdom and Third Intermediate Period, 1552–664 BC." In *Ancient Egypt: A Social History*, edited by B. G. Trigger et al. Cambridge: Cambridge University Press, 1992, pp. 183–278.
O'Connor, David, and Andrew Reid. "Introduction: Locating Ancient Egypt in Africa: Modern Theories, Past Realities." In *Ancient Egypt in Africa*, edited by David O'Connor and Andrew Reid. London: UCL Press, 2003, pp. 1–21.
Oden, Thomas C. *Early Libyan Christianity: Uncovering a North African Tradition*. Downers Grove, IL: Intervarsity Press, 2011.

Olderogge, D. "Migrations and Ethnic and Linguistic Differentiation." In *UNESCO General History of Africa, Volume I. Methodology and African Pre-History*, edited by J. Ki-Zerbo. London: Heinemann, 1981, pp. 271-291.

Oliver, Roland, and Brian Fagan. *Africa in the Iron Age: c. 500 BC to AD 1400*. Cambridge: Cambridge University Press, 1975.

O'Neil, John P. ed. *Egyptian Art in the Age of the Pyramids*. New York: The Metropolitan Museum of Art, 1999.

Ong, Walter. *Orality and Literacy: The Technologizing of the Word*. London: Metheun, 1982.

Oriji, John N. *Political Organization in Nigeria Since the Late Stone Age: A History of the Igbo People*, New York: Palgrave/Macmillan, 2011.

Osborn, F. B. "Introduction." In *The Golden Ass of Lucius Apuleius*. London: The Abbey Library, n.d. (1669), pp. 1-18.

Osman, Ahmed. *Moses: Pharaoh of Egypt: The Mysteries of Akhenaten Resolved*. London: Grafton éBooks, 1996.

Pagels, Elaine. *The Gnostic Gospels*. New York: Vintage, 1989.

Pagels, Elaine. *The Origin of Satan: How Christians Demonized Jews, Pagans, and Heretics*. New York: Random House, 1996.

Parkington, John, and Simon Hall. "The Appearance of Food Production in Southern Africa, 1000 to 2000 Years Ago." In *The Cambridge History of South Africa, Volume I, From Early Trade to 1885*, edited by Carolyn Hamilton, Bernard K. Mbenga, and Robert Ross. Cambridge: Cambridge University Press, 2010, pp. 63-111.

Parrinder, Geoffrey. *Religion in Africa*. Baltimore: Penguin Books, 1969.

Parrinder, Geoffrey. *West African Religion*. New York: Barnes and Noble, (1949) 1970.

P'Bitek, Okot. *African Religions and Western Scholarship*. Kampala: East African Literature Bureau, 1970.

Peacock, David. "The Roman Period (300 BC-AD 311)." In *The Oxford History of Ancient Egypt*, edited by Ian Shaw. Oxford: Oxford University Press, 2000, pp. 422-445.

Pelton, Robert. *The Trickster in West Africa: A Study of Myth, Irony, and Sacred Delight*. Berkeley: University of California Press, 1980.

Pernigotti, Sergio. "Priests." In *The Egyptians*, edited by Sergio Donadoni. Chicago: University of Chicago Press, 1997, pp. 121-150.

Pettitt, Paul. *The Paleolithic Origins of Human Burial*. New York: Routledge, 2011.

Philips, Jack. "Punt and Aksum: Egypt and the Horn of Africa." *Journal of African History* 38 (1997), pp. 423-457.

Phillipson David W. *African Archaeology*. 3rd ed. Cambridge: Cambridge University Press, 2005.

Phillipson David W. *Ancient Ethiopia, Aksum: Its Antecedents and Successors*. London: British Museum Press, 1998.

Phillipson David W. "Early Food Production in Sub-Saharan Africa." In *The Cambridge History of Africa, Volume I, From Earliest Times to c. 500 BC*, edited by J. Desmond Clark. London: Cambridge University Press, 1982, pp. 710-829.

Phillipson David W. *The Late Prehistory of Western and Southern Africa*. New York: Africana Publishing Company, 1977.

Pietz, William. "The Problem of the Fetish." *RES: Anthropology and Aesthetics* 9 (1985), pp. 5-17.

Pine-Coffin, R. S. "Introduction." Saint Augustine, *Confessions*. Harmondsworth, UK: Penguin, 1970, pp. 11-18.

Pohl, Walter. "The Vandals: Fragments of a Narrative." In *Vandals, Romans and Berbers: New Perspectives on Late Antique North Africa*, edited by A. H. Merrills. New York: Routledge, (2004) 2016, pp. 31-48.

Porten, Bezalel, with J. J. Farber, C. J. Martin, G. Vittman, et al. *The Elephantine Papyri in English: Three Millennia of Cross-Cultural Continuity and Change*. 2nd rev. ed. Atlanta: Society for Biblical Literature, 2011.

Portères, Roland. "Berceaux agricoles sur le continent Africain." *Journal of African History* 3 (1962), pp. 193–210.

Posnansky, Merrick. "Archaeology, Ritual and Religion." In *The Historical Study of African Religion*, edited by T. O. Ranger and In. N. Kimambo. Berkeley: University of California Press, 1972, pp. 74–88.

Preise, Karl-Heinz. "The Napatan Period." In *Africa in Antiquity: The Arts of Nubia and the Sudan, Volume I, The Essays*, edited by Sylvia Hochfield and Elizabeth Riefstahl. Brooklyn: The Brooklyn Museum of Art, 1978, pp. 125–140.

Procopius of Caesaria. *History*. Fordham Ancient History Sourcebook: Egypt, c. 550 CE.

Putnam, James S. *Egyptology: An Introduction to the History, Culture, and Art of Ancient Egypt*. New York: Quintet Publishing, 1990.

Pyysiänen, Ilka. *How Religion Works: toward a New Cognitive Science of Religion*. Leiden: Brill, 2003.

Quirke, Stephen. *Exploring Religion in Ancient Egypt*. Chichester, UK: Wiley, Blackwell, 2015.

Radin, Paul. *The Trickster: A Study in Ancient Indian Mythology*. New York: Greenwood Press, 1965.

Ranger, Terence, and I. A. Kimambo, eds. *The Historical Study of African Religions*. Berkeley: University of California Press, 1978.

Ray, Benjamin. *African Religions: Symbol, Ritual, and Community*. Englewood Cliffs, NJ: Prentice Hall, 1975.

Redford, Donald B. *Akhenaten: The Heretic King*. Princeton, NJ: Princeton University Press, 1984.

Redford, Donald B. "Egypt and the World Beyond." In *Ancient Egypt*, edited by David P Silverman. New York: Oxford University Press, 1997, pp. 40–57.

Redford, Donald B. *Egypt, Canaan, and Israel in Ancient Times*. Princeton, NJ: Princeton University Press, 1992.

Redford, Donald B. *From Slave to Pharaoh: The Black Experience of Ancient Egypt*. Baltimore: Johns Hopkins University Press, 2002.

Reeves, Nichols. *Akhenaten: Egypt's False Prophet*. London: Thames and Hudson, 2001.

Reid, Andrew. "Ancient Egypt and the Sources of the Nile." In *Egypt in Africa*, edited by David O'Connor and Andrew Reid. London: UCL Press, 1997, pp. 55–76.

Research Council of Norway. "World's Oldest Ritual Discovered—Worshipped the Python 70,000 Years Ago." *Science Daily*, November 30, 2006, www. Sciencedaily.com.

Riad, H., with J. Devisse. "Egypt in the Hellenistic Era." In *Ancient Civilizations of Africa, Volume II, UNESCO General History of Africa*, edited by G. Mokhtar. London: Heinemann, 1981, pp. 104–207.

Rice, Michael. *Egypt's Making: The Origins of Ancient Egypt, 5000–2000 BC*. London: Routledge, 1991.

Rovera, Anna Maria Donadoni. *Classic Art Tours: The Valley of Kings*. London: Atlantis, 1981.

Robbins, Larry, Alex Campbell, George Brook and Michael Murphy. "World's Oldest Ritual Site? The 'Python Cave' at Tsodilo Hills World Heritage Site, Botswana." *Nyame Akuma* 6–7 (2007).

Robbins, Larry, Mike Murphy, and Alec Campbell. "Windows into the Past: Excavating Stone Age Shelters." In *Tsodilo Hills: Copper Bracelet of the Kalahari*, edited by A. Campbell et al. East Lansing: Michigan State University Press, 2010, pp. 50–63.

Robbins, Lawrence H. "Eastern African Advanced Foragers." In *Encyclopedia of Precolonial Africa: Archaeology, History, Linguistics, Cultures, and Environment*, edited by Joseph O. Vogel. Walnut Creek, CA: Altamira, 1997.

Robbins, Lawrence H. "Lake Turkana Archaeology: The Holocene." *Ethnohistory* 53, no. 11 (2006), pp. 71–92.

Robbins, Lawrence H. "Sebillo: 19th Century Hairdos and Ancient Specularite Mining in Southern Africa." *International Journal of African Historical Studies* 49, no. 1 (2016), pp. 103–131.

Robbins, Lawrence H., Alec C. Campbell, George A. Brook, Michael L. Murphy, and Robert K. Hitchcock. "The Antiquity of the Bow and Arrow in the Kalahari Desert: Bone Points from White Paintings Rock Shelter, Botswana." *Journal of African Archaeology* 10, no. 1 (2012), pp. 7–20.

Robbins, Lawrence, Michael L. Murphy, Alec Campbell, and George A. Brook. "Excavation at the Tsodilo Hills Rhino Cave." *Botswana Notes and Records* 28 (1996), pp. 23–45.

Robbins, Lawrence, Michael L. Murphy, G. A. Brook, A. H. Iverson, and A. C. Campbell. "Archaeology, Palaeoenvironment and Chronology in the Tsodiolo Hill White Painting Rock Shelter, Northwest Kalahari Desert, Botswna," *Journal of Archaeological Science* 27 (2000), pp. 1085–1183.

Robertshaw, Peter. "Archaeology in Eastern Africa: Recent Developments and More Dates." *Journal of African History* 25, no. 4 (1984), pp. 615–617.

Robinson, David. *Muslim Societies in African History*. Cambridge: Cambridge University Press, 2004.

Robins, Gay. *Women in Ancient Egypt*. Cambridge, MA: Harvard University Press, 1993.a

Robins, Jonathan E. *Oil Palm: A Global History*. Chapel Hill: University of North Carolina Press, 2021.

Roccati, Alessandro. "Scribes." In *The Egyptians*, edited by Sergio Donadoni. Ithaca, NY: Cornell University Press, pp. 61–86.

Roscoe, John. *The Bakira of Banyoro*. Cambridge: Cambridge University Press, 1923.

Rosenberger, Bernard. "Des Origines aux Almoravides." In *Histoire de Maroc*, edited by Jean Brignon, Abdelazziz Amine, Brahim Boutaleb, Guy Martinet, Bernard Rosenberger with the assistance of Michel Terrasse. Casablanca: Librairie Nationale, 1967, pp. 87–88.

Rousseau, Philip. *Pachomius: The Making of a Community in Fourth Century Egypt*. Berkeley: University of California Press, 1985.

Rowlandson, Jane, ed. *Women and Society in Greek and Roman Egypt: A Sourcebook*. Cambridge: Cambridge University Press, 1987.

Russman, Edna R. "Egypt and the Kushite Dynasty XXV." In *Africa and Africans in Antiquity*, edited by Edwin Yamauchi. East Lansing: Michigan State University, 2001, pp. 120–131.

Saggs, H. W. E. *Civilization before Greece and Rome*. New Haven, CT: Yale University Press, 1987.

Saidi, Christine. *Women's Authority and Society in Early East-Central Africa*. Rochester: University of Rochester Press, 2010.

Salvatori, Sandro, and Donatella Usai, eds. *A Neolithic Cemetery in the Northern Dongola Reach: Excavations at Site R12*. Oxford: Archaeopress, 2008.

Sarkozy, Nicolas. "Discours du Président de la République Française, Université de Dakar Sénégal." July 26, 2007, youtube.com.

Schaav, Stuart. "The Barbary Coast." In *The Horizon History of Africa*, edited by A. M. Josephy. New York: McGraw Hill, 1971, pp. 96–135.

Schmidt, Peter R. "Archaeological Views on a History of Landscape Change in East Africa." *Journal of African History* 38, no. 3 (1997), pp. 393–421.

Schmidt, Peter R. "Archaeology of Listening: Listening and Waiting: Excavating Later." In *Archaeologies of Listening*, edited by Peter Schmidt and Alice Kehoe. Gainesville: University Press of Florida, 2019, pp. 177–201.

Schmidt, Peter R. *Community-Based Heritage in Africa: Unveiling Local Research and Development Initiatives*. New York: Routledge, 2017.

Schmidt, Peter R. *Historical Archaeology: Representation, Social Memory, and Oral Traditions*. Lanham, MD: Altamira Press, 2006.

Schmidt, Peter R. *Historical Archaeology: A Structural Approach in an African Culture*. Westport, CT: Greenwood, 1978.

Schmidt, Peter R. *Iron Technology in East Africa: Symbolism, Science, and Archaeology*. Bloomington: Indiana University Press, 1997.

Schmidt, Peter R. "Reading Gender in the Ancient Iron Technology of Africa." In *Gender in African Prehistory*, edited by Susan Kent. Walnut Creek, CA: Altamira, Press, 2001, pp. 139–162.

Schoenbrun, David Lee. *A Green Place, A Good Place: Agrarian Change, Gender, and Social Identity in the Great Lakes Region to the 15th Century*. Portsmouth, NH: Heinemann, 1998.

Schoenbrun, David Lee. "A Narrative of People and Forests between the Great Lakes, ca.1000 BC and ca. 1500." Boston: Boston University African Studies Center, #194, 1995.

Schoenbrun, David Lee. "We Are What We Eat: Ancient Agriculture between the Great Lakes." *Journal of African History* 34, no. 1, 1994, pp. 1–31.

Schoff, Wilfred H., trans. *The Periplus of the Erythraen Sea*. New York: Longman, 1912.

Schoffeleers, Matthew. *Rivers of Blood: The Genesis of a Martyr Cult in South Malawi, c.a. A.D. 1600*. Madison: University of Wisconsin Press, 1992.

Searight, Susan. *The Prehistoric Rock Art of Morocco: A Study of Its Extension, Environment, and Meaning*, BAR International Series, #1310. Oxford: Archeaopress, 2004.

Sears, Gareth. *Late Roman African Urbanism: Continuity and Transformation in the City*. Oxford: Archaeopress, 2007.

Seligman, C. G. *The Races of Africa*. London: (1930) 1960.

Serrano, Alejandro Jiménez. "Royal Festivals in the Late Predynastic Period and the First Dynasty." BAR International Archaeological Services, 1076. Oxford: Archaeopress, 2002.

Saxon, Douglas E. "Linguistic Evidence for the Eastern Spread of Ubangian." In *The Archaeological and Linguistic Reconstruction of African History*, edited by Christopher Ehret and Merrick Posnansky. Berkeley: University of California Press, 1982, pp. 66–77.

Shafer, Byron R. "Temples, Priests and Rituals: An Overview." In *Temples of Ancient Egypt*, edited by Byron R. Shafer. Ithaca, NY: Cornell University Press, 1997, pp. 1–30.

Shaw, Brent D. *Sacred Violence: African Christians and Sectarian Hatred in the Age of Augustine*. Cambridge: Cambridge University Press, 2011.

Shaw, Brent D. "Who Were the Circumcellions?" In *Vandals, Romans, and Berbers: New Perspectives on Late Antique North Africa*, edited by A. H. Merrills. New York: Routledge, 2016, pp. 227–255.

Shaw, Rosalind J. "The Invention of African Traditional Religion." *Religion* 20 (1990), pp. 339–353.

Shaw, Thurston. *Nigeria: Its Archaeology and Early History*. London: Thames and Hudson, 1978.

Sherif, N. M. "Nubia before Napata (3100 to 750). In *Ancient Civilizations of Africa, Volume II of UNESCO General History of Africa*, edited by G. Mokhtar. London: Heinemann, 1981, pp. 245–277.

Shillington, Kevin. *History of Africa*. Rev. ed. New York: St. Martin's Press, 1995.

Shinnie, Peter L. *Meroe: A Civilization of the Sudan*. London: Thames and Hudson, 1967.

Shinnie, Peter L. "The Nilotic Sudan and Ethiopia, c. 660 BC to AD 600." In *The Cambridge History of Africa, Volume II, From c. 500 BC to AD 1050*, edited by J.D. Fage. Cambridge: Cambridge University Press, 1978, pp. 210–271.

Shreve, James. "Mystery Man." *National Geographic* 228 (2015), pp. 30–57.

Silverman, David P., ed. *Ancient Egypt*. New York: Oxford University Press, 1997.

Silverman, David P. "Divinity and Deities in Ancient Egypt." In *Religion in Ancient Egypt*, edited by Byron Shafer et al. Ithaca, NY: Cornell University Press, 1991, pp. 7–87.

Silverman, David P., Josef W. Wegner, and Jennifer H. Wegner. *Akhenaten and Tutankhamun: Revolution and Restoration*. Philadelphia: University of Pennsylvania Museum of Archaeology and Anthropology, 2005.

Sindone, Harvey. *Drums of Redemption: An Introduction to African Christianity*. Westport, CT: Praeger, 1999.

Skorupski, John. *Symbol and Theory: A Philosophical Study of Religion in Social Anthropology*. Cambridge: Cambridge University Press, 1976.

Smart, Ninian. *Worldviews: Cross Cultural Explorations of Human Beliefs.* 3rd ed. Upper Saddle River, NJ: Prentice Hall, 2000.
Smith, Andrew B. *African Herders: Emergence of Pastoral Traditions.* Walnut Creek, CA: Altamira Press, 2005.
Smith, Andrew, Andrew Agrila, and Allison Galloway. "Burials and Human Skeletal Materials from Adrar Bous." In *Adrar Bous: Archaeology of a Central Saharan Granite Ring Complex in Niger,* edited by J. Desmond Clark et al. Tervuren: Royal Museum for Central Africa, 2008, pp. 355–368.
Smith, Jonathan Z. *Imagining Religion: From Babylon to Jonestown.* Chicago: University of Chicago Press, 1982.
Smith, Mark. *Following Osiris: Perspectives on the Osirian Afterlife, from Four Millennia.* Oxford: Oxford University Press, 2017.
Smith, Philip. E. L. "The Late Paleolithic and Epi-Paleolithic of Northern Africa." In *Cambridge History of Africa, Vol. I, From the Earliest Times to c. 500 BCE,* edited by J. Desmond-Clark. Cambridge: Cambridge University Press, 1982, pp. 342–409.
Snowden, Frank M. Jr. *Blacks in Antiquity: Ethiopians in the Greco-Roman Experience.* Cambridge, MA: Harvard University Press, 1971.
Soren, David. "An Ancient Overview," In *Carthage: A Mosaic of Ancient Tunisia,* edited by Aiche Ben Ahmad Ben Khadari and David Soren. New York: The American Museum of Natural History, 1987.
Speel, C. J. "The Disappearance of Christianity from North Africa in the Wake of Islam." *Church History* XXIX, no. 4 (1960), pp. 379–397.
Spencer, A. Jeffery. *Early Egypt: The Rise of Civilization in the Nile Valley.* Norman: University of Oklahoma Press, 1995.
Spencer, Patricia. "Petrie and the Discovery of Early Egypt." In *Before the Pyramids: The Origins of Egyptian Civilization,* edited by Emily Teeter. Chicago: University of Chicago Press, 2011, pp. 17–24.
Stalcup, Brenda. *Ancient Egyptian Civilization.* San Diego: Greenhaven Press, 2001.
Stanbaugh, John B. *Sarapis under the Early Ptolemies.* Leiden: Brill, 1972.
Steadman, Sharon. *The Archaeology of Religious Cultures and Their Beliefs in Worldwide Context.* Walnut Creek, CA: Left Coast Press, 2009.
Stern, M. "The Period of the Second Temple." In *A History of the Jewish People,* edited by H. H. Ben-Sasson. Cambridge, MA: Harvard University Press, 1975, pp. 185–306.
Sundkler, Bengt. *A History of the Church in Africa.* Cambridge: Cambridge University Press, 2000.
Sutton, J. F. G. "The Antecedents of the Interlacustrine Kingdoms." *Journal of African History* 34, no. 1 (1994), pp. 53–64.
Sutton, J. F. G. "East Africa before the Seventh Century." In *Ancient African Civilizations, Volume II, UNESCO General History of Africa,* edited by G. Mokhtar. London: University of California, 1981, pp. 568–592.
Suzman, James. *Affluence without Abundance: The Disappearing World of the Bushmen.* New York: Bloomsbury, 2017.
Swift, Jeremy. *The Sahara.* The Netherlands: Time-Life International, 1979.
Tacon, Paul S. C. "Identifying Ancient Religious Thought and Iconography: Problems of Definition, Preservation, and Interpretation." In *Becoming Human: Innovations in Prehistorical Material and Spiritual Cultures,* edited by Colin Renfrew and Iain Horley. Cambridge: Cambridge University Press, 2009, pp. 61–73.
Tafla, Bairu. "The Establishment of the Ethiopian Church." *Tarikh* 2, no. 2 (1967), pp. 28–42. Special issue on "Early African Christianity."
Takezawa, Shoichiro, Mamadou Cissé, Hirolaka Ode, "Mema in the History of Afar" *Journal of African Studies* 66 (2005), pp. 31–46.
Taylor, John H. *Death and the Afterlife in Ancient Egypt.* Chicago: University of Chicago Press, 2001.

Taylor, John H. "The Third Intermediate Period (1069–664) BC)." In *The Oxford History of Ancient Egypt*, edited by Ian Shaw. Oxford: Oxford University Press, 2000, pp. 330–368.

Teeter, Emily. "Change and Continuity in Egyptian Religion in Ramesside Egypt." In *Ramesses III: The Life and Times of Egypt's Last Hero*, edited by Eric H. Cline and David O'Connor. Ann Arbor: University of Michigan Press, 2012, pp. 27–65.

Teeter, Emily. *Religion and Ritual in Ancient Egypt.* Cambridge: Cambridge University Press, 2012.

Teka, Zelalem. "Distribution and Significance of Ancient Rock Art in Eritrea." In *The Archaeology of Ancient Eritrea*, edited by Peter R. Schmidt, Mathew C. Antor, and Zelalem Teka. Trenton, NJ: The Red Sea Press, 2008, pp. 49–63.

Tempels, Placide. *Bantu Philosophy.* Paris: Presence Africaine, 1946.

Tertullian. *A Treatise on the Soul.* Translated by Peter Holmes. Christian Apologetics and Resource Ministry, 1959.

Thompson, Dorothy J. *Memphis under the Ptolemies.* 2nd ed. Princeton, NJ: Princeton University Press, 2012.

Tobin, Vincent A. "Amun and Amun-Re." In *The Ancient Gods Speak: A Guide to Egyptian Religion*, edited by Donald B. Redford. Oxford: Oxford University Press, 2002, pp. 18–21.

Torjeson, Karen Jo. *When Women Were Priests: Women's Leadership in the Early Church and the Scandal of Their Subordination in the Rise of the Christianity.* San Francisco: Harper/San Francisco, 1995.

Torok, Laszlo. *The Kingdom of Kush: Handbook of the Napatan-Meroitic Civilization.* Leiden: Brill, 1997.

Trevor-Roper, Hugh. *The Rise of Christian Europe.* New York: Harcourt, Brace and World. 1965.

Trigger, Bruce G. "The Rise of Ancient Egypt." In *Ancient Egypt: A Social History*, edited by B. G. Trigger, B. J. Kemp, D. O'Connor, and A. B. Lloyd. Cambridge: Cambridge University Press, 1983, pp. 1–70.

Trigger, Bruce. "Nubian, Negro, Black, Nilotic. In *Africa in Antiquity: The Arts of Ancient Nubia and the Sudan: Volume I, The Essays*, edited by Sylvia Hirchfield and Elizabeth Riefenstahl. Brooklyn: The Brooklyn Museum, 1978.

Trimmingham, J. Spencer. *History of Islam in West Africa.* Oxford: Oxford University Press, 1969.

Tyldesley, Joyce. *Daughters of Isis: Women in Ancient Egypt.* London: Penguin, 1995.

Tyldesley, Joyce. *Hatchepsut: The Female Pharaoh,* London: Viking, 1996.

Tyldesley, Joyce. UNESCO World Heritage Sites. "Stone Circles of Senegambia." www. Whc. unesco.org/en/wst/1226,23g.

Urbanus, Jason. "Africa's Merchant Kings." *Archaeology*, July/August (2023).

Vail, Leroy, and Landeg White. *Power and the Praise Poem: Southern African Voices in History.* Charlottesville: University Press of Virginia, 1991.

Valtello, Dominic. "Craftsmen." In *The Egyptians*, edited by Sergio Donadoni. Chicago: University of Chicago Press, 1997, pp. 31–60.

Van Binsbergen, Wim. "Lykota, Liya, Bankoya: Memory, Myth, and History." *Cahiers des Etudes Africaines* XXVII (1987), pp. 353–392.

Van De Mieroop, Marc. *A History of Ancient Egypt.* Malden, MA: Wiley-Blackwell, 2011.

Van der Post, Laurens. *The Lost World of the Kalahari.* New York: Pyramid Books, 1968 (1958).

Vandier, Jacques. *La Religion Egyptienne.* Paris: Presse Universitaires de France, 1949.

Vandier, Jacques, Christiane Northcart, and Jean-Louis de Cenid. *L'Egypte avant les Pyramides: 4é millenaire.* Paris: Editions des Musées Nationales, 1973.

Van Dijk, Jacobus. "The Amarna Period and the Later New Kingdom (1352–1069 BC)." In *The Oxford History of Ancient Egypt*, edited by Ian Shaw. Oxford: Oxford University Press, 2000, pp. 272–313.

Vansina, Jan. *The Children of Woot: A History of the Kuba Peoples.* Madison: University of Wisconsin Press, 1978.

Vansina, Jan. "History of God among the Kuba." *Africa* 38 (1983), pp. 17–40.

Vansina, Jan. *How Societies Are Born: Governance in West Central Africa before 1600.* Charlottesville: University Press of Virginia, 2004.

Vansina, Jan. "Inner Africa (circa A.D. 500–1800)." In *The Horizon History of Africa*, Vol. 2, edited by Alvin Josephy. New York: McGraw Hill, 1971, pp. 261–273.

Vansina, Jan. *Oral Tradition: A Study in Historical Methodology.* Harmondsworth, UK: Penguin, 1973.

Vansina, Jan. "Oral Tradition and Its Methodology." In *UNESCO General History of Africa, Vol 1, Methodology and Prehistory*, edited by K-Zerbo. Berkeley: University of California Press, 1981, pp. 142–165.

Vansina, Jan. *Oral Tradition in History.* Madison: University of Wisconsin Press, 1985.

Vansina, Jan. *Paths into the Rainforest: Toward a History of Political Tradition in Equatorial Africa.* Madison: University of Wisconsin Press, 1990.

Vansina, Jan. "Reconstructing the Past." In *African Reflection: Art from Northeastern Zaire*, edited by Enid Schildkrout and Curtis A. Keim. Seattle: University of Washington Press, 1990, pp. 69–89.

Vérin, P. "Madagascar." In *Ancient African Civilizations, Volume II, UNESCO General History of Africa*, edited by G. Mokhtar. London: Heinemann, 1981.

Vermeersch, Pierre M. "Middle and Upper Paleolithic in the Egyptian Nile Valley." In *Southeastern Mediterranean Peoples between 150,000 and 10,000 Years Ago*, edited by Elena A. A. Garcea. Oxford: Oxford University Press, 2017, pp. 66–88.

Wagner, Jennifer H. "Shu." In *The Ancient Gods Speak: A Guide to Egyptian Religion*, edited by Donald B. Redford. Oxford: Oxford University Press, 2002, pp. 335–336.

Waldman, Marilyn R. *Prophecy and Power: Muhammad and the Qur'an in the Light of Comparison.* Edited by Bruce Lawrence with Robert M. Baum and Lindsay Jones. Sheffield, UK: Equinox, 2012.

Wallace, Marion, with John Kinahan. *A History of Namibia.* London: Hurst, 1998.

Wangila, Mary N. *Female Circumcision: The Interplay of Religion, Culture, and Gender in Kenya.* Maryknoll, NY: Orbis Books, 2007.

Warmington, B. H. *Carthage.* Rev. ed. New York: Praeger, 1969.

Warmington, B. H. "The Carthaginian Period." In *Ancient Africa, Volume II of UNESCO General History of Africa*, edited by G. Mokhtar. London: Heinemann, 1981, pp. 441–464.

Watson, Derek J. "Bosumppa Revisited: 12,500 Years of the Kwabu Plateau, Ghana, as Viewed 'from the Top of the Hill.'" *Azania Archaeological Research in Africa* 52, no. 4 (2017), pp. 437–516.

Watta, Ian. "Ochre in the Middle Stone Age: Ritualised Display or Hide Preservatives." *South African Archaeological Bulletin* 57 (2002), pp. 1–14.

Watterson, Barbara. *The Egyptians.* Oxford: Blackwell, 1997.

Watterson, Barbara. *The Gods of Ancient Egypt.* New York: Facts on File, 1986.

Weigall, Arthur. *The Life and Times of Akhnaton, Pharaoh of Egypt.* New York: Cooper Square Press, (1922) 2000.

Welsby, Derek. *The Kingdom of Kush: The Napatan and Meroitic Empires.* Princeton, NJ: Markus Wiener, 1998.

Welsby, Derek. *The Medieval Kingdoms of Nubia: Pagans, Christians, and Muslims along the Middle Nile.* London: British Museum Press, 2002.

Wendorf, Fred, and Romuald Schild. "Nabta Playa and its Role in Northeast African Prehistory." *Journal of Anthropological Archaeology* 17 (1998), pp. 107–123.

Wengrow, David. *The Archaeology of Early Egypt: Social Transformations in North Africa, 10,000 to 2650 BC.* Cambridge: Cambridge University Press, 2006.

Wenning, Steffan. *Africa in Antiquity: The Art of Ancient Nubia and the Sudan, Volume II, The Catalogue.* Brooklyn: Brooklyn Museum of Art, 1978.

Werner, Roland, William Anderson, and Andrea Wheeler. *Day of Devastation, Day of Contentment: The History of the Sudanese Church across 2,000 Years.* Nairobi: Paches Publications, 2001.

Wetterstrom, Wilson. "Foraging and Farming in Egypt: The Transition from Hunting and Gathering to Horticulture in the Nile Valley." In *The Archaeology of Africa: Foods, Metals, and Towns*, edited by Thurston Shaw et al. London: Routledge, 1993, pp. 165–226.

White, Donald. "An Archaeological Survey of the Cyrencian and Mamanican Regions of Northeast Africa." In *Africa and Africans in Antiquity*, edited by Edwin Yamauchi. East Lansing: Michigan State University Press, 2001.

Wightman, Gregory J. *The Origins of Religion in the Paleolithic*. Lanham, MD: Rowman and Littlefield, 2015.

Wilford, John Noble. "New Species in Human Lineage is Found in a South African Cave." *New York Times*, August 10, 2015.

Wildung, Dietrich. *Egyptian Saints: Deification in Ancient Egypt*. New York: New York University Press, 1977.

Wilkenson, Toby. *Lives of the Ancient Egyptians*. London: Thames and Hudson, 2003.

Wilkinson, Daryl. "Is There Such a Thing Called Animism?" *Journal of the American Academy of Religion* 85, no. 2 (2017), pp. 289–311.

Williams, Bruce, "A Perspective for Exploring the Historical Essence of Ancient Nubia." In *Egypt and Africa: Nubia from Prehistory to Islam*, edited by W. K. Davies. London: British Museum Press, 1987, pp. 90–119.

Williams, Chancellor. *The Destruction of Black Civilization: Great Issues of a Race from 4500 B.C. to 2000 A.D.* Chicago: Third World Press, 1987.

Williams, Joseph J. *Hebraisms of West Africa: From Nile to Niger with the Jews*. New York: The Dial Press, 1930.

Wills, Garry. *Saint Augustine*. New York: Penguin, 1999.

Wilmsen, Edwin N. *Land Filled with Flies: A Political Economy of the Kalahari*. Chicago: University of Chicago Press, 1989.

Winston, David. "Introduction." In *Philo of Alexandria: Contemplative Life, the Giants, and Selections*, edited by D. Winston. New York: Paulist Press, 1981, pp. 1–72.

Wolf, Eric. *Europe and the People without History*. Berkeley: University of California Press, 1982.

Wotzka, Hans-Peter. "Central Africa Neolithic." In *Encyclopedia of Prehistory, Vol. I, Africa*, edited by Peter N. Peregrine and Melvin Ember. New York: Kluwer, 2001, pp. 46–58.

Wrigley, Christopher. "Speculation on the Economic Prehistory of Africa." *Journal of African History* I, no. 2 (1960), pp. 189–213.

Yellin, Janice W. "Nubian Religions." In *Ancient Nubia: African Kingdom on the Nile*, edited by Marjorie Fisher et al. Cairo: American University in Cairo Press, 2017, pp. 125–144.

Yurco, Frank. "Egypt and Nubia: Old, Middle, and New Kingdom Eras." In *Africa and Africans in Antiquity*, edited by Edwin Yamauchi. East Lansing: Michigan State University Press, 2001, pp. 43–45.

Yurco, Frank. "Mother and Child Imagery in Egypt and Its Influence in Christianity." In *Egypt in Africa*, edited by Theodore Celenko. Indianapolis: Indianapolis Museum of Art, 1996.

Zayed, A. H., with J. Devisse. "Egypt's Relations with the Rest of Africa." In *Ancient Civilizations of Africa, Vol. I. UNESCO General History of Africa*, edited by G. Mokhtar. Paris: UNESCO, 1981, pp. 136–159.

Correspondence and Interviews

E-Mail from Professor Jeremy de Silva, Dartmouth College, Hanover, New Hampshire, 2017.

Anonymous letter addressed to Robert Baum et al., mailed from McConaugh, Georgia, December 2018.

Interview, Cairo, May 25, 2000.

Interview with M. Mengistu, guide to Axum Stelae Field, Axum, Ethiopia, July 21, 2012.

Interview with Lawrence Robbins, Okemos, Michigan, August 2021.

Films

Uys, Jamie, dir. *The Gods Must Be Crazy*. South Africa, 1980.

Site Visits

Boston, Massachusetts. Boston Museum of Fine Arts, November 19, 2017.
Washington, DC. National Gallery of Art, 2002.
Egypt, 2000.
Eswatini, 2017.
Ethiopia, 2012.
Ghana, 2017.
Morocco, 1978, 2022.
Senegal, 1973–2023, intermittently for a period of five years.
South Africa, 1992, 2000, 2017.
Tanzania, 2015.
Zimbabwe, 1992.

Index

For the benefit of digital users, indexed terms that span two pages (e.g., 52–53) may, on occasion, appear on only one of those pages.

Figures are indicated by an italic *f* following the page number.

Abraham, 70–71
Abrahamic religion, 70–71
Abu Simbel, 138–39
Abydos, 99
Acts of the Scillitan Martyrs, 215–16
Adonai, 18–19
Afro-Asiatic language family, 48–49, 76
Afrocentrism, 73–74
afterlife
    and burial practices, 19–20, 47, 53–54, 60–61, 65–66
    Egypt, 53–54, 96–97, 98–99, 104–5, 260
    Kadera, 60–61
    ordinary people, 96–97, 98–99, 104–5
    Southern Africa, 133
Agatharchides, 156
Agauw, 229
agriculture
    Cushitic, 178–79
    Egyptian, 54–55, 77
    Equatorial Africa, 247
    Interlacustrine, 241
    Madagascar, 243–44
    Mena, 173
    Neolithic, 52–53
    North Africa, 126–27, 212–13
    Nubia, 120–21
    Sabean, 163–65
    Saharan, 61
    and settlements, 48
    Southern Africa, 244–45
    Sudanic region, 62, 174–75
    West Africa, 128, 174
    Zaire River, 246–47
Aion, 226
Ajami, 10–11
Akhenaten, 70–71, 106, 112, 116, 124, 260–61
Akhtoy, 95–96
Alexander, Bishop, 202, 203
Alexander the Great, 147–48
Alexandria, 148, 185–86, 191–94, 200, 202
Alwa, 227–28

Amarna, 107
Amazigh, 166–67, 211. *See also* Berbers
Amenhotep III, 102–4, 124
Amenhotep IV, 106, 260–61
Amosis, 101
Amratian culture, 56, 258–59
Amun, 97, 102–3, 105, 107–8, 112, 123, 147–48, 152–54, 156, 157, 158–59, 189
Amun Ra/Re, 97–98, 112, 114, 124, 139–40, 141–42, 260–61. *See also* Re
ancestors, 25–26, 32, 64–65, 130–31, 214–15
Angabo, Za Besi, 162
animism, 25–26
Antony of the Desert, St., 194–95, 203
Anubis, 90–91
Anukis, 123
Apedemak, 155–56
apocalpytic, 105, 150–51
Apollo 11 Cave 49
Apollonia, 192–93
Apuleius, 215
Arabic sources, 10–11
archaeology
    Buhaya, 181–82
    and burial practices, 19–20, 40–52
    East Africa, 132–33
    Egypt, 75–76, 119
    ethnoarchaeology, 21
    Gash, 125
    Interlacustrine region, 181
    Meroe, 176–77
    Nubia, 120–21, 259
    and religious history, 19–21, 37–38, 135, 161, 257
    ritual sites, 20–21
    Southern Africa, 133
    synagogues, Libya, 213–14
    Tsodilo Hills, 258
    Turkana Turwell, 180–81
    and written sources, 19–21, 161, 176–77, 259–60
Arius, 185–86, 202–3, 224–25

INDEX

Ark of the Covenant, 163n.5
Asad, Talal, 27
Asante, Molefi Kete, 73
Asclepius, 189–90, 196–97, 214–15
Assefa, Zelalen, 20
Assmann, Jan, 14–15, 27, 70–71, 91–92, 107
assumptions about African religions, 3–6
Assyria, 144–45
Aten, 71, 103–4, 106–14, 116, 124–25, 260–61
Athanasius, 194–95, 200, 203, 229–31
Atlas Mountains, 53
Atum, 85–86, 141
Atum-Re, 91–92
Augustine, 218–19, 223–24
Australopithecus, 38–40
Awash River Valley, 43
Axial Age, 109–10
Axum, 163n.5, 211–12, 227, 228–34, 264
Aye, 113–14
Azawagh River, 62

Baal/Baal-Hammon, 168–69, 214–15
Badarians, 54–55, 258
Baker, Samuel, 24
BaKongo, 19
Ballana dynasty, 227–28
Bantu languages and migrations, 48–49, 64–65, 67, 129, 177–79, 181–83, 240, 241–42, 243–45, 246–47, 262
Batwa, the, 130, 131
Beidelman, T. O., 15
Belkis, 163
Berbers, 126–27, 166–67, 168, 171–72, 211, 218–19, 225
Berger, Iris, 181–82
Berger, Lee, 40–41
Bes, 99, 165–66
Bida, 249–50
blacksmithing, 174–76, 181–83, 239, 248–49, 262–63. *See also* iron
Blemmyes, 166, 227–28, 229
Blombos Cave, 42–43, 46–47
Border Cave, 41–42
Bowman, Alfred, 149–50
Bozo, 248–49
Brandt, S. A., 62–63
Brenner, Louis, 27
Brown, Peter, 219–20
Budge, E. Wallis, 74–75, 125–26
Buhaya, 15–16, 181–82
burial practices
    and afterlife, 19–20, 47, 53–54, 60–61, 65–66
    Amratian, 56
    and archaeology, 19–20, 40–52
    Badarian, 54–55
    Cameroun, 63–64
    Capsian, 53
    defleshing, 43
    East African, 62–63, 132–33, 179–80
    Egypt, 47, 55–56, 83–84, 89–91, 260
    Elmenteitan, 180–81
    El Omari, 57
    Equatorial Africa, 63–64
    and fertility, 56, 66
    Gogoshiis Qabe, 62–63
    Gwisho, 133–34
    Homo genus, 39–40, 257
    Homo naledi, 257
    Homo sapiens, 37, 41–43, 257
    Iberomaurusian Era, 47–48
    Kadera, 60–61
    Kadruka, 60–61
    Kerma, 122–23
    Matara, 164–65
    Naqada, 57–58
    Nile Delta, 57
    Nile Valley, 53–54
    North Africa, 127
    Nubia, 59–60, 120–21, 122–23, 154–55
    ocher 37–38, 41–42, 43–44, 45–46, 51–52, 179–80
    offerings, 55–56
    Paleolithic, 40–43, 47, 51–52
    property, 65–66
    pyramids, 89–90
    and religious history, 37–38, 65–66
    royal, 122–23
    sacrifices, 59–61
    Southern African, 62–63, 133
    Sudanic region, 62
    and sun, 65–66
    tools, 55, 57, 60, 62–63, 66, 84, 132–33
    Tsodilo Hills, 258
Burkina Faso, 175
Buto, 58–59
Byzantines, 225

Cambyses, 145–46
Camps, Gabriel, 143, 173
cannibalism, 43
Capsian religion, 53
Carthage, 168–71, 215–16, 222
Case, Shirley Jackson, 197–98
Catechetical School of Alexandria, 191–92
Catherine of Alexandra, 193
cattle, 59–60, 61. *See also* domestication

caves, Equatorial Africa, 246
Cerne, 169–70
Chalcedon, Council of, 207
Chami, Felix, 181–82
change, historical, 6–10, 14–15, 17–19, 21–22
Chidester, David, 5
Childe, Gordon, 51–52
Christianity
   and Alexandria, 202
   and Axum, 229–33, 264
   baptism, 224
   and Carthage, 215–16
   catechumenate, 217, 224
   Catholic, 203–4, 219–22, 224–25
   conversion, 197–98, 217
   Donatism, 219–22
   and Egypt, 185–87, 188, 190–99, 226–27, 263–64
   Ethiopia, 231–32, 263–64
   exorcism, 224
   flight to Egypt, Holy Family, 190–91
   Ge'ez, 232
   Gnosticism, 198–99
   and Greek, 193
   hermetic tradition, 185–86, 194–95
   and Isis, 188
   and Judaism, 203–4
   martyrdom, 193, 197–98, 211, 212–13, 215–16, 221–22
   monasticism, 185–86, 194–96
   Montanism, 217
   North Africa, 212–13, 214–26, 263–64
   orthodoxy, 203, 212–13
   and "paganism," 185–86, 197–98, 200, 204–6, 216–19, 222
   persecution, 191–96, 199–202, 217–18, 219–20, 226–27
   popular religion, 206–7
   and race, 194–95
   and Rome, 191–95, 199–202, 203–4, 217–18, 219–22
   and Septimus Severus, 216
   Son of God, 202–3
   and temples, pagan, 200–2, 203–4, 206
   Trinity, 202–3, 216–17
Circumcellions, 221–22
circumcision, 54, 64–65, 72–73, 93–94, 131, 145, 165, 178–79, 240–41, 243, 245
City of God, The (Augustine), 224
Clark, Desmond, 62
Clement, 191–92
Cleopatra, 151, 213
Cleopatra Sabine, 213

cognitive studes, 38–39
colonialism, 6, 8–9, 10
comparative religion, 26–28
Comte, Auguste, 25–26
Confessions, The (Augustine), 223–24
Constantine, 199–200, 203, 219–20
Constantius, 203
conversion, 197–98, 217
Cornelius, Izak, 74–75
Coulson, David, 50–51
Coulson, Sheila, 44–46
Craemer, W. J., 6–7
creation, 58–59, 80–81, 82, 97, 103, 105, 106–7, 114, 131
Crispina, 219
crops. *See* agriculture
cults
   blacksmithing, 239, 248–49
   Carthaginian, 171
   cattle, 61
   Cyrencia, 167
   definition, 33–34
   Egypt, 99–100, 113–14, 124
   household, 99–100, 141, 142
   Nubia, 60, 124
   and spirits, 119
cultures, African, 5, 6–7, 170, 196–97
Cushitics, 132, 178–79, 240, 241
Cyprian, 217–18
Cyrencia, 167, 213
Cyril of Alexandria, 203–4

dancing, 258
Darwin, Charles, 25–26
David, Rosalie, 88
de Brosses, Charles, 5, 23–26, 28–29
Decius, 192–93
deffufa, 121–22
definition of religion, 37–38
deities. *See* gods
de Maret, Pierre, 50, 64–65, 246
demons, 194–95
Demotic, 145–46, 189
Depression Cave, 46–47
d'Errico, Francesco, 38–39, 66–67
Descartes, René, 38–39
diffuse monotheism, 29
Dimiana, 193
Diocletian, 193, 195–96, 207, 219, 226
Diodorus, 157
Diola, 1–2, 11–12, 14, 18–19, 27–28, 31–33
Dionysius, 192–93
Diop, Cheikh Anta, 73

divinity of kings, 88, 124, 154–55, 156
Djebel Edogh, 221–22
Djoser, King, 89
D'MT, 164–65, 228–29
domestication, animals, 50–51, 52–53, 59–60, 61
Donatism, 219–22. *See also* Circumcellions
Donatus, 219–20
Dowson, T. A., 38–39
dualism, 146, 199–200
Dunand, Françoise, 149
Durkheim, Emile, 23

East Africa, 132, 161, 178, 240, 262
Ebna Hakim, 163
Edict of Milan, 199–200
education, 11–12, 17–18, 255–56
Egypt
  and African civilization, 69, 71–77, 115, 119, 134
  Afrocentrism, 73–74
  afterlife, 96–97, 98–99, 104–5, 260
  agriculture, 54–55, 77
  Archaic Period, 80
  archaeology, 75–76
  assistance, divine, 141–42
  and Assyria, 144–45
  Axial Age, 109–10
  ba, 98–99
  Book of Living and Dying (Egyptian Book of the Dead), 104–5
  burial practices, 47, 55–56, 83–84, 89–90, 260
  and Byzantine empire, 185–86
  and Christianity, 185–87, 188, 190–99, 226–27, 263–64
  circumcision, 145
  Coffin Texts, 98–99
  conversion, 197–98
  cosmology/cosmogony, 78, 81–82, 84–87, 94–95, 98–99, 189
  cults, 99–100, 113–14, 124
  and Diocletian, 193
  divine kingship, 88, 124
  dreams, 105
  and Eastern Mediterranean traditions, 185
  ethics, 96–97
  First Intermediate Period, 95
  flooding, Nile, 84
  Gnosticism, 198–99
  gods, 78–82, 84–89, 90–91, 94, 99, 105, 112–13, 115–16, 124, 141–42, 145–46, 147–48, 157, 158, 165–66, 188–90, 258–59
  Great Hymn to Khnum, 95
  and Greeks, 137–38, 146, 147–48
  Hamitic Hypothesis, 71–74

Heliopolis, 84–86
Heliopolitan Cosmogony, 85–86
Hermopolis, 94
Hermopolitan Cosmogony, 94
hieroglyphics, 10–11
household cults, 99–100, 141, 142
human elements, 82–83
human figurines, 57
hymns, 103, 108–9, 110–11, 124–25
incense, 102
Instruction for Merikare, 95–96
Instruction of Amenemope, 141
and Judaism, 146–47, 151, 189, 194
ka, 82–83, 85–86, 93
and Kerma, 121–22, 123
and Libya, 167
linguistic analysis, 76
location, 76–77
ma'at, 79–80, 96–97, 110–11, 260
Melkite Church, 227–28
Memphis, 80–81
Memphis Theology, 81
and Meroe, 211–12, 227–28
Middle, 56
Middle Kingdom, 97
monasticism, Christian, 185–86, 194–96
and Monophysitism, 185–86, 198–99, 207, 227–28
and monotheism, 70–71
New Kingdom, 101, 143
and Nubia, 120–21, 123–25, 137–38, 144, 152–53, 226–27
Old Kingdom, 84
Opet Festival, 102–3
oracles, 92, 141–42, 187–88
persecution, 200–2
and Persia, 145–46
pharaoh/king, 77–78, 83–84, 88, 90–93, 108–9
priesthood, 77–78, 93–94, 100
prophecies/prophets, 92, 100
Ptolemaic, 147
and Punt, 125, 165–66
pyramids, 89–90
Pyramid Texts, 79–80, 85–86
and race, 69, 71–73, 76–77
Ramesside Dynasty, 138
reform, 109–10, 112, 260–61
retribution, divine, 141
rituals, 108–9, 202, 206
and Rome, 185, 187, 199–202
Saites, 144–45
Second Intermediate Period, 100

Sed festival, 83–84
source materials, 78–80
states, 77
the sun/sun gods, 103–4, 106–7, 109, 114, 124
temples, 93, 113–14, 151, 187–88, 200–2, 203–4, 207
and Theodosius, 200–2
tombs, 83–84, 89–91
united kingdoms, 80–81
women priests, 93–94, 100, 144
and Zoroastrianism, 146
See also Nile Delta; Nile Valley
Ehret, Christopher, 62
Elephantine, 146–47
Eliade, Mircea, 8, 18–19, 82
Elisa, 168
Ella Amida, 229–31
Elmentaiten, 132–33, 180–81
El Omari, 57
Emitai, 2, 18–19, 31–33
Equatorial Africa, 63–64, 177, 246, 262
equilibrium, social, 6–7
Eritrea, 162, 261
Esulalu, 1–2
Ethiopia, 125–26, 162, 212, 231–34, 261, 263–64. *See also* Nubia
Ethio-Semitic, 163–64
ethnoarchaeology, 21, 180–81. *See also* archaeology
Eusebius of Caesarea, 192–93
Evans-Pritchard, E. E., 9–10
explorers, European, 23–25
Ezana, 211–12, 227, 229–31

Fabunmi, M. A., 74–75
Fagan, Brian, 74–75
Fagg, Bernard, 176
Faulkner, R., 104–5
Faustus, 223–24
Female Hill (Tsodilo Hills), 43–45
fertility, 50–51, 56, 66, 123, 164–65, 176, 182, 258–59
fetishism, 24–26
figurines, 56–57, 66
Fourshey, Catherine, 64–65, 131
Fox, R., 6–7
Frankfurter, David, 141–42, 197–98, 206–7
Freud, Sigmund, 70
Frumentius, 229–31
Fulgentius, 224–25
functionalism, 6, 12–13

Gabon, 177–78, 247
Gambia River, 250
Garamantes, 173
Garlake, Peter, 49–50
Gash, 125
Gatto, Maria, 54
Geb, 85–86
Gebel Barkal, 153–54
Geertz, Clifford, 38–39
Ge'ez, 232
Geiseric, 224–25
genital cutting. *See* circumcision
Gétules, 173
Ghana, 249–50
glottochronology, 21–22
gods
  assistance, 141–42
  Berber, 171
  Blemmye, 228
  Book of Living and Dying, 104–5
  Buhaya, 182
  Carthaginians, 168–70
  Egyptian, 78–82, 84–89, 90–91, 94, 99, 105, 112–13, 115–16, 124, 141–42, 145–46, 147–48, 153–54, 155–56, 157, 158, 165–66, 188–90, 258–59
  fertility, 176
  Gnosticism, 198–99
  Greek, 147–48
  Interlacustrine region, 242
  Israel, 146–47
  judgment, 105
  Libyan, 167
  Meroe, 155–56, 157
  Nile Delta, 58–59
  North Africa, 212–13
  Nubian, 123, 124, 153–54, 155–56
  Numidia, 214–15
  and Ptolemies, 147–50
  Punt, 165–66
  Rome, 189–90
  West Africa, 176
Gogoshiis Qabe, 62–63
Gonzalez, Rhonda, 22, 64–65, 131
Goody, Jack, 8–9, 12–13, 14, 16–18
graves. *See* burial practices
Great Lakes. *See* Interlacustrine region
Greeks, 137–38, 146, 147–48, 166–67
Greenberg, Joseph, 76
Grimal, Nicolas, 74–75
Guenther, Mathias, 46–47
Guinea, 250

Guthri, Malcolm, 129–30
Gwisho, 133–34

Hadrian, 194
Haiseb, 46–47
Halbwachs, Maurice, 17
Hapy, 84
Hardjedef, Prince, 89–90
Harvey, Graham, 26n.77
Harvey, Sheldon, 102
Hassan, Fekri, 58
Hathor, 165–66
Hatshepshut, 101–2
Hawkes, Christopher, 19
healing, 119, 129–30, 148–49, 189–90, 196–97, 206
Hebrews, 70–71, 138–39
Hegel, Georg Friedrich, 3–5
hematite, 42–43
Henshilwood, Christopher, 38–39, 66–67
Herodotus, 145, 165, 173
hijra, 233–34
history and African religion, 1–10, 13, 15, 16–17, 19, 63–64, 254, 264–65
homeostasis, 12–13, 17–19
Homo erectus, 39–40
Homo genus, 39–40, 257
Homo naledi, 40–41, 51–52, 257
Homo sapiens, 38–39, 40–42, 43, 51–52, 257
Horemheb, 113–14
Horn of Africa, 212, 228
Horton, Robin, 30–33
Horus, 84–85, 88–89, 188f, 200, 206–7
Howley, Kathryn, 75–76, 120
human origins, 38–39
Huneric, 224–25
hunting/hunter-gatherers, 51, 66–67, 246–47
husbandry. *See* domestication
Hyksos, 100–1, 123
Hypatia, 203–4

Iberomaurusian Era, 47–48
idolatry, 193
Idowu, E. Bolaji, 29
Igbo, 175–76, 250
Imazighen, the. *See* Berbers
Imhotep, 89, 90–91, 190
incubation, 214–15
indigenous religion, 1–3, 8, 254, 256–57
infibulation, 165. *See also* circumcision
Interlacustrine region, 181, 241
Invention of Africa, The (Mudimbe), 3–4, 254–55

iron, 155, 157, 174–76, 181–83, 239, 240, 242, 245, 247, 250. *See also* blacksmithing
Isichei, Elizabeth, 7–8
Isidor, 189
Isis, 87, 148–49, 157, 188, 189–90, 196–97, 200–2
Islam, 33, 233–34

Jaspers, Karl, 109–10
Jebel Sahada, 59–60
Jenné-Jenno, 248–50
Jesus Christ, 185–86, 190–91, 198–99, 206–7
Jiménez, Ana Navajas, 54
Johannan, Yosef ben, 70
John the Egyptian, St., 194–95
Juba II, 213
Judaism
  and Axum, 228–29, 231–32, 233
  and Christianity, 203–4
  Cyrencia, 213
  and Egypt, 146–47, 151, 189, 194
  Ethiopian, 233
  Libya, 213–14
  origins, 33
  and Ptolemies, 151
  and Rome, 194
judgment, postmortem, 31–32
Julian of Eclanum, 223–24
Justinian, 207

Kadera, 60–61
Kadruka, 60–61
Kaguru, 15
Kalahari, 31
Kashta, 152–53
Kaskazi, 179, 180
Kebra Nagast, 162–63
Kenherkhopshek, 105
Kerma, 121–23
Khaemwaset, 142
Khentamentiu, 99
Khnum, 123
Khoi-San, 46–47, 244–45
Khoisan language family, 48–49, 244–45
KiKongo, 246
Kintampo, 128–29
Kongo, 23–24
Kothos, 205–6
Kozloff, Arielle, 124–25
Kuhn, Thomas, 14–15
kumandwa, 182
Kumbi Saleh, 249–50
Kush, 152–55
Kusi, 183

INDEX 297

Lake Turkana, 132–33, 180–81
Lane, Peter, 49–50
Lang, Andrew, 25–26
Langer, Suzanne, 28
language, 21–23, 48–49
Lasko, Barbara, 58–59
Laviolette, Adria, 248–49
Le Corsu, Fraine, 148–49
Leptis Magna, 216
Leroi-Gourhan, André, 37–38
Lesko, Leonard, 65–66
lesser deities, 28–29, 30–31. *See also* supreme being
Levi-Strauss, Claude, 14–15
Lewis-Williams, J. David, 38–39, 42–43, 50, 133–34
Leza, 246
Libanius, 201
Libya, 143, 166–67, 213–14, 215, 216. *See also* Berbers
linguistic analysis, 64–65, 67, 76, 128, 135, 257
linguistic change. *See* glottochronology
literacy, 16–18
Louikias Andias, 213–14

Ma'at, 78–79, 90–91
Macarius, 205–6
Macedonius, 200
Mackendrick, Paul, 168–69
Madagascar, 243
Maghreb, 47–48, 224–25
Makeda, 162–63
Makuria, 227–28
Mandulis, 226
Manichaeanism, 223–24, 228–29
Marcus Aurelius, 189
Maren, Curtis, 20
Mark, St., 191
marriage, 246–47
Mary, Virgin, 217–18, 225–26
Mashariki, 178–79, 243
Massinissa, 171
Masson, John, 49
Matara, 164–65
Matory, Randy, 4–5
matrilineage, 131, 245
Maximentius, 193
Mbiti, John, 7–8
McCall, Daniel F., 174–75
McIntosh, Roderick, 174
Mecca, 233–34
Melitus, 203
Melqart, 168

memory, 18–19
Mena, 173
menorah, 221*f*
Menouthis, 200–1
Meroe, 155–57, 176–77, 211–12, 226–28, 264
Meroitic, 10–11, 152, 155–56
Meropius, 229–31
Meyerowitz, Eva, 71–72
microcosm, 30–33
Middle Paleolithic Era, 41–42, 47, 51–52
Mills, Margaret, 215–16
mining, 172
missionaries, 23–24, 28–29
Mithen, Steven, 38–39, 42–43, 50–51
Modimo, 177
Monastery of St. Simeon, 196*f*
Monica, 223
Monophysitism, 185–86, 198–99, 207, 227–28, 231–32
monotheism, 29, 70–71
Montu, 97
Moses, 70–71
Moses of Abydos, 205–6
Mudimbe, Valentin, 3–4, 254–55
Muhammad, 233–34
Mutemwia, 102–3
myth, 15, 16–17, 33–34

Nabta Playa, 48
Napata, 152–55
Naqada, 57–60
Nasrudin, Mulla, 35
Nazlet Khater, 47
Neferti, 92
Nefertiti, 106–7, 110–11
Neith, 80–81, 189
Nekhbet, 58–59
Neolithic religion, 52
Neolithic Revolution, 39–40, 52–53, 65–66, 258
Nicene Creed, 203
Niger Congo, 48–49, 128
Niger River, 174
Nile Delta, 57, 58–59
Nile Valley, 47, 53–54, 74–75
Nilo-Saharan language family, 48–49
Nilotics, 132, 180–81, 240–41
Nine Saints, 232
Nobataes, 207, 211–12
Nock, Arthur Darby, 197–98
Nok, 175–76
North Africa, 166, 212, 262, 263–64
Northeast Africa, 48–49, 120, 235–36

Nubia, 59–60, 120, 137–38, 144, 152, 158–59, 226, 259. *See also* Ethiopia
Nuer religion, 9–10
Numidia, 214–15, 223–24
Nun, 86–87
Nurse, Derek, 22
Nut, 85–86
Nyambe, 64–65

obsidian, 132–33
ocher, 37–38, 41–42, 43–44, 45–46, 51–52, 179–80
O'Connor, David, 73–74
Ogdaad, 94
Ogot, Bethwell, 4–5
Old Ngwenya Mine, 42–43
Ona, 163–64
Ong, Walter, 16, 17–18
Oracle of the Potter, The, 150–51
oral tradition, 2–3, 9, 11–19
Origen, 192
origin of religion, 23–26, 37–38
orishas, 29, 31–33
Orpen, J. M., 50
Osiris, 86–89, 96–97, 98–99, 105, 111–12, 138, 148–49, 155–56
Osman, Ahmed, 70

Pachom, St., 195–96
"paganism," 185–86, 197–98, 200, 203–6, 207, 216–19, 222
paleoanthropology, 38–39
Paleolithic religion, 10
Palomen, 195–96
Panga ya Saidi Cave, 41–42
Parenefer, 106
Parrinder, Geoffrey, 8–9, 198–99
Paul of Thebes, St., 194–95
P'Bitek, Okot, 29, 242–43
Pearson, Yves, 6, 13
Periplus of the Erythraean Sea, The, 228–29
Persia, 145–46
Phillipson, David, 47
Phillipson, John, 62–63
Philo of Alexandria, 194
Phoenicians, 167–70
Piankhy, 144, 152–53
piety, popular, 141, 154–55
Planck, Max, 14–15
polytheism, 25–26
Pomponius Mela, 214–15
popular religion, 206–7
Portugal/Portuguese, 23–25

pottery, 55–56
power objects, 24–25
prophets, 2, 92, 100, 168–69
proto-Njila, 178
Ptah, 81–82, 139–40
Ptolemy I, 149
Ptolemy II Philadelphus, 149–50
Punic, 214–15, 218–19
Punt, 125, 165–66
python (Rhino Cave), 44–47
Python Cave, 46–47

Queen of Sheba. *See* Makeda
Quirke, Stephen, 28n.84, 79–80

rain, 31–32, 48, 166–67, 248–49
rams, 53, 74–75
Re, 85–86, 91–92, 97, 114, 139–41. *See also* Amun Re
red color, 42–43. *See also* ocher
Redford, Donald, 74–75, 111, 121–23
Reeves, Nicholas, 107
reform, 109–10, 112, 260–61
Reid, Andrew, 73–74
"religion" (term), 27–29
Rhino Cave, 44–47, 51–52
rice, 128, 174
Rice, Michael, 58, 76–77
Rising Star Cave, 40–41
ritual
    Amazigh, 166–67
    and archaeology, 20–21
    Berber, 218–19
    blacksmithing, 181–82
    burial, 41–42, 47
    Demotic, 189
    Egyptian, 108–9, 202, 206
    female, 179
    Greek, 167
    initiation, 178–79, 183
    Lower Congo, 63–64
    Mashariki, 178–79
    offerings, 55–56
    propitiation, 206
    sacrifice, 50–51
    sites, 20–21, 42–46, 51–52
Robbins, Lawrence, 43–44, 46–47
rock art, 43–45, 49–52, 53, 66–67, 244–45, 258
Rome, 157, 171, 185, 187, 199–202, 203–4, 212–13, 215–16, 217–18, 219–22, 226
Roscoe, John, 72–73

INDEX 299

Sabeans, 10–11, 163–66
sacrifice
  and burial practices, 59–61
  cattle, 59–60
  child, 168–69
  human, 60–61
  Imperial (Rome), 219
  Nubia, 59–60
  Roman, 219, 220f
Sahara, 53, 61, 74–75, 127, 171, 172, 249–50
Sahel, 249
Saidi, Christine, 64–65, 131, 179, 240–41
sanctuaries, 66–67
Sarakhollé, 249–50
Sarkozy, Nicolas, 4–5
Satis, 123
Saul, 197
Schmidt, Peter, 15–16, 21, 181–82, 242–43
Schoenbrun, David, 182, 241
Schwartz, Benjamin, 109–10
Searight, Susan, 127
Sebado, Za, 162
Sed Festival, 79–80, 83–84
Seligman, C. G., 71–72
Semitic language family, 48–49
Senegal, 1–2
Septimus Severus, 192–93, 216
Serapis, 149, 189–90, 213
Seth, 78–79, 86–87, 88–89, 138, 201–2
Sety, 138
Shaw, Thurstan, 175
Shenoute, 204–5
Sheshonk, 143
Shinnie, Peter, 75–76
Shreve, James, 40–41
Shrines of the Slave Trade (Baum), 1–2
simbi, 177–78
Simeon the Cyrene, 213
Siwa Oasis, 145–46, 147–48
slave trade, 1–2, 73–74
Smart, Ninian, 27–28
Smith, Andrew, 61
Smith, Jonathan Z., 26–27
Smith, Mark, 19–20, 47
snakes, 44–47
Solomon, 162–63
sources, written, 10
  archaeology, 19–21, 161, 176–77, 259–60
  Carthaginian, 169–70
  and colonialism, 8–9
  inadequacy, 10–12, 255
  and oral tradition, 11–19
  sub-Saharan, 239–40

Southern Africa, 183, 244
Spencer, Patricia, 54–55
spirit cults, 14
spirits
  Abacwezi, 242–43
  Bantu, 64–65, 162
  Buhaya, 182
  dimo, 177
  medium, 182
  See also gods
stelae, 60–61, 99–100, 113–14, 125, 138–39, 141, 152–53, 168–69, 228–31, 230f
stone circles (Nabta Playa), 48
structuralism, 6–7
study of religion, Africa and, 1–5, 23
Sudan/Sudanic region, 62, 174–75
sun/sun gods, 71, 103–4, 106–7, 109, 114, 124, 139–41, 180, 260–61
supreme being
  and African religion, 28–29, 30–32
  and ancestors, 32
  Aten, 71, 106–7, 108–9, 110–12, 260–61
  Atum/Amun Ra, 97, 103, 105, 114, 152–53, 260–61
  Emitai, 2, 18–19, 31–32
  female, 179
  Hebrew, 71
  humanity, 114
  Leza, 246
  Mashariki, 179
  Modimo, 177
  Neith, 80–81
  Nekhbet, 58–59
  Nyambe, 64–65
  Proto-Bantu, 259
  Ptah, 81, 82
  Sudanic region, 62
Sutton, J. F. G., 242–43
Suzman, James, 43–44
symbolic behavior, 38–40, 49, 67

Tanit, 168–69
Taruqa, 175
Tassili, 50–51
Taylor, John, 55–56, 65–66
Tempels, Placide, 30
termite hills, Interlacustrine, 181
terra cotta, 175, 176
Tertullian, 216–17
Thalis, 195–96
Thebes, 84–85, 86–87, 97, 101, 112–13
Theodosius, 200, 201, 203–4
Theophilus, 203–4

Thompson, Dorothy, 149–50
Thoth, 104–5
Thutmoses II, 101
Thutmoses IV, 103–4
Tichitt, 128
time, 7–8
Tin Hinran, 247–48
tools, 60
tophet, 168–69
Torok, Laszlo, 152
trade, 161, 169–70, 176–77, 247–48
traditional societies, 6, 7–8, 11–12, 256–57
trance states, 49–50
Trevor-Roper, Hugh, 5
trickster deity, 88–89, 138
Trigger, Bruce, 71–72
Tsodilo Hills, 31, 43–45, 45f, 258
Tuareg, 247–48
Turkana Turwell culture, 180–81
Tutankhaten/Tutankhamun, 112–13
two-tiered cosmology, 30–32
Tylor, Edward Burnett, 5, 25–26, 28–29
Tyre, 168

Ubangi, 131–32
Ulfilias, 224–25

Valley of the Serpent, 249–50
Van Binsbergen, Wim, 19
Vandals, 224–25
van der Post, Laurens, 43–44
Vansina, Jan, 6–7, 9, 12–13, 15–16, 22, 130–31

Vérin, P., 243–44
Victor, Pope, 216
vital force, 30

Waimolo. *See* Waynaba
Waldman, Marilyn, 35
Walker, Nick, 44–45
Warmington, B. H., 168–69
Watt, Ian, 16–17
Watterson, Barbara, 55–56, 58, 85–86
Waynaba, 162
Welsby, Derek, 153–54
West Africa, 128, 174, 247, 262–63
West Africa's Women of God (Baum), 2
Wightman, Gregory, 46–47
Wildung, Dietrich, 89
Wilkinson, Toby, 111–12
Williams, Chancellor, 71, 73–74
witchcraft, 178
Wotzka, Hans-Peter, 63–65, 176–77
writing, 16, 58

Yahu, 146–47
Yeha, 164–65
Yellin, Janice, 120–21
Yemen, 233
Yoruba, 29, 31–32
Yurco, Frank, 60

Zaire River, 246–47
Zivi-Coche, Christiane, 58
Zoroastrianism, 146

The manufacturer's authorised representative in the EU for product safety is Oxford
University Press España S.A. of El Parque Empresarial San Fernando de Henares,
Avenida de Castilla, 2 – 28830 Madrid (www.oup.es/en or product.safety@oup.com).
OUP España S.A. also acts as importer into Spain of products made by the manufacturer.

Printed in the USA/Agawam, MA
January 17, 2025

881168.015